NISSAN
TITAN 2004-09
ARMADA 2005-10 REPAIR MANUAL

P9-CRR-050

CHILTON'S

Covers U.S. and Canadian models of Titan (2004 thru 2009)
& Armada (2005 thru 2010)
Two- and four-wheel drive

by Jay Storer

CHILTON Automotive Books

PUBLISHED BY **HAYNES NORTH AMERICA, Inc.**

Manufactured in USA
©2010 Haynes North America, Inc.
ISBN-13: 978-1-56392-841-3
ISBN-10: 1-56392-841-8
Library of Congress Control Number 2010927677

Haynes Publishing Group
Sparkford Nr Yeovil
Somerset BA22 7JJ England

Haynes North America, Inc
861 Lawrence Drive
Newbury Park
California 91320 USA

ABCDE
FGHIJ
KLMNO
PQRST

Contents

Mechanic and photographer with 2008 Nissan Armada

ACKNOWLEDGEMENTS

Technical writers who contributed to this project include Joe Hamilton, Jeff Killingsworth, Jamie Sarte and Mike Stubblefield. Wiring diagrams originated exclusively for Haynes North America, Inc. by Valley Forge Technical Information Services.

While every attempt is made to ensure that the information in this manual is correct, no liability can be accepted by the authors or publishers for loss, damage or injury caused by any errors in, or omissions from, the information given.

About this manual

ITS PURPOSE

The purpose of this manual is to help you get the best value from your vehicle. It can do so in several ways. It can help you decide what work must be done, even if you choose to have it done by a dealer service department or a repair shop; it provides information and procedures for routine maintenance and servicing; and it offers diagnostic and repair procedures to follow when trouble occurs.

We hope you use the manual to tackle the work yourself. For many simpler jobs, doing it yourself may be quicker than arranging an appointment to get the vehicle into a shop and making the trips to leave it and pick it up. More importantly, a lot of money can be saved by avoiding the expense the shop must pass on to you to cover its labor and overhead costs. An added benefit is the sense of satisfaction and accomplishment that you feel after doing the job yourself.

USING THE MANUAL

The manual is divided into Chapters. Each Chapter is divided into numbered Sections. Each Section consists of consecutively numbered paragraphs.

At the beginning of each numbered Section you will be referred to any illustrations which apply to the procedures in that Section. The reference numbers used in illustration captions pinpoint the pertinent Section and the Step within that Section. That is, illustration 3.2 means the illustration refers to Section 3 and Step (or paragraph) 2 within that Section.

Procedures, once described in the text, are not normally repeated. When it's necessary to refer to another Chapter, the reference will be given as Chapter and Section number. Cross references given without use of the word "Chapter" apply to Sections and/or paragraphs in the same Chapter. For example, "see Section 8" means in the same Chapter.

References to the left or right side of the vehicle assume you are sitting in the driver's seat, facing forward.

Even though we have prepared this manual with extreme care, neither the publisher nor the author can accept responsibility for any errors in, or omissions from, the information given.

➡**NOTE**

A *Note* provides information necessary to properly complete a procedure or information which will make the procedure easier to understand.

※※ **CAUTION**

A *Caution* provides a special procedure or special steps which must be taken while completing the procedure where the Caution is found. Not heeding a Caution can result in damage to the assembly being worked on.

※※ **WARNING**

A *Warning* provides a special procedure or special steps which must be taken while completing the procedure where the Warning is found. Not heeding a Warning can result in personal injury.

Introduction

Nissan Titan pick-ups are available in either king cab (extended cab) or crew-cab (four-door) models. The Nissan Armada SUV is available only in a four-door "wagon" style body.

The Titan pick-ups and the Armada SUVs are available only with the 5.6L V8 fuel-injected engine.

The chassis layout is conventional, with the engine mounted at the front and the power being transmitted from a five-speed automatic transmission through a driveshaft to the rear axle. On 4WD models, a transfer case directs the power through a driveshaft to the front differential and independent driveaxles to the front wheels.

Both models have the same independent front suspension design, with upper and lower control arms and shock absorber/coil spring assemblies. Titan models are equipped with a solid rear axle with leaf springs and shock absorbers. Armada models have independent rear suspension with coil springs and shock absorbers. Some Armada models are equipped with a Rear Load Leveling Air Suspension System. Steering on all models is via power-assisted rack-and-pinion steering gear.

All models have four-wheel disc brakes and four-wheel ABS (antilock brakes), with power assist standard. The parking brake system utilizes small drum brake shoes inside the rear brake discs.

Vehicle identification numbers

Modifications are a continuing and unpublicized process in vehicle manufacturing. Since spare parts manuals and lists are compiled on a numerical basis, the individual vehicle numbers are essential to correctly identify the component required.

VEHICLE IDENTIFICATION NUMBER (VIN)

The Vehicle Identification Number (VIN), which appears on the Vehicle Certificate of Title and Registration, is also embossed on a plate located in the left (driver's side) corner of the dashboard, near the windshield (see illustration). The VIN tells you when and where a vehicle was manufactured, its country of origin, make, type, passenger safety system, line, series, body style, engine and assembly plant.

VIN ENGINE AND MODEL YEAR CODES

Two particularly important pieces of information found in the VIN are the engine code and the model year code. Counting from the left, the engine code letter designation is the 4th character and the model year code is the 10th character.

On the models covered by this manual the engine codes are:

A 5.6L V8 KV56DE
B .... 5.6L V8 KV56DE FFV (Flexible Fuel Vehicle)

On the models covered by this manual the model year codes are:

4 2004
5 2005
6 2006
7 2007
8 2008
9 2009
10 2010

VEHICLE SAFETY CERTIFICATION LABEL

The Vehicle Safety Certification label is attached to the rear edge of the driver's door or on the door post (see illustration). The label contains the name of the manufacturer, the month and year of production, the Gross Vehicle Weight Rating (GVWR), the Gross Axle Weight Rating (GAWR) and the certification statement. On most models, the label also includes the OEM tire sizes and pressures.

ENGINE IDENTIFICATION NUMBER (EIN)

The Engine Identification Number (EIN) is stamped into the front of the engine block on a machined surface just behind the water pump (see illustration).

TRANSMISSION IDENTIFICATION NUMBER (TIN)

The Automatic Transmission Identification Number (TIN) is stamped into a tag and fastened to the transmission with a bolt (see illustration).

TRANSFER CASE IDENTIFICATION LABEL

The transfer case identification information is stamped into the top of the case.

The VIN plate is visible from the outside of the vehicle, through the driver's side of the windshield

The Vehicle Safety Certification label is affixed to the driver's side door end or post

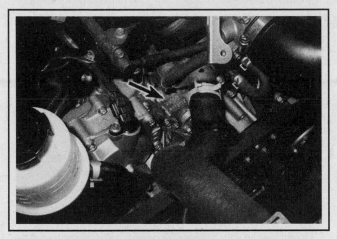

Engine identification number location

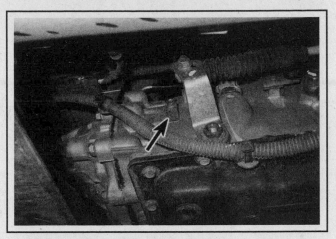

Automatic transmission identification tag

Recall information

Vehicle recalls are carried out by the manufacturer in the rare event of a possible safety-related defect. The vehicle's registered owner is contacted at the address on file at the Department of Motor Vehicles and given the details of the recall. Remedial work is carried out free of charge at a dealer service department.

If you are the new owner of a used vehicle which was subject to a recall and you want to be sure that the work has been carried out, it's best to contact a dealer service department and ask about your indi-vidual vehicle - you'll need to furnish them your Vehicle Identification Number (VIN).

The table below is based on information provided by the National Highway Traffic Safety Administration (NHTSA), the body which over-sees vehicle recalls in the United States. The recall database is updated constantly. For the latest information on vehicle recalls, check the NHTSA website at www.nhtsa.gov, www.safercar.gov, or call the NHTSA hotline at 1-888-327-4236.

Recall date	Recall campaign number	Model(s) affected	Concern
JUL 01, 2004	04V345000	2004 Titan	On certain models, an area on the rear pillar where the rear seat belt upper anchor is attached may not be sufficiently energy absorbent. This could result in an increased risk of injury if the area is struck in a crash.
AUG 09, 2004	04V408000	2004 Titan	On certain models equipped with a column shifter, the shift lever may have been damaged during assembly. This could result in failure of the portion of the assembly that holds the lever in the Park position, which could result in a crash.
NOV 22, 2006	06V459000	2004/2005/2006 Titan	On certain king cab trucks, the wires in the harness were routed through the rear doors and into the body. Over time, these wires may break. The harness contains wires for the driver seat belt pre-tensioner, the front passenger seat belt/occupant classification system and the rear audio speakers. If the wires for the seat belts and speaker wires break and make contact, there is a possibility that the pre-tensioner may deploy. If this happens when the seat belt is retracted, it will not be possible to use the seat belt. If one of the wires on the right side harness for the seat belt tension sensor breaks, the passenger side front airbag will not deploy as designed in a frontal collision increasing the risk of a crash and personal injury.

Recall date	Recall campaign number	Model(s) affected	Concern
JUN 25, 2007	07E046000	2004/2005/2006 Titan, Armada	On some Hopkins aftermarket trailer brake control connection harnesses sold for use on certain models of Nissan vehicles, a wire may have been placed in an incorrect position in the electrical connector housing. The result would be the lack of trailer braking when the towing vehicle brakes were applied. It would also result in the towing vehicle's dash lights being activated when the vehicle brakes were applied. The failure of the application of the trailer brake could result in reduced ability to stop and contribute to a possible crash.
MAR 28, 2007	07V150000	2004 Titan	On certain crew cab model trucks, the seat back shape may be such that there may not be sufficient webbing on the retractor spool for the rear center seat belt to release from the automatic locking mode (ALR) after it is engaged and the seat belt is retracted. If this occurs, there may be difficulty in pulling the seat belt out of the retractor thus preventing its usage. In the event of a crash, a seat occupant may not be properly restrained increasing the risk of personal injury.
JUN 24, 2008	08V284000	2005/2006 Titan, Armada	On some models manufactured after March 17, 2005 that are equipped with a Visteon air conditioning condenser fan motor, the fan motor may not be properly sealed allowing excessive water intrusion and inadequate drainage of moisture. This could cause corrosion in the motor leading possibly to over-heating and a fire.
FEB 28, 2006	06V064000	2006 Titan	On some models, an arc weld is missing on some right side rear door upper latch assemblies. This may result in the right side doors coming partially open, increasing the risk of injury to occupants.
SEP 21, 2007	07V449000	2007/2008 Armada	On some models, the driver's side third row seat belt upper anchor bracket may be cracked. In the event of a crash, a seat occupant may not be properly restrained increasing the risk of personal injury.
JAN 23, 2008	08V045000	2008 Titan	On some models, the tire placard lists an incorrect vehicle capacity weight. This standard specifies requirements for tire selection to prevent overloading.
APR 16, 2008	08V187000	2008 Titan, Armada	On some models equipped with manual adjustment front seats, the seat track assembly may have been manufactured out of specification. This may result in the manual seat pawl not fully engaging, increasing the risk of personal injuries in the event of a crash.

Buying parts

Replacement parts are available from many sources, which generally fall into one of two categories - authorized dealer parts departments and independent retail auto parts stores. Our advice concerning these parts is as follows:

Retail auto parts stores: Good auto parts stores will stock frequently needed components which wear out relatively fast, such as clutch components, exhaust systems, brake parts, tune-up parts, etc. These stores often supply new or reconditioned parts on an exchange basis, which can save a considerable amount of money. Discount auto parts stores are often very good places to buy materials and parts needed for general vehicle maintenance such as oil, grease, filters, spark plugs, belts, touch-up paint, bulbs, etc. They also usually sell tools and general accessories, have convenient hours, charge lower prices and can often be found not far from home.

Authorized dealer parts department: This is the best source for parts which are unique to the vehicle and not generally available elsewhere (such as major engine parts, transmission parts, trim pieces, etc.).

Warranty information: If the vehicle is still covered under warranty, be sure that any replacement parts purchased - regardless of the source - do not invalidate the warranty!

To be sure of obtaining the correct parts, have engine and chassis numbers available and, if possible, take the old parts along for positive identification.

MAINTENANCE TECHNIQUES

There are a number of techniques involved in maintenance and repair that will be referred to throughout this manual. Application of these techniques will enable the home mechanic to be more efficient, better organized and capable of performing the various tasks properly, which will ensure that the repair job is thorough and complete.

Fasteners

Fasteners are nuts, bolts, studs and screws used to hold two or more parts together. There are a few things to keep in mind when working with fasteners. Almost all of them use a locking device of some type, either a lockwasher, locknut, locking tab or thread adhesive. All threaded fasteners should be clean and straight, with undamaged threads and undamaged corners on the hex head where the wrench fits. Develop the habit of replacing all damaged nuts and bolts with new ones. Special locknuts with nylon or fiber inserts can only be used once. If they are removed, they lose their locking ability and must be replaced with new ones.

Rusted nuts and bolts should be treated with a penetrating fluid to ease removal and prevent breakage. Some mechanics use turpentine in a spout-type oil can, which works quite well. After applying the rust penetrant, let it work for a few minutes before trying to loosen the nut or bolt. Badly rusted fasteners may have to be chiseled or sawed off or removed with a special nut breaker, available at tool stores.

If a bolt or stud breaks off in an assembly, it can be drilled and removed with a special tool commonly available for this purpose. Most automotive machine shops can perform this task, as well as other repair procedures, such as the repair of threaded holes that have been stripped out.

Flat washers and lockwashers, when removed from an assembly, should always be replaced exactly as removed. Replace any damaged washers with new ones. Never use a lockwasher on any soft metal surface (such as aluminum), thin sheet metal or plastic.

Fastener sizes

For a number of reasons, automobile manufacturers are making wider and wider use of metric fasteners. Therefore, it is important to be able to tell the difference between standard (sometimes called U.S. or SAE) and metric hardware, since they cannot be interchanged.

All bolts, whether standard or metric, are sized according to diameter, thread pitch and length. For example, a standard 1/2 - 13 x 1 bolt is 1/2 inch in diameter, has 13 threads per inch and is 1 inch long. An M12 - 1.75 x 25 metric bolt is 12 mm in diameter, has a thread pitch of 1.75 mm (the distance between threads) and is 25 mm long. The two bolts are nearly identical, and easily confused, but they are not interchangeable.

In addition to the differences in diameter, thread pitch and length, metric and standard bolts can also be distinguished by examining the bolt heads. To begin with, the distance across the flats on a standard bolt head is measured in inches, while the same dimension on a metric bolt is sized in millimeters (the same is true for nuts). As a result, a standard wrench should not be used on a metric bolt and a metric wrench should not be used on a standard bolt. Also, most standard bolts have slashes radiating out from the center of the head to denote the grade or strength of the bolt, which is an indication of the amount of torque that can be applied to it. The greater the number of slashes, the greater the strength of the bolt. Grades 0 through 5 are commonly used on automobiles. Metric bolts have a property class (grade) number, rather than a slash, molded into their heads to indicate bolt strength. In this case, the higher the number, the stronger the bolt. Property class numbers 8.8, 9.8 and 10.9 are commonly used on automobiles.

Strength markings can also be used to distinguish standard hex nuts from metric hex nuts. Many standard nuts have dots stamped into one side, while metric nuts are marked with a number. The greater the number of dots, or the higher the number, the greater the strength of the nut.

Metric studs are also marked on their ends according to property class (grade). Larger studs are numbered (the same as metric bolts), while smaller studs carry a geometric code to denote grade.

It should be noted that many fasteners, especially Grades 0 through 2, have no distinguishing marks on them. When such is the case, the only way to determine whether it is standard or metric is to measure the thread pitch or compare it to a known fastener of the same size.

Standard fasteners are often referred to as SAE, as opposed to metric. However, it should be noted that SAE technically refers to a non-metric fine thread fastener only. Coarse thread non-metric fasteners are referred to as USS sizes.

Since fasteners of the same size (both standard and metric) may have different strength ratings, be sure to reinstall any bolts, studs or nuts removed from your vehicle in their original locations. Also, when replacing a fastener with a new one, make sure that the new one has a strength rating equal to or greater than the original.

Tightening sequences and procedures

Most threaded fasteners should be tightened to a specific torque value (torque is the twisting force applied to a threaded component such as a nut or bolt). Overtightening the fastener can weaken it and cause it to break, while undertightening can cause it to eventually come loose. Bolts, screws and studs, depending on the material they are made of and their thread diameters, have specific torque values, many of which are noted in the Specifications at the end of each Chapter. Be sure to follow the torque recommendations closely. For fasteners not assigned a specific torque, a general torque value chart is presented here as a guide. These torque values are for dry (unlubricated) fasteners threaded into steel or cast iron (not aluminum). As was previously mentioned, the size and grade of a fastener determine the amount of torque that can safely be applied to it. The figures listed here are approximate for Grade 2 and Grade 3 fasteners. Higher grades can tolerate higher torque values.

Fasteners laid out in a pattern, such as cylinder head bolts, oil pan bolts, differential cover bolts, etc., must be loosened or tightened in sequence to avoid warping the component. This sequence will normally be shown in the appropriate Chapter. If a specific pattern is not given, the following procedures can be used to prevent warping.

Initially, the bolts or nuts should be assembled finger-tight only. Next, they should be tightened one full turn each, in a criss-cross or diagonal pattern. After each one has been tightened one full turn, return to the first one and tighten them all one-half turn, following the same

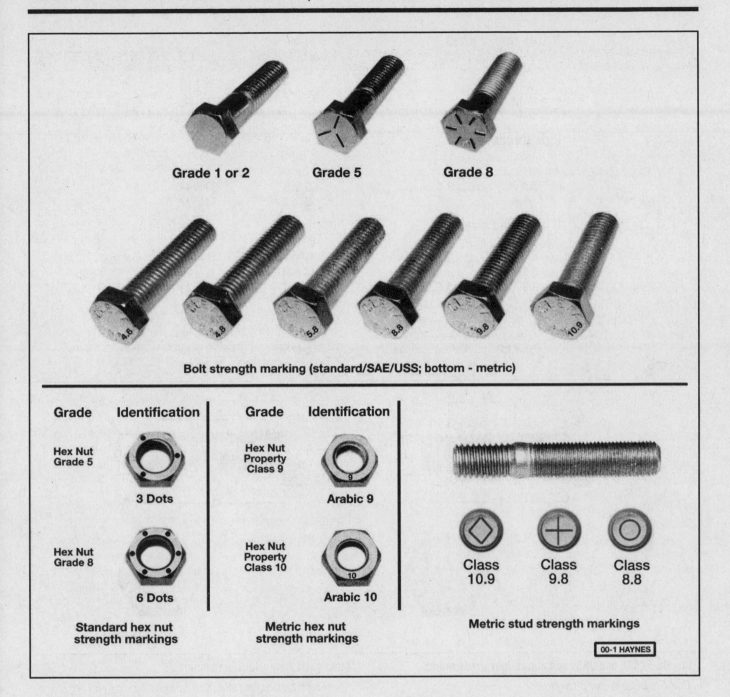

Grade 1 or 2   Grade 5   Grade 8

Bolt strength marking (standard/SAE/USS; bottom - metric)

Grade	Identification	Grade	Identification
Hex Nut Grade 5	3 Dots	Hex Nut Property Class 9	Arabic 9
Hex Nut Grade 8	6 Dots	Hex Nut Property Class 10	Arabic 10

Standard hex nut strength markings

Metric hex nut strength markings

Class 10.9   Class 9.8   Class 8.8

Metric stud strength markings

00-1 HAYNES

pattern. Finally, tighten each of them one-quarter turn at a time until each fastener has been tightened to the proper torque. To loosen and remove the fasteners, the procedure would be reversed.

Component disassembly

Component disassembly should be done with care and purpose to help ensure that the parts go back together properly. Always keep track of the sequence in which parts are removed. Make note of special characteristics or marks on parts that can be installed more than one way, such as a grooved thrust washer on a shaft. It is a good idea to lay the disassembled parts out on a clean surface in the order that they were removed. It may also be helpful to make sketches or take instant photos of components before removal.

When removing fasteners from a component, keep track of their locations. Sometimes threading a bolt back in a part, or putting the washers and nut back on a stud, can prevent mix-ups later. If nuts and bolts cannot be returned to their original locations, they should be kept in a compartmented box or a series of small boxes. A cupcake or muffin tin is ideal for this purpose, since each cavity can hold the bolts and nuts from a particular area (i.e. oil pan bolts, valve cover bolts, engine

Metric thread sizes

Metric thread sizes	Ft-lbs	Nm
M-6	6 to 9	9 to 12
M-8	14 to 21	19 to 28
M-10	28 to 40	38 to 54
M-12	50 to 71	68 to 96
M-14	80 to 140	109 to 154

Pipe thread sizes

Pipe thread sizes	Ft-lbs	Nm
1/8	5 to 8	7 to 10
1/4	12 to 18	17 to 24
3/8	22 to 33	30 to 44
1/2	25 to 35	34 to 47

U.S. thread sizes

U.S. thread sizes	Ft-lbs	Nm
1/4 - 20	6 to 9	9 to 12
5/16 - 18	12 to 18	17 to 24
5/16 - 24	14 to 20	19 to 27
3/8 - 16	22 to 32	30 to 43
3/8 - 24	27 to 38	37 to 51
7/16 - 14	40 to 55	55 to 74
7/16 - 20	40 to 60	55 to 81
1/2 - 13	55 to 80	75 to 108

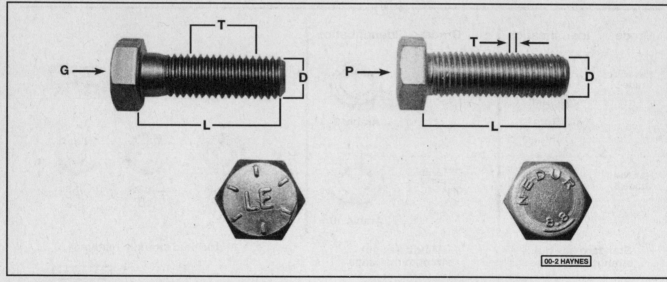

00-2 HAYNES

Standard (SAE and USS) bolt dimensions/grade marks

G   Grade marks (bolt strength)
L   Length (in inches)
T   Thread pitch (number of threads per inch)
D   Nominal diameter (in inches)

Metric bolt dimensions/grade marks

P   Property class (bolt strength)
L   Length (in millimeters)
T   Thread pitch (distance between threads in millimeters)
D   Diameter

mount bolts, etc.). A pan of this type is especially helpful when working on assemblies with very small parts, such as the carburetor, alternator, valve train or interior dash and trim pieces. The cavities can be marked with paint or tape to identify the contents.

Whenever wiring looms, harnesses or connectors are separated, it is a good idea to identify the two halves with numbered pieces of masking tape so they can be easily reconnected.

Gasket sealing surfaces

Throughout any vehicle, gaskets are used to seal the mating surfaces between two parts and keep lubricants, fluids, vacuum or pressure contained in an assembly.

Many times these gaskets are coated with a liquid or paste-type gasket sealing compound before assembly. Age, heat and pressure can sometimes cause the two parts to stick together so tightly that they are very difficult to separate. Often, the assembly can be loosened by striking it with a soft-face hammer near the mating surfaces. A regular hammer can be used if a block of wood is placed between the hammer and the part. Do not hammer on cast parts or parts that could be easily damaged. With any particularly stubborn part, always recheck to make sure that every fastener has been removed.

Avoid using a screwdriver or bar to pry apart an assembly, as they

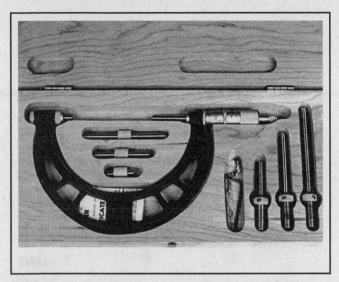

Micrometer set

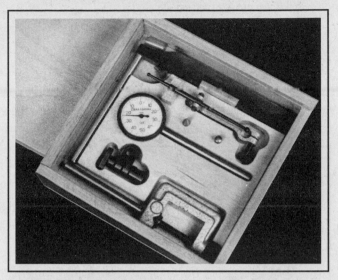

Dial indicator set

can easily mar the gasket sealing surfaces of the parts, which must remain smooth. If prying is absolutely necessary, use an old broom handle, but keep in mind that extra clean up will be necessary if the wood splinters.

After the parts are separated, the old gasket must be carefully scraped off and the gasket surfaces cleaned. Stubborn gasket material can be soaked with rust penetrant or treated with a special chemical to soften it so it can be easily scraped off.

> ✳✳ **CAUTION:**
>
> **Never use gasket removal solutions or caustic chemicals on plastic or other composite components.**

A scraper can be fashioned from a piece of copper tubing by flattening and sharpening one end. Copper is recommended because it is usually softer than the surfaces to be scraped, which reduces the chance of gouging the part. Some gaskets can be removed with a wire brush, but regardless of the method used, the mating surfaces must be left clean and smooth. If for some reason the gasket surface is gouged, then a gasket sealer thick enough to fill scratches will have to be used during reassembly of the components. For most applications, a non-drying (or semi-drying) gasket sealer should be used.

Hose removal tips

> ✳✳ **WARNING:**
>
> **If the vehicle is equipped with air conditioning, do not disconnect any of the A/C hoses without first having the system depressurized by a dealer service department or a service station.**

Hose removal precautions closely parallel gasket removal precautions. Avoid scratching or gouging the surface that the hose mates against or the connection may leak. This is especially true for radiator hoses. Because of various chemical reactions, the rubber in hoses can bond itself to the metal spigot that the hose fits over. To remove a hose, first loosen the hose clamps that secure it to the spigot. Then, with slip-joint pliers, grab the hose at the clamp and rotate it around the spigot. Work it back and forth until it is completely free, then pull it off. Silicone or other lubricants will ease removal if they can be applied

between the hose and the outside of the spigot. Apply the same lubricant to the inside of the hose and the outside of the spigot to simplify installation.

As a last resort (and if the hose is to be replaced with a new one anyway), the rubber can be slit with a knife and the hose peeled from the spigot. If this must be done, be careful that the metal connection is not damaged.

If a hose clamp is broken or damaged, do not reuse it. Wire-type clamps usually weaken with age, so it is a good idea to replace them with screw-type clamps whenever a hose is removed.

TOOLS

A selection of good tools is a basic requirement for anyone who plans to maintain and repair his or her own vehicle. For the owner who has few tools, the initial investment might seem high, but when compared to the spiraling costs of professional auto maintenance and repair, it is a wise one.

To help the owner decide which tools are needed to perform the tasks detailed in this manual, the following tool lists are offered: *Maintenance and minor repair, Repair/overhaul and Special.*

The newcomer to practical mechanics should start off with the *maintenance and minor repair* tool kit, which is adequate for the simpler jobs performed on a vehicle. Then, as confidence and experience grow, the owner can tackle more difficult tasks, buying additional tools as they are needed. Eventually the basic kit will be expanded into the *repair and overhaul* tool set. Over a period of time, the experienced do-it-yourselfer will assemble a tool set complete enough for most repair and overhaul procedures and will add tools from the special category when it is felt that the expense is justified by the frequency of use.

Maintenance and minor repair tool kit

The tools in this list should be considered the minimum required for performance of routine maintenance, servicing and minor repair work. We recommend the purchase of combination wrenches (box-end and open-end combined in one wrench). While more expensive than open end wrenches, they offer the advantages of both types of wrench.

Combination wrench set (1/4-inch to 1 inch or 6 mm to 19 mm)
Adjustable wrench, 8 inch
Spark plug wrench with rubber insert

Spark plug gap adjusting tool
Feeler gauge set
Brake bleeder wrench
Standard screwdriver (5/16-inch x 6 inch)
Phillips screwdriver (No. 2 x 6 inch)
Combination pliers - 6 inch
Hacksaw and assortment of blades
Tire pressure gauge
Grease gun

Oil can
Fine emery cloth
Wire brush
Battery post and cable cleaning tool
Oil filter wrench
Funnel (medium size)
Safety goggles
Jackstands (2)
Drain pan

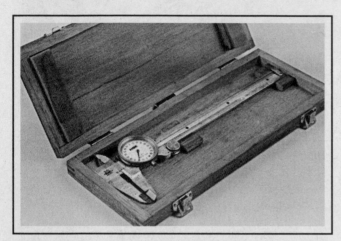

Dial caliper

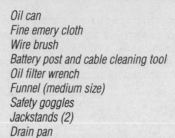
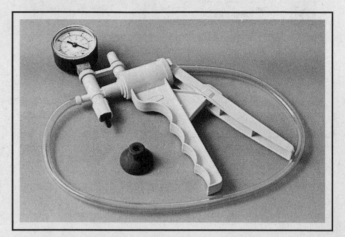

Hand-operated vacuum pump

Timing light

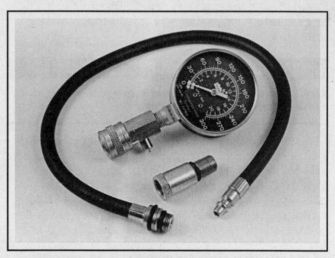

Compression gauge with spark plug hole adapter

Damper/steering wheel puller

General purpose puller

Hydraulic lifter removal tool

➡**Note: If basic tune-ups are going to be part of routine maintenance, it will be necessary to purchase a good quality stroboscopic timing light and combination tachometer/dwell meter. Although they are included in the list of special tools, it is mentioned here because they are absolutely necessary for tuning most vehicles properly.**

Repair and overhaul tool set

These tools are essential for anyone who plans to perform major repairs and are in addition to those in the maintenance and minor repair tool kit. Included is a comprehensive set of sockets which, though expensive, are invaluable because of their versatility, especially when various extensions and drives are available. We recommend the 1/2-inch drive over the 3/8-inch drive. Although the larger drive is bulky and more expensive, it has the capacity of accepting a very wide range of large sockets. Ideally, however, the mechanic should have a 3/8-inch drive set and a 1/2-inch drive set.

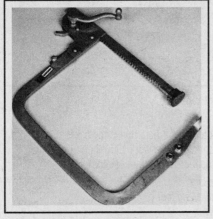

Valve spring compressor

Valve spring compressor

Ridge reamer

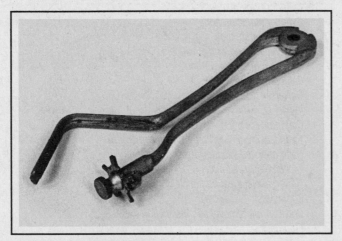

Piston ring groove cleaning tool

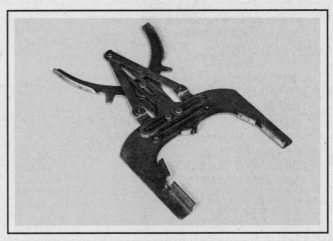

Ring removal/installation tool

Ring compressor

Cylinder hone

Brake hold-down spring tool

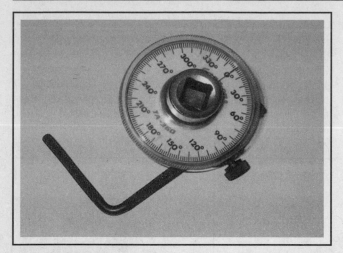

Torque angle gauge

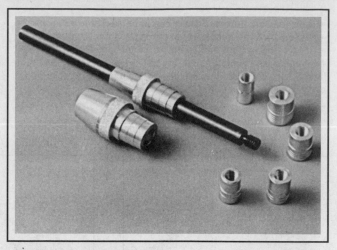

Clutch plate alignment tool

Socket set(s)
Reversible ratchet
Extension - 10 inch
Universal joint
Torque wrench (same size drive as sockets)
Ball peen hammer - 8 ounce
Soft-face hammer (plastic/rubber)
Standard screwdriver (1/4-inch x 6 inch)
Standard screwdriver (stubby - 5/16-inch)
Phillips screwdriver (No. 3 x 8 inch)
Phillips screwdriver (stubby - No. 2)
Pliers - vise grip
Pliers - lineman's
Pliers - needle nose
Pliers - snap-ring (internal and external)
Cold chisel - 1/2-inch
Scribe
Scraper (made from flattened copper tubing)
Centerpunch
Pin punches (1/16, 1/8, 3/16-inch)
Steel rule/straightedge - 12 inch
Allen wrench set (1/8 to 3/8-inch or 4 mm to 10 mm)
A selection of files
Wire brush (large)
Jackstands (second set)
Jack (scissor or hydraulic type)

➡**Note: Another tool which is often useful is an electric drill with a chuck capacity of 3/8-inch and a set of good quality drill bits.**

Special tools

The tools in this list include those which are not used regularly, are expensive to buy, or which need to be used in accordance with their manufacturer's instructions. Unless these tools will be used frequently, it is not very economical to purchase many of them. A consideration would be to split the cost and use between yourself and a friend or friends. In addition, most of these tools can be obtained from a tool rental shop on a temporary basis.

This list primarily contains only those tools and instruments widely available to the public, and not those special tools produced by the vehicle manufacturer for distribution to dealer service departments. Occasionally, references to the manufacturer's special tools are included in the text of this manual. Generally, an alternative method of doing the job without the special tool is offered. However, sometimes there is no alternative to their use. Where this is the case, and the tool cannot be purchased or borrowed, the work should be turned over to the dealer service department or an automotive repair shop.

Valve spring compressor
Piston ring groove cleaning tool
Piston ring compressor
Piston ring installation tool
Cylinder compression gauge
Cylinder ridge reamer
Cylinder surfacing hone
Cylinder bore gauge
Micrometers and/or dial calipers
Hydraulic lifter removal tool
Balljoint separator
Universal-type puller
Impact screwdriver
Dial indicator set
Stroboscopic timing light (inductive pick-up)
Hand operated vacuum/pressure pump
Tachometer/dwell meter
Universal electrical multimeter
Cable hoist
Brake spring removal and installation tools
Floor jack

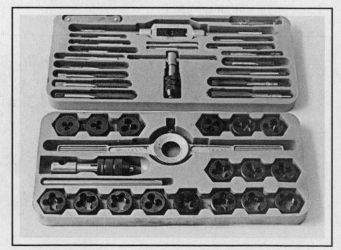

Tap and die set

Buying tools

For the do-it-yourselfer who is just starting to get involved in vehicle maintenance and repair, there are a number of options available when purchasing tools. If maintenance and minor repair is the extent of the work to be done, the purchase of individual tools is satisfactory. If, on the other hand, extensive work is planned, it would be a good idea to purchase a modest tool set from one of the large retail chain stores. A set can usually be bought at a substantial savings over the individual tool prices, and they often come with a tool box. As additional tools are needed, add-on sets, individual tools and a larger tool box can be purchased to expand the tool selection. Building a tool set gradually allows the cost of the tools to be spread over a longer period of time and gives the mechanic the freedom to choose only those tools that will actually be used.

Tool stores will often be the only source of some of the special tools that are needed, but regardless of where tools are bought, try to avoid cheap ones, especially when buying screwdrivers and sockets, because they won't last very long. The expense involved in replacing cheap tools will eventually be greater than the initial cost of quality tools.

Care and maintenance of tools

Good tools are expensive, so it makes sense to treat them with respect. Keep them clean and in usable condition and store them properly when not in use. Always wipe off any dirt, grease or metal chips before putting them away. Never leave tools lying around in the work area. Upon completion of a job, always check closely under the hood for tools that may have been left there so they won't get lost during a test drive.

Some tools, such as screwdrivers, pliers, wrenches and sockets, can be hung on a panel mounted on the garage or workshop wall, while others should be kept in a tool box or tray. Measuring instruments, gauges, meters, etc. must be carefully stored where they cannot be damaged by weather or impact from other tools.

When tools are used with care and stored properly, they will last a very long time. Even with the best of care, though, tools will wear out if used frequently. When a tool is damaged or worn out, replace it. Subsequent jobs will be safer and more enjoyable if you do.

HOW TO REPAIR DAMAGED THREADS

Sometimes, the internal threads of a nut or bolt hole can become stripped, usually from overtightening. Stripping threads is an all-too-common occurrence, especially when working with aluminum parts, because aluminum is so soft that it easily strips out.

Usually, external or internal threads are only partially stripped. After they've been cleaned up with a tap or die, they'll still work. Sometimes, however, threads are badly damaged. When this happens, you've got three choices:

1) *Drill and tap the hole to the next suitable oversize and install a larger diameter bolt, screw or stud.*

2) *Drill and tap the hole to accept a threaded plug, then drill and tap the plug to the original screw size. You can also buy a plug already threaded to the original size. Then you simply drill a hole to the specified size, then run the threaded plug into the hole with a bolt and jam nut. Once the plug is fully seated, remove the jam nut and bolt.*

3) *The third method uses a patented thread repair kit like Heli-Coil or Slimsert. These easy-to-use kits are designed to repair damaged threads in straight-through holes and blind holes. Both are available as kits which can handle a variety of sizes and thread patterns. Drill the hole, then tap it with the special included tap. Install the Heli-Coil and the hole is back to its original diameter and thread pitch.*

Regardless of which method you use, be sure to proceed calmly and carefully. A little impatience or carelessness during one of these relatively simple procedures can ruin your whole day's work and cost you a bundle if you wreck an expensive part.

WORKING FACILITIES

Not to be overlooked when discussing tools is the workshop. If anything more than routine maintenance is to be carried out, some sort of suitable work area is essential.

It is understood, and appreciated, that many home mechanics do not have a good workshop or garage available, and end up removing an engine or doing major repairs outside. It is recommended, however, that the overhaul or repair be completed under the cover of a roof.

A clean, flat workbench or table of comfortable working height is an absolute necessity. The workbench should be equipped with a vise that has a jaw opening of at least four inches.

As mentioned previously, some clean, dry storage space is also required for tools, as well as the lubricants, fluids, cleaning solvents, etc. which soon become necessary.

Sometimes waste oil and fluids, drained from the engine or cooling system during normal maintenance or repairs, present a disposal problem. To avoid pouring them on the ground or into a sewage system, pour the used fluids into large containers, seal them with caps and take them to an authorized disposal site or recycling center. Plastic jugs, such as old antifreeze containers, are ideal for this purpose.

Always keep a supply of old newspapers and clean rags available. Old towels are excellent for mopping up spills. Many mechanics use rolls of paper towels for most work because they are readily available and disposable. To help keep the area under the vehicle clean, a large cardboard box can be cut open and flattened to protect the garage or shop floor.

Whenever working over a painted surface, such as when leaning over a fender to service something under the hood, always cover it with an old blanket or bedspread to protect the finish. Vinyl covered pads, made especially for this purpose, are available at auto parts stores.

JACKING

➡**Note: On Armada models equipped with a rear auto-leveling suspension, turn the ignition key to the OFF position before raising the vehicle.**

The jack supplied with the vehicle should only be used for raising the vehicle when changing a tire or placing jackstands under the frame. NEVER work under the vehicle or start the engine when the vehicle supported only by a jack.

The vehicle should be parked on level ground with the wheels blocked, the parking brake applied and the transmission in Park (automatic) or Reverse (manual). If the vehicle is parked alongside the roadway, or in any other hazardous situation, turn on the emergency hazard flashers. If a tire is to be changed, loosen the lug nuts one-half turn before raising off the ground.

Place the jack under the vehicle in the indicated positions (see illustrations). Operate the jack with a slow, smooth motion until the wheel is raised off the ground. Remove the lug nuts, pull off the wheel, install the spare and thread the lug nuts back on with the beveled side facing in. Tighten the lug nuts snugly, lower the vehicle until some weight is on the wheel, then tighten them completely in a criss-cross pattern and remove the jack.

TOWING

Equipment specifically designed for towing should be used and attached to the main structural members of the vehicle. Optional tow hooks may be attached to the frame at both ends of the vehicle; they are intended for emergency use only, for rescuing a stranded vehicle. Do not use the tow hooks for highway towing. Stand clear when using tow straps or chains; they may break, causing serious injury.

The manufacturer recommends that these vehicles be towed only by wheel-lift equipment or a flatbed car-carrier.

Safety is a major consideration when towing and all applicable state and local laws must be obeyed. In addition to a tow bar, a safety chain must be used for all towing.

Two-wheel drive vehicles with automatic transmission may be towed with the rear wheels on a towing dolly with no mileage restriction (at posted highway speeds).

Four-wheel drive models must be towed with all four wheels off the ground or transmission damage might occur.

Front jacking location, all models - place the jack directly under the arrow stamped in the frame rail

Rear jacking location, Armada models - place the jack directly under the arrow stamped in the frame rail

Rear jacking location, Titan models

Booster battery (jump) starting

➡Note: If the vehicle is equipped with a Nissan Intelligent Key and the battery is completely discharged, the ignition key will not be able to be turned from the Lock position until the jumper cables are connected to a fully charged battery.

Observe these precautions when using a booster battery to start a vehicle:

a) *Before connecting the booster battery, make sure the ignition switch is in the Off position.*

b) *Turn off the lights, heater and other electrical loads.*

c) *Your eyes should be shielded. Safety goggles are a good idea.*

d) *Make sure the booster battery is the same voltage as the dead one in the vehicle.*

e) *The two vehicles MUST NOT TOUCH each other!*

f) *Make sure the transaxle is in Neutral (manual) or Park (automatic).*

g) *If the booster battery is not a maintenance-free type, remove the vent caps and lay a cloth over the vent holes.*

Connect the red-colored jumper cable to the positive (+) terminal of the booster battery and the other end to the positive (+) terminal of the dead battery. Then connect one end of the black jumper cable to the negative (-) terminal of the booster battery, and the other end of the cable to a good ground, such as a bolt or bracket.

Start the engine using the booster battery, then run the booster vehicle at a fast idle for a few minutes to instill some charge in the dead battery. Let the engine idle, then disconnect the jumper cables in the reverse order of connection. The vehicle with the dead battery may have to be driven for 20 minutes or more to sufficiently recharge the battery for independent starting.

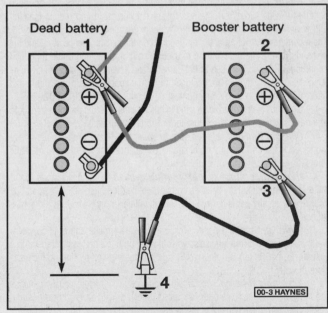

Make the booster battery cable connections in the numerical order shown (note that the negative cable of the booster battery is NOT attached to the negative terminal of the dead battery)

Automotive chemicals and lubricants

A number of automotive chemicals and lubricants are available for use during vehicle maintenance and repair. They include a wide variety of products ranging from cleaning solvents and degreasers to lubricants and protective sprays for rubber, plastic and vinyl.

CLEANERS

Carburetor cleaner and choke cleaner is a strong solvent for gum, varnish and carbon. Most carburetor cleaners leave a dry-type lubricant film which will not harden or gum up. Because of this film it is not recommended for use on electrical components.

Brake system cleaner is used to remove brake dust, grease and brake fluid from the brake system, where clean surfaces are absolutely necessary. It leaves no residue and often eliminates brake squeal caused by contaminants.

Electrical cleaner removes oxidation, corrosion and carbon deposits from electrical contacts, restoring full current flow. It can also be used to clean spark plugs, carburetor jets, voltage regulators and other parts where an oil-free surface is desired.

Demoisturants remove water and moisture from electrical components such as alternators, voltage regulators, electrical connectors and fuse blocks. They are non-conductive and non-corrosive.

Degreasers are heavy-duty solvents used to remove grease from the outside of the engine and from chassis components. They can be sprayed or brushed on and, depending on the type, are rinsed off either with water or solvent.

LUBRICANTS

Motor oil is the lubricant formulated for use in engines. It normally contains a wide variety of additives to prevent corrosion and reduce foaming and wear. Motor oil comes in various weights (viscosity ratings) from 0 to 50. The recommended weight of the oil depends on the season, temperature and the demands on the engine. Light oil is used in cold climates and under light load conditions. Heavy oil is used in hot climates and where high loads are encountered. Multi-viscosity oils are designed to have characteristics of both light and heavy oils and are available in a number of weights from 0W-20 to 20W-50.

Gear oil is designed to be used in differentials, manual transmissions and other areas where high-temperature lubrication is required.

Chassis and wheel bearing grease is a heavy grease used where increased loads and friction are encountered, such as for wheel bearings, ball-joints, tie-rod ends and universal joints.

High-temperature wheel bearing grease is designed to withstand the extreme temperatures encountered by wheel bearings in disc brake equipped vehicles. It usually contains molybdenum disulfide (moly), which is a dry-type lubricant.

White grease is a heavy grease for metal-to-metal applications where water is a problem. White grease stays soft under both low and high temperatures (usually from -100 to +190-degrees F), and will not wash off or dilute in the presence of water.

Assembly lube is a special extreme pressure lubricant, usually containing moly, used to lubricate high-load parts (such as main and rod bearings and cam lobes) for initial start-up of a new engine. The assembly lube lubricates the parts without being squeezed out or washed away until the engine oiling system begins to function.

Silicone lubricants are used to protect rubber, plastic, vinyl and nylon parts.

Graphite lubricants are used where oils cannot be used due to contamination problems, such as in locks. The dry graphite will lubricate metal parts while remaining uncontaminated by dirt, water, oil or acids. It is electrically conductive and will not foul electrical contacts in locks such as the ignition switch.

Moly penetrants loosen and lubricate frozen, rusted and corroded fasteners and prevent future rusting or freezing.

Heat-sink grease is a special electrically non-conductive grease that is used for mounting electronic ignition modules where it is essential that heat is transferred away from the module.

SEALANTS

RTV sealant is one of the most widely used gasket compounds. Made from silicone, RTV is air curing, it seals, bonds, waterproofs, fills surface irregularities, remains flexible, doesn't shrink, is relatively easy to remove, and is used as a supplementary sealer with almost all low and medium temperature gaskets.

Anaerobic sealant is much like RTV in that it can be used either to seal gaskets or to form gaskets by itself. It remains flexible, is solvent resistant and fills surface imperfections. The difference between an anaerobic sealant and an RTV-type sealant is in the curing. RTV cures when exposed to air, while an anaerobic sealant cures only in the absence of air. This means that an anaerobic sealant cures only after the assembly of parts, sealing them together.

Thread and pipe sealant is used for sealing hydraulic and pneumatic fittings and vacuum lines. It is usually made from a Teflon compound, and comes in a spray, a paint-on liquid and as a wrap-around tape.

CHEMICALS

Anti-seize compound prevents seizing, galling, cold welding, rust and corrosion in fasteners. High-temperature anti-seize, usually made with copper and graphite lubricants, is used for exhaust system and exhaust manifold bolts.

Anaerobic locking compounds are used to keep fasteners from vibrating or working loose and cure only after installation, in the absence of air. Medium strength locking compound is used for small nuts, bolts and screws that may be removed later. High-strength locking compound is for large nuts, bolts and studs which aren't removed on a regular basis.

Oil additives range from viscosity index improvers to chemical treatments that claim to reduce internal engine friction. It should be noted that most oil manufacturers caution against using additives with their oils.

Gas additives perform several functions, depending on their chemical makeup. They usually contain solvents that help dissolve gum and varnish that build up on carburetor, fuel injection and intake parts. They also serve to break down carbon deposits that form on the inside surfaces of the combustion chambers. Some additives contain upper cylinder lubricants for valves and piston rings, and others contain chemicals to remove condensation from the gas tank.

MISCELLANEOUS

Brake fluid is specially formulated hydraulic fluid that can withstand the heat and pressure encountered in brake systems. Care must be taken so this fluid does not come in contact with painted surfaces or plastics. An opened container should always be resealed to prevent contamination by water or dirt.

Weatherstrip adhesive is used to bond weatherstripping around doors, windows and trunk lids. It is sometimes used to attach trim pieces.

Undercoating is a petroleum-based, tar-like substance that is designed to protect metal surfaces on the underside of the vehicle from corrosion. It also acts as a sound-deadening agent by insulating the bottom of the vehicle.

Waxes and polishes are used to help protect painted and plated surfaces from the weather. Different types of paint may require the use of different types of wax and polish. Some polishes utilize a chemical or abrasive cleaner to help remove the top layer of oxidized (dull) paint on older vehicles. In recent years many non-wax polishes that contain a wide variety of chemicals such as polymers and silicones have been introduced. These non-wax polishes are usually easier to apply and last longer than conventional waxes and polishes.

CONVERSION FACTORS

LENGTH (distance)

Inches (in)	X 25.4	= Millimeters (mm)	X 0.0394	= Inches (in)
Feet (ft)	X 0.305	= Meters (m)	X 3.281	= Feet (ft)
Miles	X 1.609	= Kilometers (km)	X 0.621	= Miles

VOLUME (capacity)

Cubic inches (cu in; in^3)	X 16.387	= Cubic centimeters (cc; cm^3)	X 0.061	= Cubic inches (cu in; in^3)
Imperial pints (Imp pt)	X 0.568	= Liters (l)	X 1.76	= Imperial pints (Imp pt)
Imperial quarts (Imp qt)	X 1.137	= Liters (l)	X 0.88	= Imperial quarts (Imp qt)
Imperial quarts (Imp qt)	X 1.201	= US quarts (US qt)	X 0.833	= Imperial quarts (Imp qt)
US quarts (US qt)	X 0.946	= Liters (l)	X 1.057	= US quarts (US qt)
Imperial gallons (Imp gal)	X 4.546	= Liters (l)	X 0.22	= Imperial gallons (Imp gal)
Imperial gallons (Imp gal)	X 1.201	= US gallons (US gal)	X 0.833	= Imperial gallons (Imp gal)
US gallons (US gal)	X 3.785	= Liters (l)	X 0.264	= US gallons (US gal)

MASS (weight)

Ounces (oz)	X 28.35	= Grams (g)	X 0.035	= Ounces (oz)
Pounds (lb)	X 0.454	= Kilograms (kg)	X 2.205	= Pounds (lb)

FORCE

Ounces-force (ozf; oz)	X 0.278	= Newtons (N)	X 3.6	= Ounces-force (ozf; oz)
Pounds-force (lbf; lb)	X 4.448	= Newtons (N)	X 0.225	= Pounds-force (lbf; lb)
Newtons (N)	X 0.1	= Kilograms-force (kgf; kg)	X 9.81	= Newtons (N)

PRESSURE

Pounds-force per square inch (psi; lbf/in^2; lb/in^2)	X 0.070	= Kilograms-force per square centimeter (kgf/cm^2; kg/cm^2)	X 14.223	= Pounds-force per square inch (psi; lbf/in^2; lb/in^2)
Pounds-force per square inch (psi; lbf/in^2; lb/in^2)	X 0.068	= Atmospheres (atm)	X 14.696	= Pounds-force per square inch (psi; lbf/in^2; lb/in^2)
Pounds-force per square inch (psi; lbf/in^2; lb/in^2)	X 0.069	= Bars	X 14.5	= Pounds-force per square inch (psi; lbf/in^2; lb/in^2)
Pounds-force per square inch (psi; lbf/in^2; lb/in^2)	X 6.895	= Kilopascals (kPa)	X 0.145	= Pounds-force per square inch (psi; lbf/in^2; lb/in^2)
Kilopascals (kPa)	X 0.01	= Kilograms-force per square centimeter (kgf/cm^2; kg/cm^2)	X 98.1	= Kilopascals (kPa)

TORQUE (moment of force)

Pounds-force inches (lbf in; lb in)	X 1.152	= Kilograms-force centimeter (kgf cm; kg cm)	X 0.868	= Pounds-force inches (lbf in; lb in)
Pounds-force inches (lbf in; lb in)	X 0.113	= Newton meters (Nm)	X 8.85	= Pounds-force inches (lbf in; lb in)
Pounds-force inches (lbf in; lb in)	X 0.083	= Pounds-force feet (lbf ft; lb ft)	X 12	= Pounds-force inches (lbf in; lb in)
Pounds-force feet (lbf ft; lb ft)	X 0.138	= Kilograms-force meters (kgf m; kg m)	X 7.233	= Pounds-force feet (lbf ft; lb ft)
Pounds-force feet (lbf ft; lb ft)	X 1.356	= Newton meters (Nm)	X 0.738	= Pounds-force feet (lbf ft; lb ft)
Newton meters (Nm)	X 0.102	= Kilograms-force meters (kgf m; kg m)	X 9.804	= Newton meters (Nm)

VACUUM

Inches mercury (in. Hg)	X 3.377	= Kilopascals (kPa)	X 0.2961	= Inches mercury
Inches mercury (in. Hg)	X 25.4	= Millimeters mercury (mm Hg)	X 0.0394	= Inches mercury

POWER

Horsepower (hp)	X 745.7	= Watts (W)	X 0.0013	= Horsepower (hp)

VELOCITY (speed)

Miles per hour (miles/hr; mph)	X 1.609	= Kilometers per hour (km/hr; kph)	X 0.621	= Miles per hour (miles/hr; mph)

FUEL CONSUMPTION *

Miles per gallon, Imperial (mpg)	X 0.354	= Kilometers per liter (km/l)	X 2.825	= Miles per gallon, Imperial (mpg)
Miles per gallon, US (mpg)	X 0.425	= Kilometers per liter (km/l)	X 2.352	= Miles per gallon, US (mpg)

TEMPERATURE

Degrees Fahrenheit = (°C x 1.8) + 32   Degrees Celsius (Degrees Centigrade; °C) = (°F - 32) x 0.56

*It is common practice to convert from miles per gallon (mpg) to liters/100 kilometers (l/100km),
where mpg (Imperial) x l/100 km = 282 and mpg (US) x l/100 km = 235

FRACTION/DECIMAL/MILLIMETER EQUIVALENTS

DECIMALS TO MILLIMETERS

Decimal	mm	Decimal	mm
0.001	0.0254	0.500	12.7000
0.002	0.0508	0.510	12.9540
0.003	0.0762	0.520	13.2080
0.004	0.1016	0.530	13.4620
0.005	0.1270	0.540	13.7160
0.006	0.1524	0.550	13.9700
0.007	0.1778	0.560	14.2240
0.008	0.2032	0.570	14.4780
0.009	0.2286	0.580	14.7320
		0.590	14.9860
0.010	0.2540		
0.020	0.5080		
0.030	0.7620		
0.040	1.0160	0.600	15.2400
0.050	1.2700	0.610	15.4940
0.060	1.5240	0.620	15.7480
0.070	1.7780	0.630	16.0020
0.080	2.0320	0.640	16.2560
0.090	2.2860	0.650	16.5100
		0.660	16.7640
0.100	2.5400	0.670	17.0180
0.110	2.7940	0.680	17.2720
0.120	3.0480	0.690	17.5260
0.130	3.3020		
0.140	3.5560		
0.150	3.8100		
0.160	4.0640	0.700	17.7800
0.170	4.3180	0.710	18.0340
0.180	4.5720	0.720	18.2880
0.190	4.8260	0.730	18.5420
		0.740	18.7960
0.200	5.0800	0.750	19.0500
0.210	5.3340	0.760	19.3040
0.220	5.5880	0.770	19.5580
0.230	5.8420	0.780	19.8120
0.240	6.0960	0.790	20.0660
0.250	6.3500		
0.260	6.6040		
0.270	6.8580	0.800	20.3200
0.280	7.1120	0.810	20.5740
0.290	7.3660	0.820	21.8280
		0.830	21.0820
0.300	7.6200	0.840	21.3360
0.310	7.8740	0.850	21.5900
0.320	8.1280	0.860	21.8440
0.330	8.3820	0.870	22.0980
0.340	8.6360	0.880	22.3520
0.350	8.8900	0.890	22.6060
0.360	9.1440		
0.370	9.3980		
0.380	9.6520		
0.390	9.9060		
		0.900	22.8600
0.400	10.1600	0.910	23.1140
0.410	10.4140	0.920	23.3680
0.420	10.6680	0.930	23.6220
0.430	10.9220	0.940	23.8760
0.440	11.1760	0.950	24.1300
0.450	11.4300	0.960	24.3840
0.460	11.6840	0.970	24.6380
0.470	11.9380	0.980	24.8920
0.480	12.1920	0.990	25.1460
0.490	12.4460	1.000	25.4000

FRACTIONS TO DECIMALS TO MILLIMETERS

Fraction	Decimal	mm	Fraction	Decimal	mm
1/64	0.0156	0.3969	33/64	0.5156	13.0969
1/32	0.0312	0.7938	17/32	0.5312	13.4938
3/64	0.0469	1.1906	35/64	0.5469	13.8906
1/16	0.0625	1.5875	9/16	0.5625	14.2875
5/64	0.0781	1.9844	37/64	0.5781	14.6844
3/32	0.0938	2.3812	19/32	0.5938	15.0812
7/64	0.1094	2.7781	39/64	0.6094	15.4781
1/8	0.1250	3.1750	5/8	0.6250	15.8750
9/64	0.1406	3.5719	41/64	0.6406	16.2719
5/32	0.1562	3.9688	21/32	0.6562	16.6688
11/64	0.1719	4.3656	43/64	0.6719	17.0656
3/16	0.1875	4.7625	11/16	0.6875	17.4625
13/64	0.2031	5.1594	45/64	0.7031	17.8594
7/32	0.2188	5.5562	23/32	0.7188	18.2562
15/64	0.2344	5.9531	47/64	0.7344	18.6531
1/4	0.2500	6.3500	3/4	0.7500	19.0500
17/64	0.2656	6.7469	49/64	0.7656	19.4469
9/32	0.2812	7.1438	25/32	0.7812	19.8438
19/64	0.2969	7.5406	51/64	0.7969	20.2406
5/16	0.3125	7.9375	13/16	0.8125	20.6375
21/64	0.3281	8.3344	53/64	0.8281	21.0344
11/32	0.3438	8.7312	27/32	0.8438	21.4312
23/64	0.3594	9.1281	55/64	0.8594	21.8281
3/8	0.3750	9.5250	7/8	0.8750	22.2250
25/64	0.3906	9.9219	57/64	0.8906	22.6219
13/32	0.4062	10.3188	29/32	0.9062	23.0188
27/64	0.4219	10.7156	59/64	0.9219	23.4156
7/16	0.4375	11.1125	15/16	0.9375	23.8125
29/64	0.4531	11.5094	61/64	0.9531	24.2094
15/32	0.4688	11.9062	31/32	0.9688	24.6062
31/64	0.4844	12.3031	63/64	0.9844	25.0031
1/2	0.5000	12.7000	1	1.0000	25.4000

Safety first!

Regardless of how enthusiastic you may be about getting on with the job at hand, take the time to ensure that your safety is not jeopardized. A moment's lack of attention can result in an accident, as can failure to observe certain simple safety precautions. The possibility of an accident will always exist, and the following points should not be considered a comprehensive list of all dangers. Rather, they are intended to make you aware of the risks and to encourage a safety conscious approach to all work you carry out on your vehicle.

ESSENTIAL DOS AND DON'TS

DON'T rely on a jack when working under the vehicle. Always use approved jackstands to support the weight of the vehicle and place them under the recommended lift or support points.

DON'T attempt to loosen extremely tight fasteners (i.e. wheel lug nuts) while the vehicle is on a jack - it may fall.

DON'T start the engine without first making sure that the transmission is in Neutral (or Park where applicable) and the parking brake is set.

DON'T remove the radiator cap from a hot cooling system - let it cool or cover it with a cloth and release the pressure gradually.

DON'T attempt to drain the engine oil until you are sure it has cooled to the point that it will not burn you.

DON'T touch any part of the engine or exhaust system until it has cooled sufficiently to avoid burns.

DON'T siphon toxic liquids such as gasoline, antifreeze and brake fluid by mouth, or allow them to remain on your skin.

DON'T inhale brake lining dust - it is potentially hazardous (see Asbestos below).

DON'T allow spilled oil or grease to remain on the floor - wipe it up before someone slips on it.

DON'T use loose fitting wrenches or other tools which may slip and cause injury.

DON'T push on wrenches when loosening or tightening nuts or bolts. Always try to pull the wrench toward you. If the situation calls for pushing the wrench away, push with an open hand to avoid scraped knuckles if the wrench should slip.

DON'T attempt to lift a heavy component alone - get someone to help you.

DON'T rush or take unsafe shortcuts to finish a job.

DON'T allow children or animals in or around the vehicle while you are working on it.

DO wear eye protection when using power tools such as a drill, sander, bench grinder, etc. and when working under a vehicle.

DO keep loose clothing and long hair well out of the way of moving parts.

DO make sure that any hoist used has a safe working load rating adequate for the job.

DO get someone to check on you periodically when working alone on a vehicle.

DO carry out work in a logical sequence and make sure that everything is correctly assembled and tightened.

DO keep chemicals and fluids tightly capped and out of the reach of children and pets.

DO remember that your vehicle's safety affects that of yourself and others. If in doubt on any point, get professional advice.

STEERING, SUSPENSION AND BRAKES

These systems are essential to driving safety, so make sure you have a qualified shop or individual check your work. Also, compressed suspension springs can cause injury if released suddenly - be sure to use a spring compressor.

AIRBAGS

Airbags are explosive devices that can CAUSE injury if they deploy while you're working on the vehicle. Follow the manufacturer's instructions to disable the airbag whenever you're working in the vicinity of airbag components.

ASBESTOS

Certain friction, insulating, sealing, and other products - such as brake linings, brake bands, clutch linings, torque converters, gaskets, etc. - may contain asbestos or other hazardous friction material. Extreme care must be taken to avoid inhalation of dust from such products, since it is hazardous to health. If in doubt, assume that they do contain asbestos.

FIRE

Remember at all times that gasoline is highly flammable. Never smoke or have any kind of open flame around when working on a vehicle. But the risk does not end there. A spark caused by an electrical short circuit, by two metal surfaces contacting each other, or even by static electricity built up in your body under certain conditions, can ignite gasoline vapors, which in a confined space are highly explosive. Do not, under any circumstances, use gasoline for cleaning parts. Use an approved safety solvent.

Always disconnect the battery ground (-) cable at the battery before working on any part of the fuel system or electrical system. Never risk spilling fuel on a hot engine or exhaust component. It is strongly recommended that a fire extinguisher suitable for use on fuel and electrical fires be kept handy in the garage or workshop at all times. Never try to extinguish a fuel or electrical fire with water.

FUMES

Certain fumes are highly toxic and can quickly cause unconsciousness and even death if inhaled to any extent. Gasoline vapor falls into this category, as do the vapors from some cleaning solvents. Any draining or pouring of such volatile fluids should be done in a well ventilated area.

When using cleaning fluids and solvents, read the instructions on the container carefully. Never use materials from unmarked containers.

Never run the engine in an enclosed space, such as a garage. Exhaust fumes contain carbon monoxide, which is extremely poisonous. If you need to run the engine, always do so in the open air, or at least have the rear of the vehicle outside the work area.

THE BATTERY

Never create a spark or allow a bare light bulb near a battery. They normally give off a certain amount of hydrogen gas, which is highly explosive.

Always disconnect the battery ground (-) cable at the battery before working on the fuel or electrical systems.

If possible, loosen the filler caps or cover when charging the battery from an external source (this does not apply to sealed or maintenance-free batteries). Do not charge at an excessive rate or the battery may burst.

Take care when adding water to a non maintenance-free battery and when carrying a battery. The electrolyte, even when diluted, is very corrosive and should not be allowed to contact clothing or skin.

Always wear eye protection when cleaning the battery to prevent the caustic deposits from entering your eyes.

HOUSEHOLD CURRENT

When using an electric power tool, inspection light, etc., which operates on household current, always make sure that the tool is correctly connected to its plug and that, where necessary, it is properly grounded. Do not use such items in damp conditions and, again, do not create a spark or apply excessive heat in the vicinity of fuel or fuel vapor.

SECONDARY IGNITION SYSTEM VOLTAGE

A severe electric shock can result from touching certain parts of the ignition system (such as the spark plug wires) when the engine is running or being cranked, particularly if components are damp or the insulation is defective. In the case of an electronic ignition system, the secondary system voltage is much higher and could prove fatal.

HYDROFLUORIC ACID

This extremely corrosive acid is formed when certain types of synthetic rubber, found in some O-rings, oil seals, fuel hoses, etc. are exposed to temperatures above 750-degrees F (400-degrees C). The rubber changes into a charred or sticky substance containing the acid. *Once formed, the acid remains dangerous for years. If it gets onto the skin, it may be necessary to amputate the limb concerned.*

When dealing with a vehicle which has suffered a fire, or with components salvaged from such a vehicle, wear protective gloves and discard them after use.

Troubleshooting

CONTENTS

This section provides an easy reference guide to the more common problems that may occur during the operation of your vehicle. These problems and possible causes are grouped under various components or systems; i.e. Engine, Cooling System, etc., and also refer to the Chapter and/or Section that deals with the problem.

Remember that successful troubleshooting is not a mysterious black art practiced only by professional mechanics. It's simply the result of a bit of knowledge combined with an intelligent, systematic approach to the problem. Always work by a process of elimination, starting with the simplest solution and working through to the most complex - and never overlook the obvious. Anyone can forget to fill the gas tank or leave the lights on overnight, so don't assume that you are above such oversights.

Finally, always get clear in your mind why a problem has occurred and take steps to ensure that it doesn't happen again. If the electrical system fails because of a poor connection, check all other connections in the system to make sure that they don't fail as well. If a particular fuse continues to blow, find out why - don't just go on replacing fuses. Remember, failure of a small component can often be indicative of potential failure or incorrect functioning of a more important component or system.

ENGINE

1   Engine will not rotate when attempting to start

1   Battery terminal connections loose or corroded. Check the cable terminals at the battery. Tighten the cable or remove corrosion as necessary.
2   Battery discharged or faulty. If the cable connections are clean and tight on the battery posts, turn the key to the On position and switch on the headlights and/or windshield wipers. If they fail to function, the battery is discharged.
3   Automatic transmission not completely engaged in Park or Neutral.
4   Broken, loose or disconnected wiring in the starting circuit. Inspect all wiring and connectors at the battery, starter solenoid and ignition switch.
5   Starter motor pinion jammed in driveplate ring gear. Remove the starter (Chapter 5) and inspect the pinion and driveplate.
6   Starter solenoid faulty (Chapter 5).
7   Starter motor faulty (Chapter 5).
8   Ignition switch faulty (Chapter 12).
9   Intelligent Power Distribution Module (IPDM) faulty (Chapter 12).
10 Starter relay faulty (Chapter 12).

2   Engine rotates but will not start

1   Fuel tank empty, fuel filter plugged or fuel line restricted.
2   Fault in the fuel injection system (Chapter 4).
3   Battery discharged (engine rotates slowly). Check the operation of electrical components as described in the previous Section.
4   Battery terminal connections loose or corroded (see previous Section).
5   Fuel pump faulty (Chapter 4).
6   Ignition system or engine control system problem (see Chapters 5 and 6).
7   Worn, faulty or incorrectly gapped spark plugs (Chapter 1).

3   Starter motor operates without rotating engine

1   Starter pinion sticking. Remove the starter (Chapter 5) and inspect.
2   Starter pinion or driveplate teeth worn or broken. Remove the driveplate/driveplate access cover and inspect.

4   Engine hard to start when cold

1   Discharged or low battery. Check as described in Section 1.

2   Fault in the fuel, ignition or engine management system (Chapters 4, 5 and 6).
3   Injector(s) leaking (Chapter 4).

5   Engine hard to start when hot

1   Air filter clogged (Chapter 1).
2   Fault in the fuel, ignition or engine management system (Chapters 4, 5 and 6).
3   Fuel not reaching the injectors (see Chapter 4).
4   Low cylinder compression (Chapter 2B).
5   Malfunctioning EVAP system (Chapter 6).

6   Starter motor noisy or excessively rough in engagement

1   Pinion or driveplate gear teeth worn or broken. Remove the cover at the rear of the engine (if equipped) and inspect.
2   Starter motor mounting bolts loose or missing.

7   Engine starts but stops immediately

1   Fault in the fuel or ignition systems (Chapters 4 and 5).
2   Vacuum leak at the gasket surfaces of the intake manifold. Make sure all mounting bolts/nuts are tightened securely and all vacuum hoses connected to the manifold are positioned properly and in good condition.
3   Restricted intake or exhaust systems (Chapter 4).

8   Engine lopes while idling or idles erratically

1   Vacuum leakage. Check the mounting bolts/nuts at the throttle body and intake manifold for tightness. Make sure all vacuum hoses are connected and in good condition. Use a stethoscope or a length of fuel hose held against your ear to listen for vacuum leaks while the engine is running. A hissing sound will be heard. A soapy water solution will also detect leaks.
2   Fault in the fuel, ignition or engine management system (Chapters 4, 5 and 6).
3   Plugged PCV valve or hose (see Chapters 1 and 6).
4   Air filter clogged (Chapter 1).
5   Fuel pump not delivering sufficient fuel to the fuel injectors (see Chapter 4).
6   Leaking head gasket. Perform a compression check (Chapter 2B).
7   Camshaft lobes worn (Chapter 2).

9 Engine misses at idle speed

1 Spark plugs worn, fouled or not gapped properly (Chapter 1).
2 Fault in the fuel, ignition or engine management system (Chapters 4, 5 and 6).
3 Faulty ignition coil(s) (Chapter 1).
4 Vacuum leaks at intake or hose connections. Check as described in Section 8.
5 Uneven or low cylinder compression. Check compression as described in Chapter 2B.

10 Engine misses throughout driving speed range

1 Fuel filter clogged and/or impurities in the fuel system (Chapter 1).
2 Faulty or incorrectly gapped spark plugs (Chapter 1).
3 Fault in the fuel, ignition or engine management system (Chapters 4, 5 and 6).
4 Defective spark plug boots or coils (Chapter 1).
5 Faulty emissions system components (Chapter 6).
6 Low or uneven cylinder compression pressures. Check compression as described in Chapter 2B.
7 Vacuum leaks at the throttle body, intake manifold or vacuum hoses (see Section 8).

11 Engine stalls

1 Fuel filter clogged and/or water and impurities in the fuel system (Chapter 1).
2 Fault in the fuel, ignition or engine management system (Chapters 4, 5 and 6).
3 Faulty emissions system components (Chapter 6).
4 Faulty or incorrectly gapped spark plugs (Chapter 1). Also check the ignition coils (Chapter 1).
5 Vacuum leak at the throttle body, intake manifold or vacuum hoses. Check as described in Section 8.

12 Engine lacks power

1 Fault in the fuel, ignition or engine management system (Chapters 4, 5 and 6).
2 Faulty or incorrectly gapped spark plugs (Chapter 1).
3 Brakes binding (Chapter 1).
4 Automatic transmission fluid level incorrect (Chapter 1).
5 Fuel filter clogged and/or impurities in the fuel system (Chapter 1).
6 Emissions control system not functioning properly (Chapter 6).
7 Use of substandard fuel. Fill the tank with the proper fuel.
8 Low or uneven cylinder compression pressures (Chapter 2B).
9 Restriction in the intake or exhaust system (Chapter 4).

13 Engine backfires

1 Emissions system not functioning properly (Chapter 6).
2 Fault in the fuel or ignition systems (Chapters 4 and 5).
3 Fuel injection system not functioning properly (Chapter 4).
4 Vacuum leak at the throttle body, intake manifold or vacuum hoses. Check as described in Section 8.
5 Valves sticking (Chapter 2).

14 Pinging or knocking engine sounds during acceleration or uphill

1 Incorrect grade of fuel. Fill the tank with fuel of the proper octane rating.
2 Fault in the fuel or ignition systems (Chapters 4 and 5).
3 Improper spark plugs (Chapter 1).
4 Faulty emissions system or knock sensor (Chapter 6).
5 Vacuum leak. Check as described in Section 9.

15 Engine diesels (continues to run) after switching off

1 Idle speed too high (Chapter 4).
2 Fault in the fuel or ignition systems (Chapters 4 and 5).
3 Excessive engine operating temperature. Probable causes of this are a low coolant level (see Chapter 1), malfunctioning thermostat, clogged radiator or faulty water pump (see Chapter 3).

ENGINE ELECTRICAL SYSTEM

16 Battery will not hold a charge

1 Alternator drivebelt defective or not adjusted properly (Chapter 1).
2 Electrolyte level low or battery discharged (Chapter 1).
3 Battery terminals loose or corroded (Chapter 1).
4 Alternator not charging properly (Chapter 5).
5 Loose, broken or faulty wiring in the charging circuit (Chapter 5).
6 Battery defective internally.

17 Alternator light fails to go out

1 Fault in the alternator or charging circuit (Chapter 5).
2 Alternator drivebelt defective or not properly adjusted (Chapter 1).

18 Alternator light fails to come on when key is turned on

1 Instrument cluster warning light bulb defective (Chapter 12).
2 Alternator faulty (Chapter 5).
3 Fault in the instrument cluster printed circuit, dashboard wiring or bulb holder (Chapter 12).

FUEL SYSTEM

19 Excessive fuel consumption

1 Dirty or clogged air filter element (Chapter 1).
2 Emissions system not functioning properly (Chapter 6).
3 Fault in the fuel, ignition or engine management system (Chapters 4, 5 and 6).
4 Low tire pressure or incorrect tire size (Chapter 1).
5 Restricted exhaust system (Chapter 4).

20   Fuel leakage and/or fuel odor

1   Leak in a fuel feed or vent line (Chapter 4).
2   Tank overfilled. Fill only to automatic shut-off.
3   Evaporative emissions control system problem (Chapter 6).
4   Vapor leaks from system lines or injectors (Chapter 4).

COOLING SYSTEM

21   Overheating

1   Insufficient coolant in the system (Chapter 1).
2   Water pump drivebelt defective or belt tensioner faulty (Chapter 1).
3   Radiator core blocked or radiator grille dirty and restricted (see Chapter 3).
4   Thermostat faulty (Chapter 3).
5   Fan blades broken (Chapter 3).
6   Cooling system pressure cap leaking. Have the cap pressure tested by a gas station or repair shop.
7   Problem in the electric cooling fan circuit (see Chapter 3).

22   Overcooling

1   Thermostat faulty (Chapter 3).
2   Inaccurate temperature gauge (Chapter 12).
3   Defective fan clutch (see Chapter 3).

23   External coolant leakage

1   Deteriorated or damaged hoses or loose clamps. Replace hoses and/or tighten the clamps at the hose connections (Chapter 1).
2   Water pump seals defective (Chapter 3).
3   Leakage from the radiator core or tank(s). This will require the radiator to be professionally repaired (see Chapter 3 for removal procedures).
4   Engine drain plug(s) leaking (Chapter 1) or water jacket core plugs leaking.
5   Leakage at the heater core. Signs of leakage should show up on interior carpeting (Chapter 3).

24   Internal coolant leakage

➡Note: Internal coolant leaks can usually be detected by examining the oil. Check the dipstick and inside of the valve cover for water deposits and an oil consistency like that of a milkshake.

1   Leaking cylinder head gasket. Have the cooling system pressure tested.
2   Cracked cylinder bore or cylinder head. Remove the head(s) and inspect (Chapter 2).

25   Coolant loss

1   Too much coolant in the system (Chapter 1).
2   Coolant boiling away due to overheating (see Section 15).
3   External or internal leakage (see Sections 23 and 24).
4   Faulty cooling system pressure cap. Have the cap pressure tested.

26   Poor coolant circulation

1   Inoperative water pump. A quick test is to pinch the top radiator hose closed with your hand while the engine is idling, then let it loose. You should feel the surge of coolant if the pump is working properly (see Chapter 1).
2   Restriction in the cooling system. Drain, flush and refill the system (Chapter 1). If necessary, remove the radiator (Chapter 3) and have it reverse flushed.
3   Water pump drivebelt defective or belt tensioner faulty (Chapter 1).
4   Thermostat sticking (Chapter 3).

AUTOMATIC TRANSMISSION

➡**Note: Due to the complexity of the automatic transmission, it's difficult for the home mechanic to properly diagnose and service this component. For problems other than the following, the vehicle should be taken to a dealer service department or a transmission shop.**

27   General shift mechanism problems

1   Chapter 7A deals with checking and adjusting the shift cable on automatic transmissions. Common problems that may be attributed to poorly adjusted cable are:
   a)   *Engine starting in gears other than Park or Neutral.*
   b)   *Indicator on shifter pointing to a gear other than the one actually being selected.*
   c)   *Vehicle moves when in Park.*
2   Refer to Chapter 7A to adjust the cable.

28   Transmission will not downshift with accelerator pedal pressed to the floor

Transmission pressure control solenoid valve faulty. Check for Diagnostic Trouble Codes (Chapter 6).

29   Transmission slips, shifts rough, is noisy or has no drive in forward or reverse gears

1   Of the many probable causes for the above problems, the home mechanic should be concerned with only one possibility - fluid level.
2   Before taking the vehicle to a repair shop, check the level and condition of the fluid as described in Chapter 1. Correct fluid level as necessary or change the fluid and filter if needed. If the problem persists, have a professional diagnose the probable cause.
3   If the transmission shifts late and the shifts are harsh, suspect a faulty transmission pressure control solenoid valve. Check for Diagnostic Trouble Codes (Chapter 6).

30   Fluid leakage

1   Automatic transmission fluid is a deep red color. Fluid leaks should not be confused with engine oil, which can easily be blown by airflow to the transmission.
2   To pinpoint a leak, first remove all built-up dirt and grime from around the transmission. Degreasing agents and/or steam cleaning will achieve this. With the underside clean, drive the vehicle at low speeds

so airflow will not blow the leak far from its source. Raise the vehicle and determine where the leak is coming from. Common areas of leakage are:

a) **Pan:** *Tighten the mounting bolts and/or replace the pan gasket as necessary (see Chapter 1).*

b) **Filler pipe:** *Replace the rubber seal where the pipe enters the transmission case.*

c) **Transmission oil lines:** *Tighten the connectors where the lines enter the transmission case and/or replace the lines.*

d) **Vent pipe:** *Transmission overfilled and/or water in fluid (see checking procedures, Chapter 1).*

e) **Speed sensor connector:** *Replace the O-ring where the vehicle speed sensor enters the transmission case (Chapter 6).*

TRANSFER CASE

31 Transfer case is difficult to shift into the desired range

1 Speed may be too great to permit engagement. Stop the vehicle and shift into the desired range.

2 If the vehicle has been driven on a paved surface for some time, the driveline torque can make shifting difficult. Stop and shift into two-wheel drive on paved or hard surfaces.

3 Insufficient or incorrect grade of lubricant. Drain and refill the transfer case with the specified lubricant (Chapter 1).

4 Worn or damaged internal components. Disassembly and overhaul of the transfer case, by a qualified shop, may be necessary.

32 Transfer case noisy in all gears

Insufficient or incorrect grade of lubricant. Drain and refill (Chapter 1).

33 Noisy or jumps out of four-wheel drive Low range

1 Transfer case not fully engaged. Stop the vehicle, shift into Neutral and then engage 4L.

2 Shift linkage loose, worn or binding. Tighten, repair or lubricate linkage as necessary.

3 Shift fork cracked, inserts worn or fork binding on the rail.

34 Lubricant leaks from the vent or output shaft seals

1 Transfer case is overfilled. Drain to the proper level (Chapter 1).

2 Vent is clogged or jammed closed. Clear or replace the vent.

3 Output shaft seal incorrectly installed or damaged. Replace the seal and check contact surfaces for nicks and scoring.

DRIVESHAFT

35 Oil leak at seal end of driveshaft

Defective transmission or transfer case oil seal. See Chapter 7 for replacement procedures. While this is done, check the splined yoke for burrs or a rough condition that may be damaging the seal. Burrs can be removed with crocus cloth or a fine whetstone.

36 Knock or clunk when the transmission is under initial load (just after transmission is put into gear)

1 Loose or disconnected rear suspension components. Check all mounting bolts, nuts and bushings (see Chapter 10).

2 Loose driveshaft bolts. Inspect all bolts and nuts and tighten them to the specified torque.

3 Worn or damaged universal joint bearings. Check for wear (see Chapter 8).

37 Metallic grinding sound consistent with vehicle speed

Pronounced wear in the universal joint bearings. Check as described in Chapter 8.

38 Vibration

➡**Note: Before assuming that the driveshaft is at fault, make sure the tires are perfectly balanced and perform the following test.**

1 Install a tachometer inside the vehicle to monitor engine speed as the vehicle is driven. Drive the vehicle and note the engine speed at which the vibration (roughness) is most pronounced. Now shift the transmission to a different gear and bring the engine speed to the same point.

2 If the vibration occurs at the same engine speed (rpm) regardless of which gear the transmission is in, the driveshaft is NOT at fault since the driveshaft speed varies.

3 If the vibration decreases or is eliminated when the transmission is in a different gear at the same engine speed, refer to the following probable causes.

4 Bent or dented driveshaft. Inspect and replace as necessary (see Chapter 8).

5 Undercoating or built-up dirt, etc. on the driveshaft. Clean the shaft thoroughly and recheck.

6 Worn universal joint bearings. Remove and inspect (see Chapter 8).

7 Driveshaft and/or companion flange out of balance. Check for missing weights on the shaft. Remove the driveshaft (see Chapter 8) and reinstall 180-degrees from original position, then retest. Have the driveshaft professionally balanced if the problem persists.

8 Center support bearing worn out (two-piece driveshafts) (Chapter 8).

AXLES

39 Noise

1 Road noise. No corrective procedures available.

2 Tire noise. Inspect tires and check tire pressures (Chapter 1).

3 Rear axle bearings worn or damaged (Chapter 8).

40 Vibration

See probable causes under *Driveshaft*. Proceed under the guidelines listed for the driveshaft. If the problem persists, check the rear wheel bearings by raising the rear of the vehicle and spinning the rear wheels by hand. Listen for evidence of rough (noisy) bearings. Remove and inspect (see Chapter 8).

41 Oil leakage

1   Pinion seal damaged (see Chapter 8).
2   Axleshaft oil seals damaged (see Chapter 8).
3   Differential inspection cover leaking. Tighten the bolts or replace the gasket as required (see Chapter 8).

DRIVEAXLES

42 Clicking noise on turns

Worn or damaged outboard CV joints (Chapter 8).

43 Shudder or vibration during acceleration

1   Excessive toe-in. Have alignment checked.
2   Incorrect spring heights (Chapter 10).
3   Worn or damaged inboard or outboard CV joints (Chapter 8).
4   Sticking inboard CV joint assembly (Chapter 8).

44 Vibration at highway speeds

1   Out-of-balance front wheels and/or tires (Chapters 1 and 10).
2   Out-of-round front tires (Chapters 1 and 10).
3   Worn CV joints (Chapter 8).

BRAKES

➡Note: **Before assuming that a brake problem exists, make sure that the tires are in good condition and inflated properly (see Chapter 1), that the front-end alignment is correct and that the vehicle is not loaded with weight in an unequal manner.**

45 Vehicle pulls to one side during braking

1   Defective, damaged or oil contaminated disc brake pads on one side. Inspect as described in Chapter 9.
2   Excessive wear of brake pad material or drum/disc on one side. Inspect and correct as necessary.
3   Loose or disconnected front suspension components. Inspect and tighten all bolts to the specified torque (Chapter 10).
4   Defective brake caliper. Remove the caliper and inspect for a stuck piston or other damage (Chapter 9).
5   Inadequate lubrication of front brake caliper slide pins. Remove caliper and lubricate slide pins (Chapter 9).

46 Noise (high-pitched squeal or grinding with the brakes applied)

1   Disc brake pads worn out. The noise comes from the wear sensor rubbing against the disc (does not apply to all vehicles) or the actual pad backing plate itself if the material is completely worn away. Replace the pads with new ones immediately (Chapter 9). If the pad material has worn completely away, the brake discs should be inspected for damage as described in Chapter 9.
2   Missing or damaged brake pad insulators. Replace pad insulators (see Chapter 9).
3   Linings contaminated with dirt or grease. Replace pads.
4   Incorrect linings. Replace with correct linings.

47 Excessive brake pedal travel

1   Partial brake system failure. Inspect the entire system (Chapter 9) and correct as required.
2   Insufficient fluid in the master cylinder. Check (Chapter 1), add fluid and bleed the system if necessary (Chapter 9).

48 Brake pedal feels spongy when depressed

1   Air in the hydraulic lines. Bleed the brake system (Chapter 9).
2   Faulty flexible hoses. Inspect all system hoses and lines. Replace parts as necessary.
3   Master cylinder mounting bolts/nuts loose.
4   Master cylinder defective (Chapter 9).

49 Excessive effort required to stop vehicle

1   Power brake booster not operating properly (see check in Chapter 1, repairs in Chapter 9).
2   Excessively worn pads. Inspect and replace if necessary (Chapter 9).
3   One or more caliper pistons seized or sticking. Inspect and replace as required (Chapter 9).
4   Brake pads contaminated with oil or grease. Inspect and replace as required (Chapter 9).
5   New pads installed and not yet seated. It will take a while for the new material to seat against the disc.

50 Pedal travels to the floor with little resistance

1   Little or no fluid in the master cylinder reservoir caused by leaking caliper piston(s), loose, damaged or disconnected brake lines. Inspect the entire system and correct as necessary.
2   Worn master cylinder seals (Chapter 9).

51 Brake pedal pulsates during brake application

Disc(s) defective. Check for excessive lateral runout and parallelism (Chapter 9). Have the disc(s) resurfaced or replace it with a new one.

SUSPENSION AND STEERING SYSTEMS

52 Vehicle pulls to one side

1 Tire pressures uneven or tires mismatched (Chapter 1).
2 Defective tire (Chapter 1).
3 Excessive wear in suspension or steering components (Chapter 10).
4 Front end in need of alignment.
5 Front brakes dragging (Chapter 9).

53 Shimmy, shake or vibration

1 Tire or wheel out-of-balance or out-of-round. Have professionally balanced.
2 Loose, worn or out-of-adjustment front wheel bearings (Chapter 1).
3 Shock absorbers and/or suspension components worn or damaged (Chapter 10).

54 Excessive pitching and/or rolling around corners or during braking

1 Defective shock absorbers. Replace as a set (Chapter 10).
2 Stabilizer bar bushings or links worn (Chapter 10).
3 Broken or weak springs. Inspect as described in Chapters 1 and 10.

55 Excessively stiff steering

1 Lack of fluid in power steering fluid reservoir (Chapter 1).
2 Incorrect tire pressures (Chapter 1).
3 Lack of lubrication at steering joints (see Chapter 1).
4 Front end out of alignment.
5 Lack of power assistance (see Section 57).

56 Excessive play in steering

1 Loose front wheel bearings (Chapters 1 and 10).
2 Excessive wear in suspension or steering components (Chapter 10).
3 Steering gear damaged (Chapter 10).

57 Lack of power assistance

1 Drivebelt or tensioner faulty (Chapter 1).
2 Fluid level low (Chapter 1).
3 Hoses or lines restricted. Inspect and replace parts as necessary.
4 Air in power steering system. Bleed the system (Chapter 10).

58 Excessive tire wear (not specific to one area)

1 Incorrect tire pressure (Chapter 1).
2 Tires out-of-balance. Have professionally balanced.
3 Wheels damaged. Inspect and replace as necessary.
4 Suspension or steering components excessively worn (Chapter 10).

59 Excessive tire wear on outside edge

1 Inflation pressures incorrect (Chapter 1).
2 Excessive speed in turns.
3 Alignment incorrect.
4 Suspension arm bent or twisted (Chapter 10).

60 Excessive tire wear on inside edge

1 Inflation pressures incorrect (Chapter 1).
2 Front-end alignment incorrect. Have the front end professionally aligned.
3 Loose or damaged steering components (Chapter 10).

61 Tire tread worn in one place

1 Tires out-of-balance.
2 Damaged wheel. Inspect and replace if necessary.
3 Defective tire (Chapter 1).

1

TUNE-UP AND ROUTINE MAINTENANCE

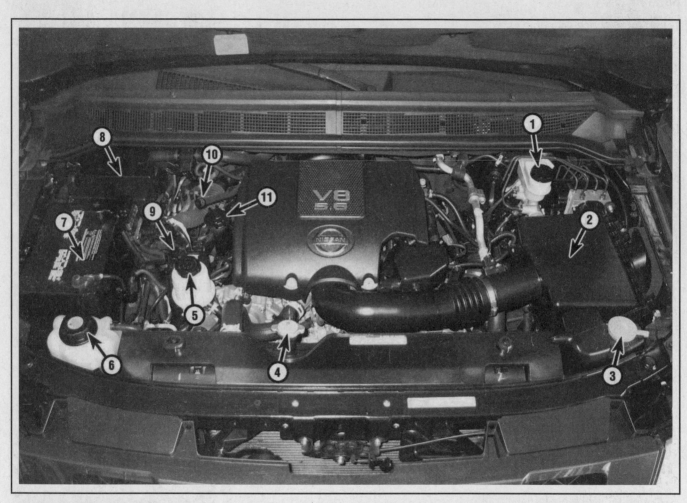

Engine compartment components

1	Brake fluid reservoir	5	Power steering fluid reservoir	9	Engine oil dipstick
2	Air filter housing	6	Expansion tank pressure cap	10	Automatic transmission fluid dipstick
3	Windshield washer fluid reservoir	7	Battery	11	Engine oil filler cap
4	Radiator cap	8	Fuse/relay box		

Engine compartment underside components

1	Radiator drain plug	4	Engine oil drain plug	7	Lower control arm balljoint
2	Drivebelt	5	Automatic transmission drain plug	8	Tie-rod end
3	Engine oil filter	6	Front brake caliper		

Rear underside components - Titan

1	Shock absorber	4	Differential lubricant check/fill plug	7	Muffler
2	Brake hose	5	Differential lubricant drain plug	8	Fuel tank
3	Leaf springs	6	Universal joint		

Rear underside components - Armada

1	Lower balljoint	4	Muffler	6	Differential lubricant drain plug
2	Driveaxle boot	5	Universal joint	7	Differential lubricant check/fill plug
3	Fuel tank				

1 Maintenance schedule

The following maintenance intervals are based on the assumption that the vehicle owner will be doing the maintenance or service work, as opposed to having a dealer service department do the work. These are the minimum maintenance intervals recommended by the factory for vehicles that are driven daily. If you wish to keep your vehicle in peak condition at all times, you may wish to perform some of these procedures even more often. Because frequent maintenance enhances the efficiency, performance and resale value of your car, we encourage you to do so. If you drive in dusty areas, tow a trailer, idle or drive at low speeds for extended periods or drive for short distances (less than four miles) in below freezing temperatures, shorter intervals are also recommended.

When the vehicle is new, follow the maintenance schedule to the letter, record the maintenance performed in your owner's manual and keep all receipts to protect the new vehicle warranty. In many cases the initial maintenance check is done at no cost to the owner (check with your dealer service department for more information).

EVERY 250 MILES OR WEEKLY, WHICHEVER COMES FIRST

Check the engine oil level (Section 4)
Check the coolant level (Section 4)
Check the windshield washer fluid level (Section 4)
Check the brake fluid level (Section 4)
Check the tires and tire pressures (Section 5)

EVERY 3000 MILES OR 3 MONTHS, WHICHEVER COMES FIRST

All items listed above, plus . . .
Check the power steering fluid level (Section 6)
Check the automatic transmission fluid level (Section 7)
Change the engine oil and filter (Section 8)

EVERY 6000 MILES OR 6 MONTHS, WHICHEVER COMES FIRST

All items listed above, plus . . .
Check the seat belts (Section 9)
Inspect the windshield wiper blades (Section 10)
Check and service the battery (Section 11)
Check the engine drivebelt (Section 12)
Inspect underhood hoses (Section 13)
Check the cooling system (Section 14)
Rotate the tires (Section 15)
Check the exhaust system (Section 16)

EVERY 15,000 MILES OR 12 MONTHS, WHICHEVER COMES FIRST

All items listed above, plus . . .
Check the lubricant level in the front (4x4) and rear axles (Section 17)

Check the transfer case lubricant level - 4WD models (Section 18)
Lubricate the chassis (Section 19)
Check the fuel system (Section 20)
Check the suspension, steering, and driveaxle boots (Section 21)
Check the brake system (Section 22)*
Replace the cabin air filters (Section 23)

EVERY 30,000 MILES OR 24 MONTHS, WHICHEVER COMES FIRST

All items listed above, plus . . .
Change the brake fluid (Section 24)
Replace the air filter (Section 25)*
Inspect the front and rear wheel bearings (Section 26)
Check the evaporative emissions control system (Section 27)
Replace the spark plugs (conventional, non-platinum) (Section 28)
Service the cooling system (drain, flush and refill) (green-colored ethylene glycol antifreeze only) (Section 29)
Change the automatic transmission fluid (Section 30)**
Replace the Positive Crankcase Ventilation (PCV) valve (Section 31)
If noisy, check and, if necessary, adjust the valve clearances (Chapter 2A).

EVERY 60,000 MILES OR 48 MONTHS, WHICHEVER COMES FIRST

Inspect the spark plug boots and ignition coils (Section 32)
Change the transfer case lubricant - 4WD models (Section 33)
Change the differential lubricant (Section 34)**

EVERY 100,000 MILES OR 60 MONTHS, WHICHEVER COMES FIRST

Replace the spark plugs (platinum type) (Section 28)
* *This item is affected by "severe" operating conditions, as described below. If the vehicle is operated under severe conditions, perform all maintenance indicated with an asterisk (*) at half the indicated intervals. Severe conditions exist if you mainly operate the vehicle . . .*
  in dusty areas
  towing a trailer
  idling for extended periods
  driving at low speeds when outside temperatures remain below freezing and most trips are less than four miles long
** *Perform this procedure at half the recommended interval if operated under one or more of the following conditions:*
  in heavy city traffic where the outside temperature regularly reaches 90-degrees F or higher in hilly or mountainous terrain
  frequent trailer towing
  if the vehicle has been driven through deep water

2 Introduction

This Chapter is designed to help the home mechanic maintain the Nissan Titan and Armada with the goals of maximum performance, economy, safety and reliability in mind.

Included is a master maintenance schedule, followed by procedures dealing specifically with each item on the schedule. Visual checks, adjustments, component replacement and other helpful items are included. Refer to the accompanying illustrations of the engine compartment and the underside of the vehicle for the locations of various components.

Servicing your vehicle in accordance with the mileage/time maintenance schedule and the step-by-step procedures will result in a planned maintenance program that should produce a long and reliable service life. Keep in mind that it's a comprehensive plan, so maintaining some items but not others at the specified intervals will not produce the same results.

As you service your vehicle, you will discover that many of the procedures can - and should - be grouped together because of the nature of the particular procedure you're performing or because of the close proximity of two otherwise unrelated components to one another.

For example, if the vehicle is raised for chassis lubrication, you should inspect the exhaust, suspension, steering and fuel systems while you're under the vehicle. When you're rotating the tires, it makes good sense to check the brakes since the wheels are already removed. Finally, let's suppose you have to borrow or rent a torque wrench. Even if you only need it to tighten the spark plugs, you might as well check the torque of as many critical fasteners as time allows.

The first step in this maintenance program is to prepare yourself before the actual work begins. Read through all the procedures you're planning to do, then gather up all the parts and tools needed. If it looks like you might run into problems during a particular job, seek advice from a mechanic or an experienced do-it-yourselfer.

3 Tune-up general information

The term tune-up is used in this manual to represent a combination of individual operations rather than one specific procedure that will maintain a gasoline engine in proper tune.

If, from the time the vehicle is new, the routine maintenance schedule is followed closely and frequent checks are made of fluid levels and high wear items, as suggested throughout this manual, the engine will be kept in relatively good running condition and the need for additional work will be minimized.

More likely than not, however, there may be times when the engine is running poorly due to lack of regular maintenance. This is even more likely if a used vehicle, which has not received regular and frequent maintenance checks, is purchased. In such cases, an engine tune-up will be needed outside of the regular routine maintenance intervals.

The first step in any tune-up or diagnostic procedure to help correct a poor running engine is a cylinder compression check. A compression check (see Chapter 2B) will help determine the condition of internal engine components and should be used as a guide for tune-up and repair procedures. If, for instance, the compression check indicates serious internal engine wear, a conventional tune-up won't improve the performance of the engine and would be a waste of time and money. Because of its importance, the compression check should be done by someone with the right equipment and the knowledge to use it properly.

The following procedures are those most often needed to bring a generally poor running engine back into a proper state of tune.

MINOR TUNE-UP

Check all engine related fluids (Section 4)
Clean, inspect and test the battery (Section 11)
Check the drivebelt (Section 12)
Check all underhood hoses (Section 13)
Check the cooling system (Section 14)
Check the air filter (Section 25)

MAJOR TUNE-UP

All items listed under Minor tune-up, plus . . .
Replace the air filter (Section 25)
Replace the spark plugs (Section 28)
Check the ignition system (Chapter 5)
Check the charging system (Chapter 5)

4 Fluid level checks (every 250 miles or weekly)

➡**Note: The following are fluid level checks to be done on a 250 mile or weekly basis. Additional fluid level checks can be found in specific maintenance procedures that follow. Regardless of intervals, be alert to fluid leaks under the vehicle, which would indicate a fault to be corrected immediately.**

1   Fluids are an essential part of the lubrication, cooling, brake, clutch and windshield washer systems. Because the fluids gradually become depleted and/or contaminated during normal operation of the vehicle, they must be periodically replenished. See *Recommended lubricants and fluids* in this Chapter's Specifications before adding fluid to any of the following components.

➡**Note: The vehicle must be on level ground when fluid levels are checked.**

ENGINE OIL

▶ **Refer to illustrations 4.2, 4.4 and 4.6**

2   The engine oil level is checked with a dipstick that extends through a tube and into the oil pan at the bottom of the engine (see illustration).

3   The oil level should be checked before the vehicle has been driven, or about 5 minutes after the engine has been shut off. If the oil is checked immediately after driving the vehicle, some of the oil will remain in the upper engine components, resulting in an inaccurate reading on the dipstick.

4   Pull the dipstick out of the tube and wipe all the oil from the end with a clean rag or paper towel. Insert the clean dipstick all the way back into the tube, then pull it out again. Note the oil at the end of the dipstick. Add oil as necessary to keep the level between the L and H

marks or within the cross-hatched zone on the dipstick (see illustration).

5   Do not overfill the engine by adding too much oil since this may result in oil-fouled spark plugs, oil leaks or oil seal failures.

6   Oil is added to the engine after unscrewing a cap from the valve cover (see illustration). A funnel may help to reduce spills.

7   Checking the oil level is an important preventive maintenance step. A consistently low oil level indicates oil leakage through damaged seals, defective gaskets or past worn rings or valve guides. If the oil looks milky or has water droplets in it, the cylinder head gasket(s) may be blown or the head(s) or block may be cracked. The engine should be checked immediately. The condition of the oil should also be checked. Whenever you check the oil level, slide your thumb and index finger up the dipstick before wiping off the oil. If you see small dirt or metal particles clinging to the dipstick, the oil should be changed (see Section 8).

ENGINE COOLANT

▶ **Refer to illustration 4.8**

✳✳ WARNING:

Do not allow antifreeze to come in contact with your skin or painted surfaces of the vehicle. Rinse off spills immediately with plenty of water. Antifreeze is highly toxic if ingested. Never leave antifreeze lying around in an open container or in puddles on the floor; children and pets are attracted by its sweet smell and may drink it. Check with local authorities on disposing of used antifreeze. Many communities have collection centers that will see that antifreeze is disposed of safely.

➡ **Note: Non-toxic antifreeze is now manufactured and available at local auto parts stores, but even this type should be disposed of properly.**

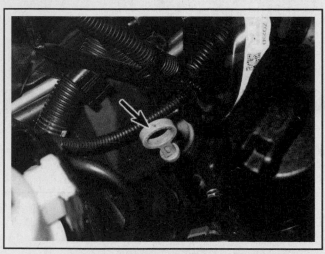

4.2 Location of the engine oil dipstick

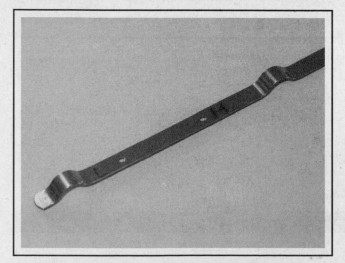

4.4 The oil level must be maintained between the marks at all times - it takes about one quart of oil to raise the level from the L to the H mark

4.6 Oil is added to the engine after unscrewing the oil filler cap from the valve cover - always make sure the area around the opening is clean before removing the cap to prevent dirt from contaminating the engine

4.8 Keep the coolant level near the MAX mark or MIN mark on the side of the reservoir, depending on engine temperature

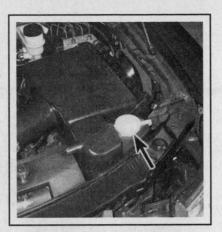

4.14 The windshield washer fluid reservoir is located in the left front corner of the engine compartment

4.16 The electrolyte level can be checked on original equipment batteries; some have individual cell plugs that can be unscrewed, while others have caps which must be pried off

8   All vehicles covered by this manual are equipped with a pressurized coolant recovery system. A white plastic coolant reservoir/expansion tank located in the engine compartment is connected by hoses to the radiator filler neck and the thermostat housing (see illustration).

9   The coolant level in the reservoir should be checked regularly.

❄ WARNING:

Do not remove the pressure cap on the radiator or the reservoir/expansion tank to check the coolant level when the engine is warm.

The level of coolant in the reservoir varies with the temperature of the engine. When the engine is cold, the coolant level should be at or slightly above the MIN mark on the reservoir. Once the engine has warmed up, the level should be at or near the MAX mark. If it isn't, add coolant to the reservoir. To add coolant, simply twist open the cap and add a 50/50 mixture of ethylene glycol based antifreeze and water.

10   Drive the vehicle and recheck the coolant level. If only a small amount of coolant is required to bring the system up to the proper level, water can be used. However, repeated additions of water will dilute the antifreeze and water solution. In order to maintain the proper ratio of antifreeze and water, always top up the coolant level with the correct mixture. An empty plastic milk jug or bleach bottle makes an excellent container for mixing coolant. Do not use rust inhibitors or additives.

11   If the coolant level drops consistently, there may be a leak in the system. Inspect the radiator, hoses, filler cap, drain plugs and water pump (see Section 14). If no leaks are noted, have the radiator cap tested by a service station.

12   If you have to remove the radiator cap or the reservoir/expansion tank cap, wait until the engine has cooled completely, then wrap a thick cloth around the cap and turn it to the first stop. If coolant or steam escapes, let the engine cool down longer, then remove the cap.

13   Check the condition of the coolant as well. It should be relatively clear. If it is brown or rust colored, the system should be drained, flushed and refilled. Even if the coolant appears to be normal, the corrosion inhibitors wear out, so it must be replaced at the specified intervals.

WINDSHIELD WASHER FLUID

▶ **Refer to illustration 4.14**

14 Fluid for the windshield washer system is located in a plastic reservoir on the right side of the engine compartment (see illustration).

15 In milder climates, plain water can be used in the reservoir, but it should be kept no more than 2/3 full to allow for expansion if the water freezes. In colder climates, use windshield washer system antifreeze, available at any auto parts store, to lower the freezing point of the fluid. Mix the antifreeze with water in accordance with the manufacturer's directions on the container.

❄ CAUTION:

Don't use cooling system antifreeze - it will damage the vehicle's paint.

➡Note: To help prevent icing in cold weather, warm the windshield with the defroster before using the washer.

BATTERY ELECTROLYTE

▶ **Refer to illustration 4.16**

16 On models not equipped with a sealed battery, check the electrolyte level of all six battery cells. On models with a translucent battery case, minimum and maximum level marks are present on the side of the case; keep the electrolyte level at the MAX mark. On models with an opaque case, carefully remove the cell caps to check the level or add water. Some batteries have six individual cell plugs that can be unscrewed, but others have two cell caps that must be carefully pried off (see illustration).

17 If the level is low, add distilled water until the level is up to the MAX mark (translucent batteries) or up to the bottom of the split-ring indicators or filler neck (opaque batteries).

BRAKE FLUID

▶ **Refer to illustration 4.18**

18 The brake master cylinder is mounted on the front of the power brake booster, on the left (driver's) side of the engine compartment firewall (see illustration).

19 The translucent plastic reservoir allows the fluid inside to be checked without removing the cap. Be sure to wipe the area around the reservoir cap with a clean rag to prevent contamination of the brake system before removing the cap. Don't allow the fluid level to fall below the MIN mark.

20 When adding fluid, pour it carefully into the reservoir to avoid spilling it on surrounding painted surfaces. Be sure the specified fluid is used, since mixing different types of brake fluid can cause damage to the system. See *Recommended lubricants and fluids* in this Chapter's Specifications or your owner's manual.

❊❊ **WARNING:**

Brake fluid can harm your eyes and damage painted surfaces, so use extreme caution when handling or pouring it. Do not use brake fluid that has been standing open or is more than one year old. Brake fluid absorbs moisture from the air. Moisture in the system can cause a dangerous loss of brake performance.

21 At this time, the fluid and master cylinder can be inspected for contamination. The system should be drained and refilled if deposits, dirt particles or water droplets are seen in the fluid.

22 After filling the reservoir to the proper level, make sure the cap is on tight to prevent fluid leakage.

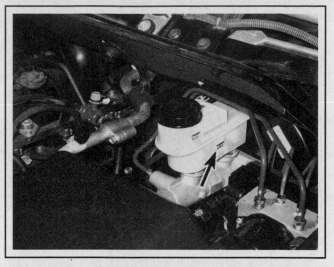

4.18 Never let the brake fluid level drop below the MIN mark

23 The brake fluid level in the master cylinder will drop slightly as the brake pads wear down during normal operation. If the master cylinder requires repeated additions to keep it at the proper level, it's an indication of leakage in the brake system, which should be corrected immediately. Check all brake lines and connections (see Section 22 for more information).

24 If, upon checking the master cylinder fluid level, you discover the reservoir empty or nearly empty, the brake system should be bled and thoroughly inspected (see Chapter 9).

5 Tire and tire pressure checks (every 250 miles or weekly)

▶ **Refer to illustrations 5.2, 5.3, 5.4a, 5.4b and 5.8**

1 Periodic inspection of the tires may spare you the inconvenience of being stranded with a flat tire. It can also provide you with vital information regarding possible problems in the steering and suspension systems before major damage occurs.

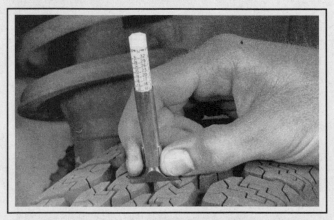

5.2 Use a tire tread depth indicator to monitor tire wear - they are available at auto parts stores and service stations and cost very little

2 The original tires on this vehicle are equipped with 1/2-inch wide wear bands that will appear when tread depth reaches 1/16-inch, at which point the tires can be considered worn out. Tread wear can be monitored with a simple, inexpensive device known as a tread depth indicator (see illustration).

3 Note any abnormal tread wear (see illustration). Tread pattern irregularities such as cupping, flat spots and more wear on one side than the other are indications of front end alignment and/or balance problems. If any of these conditions are noted, take the vehicle to a tire shop or service station to correct the problem.

4 Look closely for cuts, punctures and embedded nails or tacks. Sometimes a tire will hold air pressure for a short time or leak down very slowly after a nail has embedded itself in the tread. If a slow leak persists, check the valve stem core to make sure it's tight (see illustration). Examine the tread for an object that may have embedded itself in the tire or for a plug that may have begun to leak (radial tire punctures are repaired with a plug that's installed in a puncture). If a puncture is suspected, it can be easily verified by spraying a solution of soapy water onto the puncture area (see illustration). The soapy solution will bubble if there's a leak. Unless the puncture is unusually large, a tire shop or service station can usually repair the tire.

5 Carefully inspect the inner sidewall of each tire for evidence of brake fluid leakage. If you see any, inspect the brakes immediately.

6 Correct air pressure adds miles to the lifespan of the tires,

UNDERINFLATION

CUPPING

OVERINFLATION

Cupping may be caused by:
- Underinflation and/or mechanical irregularities such as out-of-balance condition of wheel and/or tire, and bent or damaged wheel.
- Loose or worn steering tie-rod or steering idler arm.
- Loose, damaged or worn front suspension parts.

INCORRECT TOE-IN OR EXTREME CAMBER

FEATHERING DUE TO MISALIGNMENT

5.3 This chart will help you determine the condition of the tires and the probable cause(s) of abnormal wear

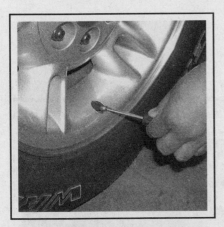

5.4a If a tire loses air on a steady basis, check the valve stem core first to make sure it's snug (special inexpensive wrenches are commonly available at auto parts stores)

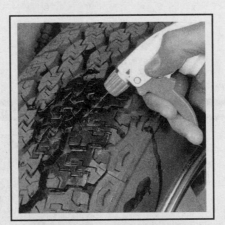

5.4b If the valve stem core is tight, raise the corner of the vehicle with the low tire and spray a soapy water solution onto the tread as the tire is turned slowly - leaks will cause small bubbles to appear

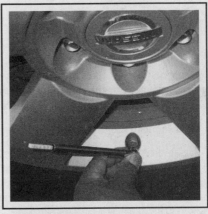

5.8 To extend the life of the tires, check the air pressure at least once a week with an accurate gauge (don't forget the spare!)

improves mileage and enhances overall ride quality. Tire pressure cannot be accurately estimated by looking at a tire, especially if it's a radial. A tire pressure gauge is essential. Keep an accurate gauge in the vehicle. The pressure gauges attached to the nozzles of air hoses at gas stations are often inaccurate.

7   Always check tire pressure when the tires are cold. Cold, in this case, means the vehicle has not been driven over a mile in the three hours preceding a tire pressure check. A pressure rise of four to eight pounds is not uncommon once the tires are warm.

8   Unscrew the valve cap protruding from the wheel or hubcap and push the gauge firmly onto the valve stem (see illustration). Note the reading on the gauge and compare the figure to the recommended tire pressure shown on the placard on the driver's side door pillar. Be sure to reinstall the valve cap to keep dirt and moisture out of the valve stem mechanism. Check all four tires and, if necessary, add enough air to bring them up to the recommended pressure.

9   Don't forget to keep the spare tire inflated to the specified pressure (refer to your owner's manual or the tire sidewall).

6   Power steering fluid level check (every 3000 miles or 3 months)

▶ **Refer to illustration 6.4**

1   Unlike manual steering, the power steering system relies on fluid which may, over a period of time, require replenishing.

2   All models have a remote power steering fluid reservoir mounted to a bracket on the right (passenger's) front corner of the engine. The translucent reservoir allows the fluid to be checked without removing the cap. For the check, the front wheels should be pointed straight ahead and the engine should be off.

3   Use a clean rag to wipe off the reservoir and the area around the cap. This will help prevent any foreign matter from entering the reservoir during the check.

4   Feel the reservoir to check the temperature of the fluid. Check the level of the fluid on the side of the reservoir (see illustration). The level should be at the HOT or MAX mark if the reservoir was hot to the touch. If the reservoir felt cool, the level should be at the COLD mark (but not below the MIN level).

5   The fluid should be at the proper level, depending on whether it was checked hot or cold. Never allow the fluid level to drop below the MIN mark on the reservoir.

6   If additional fluid is required, pour the specified type directly into the reservoir, using a funnel to prevent spills.

6.4 The power steering fluid level can be checked through the translucent reservoir

7   If the reservoir requires frequent fluid additions, all power steering hoses, hose connections, steering gear and the power steering pump should be carefully checked for leaks.

7   Automatic transmission fluid level check (every 3000 miles or 3 months)

▶ **Refer to illustrations 7.3 and 7.6**

1   The automatic transmission fluid level should be carefully maintained. Low fluid level can lead to slipping or loss of drive, while overfilling can cause foaming and loss of fluid.

2   With the parking brake set, start the engine, then move the shift lever through all the gear ranges, ending in Park. The fluid level must be checked with the vehicle level and the engine running at idle.

➡**Note: Incorrect fluid level readings will result if the vehicle has just been driven at high speeds for an extended period, in hot weather in city traffic, or if it has been pulling a trailer. If any of these conditions apply, wait until the fluid has cooled (about 30 minutes).**

3   With the transmission at normal operating temperature, remove the dipstick retaining bolt and remove the dipstick from the filler tube. The dipstick is located at the rear of the engine on the passenger's side (see illustration).

➡**Note: Normal operating temperature is considered to be approximately 176-degrees F (80-degrees C). The fluid level can be checked when it's cold, in the range of 86 to 122-degrees F (30 to 50-degrees C), but the check is much more accurate when the fluid is at normal operating temperature.**

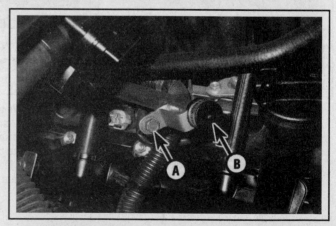

7.3 Remove the bolt (A) securing the automatic transmission dipstick (B) to its tube, then pull out the dipstick

4   Wipe the fluid from the dipstick with a clean rag and push it back into the filler tube until the cap seats.

5   Pull the dipstick out again and note the fluid level.

6   If the fluid is cool to warm, the level should be between the notches on the COLD side of the dipstick; if it's hot, the level should be in the cross-hatched area on the HOT side of the dipstick (see illustration). If additional fluid is required, add it directly into the tube using a funnel. Add the fluid a little at a time and keep checking the level until it's correct.

※ CAUTION:

Do not overfill the transmission.

7   The condition of the fluid should also be checked along with the level. If the fluid at the end of the dipstick is a dark reddish-brown color, or if it smells burned, it should be changed. If you are in doubt about the condition of the fluid, purchase some new fluid and compare the two for color and smell.

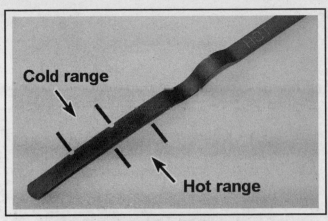

7.6 The automatic transmission fluid can be checked when at normal operating temperature using the HOT range (cross-hatched area), or before the transmission is fully warmed-up by using the COLD range (between the notches)

8   Engine oil and filter change (every 3000 miles or 3 months)

♦ Refer to illustrations 8.3, 8.8, 8.9, 8.14 and 8.18

1   Frequent oil changes are the most important preventive maintenance procedures that can be done by the home mechanic. As engine oil ages, it becomes diluted and contaminated, which leads to premature engine wear.

2   Although some sources recommend oil filter changes every other oil change, we feel that the minimal cost of an oil filter and the relative ease with which it is installed dictate that a new filter be installed every time the oil is changed.

3   Gather together all necessary tools and materials before beginning this procedure (see illustration).

4   You should have plenty of clean rags and newspapers handy to mop up any spills. Access to the under side of the vehicle may be improved if the vehicle can be lifted on a hoist, driven onto ramps or supported by jackstands.

※ WARNING:

Do not work under a vehicle which is supported only by a jack.

5   If this is your first oil change, familiarize yourself with the locations of the oil drain plug and the oil filter.

6   Warm the engine to normal operating temperature. If the new oil or any tools are needed, use this warm-up time to gather everything necessary for the job. The correct type of oil for your application can be found in *Recommended lubricants and fluids* in this Chapter's Specifications.

7   With the engine oil warm (warm engine oil will drain better and more built-up sludge will be removed with it), raise and support the vehicle. Make sure it's safely supported!

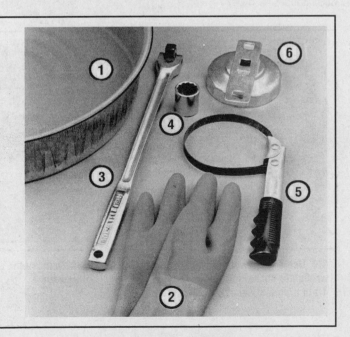

8.3 These tools are required when changing the engine oil and filter

1   *Drain pan* - It should be fairly shallow in depth, but wide to prevent spills
2   *Rubber gloves* - When removing the drain plug and filter, you will get oil on your hands (the gloves will prevent burns)
3   *Breaker bar* - Sometimes the oil drain plug is tight, and a long breaker bar is needed to loosen it
4   *Socket* - To be used with the breaker bar or a ratchet (must be the correct size to fit the drain plug - six-point preferred)
5   *Filter wrench* - This is a metal band-type wrench, which requires clearance around the filter to be effective
6   *Filter wrench* - This type fits on the bottom of the filter and can be turned with a ratchet or breaker bar (different-size wrenches are available for different types of filters)

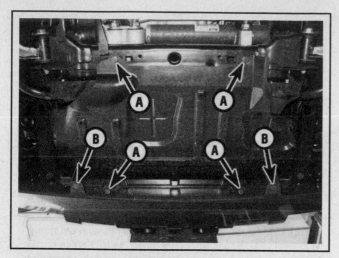

8.8 Engine undercover details

A   Bolts
B   Push fasteners (models with one-piece bumper covers)

8 Remove the engine undercover (see illustration).

9 Set the drain pan under the drain plug. Keep in mind that the oil will initially flow from the pan with some force; position the pan accordingly. Being careful not to touch any of the hot exhaust components, use a box-end wrench or a socket to remove the drain plug near the bottom of the oil pan (see illustration). Depending on how hot the oil is, you may want to wear gloves while unscrewing the plug the final few turns.

10 Allow the oil to drain into the pan. It may be necessary to move the pan as the oil flow slows to a trickle.

11 After all the oil has drained, wipe off the drain plug with a clean rag. Small metal particles may cling to the plug and would immediately contaminate the new oil.

12 Clean the area around the drain plug opening and reinstall the plug. Tighten the plug securely with the wrench. If a torque wrench is available, use it to tighten the plug to the torque listed in this Chapter's Specifications.

13 Move the drain pan into position under the oil filter.

14 Use the oil filter wrench to loosen the oil filter (see illustration).

15 Completely unscrew the old filter. Be careful: it's full of oil. Empty the oil inside the filter into the drain pan, then lower the filter.

16 Compare the old filter with the new one to make sure they're the same type.

17 Use a clean rag to remove all oil, dirt and sludge from the area where the oil filter mounts to the engine. Check the old filter to make sure the rubber gasket isn't stuck to the engine. If the gasket is stuck to the engine, remove it.

18 Apply a light coat of clean oil to the rubber gasket on the new oil filter (see illustration).

19 Attach the new filter to the engine, following the tightening directions printed on the filter canister or packing box. Most filter manufacturers recommend against using a filter wrench due to the possibility of overtightening and damage to the seal.

20 Remove all tools, rags, etc. from under the vehicle, being careful not to spill the oil in the drain pan, then lower the vehicle.

21 Move to the engine compartment and locate the oil filler cap.

22 Refer to the engine oil capacity in this Chapter's Specifications and add the proper amount of fresh oil into the engine. Wait a few minutes to allow the oil to drain into the pan, then check the level on the oil dipstick (see Section 4 if necessary). If the oil level is above the hatched area, start the engine and allow the new oil to circulate.

23 Run the engine for only about a minute, then shut it off. Immediately look under the vehicle and check for leaks at the oil pan drain plug and around the oil filter.

24 With the new oil circulated and the filter now completely full, recheck the level on the dipstick and add more oil as necessary.

25 During the first few trips after an oil change, make it a point to check frequently for leaks and proper oil level.

26 The old oil drained from the engine cannot be reused in its present state and should be disposed of. Check with your local auto parts store, disposal facility or environmental agency to see if they will accept the oil for recycling. After the oil has cooled it can be drained into a container (capped plastic jugs, topped bottles, milk cartons, etc.) for transport to one of these disposal sites. Don't dispose of the oil by pouring it on the ground or down a drain!

8.9 Use a proper size box-end wrench or socket to remove the oil drain plug and avoid rounding it off

8.14 Remove the oil filter with a filter wrench

8.18 Lubricate the oil filter gasket with clean engine oil before installing the filter on the engine

9 Seat belt check (every 6000 miles or 6 months)

1 Check the seat belts, buckles, latch plates and guide loops for obvious damage and signs of wear.

2 Where the seat belt receptacle bolts to the floor of the vehicle, check that the bolts are secure.

3 See if the seat belt reminder light comes on when the key is turned to the Run or Start position. A chime should also sound.

10 Wiper blade inspection and replacement (every 6000 miles or 6 months)

▶ **Refer to illustration 10.3**

1 The windshield wiper blade elements should be checked periodically for cracks and deterioration.

2 Lift the wiper blade assembly away from the glass.

3 Press the release lever and slide the blade assembly out of the hook in the end of the wiper arm (see illustration).

4 Reinstall the blade assembly on the arm, wet the windshield and test for proper operation.

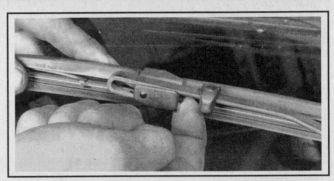

10.3 Depress the release lever (finger is on it here) and slide the wiper assembly down the wiper arm and out of the hook in the end of the arm

11 Battery check, maintenance and charging (every 6000 miles or 6 months)

▶ **Refer to illustrations 11.1, 11.5, 11.6a, 11.6b, 11.7a and 11.7b**

❊❊ WARNING:

Certain precautions must be followed when checking and servicing the battery. Hydrogen gas, which is highly flammable, is always present in the battery cells, so keep lighted tobacco and all other open flames and sparks away from the battery. The electrolyte inside the battery is actually dilute sulfuric acid, which will cause injury if splashed on your skin or in your eyes. It will also ruin clothes and painted surfaces. When removing the battery cables, always detach the negative cable first and hook it up last!

1 A routine preventive maintenance program for the battery in your vehicle is the only way to ensure quick and reliable starts. But before performing any battery maintenance, make sure that you have the proper equipment necessary to work safely around the battery (see illustration).

11.1 Tools and materials required for battery maintenance

1 *Face shield/safety goggles* - When removing corrosion with a brush, the acidic particles can easily fly up into your eyes

2 *Baking soda* - A solution of baking soda and water can be used to neutralize corrosion

3 *Petroleum jelly* - A layer of this on the battery posts will help prevent corrosion

4 *Battery post/cable cleaner* - This wire brush cleaning tool will remove all traces of corrosion from the battery posts and cable clamps

5 *Treated felt washers* - Placing one of these on each post, directly under the cable clamps, will help prevent corrosion

6 *Puller* - Sometimes the cable clamps are very difficult to pull off the posts, even after the nut/bolt has been completely loosened. This tool pulls the clamp straight up and off the post without damage

7 *Battery post/cable cleaner* - Here is another cleaning tool that is a slightly different version of Number 4 above, but it does the same thing

8 *Rubber gloves* - Another safety item to consider when servicing the battery; remember that's acid inside the battery!

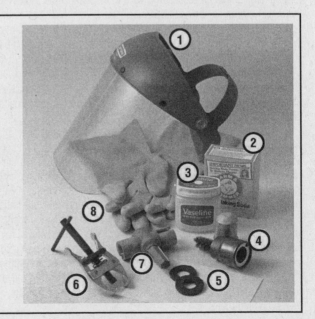

Terminal end corrosion or damage.

Insulation cracks.

Chafed insulation or exposed wires.

Burned or melted insulation.

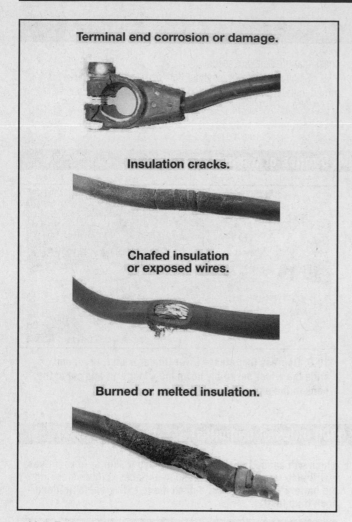

11.5 Typical battery cable problems

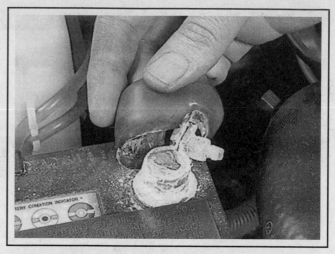

11.6a Battery terminal corrosion usually appears as light, fluffy powder

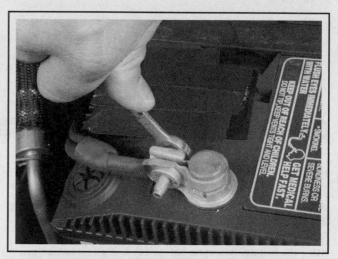

11.6b If the battery cable terminal is in good shape and not corroded, it can usually be loosened with a wrench - sometimes special battery pliers are required if corrosion has caused deterioration of the nut hex (always remove the ground cable first and hook it up last!)

2   There are also several precautions that should be taken whenever battery maintenance is performed. Before servicing the battery, always turn the engine and all accessories off and disconnect the cable from the negative terminal of the battery.

3   The battery produces hydrogen gas, which is both flammable and explosive. Never create a spark, smoke or light a match around the battery. Always charge the battery in a ventilated area.

4   Electrolyte contains poisonous and corrosive sulfuric acid. Do not allow it to get in your eyes, on your skin or on your clothes. Never ingest it. Wear protective safety glasses when working near the battery. Keep children away from the battery.

5   Note the external condition of the battery. If the positive terminal and cable clamp on your vehicle's battery is equipped with a rubber protector, make sure that it's not torn or damaged. It should completely cover the terminal. Look for any corroded or loose connections, cracks in the case or cover or loose hold-down clamps. Also check the entire length of each cable for cracks and frayed conductors (see illustration).

6   If corrosion, which looks like white, fluffy deposits is evident, particularly around the terminals, the battery should be removed for cleaning (see illustration). Loosen the cable nuts with a wrench or battery pliers, being careful to remove the ground cable first, and slide them off the terminals (see illustration). Then disconnect the hold-down clamp bolt and nut, remove the clamp and lift the battery from the engine compartment.

7   Clean the cable ends thoroughly with a battery brush or a terminal cleaner and a solution of warm water and baking soda. Wash the terminals and the battery case with the same solution but make sure that the solution doesn't get into the battery. When cleaning the cables, terminals and battery case, wear safety goggles and rubber gloves to prevent any solution from coming in contact with your eyes or hands. Wear old clothes too - even diluted, sulfuric acid splashed onto clothes will burn holes in them. If the terminals have been corroded, clean them up with a terminal cleaner (see illustrations). Thoroughly wash all cleaned areas with plain water.

8   Make sure that the battery tray is in good condition and the hold-down clamp bolts are tight. If the battery is removed from the tray, make sure no parts remain in the bottom of the tray when the battery is reinstalled. When reinstalling the hold down clamp bolts, do not over-tighten them.

9   Any metal parts of the vehicle damaged by corrosion should be covered with a zinc-based primer, then painted.

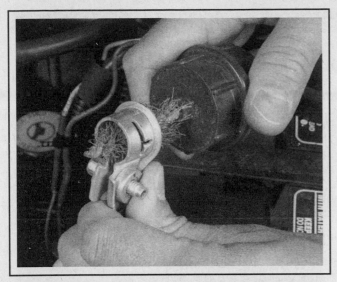

11.7a When cleaning the cable clamps, all corrosion must be removed (the inside of the clamp is tapered to match the taper on the post, so don't remove too much material)

11.7b Regardless of the type of tool used on the battery posts, a clean, shiny surface should be the result

10 Information on removing and installing the battery can be found in Chapter 5. Information on jump starting can be found at the front of this manual.

CHARGING

✳✳ WARNING:

When batteries are being charged, hydrogen gas, which is very explosive and flammable, is produced. Do not smoke or allow open flames near a charging or a recently charged battery. Wear eye protection when near the battery during charging. Also, make sure the charger is unplugged before connecting or disconnecting the battery from the charger.

➡Note: It is recommended that the battery be removed from the vehicle for charging because the gas that escapes during this procedure can damage the paint. Fast charging with the battery cables connected can result in damage to the electrical system.

11 Slow-rate charging is the best way to restore a battery that's discharged to the point where it will not start the engine. It's also a good way to maintain the battery charge in a vehicle that's only driven a few miles between starts. Maintaining the battery charge is particularly important in the winter when the battery must work harder to start the engine and electrical accessories that drain the battery are in greater use.

12 It's best to use a one or two-amp battery charger (sometimes called a "trickle" charger). They are the safest and put the least strain on the battery. They are also the least expensive. For a faster charge, you can use a higher amperage charger, but don't use one rated more than 1/10th the amp/hour rating of the battery. Rapid boost charges that claim to restore the power of the battery in one to two hours are hardest

on the battery and can damage batteries not in good condition. This type of charging should only be used in emergency situations.

13 The average time necessary to charge a battery should be listed in the instructions that come with the charger. As a general rule, a trickle charger will charge a battery in 12 to 16 hours.

14 Remove all the cell caps (if equipped - see Section 4) and cover the holes with a clean cloth to prevent spattering electrolyte. Disconnect the negative battery cable and hook the battery charger cable clamps up to the battery posts (positive-to-positive, negative-to-negative), then plug in the charger. Make sure it is set at 12-volts if it has a selector switch.

15 If you're using a charger with a rate higher than two amps, check the battery regularly during charging to make sure it doesn't overheat. If you're using a trickle charger, you can safely let the battery charge overnight after you've checked it regularly for the first couple of hours.

16 If the battery has removable cell caps, measure the specific gravity with a hydrometer every hour during the last few hours of the charging cycle. Hydrometers are available inexpensively from auto parts stores - follow the instructions that come with the hydrometer. Consider the battery charged when there's no change in the specific gravity reading for two hours and the electrolyte in the cells is gassing (bubbling) freely. The specific gravity reading from each cell should be very close to the others. If not, the battery probably has a bad cell(s).

17 Some batteries with sealed tops have built-in hydrometers on the top that indicate the state of charge by the color displayed in the hydrometer window. Normally, a bright-colored hydrometer indicates a full charge and a dark hydrometer indicates the battery still needs charging.

18 If the battery has a sealed top and no built-in hydrometer, you can hook up a digital voltmeter across the battery terminals to check the charge. A fully charged battery should read 12.5 volts or higher.

19 Further information on the battery and jump-starting can be found in Chapter 5 and at the front of this manual.

12 Drivebelt check and replacement (every 6000 miles or 6 months)

▶ **Refer to illustration 12.1**

1 A drivebelt is located at the front of the engine (see illustration) and plays an important role in the overall operation of the engine and its components. Due to its function and material make up, the belt is prone to wear and should be periodically inspected. All models have a single, ribbed serpentine belt to drive all the engine accessories.

CHECK

▶ **Refer to illustrations 12.2 and 12.4**

2 With the engine off, open the hood and use your fingers (and a flashlight, if necessary) to move along the belt, checking for cracks and

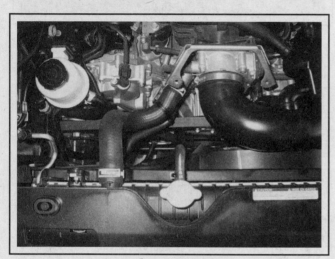

12.1 Always note the routing of the drivebelt before removing

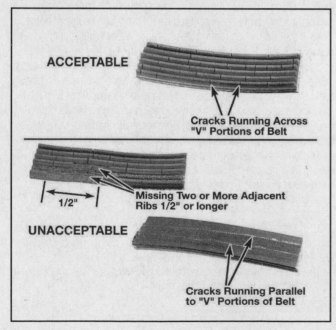

12.2 Check ribbed belts for signs of wear like these

separation of the belt plies. Also check for fraying and glazing, which gives the belt a shiny appearance (see illustration). Both sides of the belt should be inspected, which means you will have to twist the belt to check the underside.

3 Check the ribs on the underside of the belt. They should all be the same depth, with none of the surface uneven.

4 Inspect the indicator marks next to the automatic belt tensioner. If the stationary mark is aligned with the outer limit of the tensioner's travel, the belt must be replaced (see illustration).

REPLACEMENT

▶ **Refer to illustrations 12.5 and 12.7**

5 Refer to the accompanying illustration for the belt routing diagram for your vehicle (see illustration).

6 Disconnect the cable from the negative terminal of the battery. Remove the intake air duct and intake air resonator (see Chapter 4).

7 To replace the belt, rotate the tensioner to relieve the tension on the belt (see illustration).

8 Remove the belt from the auxiliary components and carefully release the tensioner.

9 Route the new belt over the various pulleys, again rotating the tensioner to allow the belt to be installed, then release the belt tensioner. Make sure the belt fits properly into the pulley grooves - it must be completely engaged.

10 Reconnect the battery.

TENSIONER REPLACEMENT

11 Remove the drivebelt.

12 Remove the three bolts and remove the tensioner assembly.

13 Installation is the reverse of removal. Tighten the bolts to the torque listed in this Chapter's Specifications.

12.4 Observe the scale at the belt tension automatic adjuster; if the maximum wear mark is aligned with the stationary mark, replace the belt

A	Stationary mark
B	New belt range
C	Wear limit mark

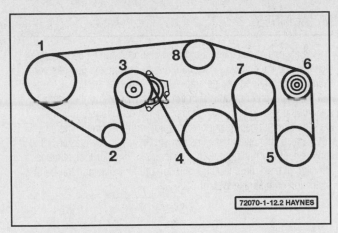

12.5 Drivebelt routing diagram

1	Power steering pump	5	Air conditioning
2	Alternator		compressor (if equipped)
3	Tensioner pulley		or idler pulley
4	Crankshaft pulley	6	Idler pulley
		7	Water pump
		8	Idler pulley

12.7 Use a socket and ratchet or breaker bar to rotate the tensioner counterclockwise far enough to remove the drivebelt, then slowly release the tensioner

13 Underhood hose check and replacement (every 6000 miles or 6 months)

GENERAL

> ※ **CAUTION:**
>
> **Replacement of air conditioning hoses must be left to a dealer service department or air conditioning shop that has the equipment to depressurize the system safely and recover the refrigerant. Never remove air conditioning components or hoses until the system has been depressurized.**

1 High temperatures in the engine compartment can cause the deterioration of the rubber and plastic hoses used for engine, accessory and emission systems operation. Periodic inspection should be made for cracks, loose clamps, material hardening and leaks. Information specific to the cooling system hoses can be found in Section 14.

2 Some, but not all, hoses are secured to their fittings with clamps. Where clamps are used, check to be sure they haven't lost their tension, allowing the hose to leak. If clamps aren't used, make sure the hose has not expanded and/or hardened where it slips over the fitting, allowing it to leak.

VACUUM HOSES

3 It's quite common for vacuum hoses, especially those in the emissions system, to be color-coded or identified by colored stripes molded into them. Various systems require hoses with different wall thickness, collapse resistance and temperature resistance. When replacing hoses, be sure the new ones are made of the same material.

4 Often the only effective way to check a hose is to remove it completely from the vehicle. If more than one hose is removed, be sure to label the hoses and fittings to ensure correct installation.

5 When checking vacuum hoses, be sure to include any plastic T-fittings in the check. Inspect the fittings for cracks and the hose where it fits over the fitting for distortion, which could cause leakage.

6 A small piece of vacuum hose (1/4-inch inside diameter) can be used as a stethoscope to detect vacuum leaks. Hold one end of the hose to your ear and probe around vacuum hoses and fittings, listening for the hissing sound characteristic of a vacuum leak.

> ※ **WARNING:**
>
> **When probing with the vacuum hose stethoscope, be very careful not to come into contact with moving engine components such as the drivebelt, cooling fan, etc.**

FUEL HOSE

> ※ **WARNING:**
>
> **Gasoline is extremely flammable, so take extra precautions when you work on any part of the fuel system. Don't smoke or allow open flames or bare light bulbs near the work area, and don't work in a garage where a gas-type appliance (such as a water heater or clothes dryer) is present. Since gasoline is carcinogenic, wear fuel-resistant gloves when there's a possibility of being exposed to fuel, and, if you spill any fuel on your skin, rinse it off immediately with soap and water. Mop up any spills immediately and do not store fuel-soaked rags where they could ignite. When you perform any kind of work on the fuel system, wear safety glasses and have a Class B type fire extinguisher on hand. The fuel system is under pressure, so if any lines must be disconnected, the pressure in the system must be relieved first (see Chapter 4 for more information).**

7   Check all rubber fuel lines for deterioration and chafing. Check especially for cracks in areas where the hose bends and just before fittings, such as where a hose attaches to the fuel filter and fuel injection unit.

8   High quality fuel line, specifically designed for high-pressure fuel injection applications, must be used for fuel line replacement. Never, under any circumstances, use regular fuel line, unreinforced vacuum line, clear plastic tubing or water hose for fuel lines.

9   Spring-type (pinch) clamps are commonly used on fuel lines. These clamps often lose their tension over a period of time, and can be sprung during removal. Replace all spring-type clamps with screw clamps whenever a hose is replaced.

METAL LINES

10 Sections of metal line are routed along the frame, between the fuel tank and the engine. Check carefully to be sure the line has not been bent or crimped and no cracks have started in the line.

11 If a section of metal fuel line must be replaced, only seamless steel tubing should be used, since copper and aluminum tubing don't have the strength necessary to withstand normal engine vibration.

12 Check the metal brake lines where they enter the master cylinder and brake proportioning unit for cracks in the lines or loose fittings. Any sign of brake fluid leakage calls for an immediate and thorough inspection of the brake system.

14 Cooling system check (every 6000 miles or 6 months)

▶ **Refer to illustration 14.4**

1   Many major engine failures can be attributed to a faulty cooling system. If the vehicle is equipped with an automatic transmission, the cooling system also cools the transmission fluid and thus plays an important role in prolonging transmission life.

2   The cooling system should be checked with the engine cold. Do this before the vehicle is driven for the day or after it has been shut off for at least three hours.

3   Remove the coolant reservoir/expansion tank cap by turning it counterclockwise until it reaches a stop. If you hear any hissing sounds (indicating there is still pressure in the system), wait until it stops, then depress the cap and continue turning until it can be removed. Thoroughly clean the cap, inside and out, with clean water. Also remove the radiator cap and clean the filler neck on the radiator. All traces of corrosion should be removed. The coolant inside the radiator (and coolant reservoir) should be relatively transparent. If it is rust colored, the system should be drained and refilled (see Section 29). If the coolant level is low, add additional antifreeze/coolant mixture (see Section 4).

4   Carefully check the large upper and lower radiator hoses along with any smaller diameter heater hoses that run from the engine to the firewall. Inspect each hose along its entire length, replacing any hose that is cracked, swollen or shows signs of deterioration. Cracks may become more apparent if the hose is squeezed (see illustration).

5   Make sure all hose connections are tight. A leak in the cooling system will usually show up as white or rust-colored deposits on the areas adjoining the leak. If spring-type clamps are used at the ends of the hoses, it may be wise to replace them with more secure, screw-type clamps.

6   Use compressed air or a soft brush to remove bugs, leaves, etc. from the front of the radiator or air conditioning condenser. Be careful not to damage the delicate cooling fins or cut yourself on them.

7   Every other inspection, or at the first indication of cooling system problems, have the cap and system pressure tested. If you don't have a pressure tester, most gas stations and repair shops will do this for a minimal charge.

Check for a chafed area that could fail prematurely.

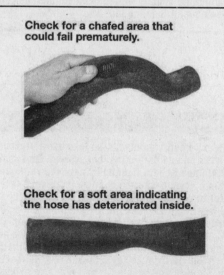

Check for a soft area indicating the hose has deteriorated inside.

Overtightening the clamp on a hardened hose will damage the hose and cause a leak.

Check each hose for swelling and oil-soaked ends. Cracks and breaks can be located by squeezing the hose.

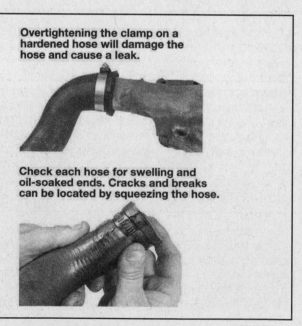

14.4 Hoses, like drivebelts, have a habit of failing at the worst possible time - to prevent the inconvenience of a blown radiator or heater hose, inspect them carefully as shown here

15 Tire rotation (every 6000 miles or 6 months)

▶ **Refer to illustration 15.2**

1   The tires should be rotated at the specified intervals and whenever uneven wear is noticed.

2   Tires must be rotated in the recommended pattern (see illustration).

3   Refer to the information in *Jacking and towing* at the front of this manual for the proper procedures to follow when raising the vehicle and changing a tire. If the brakes are to be checked, don't apply the parking brake as stated. Make sure the tires are blocked to prevent the vehicle from rolling as it's raised. Before raising the vehicle, loosen the wheel lug nuts slightly.

4   Preferably, the entire vehicle should be raised at the same time. This can be done on a hoist or by jacking up each corner, then lowering the vehicle onto jackstands placed under the frame rails. Always use four jackstands and make sure the vehicle is safely supported.

5   After rotation, check and adjust the tire pressures as necessary. Tighten the lug nuts to the torque listed in this Chapter's Specifications.

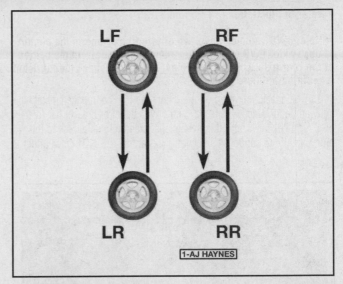

15.2 The recommended tire rotation pattern

16 Exhaust system check (every 6,000 miles or 6 months)

▶ **Refer to illustrations 16.2a and 16.2b**

1   With the engine cold (at least three hours after the vehicle has been driven), check the complete exhaust system from the manifold to the end of the tailpipe. Be careful around the catalytic converter, which may be hot even after three hours. The inspection should be done with the vehicle on a hoist to permit unrestricted access. If a hoist isn't available, raise the vehicle and support it securely on jackstands.

2   Check the exhaust pipes and connections for signs of leakage and/or corrosion indicating a potential failure. Make sure that all brackets and hangers are in good condition and tight (see illustrations).

3   Inspect the underside of the body for holes, corrosion, open seams, etc. which may allow exhaust gasses to enter the passenger compartment. Seal all body openings with silicone sealant or body putty.

4   Rattles and other noises can often be traced to the exhaust system, especially the hangers, mounts and heat shields. Try to move the pipes, mufflers and catalytic converter. If the components can come in contact with the body or suspension parts, secure the exhaust system with new brackets and hangers.

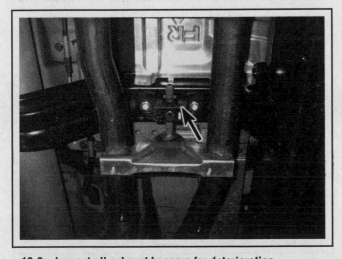

16.2a Inspect all exhaust hangers for deterioration

16.2b Inspect all flanged joints for signs of exhaust gas leakage

17 Differential lubricant level check (every 15,000 miles or 12 months)

▶ **Refer to illustrations 17.2a and 17.2b**

➡**Note: 4WD vehicles have two differentials - one in the center of each axle. 2WD vehicles have one differential - in the center of the rear axle. On 4WD vehicles, be sure to check the lubricant level in both differentials.**

1 The check/filler plug on the differential(s) is a threaded metal type and can be loosened with a 1/2-inch drive ratchet or breaker bar (rear) or a large hex bit (front). If the vehicle is raised to gain access to the plug, be sure to support it safely on jackstands - DO NOT crawl under the vehicle when it's supported only by the jack. Be sure the vehicle is level or the check may not be accurate.

2 Remove the plug from the filler hole in the differential housing or cover (see illustrations).

3 The lubricant level should be up to the bottom of the filler hole. If not, use a pump or squeeze bottle to add the recommended lubricant until it just starts to run out of the opening.

4 Install the plug in the filler hole and tighten it to the torque listed in this Chapter's Specifications.

17.2a Rear differential check/filler plug (A) and drain plug (B) - Armada

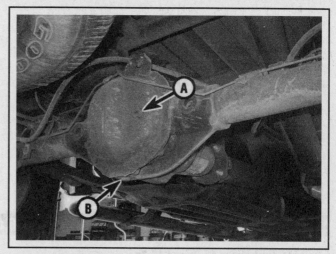

17.2b Rear differential check/filler plug (A) and drain plug (B) - Titan

18 Transfer case lubricant level check (4WD models) (every 15,000 miles or 12 months)

▶ **Refer to illustration 18.1**

1 The transfer case lubricant level is checked by removing the upper plug located at the rear of the case (see illustration).

2 After removing the plug, reach inside the hole. The lubricant level should be just at the bottom of the hole. If not, add the appropriate lubricant through the opening.

18.1 Transfer case filler plug (A) (the drain plug is on the other side)

19 Chassis lubrication (every 15,000 miles or 12 months)

▶ **Refer to illustration 19.1**

1   Refer to *Recommended lubricants and fluids* in this Chapter's Specifications to obtain the necessary grease, etc. You'll also need a grease gun (see illustration). If a suspension component has no grease fitting in place, this indicates the part is sealed and doesn't require periodic lubrication.

2   Look under the vehicle and locate the grease fittings. Occasionally, plugs may be installed rather than grease fittings. If so, grease fittings will have to be purchased and installed (they're available at auto parts stores).

3   For easier access under the vehicle, raise it with a jack and place jackstands under the frame. Make sure it's safely supported by the stands. If the wheels are to be removed at this interval for tire rotation or brake inspection, loosen the lug nuts slightly while the vehicle is still on the ground.

4   Before beginning, force a little grease out of the nozzle to remove any dirt from the end of the gun. Wipe the nozzle clean with a rag.

5   With the grease gun and plenty of clean rags, crawl under the vehicle and begin lubricating the components.

6   Wipe one of the grease fittings clean and push the nozzle firmly over it. Pump the gun until the component is completely lubricated. On balljoints, stop pumping when the rubber seal is firm to the touch. Do not pump too much grease into the fitting as it could rupture the seal. For all other suspension and steering components, continue pumping grease into the fitting until it oozes out of the joint between the two components. If it escapes around the grease gun nozzle, the fitting is clogged or the nozzle is not completely seated on the fitting. Resecure the gun nozzle to the fitting and try again. If necessary, replace the fitting with a new one.

7   Wipe the excess grease from the components and the grease fitting. Repeat the procedure for the remaining fittings.

8   Clean the fitting and pump grease into the driveline universal joints until the grease can be seen coming out of the contact points. The other U-joints are sealed and do not require lubrication.

➡**Note: Most replacement driveshaft U-joints aren't permanently sealed, and are sold with grease fittings. If your U-joints have been replaced, make sure you include them in your routine chassis lubrication.**

19.1 Materials required for chassis and body lubrication

1   Engine oil - Light engine oil in a can like this can be used for door and hood hinges
2   Graphite spray - Used to lubricate lock cylinders
3   Grease - Grease, in a variety of types and weights, is available for use in a grease gun. Check the Specifications for your requirements
4   Grease gun - A common grease gun, shown here with a detachable hose and nozzle, is needed for chassis lubrication. After use, clean it thoroughly!

9   Also clean and lubricate the parking brake cable guides and levers.

❋❋ CAUTION:

Do not use chassis lubrication on the brake cables themselves. The grease will cause the cable housings to deteriorate.

20 Fuel system check (every 15,000 miles or 12 months)

❋❋ WARNING:

Gasoline is extremely flammable, so take extra precautions when you work on any part of the fuel system. Don't smoke or allow open flames or bare light bulbs near the work area, and don't work in a garage where a gas-type appliance (such as a water heater or clothes dryer) is present. Since gasoline is carcinogenic, wear fuel-resistant gloves when there's a possibility of being exposed to fuel, and, if you spill any fuel on your skin, rinse it off immediately with soap and water. Mop up any spills immediately and do not store fuel-soaked rags where they could ignite. When you perform any kind of work on the fuel system, wear safety glasses and have a Class B type fire extinguisher on hand. The fuel system is under constant pressure, so, before any lines are disconnected, the fuel system pressure must be relieved (see Chapter 4).

1   If you smell gasoline while driving or after the vehicle has been sitting in the sun, inspect the fuel system immediately.

2   Remove the fuel filler cap and inspect it for damage and corrosion. The gasket should have an unbroken sealing imprint. If the gasket is damaged or corroded, install a new cap.

3   Inspect the fuel feed and return lines for cracks. Make sure that the connections between the fuel lines and the fuel injection system are tight.

❋❋ WARNING:

Your vehicle is fuel injected, so you must relieve the fuel system pressure before servicing fuel system components. The fuel system pressure relief procedure is described in Chapter 4.

4   If the fuel injectors are visible, look for signs of fuel leakage (wet spots) around any of the injectors - they may need new O-rings (see Chapter 4).

5   Since some components of the fuel system - the fuel tank and part of the fuel feed and return lines, for example - are underneath the vehicle, they can be inspected more easily with the vehicle raised on a hoist. If that's not possible, raise the vehicle and support it securely on jackstands.

6   With the vehicle raised and safely supported, inspect the fuel tank and filler neck for punctures, cracks and other damage. The connection between the filler neck and the tank is particularly critical. Sometimes a rubber filler neck will leak because of loose clamps or deteriorated rubber. Inspect all fuel tank mounting brackets and straps to be sure that the tank is securely attached to the vehicle.

✳✳ WARNING:

Do not, under any circumstances, try to repair a fuel tank (except rubber components). A welding torch or any open flame can easily cause fuel vapors inside the tank to explode.

7   Carefully check all rubber hoses and metal lines leading away from the fuel tank. Check for loose connections, deteriorated hoses, crimped lines and other damage. Repair or replace damaged sections as necessary (see Chapter 4).

8   The evaporative emissions control system can also be a source of fuel odors. The function of the system is to store fuel vapors from the fuel tank in a charcoal canister until they can be routed to the intake manifold, where they mix with incoming air before being burned in the combustion chambers.

9   The most common symptom of a faulty evaporative emissions system is a strong odor of fuel near the charcoal canister, which is mounted under the rear of the vehicle on all models. If a fuel odor has been detected, and you have already checked the areas described above, check the charcoal canister and the hoses connected to it (see Section 27).

21 Suspension, steering and driveaxle boot check (every 15,000 miles or 12 months)

→**Note: The steering linkage and suspension components should be checked periodically. Worn or damaged suspension and steering linkage components can result in excessive and abnormal tire wear, poor ride quality and vehicle handling and reduced fuel economy. For detailed illustrations of the steering and suspension components, refer to Chapter 10.**

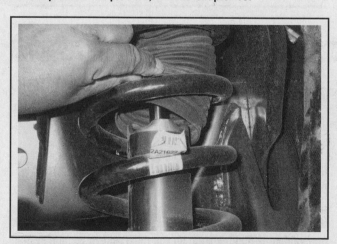

21.6 Check the shock absorbers for fluid leakage where the piston rod enters the shock body (front shock absorber shown)

SHOCK ABSORBER CHECK

▶ **Refer to illustration 21.6**

1   Park the vehicle on level ground, turn the engine off and set the parking brake. Check the tire pressures.

2   Push down at one corner of the vehicle, then release it while noting the movement of the body. It should stop moving and come to rest in a level position within one or two bounces.

3   If the vehicle continues to move up-and-down or if it fails to return to its original position, a worn or weak shock absorber is probably the reason.

4   Repeat the above check at each of the three remaining corners of the vehicle.

5   Raise the vehicle and support it securely on jackstands.

6   Check the shock absorbers for evidence of fluid leakage (see illustration). A light film of fluid is no cause for concern. Make sure that any fluid noted is from the shocks and not from some other source. If leakage is noted, replace the shocks as a set (front or rear).

7   Check the shocks to be sure they are securely mounted and undamaged. Check the upper mounts for damage and wear. If damage or wear is noted, replace the shocks as a set (front or rear).

8   If the shocks must be replaced, refer to Chapter 10 for the procedure.

21.9a Check the bushings at the inner ends of the control arms for deterioration

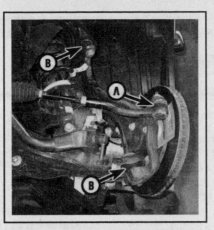

21.9b Inspect the tie-rod ends (A) and the balljoints (B)

21.9c Inspect the steering gear boots for signs of cracking or fluid leakage (if fluid leakage is noted, the rack seals are faulty)

21.11 With the steering wheel in the locked position and the vehicle raised, grasp the front tire as shown and try to move it back-and-forth - if any play is noted, check the steering gear mounts and tie-rod ends for looseness

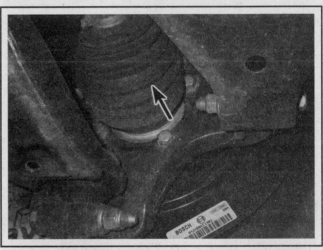

21.14 Inspect the inner and outer driveaxle boots for loose clamps, cracks or signs of leaking lubricant

STEERING AND SUSPENSION CHECK

♦ **Refer to illustrations 21.9a, 21.9b, 21.9c and 21.11**

9   Visually inspect the steering and suspension components (front and rear) for damage and distortion. Look for damaged seals, boots and bushings and leaks of any kind. Examine the bushings where the control arms meet the chassis (see illustrations).

10 Clean the lower end of the steering knuckle. Have an assistant grasp the lower edge of the tire and move the wheel in-and-out while you look for movement at the steering knuckle-to-control arm balljoint. If there is any movement, the suspension balljoint(s) must be replaced.

11 Grasp each front tire at the front and rear edges, push in at the front, pull out at the rear and feel for play in the steering system components. If any freeplay is noted, check the idler arm and the tie-rod ends for looseness (see illustration).

12 Additional steering and suspension system information and illus-

trations can be found in Chapter 10.

DRIVEAXLE BOOT CHECK (FRONT - ALL 4WD MODELS, REAR - ALL ARMADA MODELS)

♦ **Refer to illustration 21.14**

13 The driveaxle boots are very important because they prevent dirt, water and foreign material from entering and damaging the constant velocity (CV) joints. Oil and grease can cause the boot material to deteriorate prematurely, so it's a good idea to wash the boots with soap and water. Because it constantly pivots back and forth following the steering action of the front hub, the outer CV boot wears out sooner and should be inspected regularly.

14 Inspect the boots for tears and cracks as well as loose clamps (see illustration). If there is any evidence of cracks or leaking lubricant, they must be replaced as described in Chapter 8.

22 Brake system check (every 15,000 miles or 12 months)

✳✳ WARNING:

The dust created by the brake system is harmful to your health. Never blow it out with compressed air and don't inhale any of it. An approved filtering mask should be worn when working on the brakes. Do not, under any circumstances, use petroleum-based solvents to clean brake parts. Use brake system cleaner only! Try to use non-asbestos replacement parts whenever possible.

➡**Note: For detailed photographs of the brake system, refer to Chapter 9.**

1   In addition to the specified intervals, the brakes should be inspected every time the wheels are removed or whenever a defect is suspected.

2   Any of the following symptoms could indicate a potential brake system defect: The vehicle pulls to one side when the brake pedal is depressed; the brakes make squealing or dragging noises when applied; brake pedal travel is excessive; the pedal pulsates; or brake fluid leaks, usually onto the inside of the tire or wheel.

3   Loosen the wheel lug nuts.

4   Raise the vehicle and place it securely on jackstands.

5   Remove the wheels.

22.7a With the wheel off, check the thickness of the inner brake pads through the inspection hole

22.7b Check the thickness of the outer pad material, too

DISC BRAKES

▶ **Refer to illustrations 22.7a, 22.7b, 22.9 and 22.11**

6   There are two pads (an outer and an inner) in each caliper. The pads are visible with the wheels removed.

7   Check the pad thickness by looking through the inspection window in the caliper body and along the edge of the outer pad (see illustrations). If the lining material is less than the thickness listed in this Chapter's Specifications, replace the pads.

➡**Note: Keep in mind that the lining material is riveted or bonded to a metal backing plate and the metal portion is not included in this measurement.**

8   If it is difficult to determine the exact thickness of the remaining pad material by the above method, or if you are at all concerned about the condition of the pads, remove the pads for further inspection (see Chapter 9).

9   Once the pads are removed from the calipers, clean them with brake cleaner and re-measure them with a ruler or a vernier caliper (see illustration).

10 Measure the disc thickness with a micrometer to make sure that it still has service life remaining. If any disc is thinner than the specified minimum thickness, replace it (see Chapter 9). Even if the disc has service life remaining, check its condition. Look for scoring, gouging and burned spots. If these conditions exist, remove the disc and have it resurfaced (see Chapter 9).

11 Before installing the wheels, check all brake lines and hoses for damage, wear, deformation, cracks, corrosion, leakage, bends and twists, particularly in the vicinity of the rubber hoses at the calipers (see illustration). Check the clamps for tightness and the connections for leakage. Make sure that all hoses and lines are clear of sharp edges, moving parts and the exhaust system. If any of the above conditions are noted, repair, reroute or replace the lines and/or fittings as necessary (see Chapter 9).

BRAKE BOOSTER CHECK

12 Sit in the driver's seat and perform the following sequence of tests.

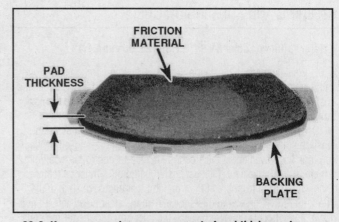

22.9 If a more precise measurement of pad thickness is necessary, remove the pads and measure the remaining friction material

13 With the brake fully depressed, start the engine - the pedal should move down a little when the engine starts.

14 With the engine running, depress the brake pedal several times - the travel distance should not change.

15 Depress the brake, stop the engine and hold the pedal in for about 30 seconds - the pedal should neither sink nor rise.

16 Restart the engine, run it for about a minute and turn it off. Then firmly depress the brake several times - the pedal travel should decrease with each application.

17 If your brakes do not operate as described, the brake booster has failed. Refer to Chapter 9 for the replacement procedure.

PARKING BRAKE

18 One method of checking the parking brake is to park the vehicle on a steep hill with the parking brake set and the transmission in Neutral (be sure to stay in the vehicle during this check!). If the parking brake cannot prevent the vehicle from rolling, it's in need of adjustment (see Chapter 9).

BRAKE PEDAL

→Note: On vehicles equipped with electrically adjustable pedals, move the pedals to their lowest position (closest to the floor) before checking or adjusting the pedal height.

Brake pedal released height

♦ Refer to illustrations 22.19 and 22.21

19 Remove the brake light and speed control switches (see Chapter 9). Peel back the carpet and insulator pad. With the brake pedal fully released, measure the distance from the top of the pad to the floor (see illustration).

20 If the height is not as listed in this Chapter's Specifications, it must be adjusted.

21 Loosen the locknut just in front of the power brake booster clevis (see illustration).

22 Turn the booster input rod until the pedal height is correct.

23 Tighten the locknut.

24 After adjusting the pedal height, check the freeplay. It may also be

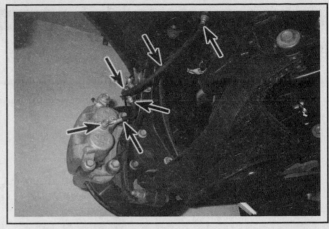

22.11 Check along the brake hoses and at each fitting for seepage, deterioration and cracks

necessary to adjust the brake light switch (see Chapter 9).

Brake pedal freeplay

♦ Refer to illustration 22.25

25 Press down lightly on the brake pedal and measure the distance that it moves freely before resistance is felt (see illustration). The freeplay should be within the specified limits. If it isn't, it must be adjusted.

26 Loosen the locknut for the brake booster clevis (see illustration 22.21).

27 Turn the booster input rod until the pedal freeplay is correct.

28 Tighten the locknut.

Brake pedal depressed height

29 After checking and, if necessary, adjusting the pedal released height and freeplay, the pedal depressed height must be checked.

30 With the engine running, press the brake pedal fully and measure the pedal pad-to-floor distance.

31 If the minimum depressed height is below that listed in this Chapter's Specifications, check the brake system for leaks or other damage.

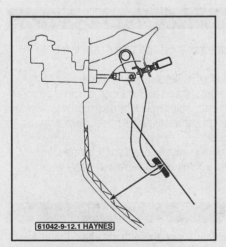

22.19 With the brake pedal fully released, measure the distance from the top of the pad to the floor

22.21 To adjust brake pedal released height, loosen the locknut (A) in front of the brake booster clevis (B) and turn the input rod until free height is correct (this procedure is also used to adjust brake pedal freeplay)

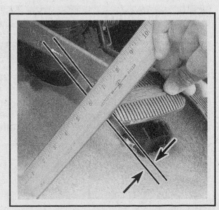

22.25 To measure brake pedal freeplay, press down lightly on the brake pedal and measure the distance that it moves freely before resistance is felt

23 Cabin air filters - replacement (every 15,000 miles or 12 months)

▶ **Refer to illustrations 23.3 and 23.5**

1   The manufacturer recommends replacing the cabin air filters at the specified interval, to maintain the performance of the HVAC system.

2   Remove the glove box (see Chapter 11, Section 28).

3   Remove the bolt securing the cover of the filter drawer in the heating/air conditioning unit, then remove the cover (see illustration).

4   Withdraw the two filters.

5   Install the new filters, which are marked with arrows to indicate which side faces down. The ends marked with the arrow should be visible when the new filters are installed (see illustration).

➡**Note: Install one filter first and nudge it to the right as far as it will go before installing the second filter.**

6   The remainder of installation is the reverse of the removal procedure.

23.3 Remove the filter cover bolt, then remove the cover

23.5 When the two new filters are inserted properly, the airflow indicator arrows should point down

24 Brake fluid change (every 30,000 miles or 24 months)

❋❋ **WARNING:**

Brake fluid can harm your eyes and damage painted surfaces, so use extreme caution when handling or pouring it. Do not use brake fluid that has been standing open or is more than one year old. Brake fluid absorbs moisture from the air. Excess moisture can cause a dangerous loss of braking effectiveness.

1   At the specified intervals, the brake fluid should be drained and replaced. Since the brake fluid may drip or splash when pouring it, place plenty of rags around the master cylinder to protect any surrounding painted surfaces.

2   Before beginning work, purchase the specified brake fluid (see *Recommended lubricants and fluids* in this Chapter's Specifications).

3   Remove the cap from the master cylinder reservoir.

4   Using a hand suction pump or similar device, withdraw the fluid from the master cylinder reservoir.

5   Add new fluid to the master cylinder until it rises to the line indicated on the reservoir.

6   Bleed the brake system as described in Chapter 9 at all four brakes until new and uncontaminated fluid is expelled from the bleeder screw. Be sure to maintain the fluid level in the master cylinder as you perform the bleeding process. If you allow the master cylinder to run dry, air will enter the system.

7   Refill the master cylinder with fluid and check the operation of the brakes. The pedal should feel solid when depressed, with no sponginess.

❋❋ **WARNING:**

Do not operate the vehicle if you are in doubt about the effectiveness of the brake system.

25 Air filter replacement (every 30,000 miles or 24 months)

▶ **Refer to illustrations 25.1a and 25.1b**

1 The air filter is contained within a housing near the left-front of the engine compartment. To replace the filter, release the clips securing the housing halves and pull the upper half away enough to remove the filter element (see illustrations).

2 Inspect the outer surface of the filter element. If it is dirty, replace it. If it is only moderately dusty, it can be reused by blowing it clean from the back to the front surface with compressed air. Because it is a pleated paper type filter, it cannot be washed or oiled. If it cannot be cleaned satisfactorily with compressed air, discard and replace it. While the cover is off, be careful not to drop anything down into the housing.

❊❊ CAUTION:

Never drive the vehicle with the air cleaner removed. Excessive engine wear could result and backfiring could even cause a fire under the hood.

3 Wipe out the inside of the air cleaner housing.

4 Place the new filter into the air cleaner housing, making sure it seats properly.

5 Installation of the cover is the reverse of removal.

25.1a Release the clips on the filter housing . . .

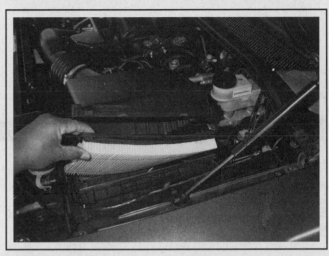

25.1b . . . then lift the cover, slide the old filter out and insert a new filter

26 Wheel bearings - inspection (every 30,000 miles or 24 months)

FRONT (ALL MODELS) AND REAR (ARMADA MODELS)

1 Loosen the wheel lug nuts. Raise the vehicle and support it securely on jackstands, then chock the wheels at the other end of the vehicle.

2 Remove the wheel and inspect the wheel bearing for signs of damage or excessive rust. The wheel bearings are inside a sealed housing with permanent lubrication and require no adjustment. Spin the wheel bearing assembly, listening for unusual noise and feeling for any roughness Try to move the bearing assembly in or out, and try to tilt it relative to the knuckle. If there is any noise or play in the assembly, it must be replaced.

3 Refer to Chapter 10 for the hub and bearing assembly replacement procedure.

REAR (TITAN MODELS)

4 On Titan models, the rear wheel bearings are mounted at the outboard ends of the axle housing. Check the axle bearings with both rear wheels removed and the transmission in Neutral. Make sure the vehicle is properly supported and the front wheels are chocked to prevent movement. Listen and feel for noise or roughness in the rear axle bearings. There should be no axial play when trying to move the axle.

5 The axle bearings are secured to the axle and must be pressed off and new ones pressed on. Refer to Chapter 8 for the replacement procedure.

27 Evaporative emissions control system check (every 30,000 miles or 24 months)

▶ **Refer to illustration 27.2**

1   The function of the evaporative emissions control system is to draw fuel vapors from the gas tank and fuel system, store them in a charcoal canister and route them to the intake manifold during normal engine operation.

2   The most common symptom of a fault in the evaporative emissions system is a strong fuel odor. If a fuel odor is detected, inspect the charcoal canister, located inboard of the left rear wheel, near the rear of the fuel tank. Check the canister and hoses for damage, leaks or deterioration (see illustration).

3   The evaporative emissions control system component replacement procedures are in Chapter 6.

27.2 Check the charcoal canister (A) for damage and the hose connections (B) for cracks and deterioration

28 Spark plug replacement (see Maintenance schedule for replacement interval)

▶ **Refer to illustrations 28.1, 28.4, 28.6, 28.7a, 28.7b and 28.8**

➡**Note: The manufacturer recommends against checking the spark plug gap on used spark plugs, as the platinum or iridium coating could be scraped off, thereby greatly reducing the life of the spark plugs.**

1   In most cases, the tools necessary for spark plug replacement include a spark plug socket which fits onto a ratchet (spark plug sockets are padded inside to prevent damage to the porcelain insulators on the new plugs), and various extensions (see illustration).

2   When buying the new spark plugs, be sure to obtain the correct plug type for your particular engine. This information can be found in the vehicle owner's manual and this Chapter's Specifications.

3   Allow the engine to cool completely before attempting to remove any of the plugs. While you're waiting for the engine to cool, check the new plugs for defects.

4   Disconnect the electrical connector at the ignition coil for one cylinder, then remove the bolt and pull up on the coil/plug boot assembly (see illustration). Replace one plug at a time.

5   If compressed air is available, use it to blow any dirt or foreign material away from the spark plug hole. The idea here is to eliminate the possibility of debris falling into the cylinder as the spark plug is removed.

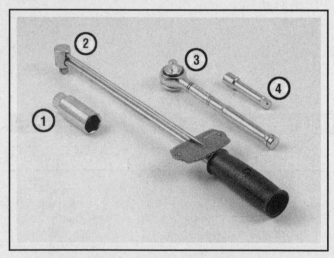

28.1 Tools required for changing spark plugs

1   *Spark plug socket* - This will have special padding inside to protect the spark plug's porcelain insulator
2   *Torque wrench* - Although not mandatory, using this tool is the best way to ensure the plugs are tightened properly
3   *Ratchet* - Standard hand tool to fit the spark plug socket
4   *Extension* - Depending on model and accessories, you may need special extensions and universal joints to reach one or more of the plugs

28.4 Disconnect the electrical connector (A) at an ignition coil, then remove the mounting bolt (B) and pull up on the coil/boot assembly to access the spark plug below

6   Place the spark plug socket over the plug and remove it from the engine by turning it in a counterclockwise direction (see illustration).

7   Compare the spark plug with the chart shown (see illustration) to get an indication of the general running condition of the engine. Before installing the new plugs, apply a thin coat of anti-seize compound to the threads (see illustration).

8   Thread one of the new plugs into the hole until you can no longer turn it with your fingers, then tighten it with a torque wrench (if available) or the ratchet. It is a good idea to slip a short length of rubber hose over the end of the plug to use as a tool to thread it into place (see illustration). The hose will grip the plug well enough to turn it, but will start to slip if the plug begins to cross-thread in the hole - this will prevent damaged threads and the accompanying repair costs.

9   Attach the ignition coil to the new spark plug, again using a twisting motion on the boot until it's seated on the spark plug. Install the bolt and tighten it securely.

10 Repeat the procedure for the remaining spark plugs.

28.6 Use a socket and extension to unscrew the spark plugs

A **normally worn** spark plug should have light tan or gray deposits on the firing tip.

A **carbon fouled** plug, identified by soft, sooty, black deposits, may indicate an improperly tuned vehicle. Check the air cleaner, ignition components and engine control system.

An **oil fouled** spark plug indicates an engine with worn piston rings and/or bad valve seals allowing excessive oil to enter the chamber.

This spark plug has been **left in the engine too long,** as evidenced by the extreme gap- Plugs with such an extreme gap can cause misfiring and stumbling accompanied by a noticeable lack of power.

A **physically damaged** spark plug may be evidence of severe detonation in that cylinder. Watch that cylinder carefully between services, as a continued detonation will not only damage the plug, but could also damage the engine.

A **bridged or almost bridged** spark plug, identified by a build-up between the electrodes caused by excessive carbon or oil build-up on the plug.

28.7a Inspect the spark plug to determine engine running conditions

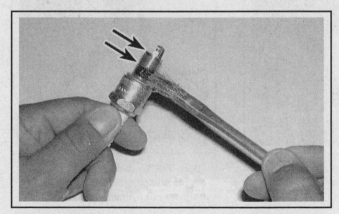

28.7b Apply a thin coat of anti-seize compound to the spark plug threads, being careful not to get any near the lower threads

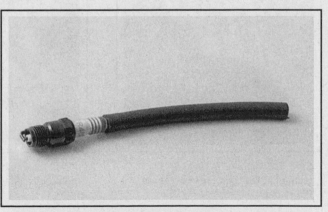

28.8 A length of snug-fitting rubber hose will save time and prevent damaged threads when installing the spark plugs

29 Cooling system servicing (draining, flushing and refilling) (every 30000 miles or 24 months)

✳✳ WARNING:

Do not allow antifreeze to come in contact with your skin or painted surfaces of the vehicle. Flush contacted areas immediately with plenty of water. Do not store new coolant or leave old coolant lying around where it is easily accessible to children and pets, because they are attracted by its sweet smell. Ingestion of even a small amount can be fatal. Wipe up the garage floor and drip pan coolant spills immediately. Keep antifreeze containers covered and repair leaks in your cooling system immediately. Antifreeze is flammable - be sure to read the precautions on the container.

➡Note: Non-toxic coolant is available at local auto parts stores. Although the coolant is non-toxic when fresh, proper disposal is still required.

DRAINING

▸ Refer to illustrations 29.3, 29.4a and 29.4b

1 Periodically, the cooling system should be drained, flushed and refilled to replenish the antifreeze mixture and prevent formation of rust and corrosion, which can impair the performance of the cooling system and cause engine damage. When the cooling system is serviced, all hoses and the radiator cap should be checked and replaced if necessary.

2 Apply the parking brake and block the wheels.

✳✳ WARNING:

If the vehicle has just been driven, wait several hours to allow the engine to cool down before beginning this procedure. Turn the ignition key to the On position, then set the heater control to the maximum heat position. Wait at least ten seconds, then turn the ignition Off.

3 Move a large container under the radiator drain to catch the coolant. Remove the engine under-cover (see illustration 8.8) for access to the drain plug, which is located in the radiator's lower tank (see illustration). Unscrew the drain plug, then remove the radiator cap.

4 After coolant stops flowing out of the radiator, move the container under the right-side engine block drain plug (see illustration). Remove the plug and allow the coolant in the block to drain. To drain the left-side cylinder bank, detach the coolant hose from the engine oil cooler (see illustration).

5 While the coolant is draining, check the condition of the radiator hoses, heater hoses and clamps (refer to Section 14 if necessary).

6 Once the coolant has drained completely, replace any damaged clamps or hoses. Apply thread sealant to the drain plug, reinstall it and tighten it securely. Reconnect the coolant hose to the engine oil cooler.

FLUSHING

▸ Refer to illustration 29.9

➡Note 1: In severe cases of contamination or clogging of the radiator, remove the radiator (see Chapter 3) and have a radiator repair facility clean and repair it if necessary.

➡Note 2: Many deposits can be removed by the chemical action of a cleaner available at auto parts stores. Follow the procedure outlined in the manufacturer's instructions. However, when the coolant is regularly drained and the system refilled with the correct antifreeze/water mixture, there should be no need to use chemical cleaners or descalers.

7 Make sure your heating system controls are set to Hot, so that the heater core will be flushed at the same time as the rest of the cooling system.

8 Once the system is completely drained, remove the thermostat from the engine (see Chapter 3). Reinstall the thermostat housing without the thermostat. This will allow the system to be thoroughly flushed.

9 Disconnect the upper radiator hose, then place a garden hose in

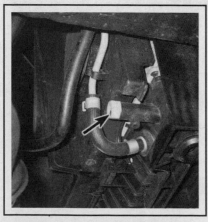

29.3 The radiator drain plug is located at the right lower corner of the radiator

29.4a Engine block drain plug for the right-side cylinder bank

29.4b Detach this hose from the engine oil cooler to drain the coolant from the left cylinder bank

the upper radiator inlet and flush the system until the water runs clear at the upper radiator hose (see illustration).

REFILLING

10 Install the thermostat (if removed) and reconnect the upper radiator hose.

11 Place the heater temperature control in the maximum heat position.

12 Make sure to use the proper coolant listed in this Chapter's Specifications. Slowly fill the radiator with the recommended mixture of antifreeze and water until coolant reaches the base of the radiator filler neck. Then add coolant to the reservoir until it reaches the FULL COLD mark. Wait five minutes and recheck the coolant level in the radiator, adding if necessary.

13 Leave the radiator cap off and run the engine in a well-ventilated area until the thermostat opens (coolant will begin flowing through the radiator and the upper radiator hose will become hot).

14 Rev the engine to approximately 2500 rpm for ten seconds then let it idle; do this a few times.

15 Turn the engine off and let it cool. Add more coolant mixture to bring the level back up to the base of the filler neck.

16 Squeeze the upper radiator hose to expel air, then add more coolant mixture if necessary. Reinstall the radiator cap. Add coolant to the reservoir, if necessary.

17 Start the engine, allow it to reach normal operating temperature and check for leaks.

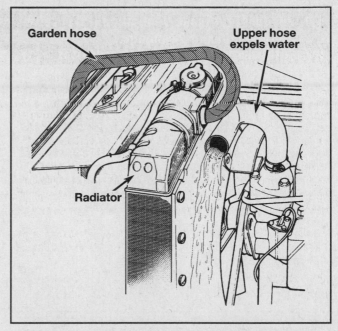

29.9 With the thermostat removed, disconnect the upper radiator hose and flush the radiator and engine block with a garden hose

30 Automatic transmission fluid change (every 30,000 miles or 24 months)

▶ **Refer to illustration 30.5**

1 At the specified intervals, the transmission fluid should be drained and replaced. Since the fluid will remain hot long after driving, perform this procedure only after the engine has cooled down completely.

2 Before beginning work, purchase the specified transmission fluid (see *Recommended lubricants and fluids* in this Chapter's Specifications) and a new filter and pan gasket.

3 Other tools necessary for this job include a floor jack, jackstands to support the vehicle in a raised position, a drain pan capable of holding at least eight quarts, newspapers and clean rags.

4 Raise the vehicle and support it securely on jackstands.

5 Place the drain pan underneath the transmission pan. Remove the drain plug and allow the fluid to drain, then reinsert the plug and tighten it securely (see illustration). Measure the amount of fluid drained (the same amount will be added to the transmission later, assuming that the fluid level was correct to begin with).

6 Lower the vehicle and add the specified type of automatic transmission fluid (the same amount that was drained in Step 5), through the filler tube (see Section 7).

7 With the transmission in Park and the parking brake set, run the engine at a fast idle, but don't race it.

8 Move the gear selector through each range and back to Park, then let the engine idle for a few minutes. Check the fluid level. It may be low. Add enough fluid to bring the level the COLD range on the dip-

30.5 Location of the automatic transmission fluid drain plug

stick. Be careful not to overfill.

9 Check under the vehicle for leaks during the first few trips. Check the fluid level again when the transmission is hot (see Section 7).

10 If desired, repeat Steps 4 through 8 once to flush any contaminated fluid from the torque converter and transmission cooler.

31 Positive Crankcase Ventilation (PCV) valve and hose check and replacement (30,000 miles or 24 months)

♦ Refer to illustration 31.1

1   Remove the engine cover (see Chapter 2A, illustration 4.2). The PCV valve is located in the valve cover (see illustration). Detach the hose from the valve, then pull the valve from the grommet in the valve cover.

2   Shake the PCV valve, listening for a rattle. If the valve doesn't rattle, replace it with a new one.

3   When purchasing a replacement PCV valve, make sure it's for your particular vehicle and engine size. Compare the old valve with the new one to make sure they're the same.

31.1 The PCV valves are located on the valve covers

32 Spark plug boots and ignition coils - cleaning and inspection (every 60,000 miles or 48 months)

♦ Refer to illustration 32.2

1   The engines in these models have individual ignition coils for each cylinder. Each coil has a boot on the bottom that connects directly to the top of its spark plug.

2   Whenever spark plugs are replaced (see Section 28), the coils/ boots are removed to access the plugs. Examine both the boots and the coils for any signs of carbon tracking, cracks or other damage (see illustration). Clean them with a dampened cloth and dry them thoroughly before installation.

32.2 Examine the spark plug boots and the individual ignition coils for signs of damage

33 Transfer case lubricant change (4WD models) (every 60,000 miles or 48 months)

1   This procedure should be performed after the vehicle has been driven so the lubricant will be warm and therefore will flow out of the transfer case more easily.

2   Raise the vehicle and support it securely on jackstands.

3   Remove the filler plug from the case (see Section 18).

4   Remove the drain plug from the lower part of the case and allow the lubricant to drain completely.

5   After the case is completely drained, carefully clean and install the drain plug. Tighten the plug to the torque listed in this Chapter's Specifications.

6   Using a hand pump, syringe or squeeze bottle, fill the transfer case with the specified lubricant until it is level with the lower edge of the filler hole.

7   Install the filler plug and tighten it to the torque listed in this Chapter's Specifications.

8   Drive the vehicle for a short distance and recheck the lubricant level. In some instances a small amount ot additional lubricant will have to be added.

34 Differential lubricant change (every 60,000 miles or 48 months)

1   This procedure should be performed after the vehicle has been driven, so the lubricant will be warm and therefore will flow out of the differential more easily.

2   Raise the vehicle and support it securely on jackstands. You'll be draining the lubricant by removing the drain plug, so move a drain pan, rags, newspapers and wrenches under the vehicle.

3   Remove the fill plug, then remove the drain plug (see Section 17)

and allow the lubricant to drain into the pan, then clean and reinstall the drain plug. Tighten the plug to the torque listed in this Chapter's Specifications.

4   Using a hand pump, syringe or squeeze bottle, fill the differential housing with the specified lubricant until it's level with the bottom of the fill-plug hole. Install the plug and tighten it to the torque listed in this Chapter's Specifications.

Specifications

Recommended lubricants and fluids

➡**Note: Listed here are manufacturer recommendations at the time this manual was written. Manufacturers occasionally upgrade their fluid and lubricant specifications, so check with your local auto parts store for current recommendations.**

Engine oil .... API "certified for gasoline engines"
Viscosity .... See accompanying chart

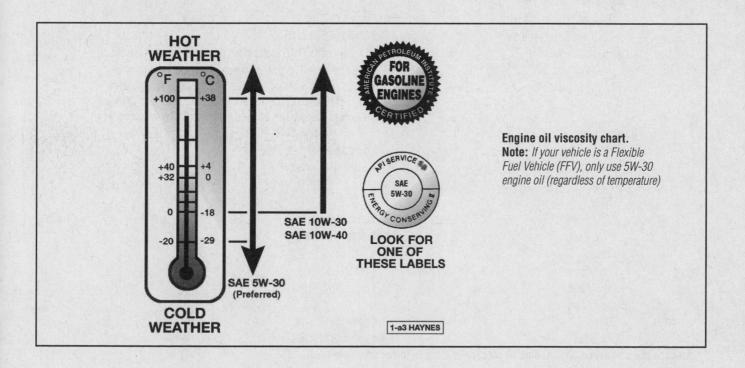

Engine oil viscosity chart.
Note: *If your vehicle is a Flexible Fuel Vehicle (FFV), only use 5W-30 engine oil (regardless of temperature)*

Recommended lubricants and fluids (continued)

Fuel	87 octane minimum
Automatic transmission fluid	
2008 and earlier models	Nissan Matic J automatic transmission fluid
2009 and later models	Nissan Matic S automatic transmission fluid
Power steering fluid	
U.S. models	Nissan PSF or equivalent
Canadian models	Nissan PSF, Nissan ATF, DEXRON III/MERCON (2007 and earlier), DEXRON VI (2008 and later) automatic transmission fluid
Transfer case lubricant	Nissan Matic D automatic transmission fluid or equivalent
Differential lubricant	
Front (4WD models)	
Titan	API GL-5 synthetic 80W-90 gear oil
Armada	API GL-5 synthetic 80W-90 gear oil
Rear	
Titan	
2004 models	API GL-5 synthetic 80W-90 gear oil
2005 and later models	API GL-5 synthetic 75W-140 gear oil
Armada	
2006 and earlier models	API GL-5 synthetic 80W-90 gear oil
2007 and later models	API GL-5 synthetic 75W-90 gear oil
Brake fluid	DOT 3 brake fluid
Engine coolant	50/50 mixture of ethylene glycol-based antifreeze and distilled or demineralized water
Chassis lubrication grease	NLGI No. 2 moly-based chassis grease
Key lock cylinder lubricant	Graphite spray

Capacities*

Engine oil (including filter)	
2008 and earlier models	6-1/2 quarts (6.2 liters)
2009 and later models	6-4/5 quarts (6.5 liters)
Automatic transmission	Up to 11-1/4 quarts (10.6 liters) (This is a dry fill capacity, incluing the torque converter. The amount needed for a routine fluid and filter change will be substantially less. The best way to determine the amount of fluid to add during a routine fluid change is to mea sure the amount drained. This way you won't overfill the transmission.)
Transfer case	
Titan	2-1/8 quarts (2.0 liters)
Armada	3-1/8 quarts (3.0 liters)
Differential	
Titan	
Front	3-3/8 pints (1.6 liters)
Rear	4-1/4 pints (2.01 liters)
Armada	
Front	3-3/8 pints (1.6 liters)
Rear	3-3/4 pints (1.75 liters)
Cooling system	
Titan	3-1/4 gallons (12.2 liters)
Armada	3-3/4 gallons (14.4 liters)

* All capacities approximate. Add as necessary to bring to the appropriate level.

Brakes

Disk brake pad lining thickness (minimum)	0.039 inch (1.0 mm)
Brake pedal adjustments	
Free height (from dash panel top surface)	7.18 to 7.57 inches (182 to 192 mm)
Reserve distance	3.55 inches (90.3 mm)
Freeplay	0.12 to 0.43 inch (3 to 11 mm)

Ignition system

Cylinder numbering diagram

Spark plug type	
Titan	
All except Flexible Fuel Vehicle (FFV) models	
2006 and earlier models	NGK PLFR5A-11
2007 models	NGK DIFR5A-11
2008 and later models	NGK DILFR5A-11
Flexible Fuel Vehicle (FFV) models	
2006 and earlier models	NGK PLFR5A-11D
2007 models	NGK DIFR5A-11D
2008 and later models	NGK DILFR5A-11D
Armada	
All except Flexible Fuel Vehicle (FFV) models	
2006 and earlier models	NGK PLFR5A-11
2007 and 2008 models	NGK DIFR5A-11
2009 and later models	NGK DILFR5A-11
Flexible Fuel Vehicle (FFV) models	
2007 and 2008 models	NGK DIFR5A-11D
2009 and later models	NGK DILFR5A-11D
Spark plug gap	0.043 inch (1.1 mm)

Torque specifications	Ft-lbs (unless otherwise indicated)	Nm

➡**Note: One foot-pound (ft-lb) of torque is equivalent to 12 inch-pounds (in-lbs) of torque. Torque values below approximately 15 ft-lbs are expressed in inch-pounds, since most foot-pound torque wrenches are not accurate at these smaller values.**

	Ft-lbs (unless otherwise indicated)	Nm
Engine oil drain plug	25	34
Drivebelt tensioner bolts	16	22
Drivebelt idler pulley bolt	26	35
Automatic transmission		
Pan bolts	70 in-lbs	8
Drain plug	25	34
Transfer case drain/fill plugs	26	35
Differential drain/fill plugs		
Front	25	34
Rear	32	43
Spark plugs	168 in-lbs	19
Wheel lug nuts	98	133
Radiator drain plug	11 in-lbs	1
Engine cylinder block drain plug (right bank)	15	20

Notes

2A

5.6L V8 ENGINE

Section

Reference to other Chapters

1 General information

This Part of Chapter 2 is devoted to in-vehicle repair procedures for the 5.6L Dual Overhead Camshaft (DOHC) V8 engine. Information concerning engine removal, installation and overhaul can be found in Part B of this Chapter.

Most of the following repair procedures are based on the assumption that the engine is installed in the vehicle. If the engine has been removed from the vehicle and mounted on a stand, many of the steps outlined in this Part of Chapter 2 will not apply.

2 Repair operations possible with the engine in the vehicle

➡**Note: Many major repair operations can be accomplished only by removing the engine from the vehicle.**

Clean the engine compartment and the exterior of the engine with some type of degreaser before any work is done. It will make the job easier and help keep dirt out of the internal areas of the engine.

Depending on the components involved, it may be helpful to remove the hood to improve access to the engine as repairs are performed (refer to Chapter 11 if necessary). Cover the fenders to prevent damage to the paint. Special pads are available, but an old bedspread or blanket will also work.

If vacuum, exhaust, oil or coolant leaks develop, indicating a need for gasket or seal replacement, the repairs can generally be made with the engine in the vehicle. The intake and exhaust manifold gaskets are accessible with the engine in place, but the upper oil pan gasket and cylinder head gaskets can't be replaced with the engine in the vehicle.

Exterior engine components, such as the intake and exhaust manifolds, the water pump (see Chapter 3), the starter motor, the alternator and the fuel system components (see Chapter 4) can be removed for repair with the engine in place. Removal of the camshafts and lifters can be accomplished with the engine in the vehicle.

Since the cylinder heads cannot be removed without pulling the engine, valve servicing also requires the engine to be removed from the vehicle. Replacement of the timing chains and sprockets are also possible only with the engine out of the vehicle.

3 Top Dead Center (TDC) for number one piston - locating

▶ **Refer to illustration 3.8**

1 Top Dead Center (TDC) is the highest point in the cylinder that each piston reaches as it travels up the cylinder bore. Each piston reaches TDC on the compression stroke and again on the exhaust stroke, but TDC generally refers to piston position on the compression stroke.

2 Positioning the piston(s) at TDC is an essential part of many procedures such as valve timing, camshaft and timing chain/sprocket removal.

3 Before beginning this procedure, be sure to place the transmission in Park (automatic) and apply the parking brake or block the rear wheels. Disable the ignition system by disconnecting the primary electrical connectors at the ignition coil packs, then remove the coil packs and spark plugs (see Chapter 1). If method b) or c) will be used to rotate the engine in the next step, also disable the fuel system (see Chapter 4, Section 3).

4 In order to bring any piston to TDC, the crankshaft must be turned using one of the methods outlined below. When looking at the front of the engine, normal crankshaft rotation is clockwise.

a) *The preferred method is to turn the crankshaft with a socket and ratchet attached to the bolt threaded into the front of the crankshaft. Turn the bolt in a clockwise direction.*

b) *A remote starter switch, which may save some time, can also be used. Follow the instructions included with the switch. Once the piston is close to TDC, use a socket and ratchet as described in the previous paragraph.*

c) *If an assistant is available to turn the ignition switch to the Start position in short bursts, you can get the piston close to TDC without a remote starter switch. Make sure your assistant is out of the vehicle, away from the ignition switch, then use a socket and ratchet as described in Paragraph (a) to complete the procedure.*

5 Install a compression pressure gauge in the number one spark

plug hole (see Chapter 2B). It should be a gauge with a screw-in fitting and a hose at least six inches long.

6   Rotate the crankshaft using one of the methods described above while observing for pressure on the compression gauge. The moment the gauge shows pressure indicates that the number one cylinder has begun the compression stroke.

7   Once the compression stroke has begun, TDC for the compression stroke is reached by bringing the piston to the top of the cylinder.

8   Continue turning the crankshaft until the TDC notch in the crankshaft damper (the only notch that is not painted) is aligned with the pointer on the front cover (see illustration). At this point, the number one cylinder is at TDC on the compression stroke. If the marks are aligned but there was no compression, the piston was on the exhaust stroke. Continue rotating the crankshaft 360-degrees (1-turn).

9   After the number one piston has been positioned at TDC on the compression stroke, TDC for any of the remaining cylinders can be located by turning the crankshaft 90-degrees and following the firing order (refer to the Specifications). Rotating the engine 90-degrees past TDC no. 1 will put the engine at TDC compression for cylinder no. 8, another 90 degrees puts cylinder no. 7 at TDC, etc.

3.8 Align the TDC notch on the crankshaft pulley with the pointer on the timing chain cover - the TDC notch is the one farthest to the left when facing the front of the engine, and is typically the line without color

---

4   Valve covers - removal and installation

REMOVAL

▶ **Refer to illustrations 4.2, 4.6 and 4.7**

1   Disconnect the cable from the negative terminal of the battery (see Chapter 5).

2   Remove the engine cover (see illustration).

3   Disconnect the PCV hose from the PCV valve in each valve cover.

4   Remove the ignition coils from the valve cover (see Chapter 5). If both valve covers are being removed, remove all eight coils.

5   If you're removing the left valve cover, removing the air filter housing cover will make access easier (see Chapter 4).

6   Detach any wiring or hoses which would interfere with valve cover removal (see illustration).

7   Remove the valve cover bolts (see illustration).

4.2 Remove the fasteners and detach the engine cover

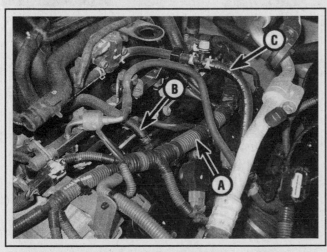

4.6 On the left-side valve cover, disconnect the main harness (A) and the PCV hose (B), then disconnect and set aside the EVAP purge control solenoid hose (C)

4.7 Remove the valve cover bolts

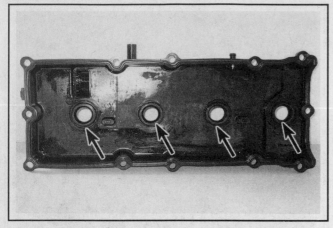

4.11 Install new spark plug tube seals if they're cracked or hardened

4.12 Apply a thin line of RTV around the gasket groove and press in the new valve cover gasket

8 Detach the valve cover.

➡Note: If the cover is stuck to the cylinder head, bump one end with a block of wood and a hammer to jar it loose. If that doesn't work, try to slip a flexible putty knife between the cylinder head and cover to break the gasket seal. Don't pry at the cover-to-cylinder head joint or damage to the sealing surfaces may occur (leading to oil leaks in the future).

INSTALLATION

▶ Refer to illustrations 4.11 and 4.12

9 The mating surfaces of each cylinder head and valve cover must be perfectly clean when the covers are installed. Use a gasket scraper to remove all traces of sealant and old gasket material, then clean the mating surfaces with brake cleaner. If there's sealant or oil on the mating surfaces when the cover is installed, oil leaks may develop.

10 If necessary, clean the bolt threads with a wire wheel to remove

any corrosion. Make sure the threaded holes in the cylinder head are clean.

11 Inspect and replace, if necessary, the spark plug tube seals (see illustration).

12 The valve cover gaskets should be mated to the covers before the covers are installed. Apply a thin coat of RTV sealant to the cover groove and to the corners on the front camshaft journal cap, then position the gasket inside the cover and allow the sealant to set up so the gasket adheres to the cover (see illustration). If the sealant isn't allowed to set, the gasket may fall out of the cover as it's installed on the engine.

13 Carefully position the cover on the cylinder head and install the bolts.

14 Tighten the bolts, in two steps, to the torque listed in this Chapter's Specifications. Start with the bolts in the center of the cover and work outwards in a criss-cross pattern.

15 The remaining installation steps are the reverse of removal.

16 Start the engine and check for oil leaks.

5   Valve clearance - check and adjustment

▶ Refer to illustrations 5.5, 5.6a, 5.6b, 5.7, 5.8 and 5.10

➡Note: The manufacturer recommends checking and, if necessary, adjusting the valve clearance after replacement of the camshaft(s) or other valve-related parts, or if the valve train is making excessive noise.

1 Disconnect the cable from the negative terminal of the battery (see Chapter 5).

2 Remove the spark plugs (see Chapter 1).

3 Position the number 1 piston at TDC on the compression stroke and align the timing marks (see Section 3).

4 Remove the valve covers (see Section 4).

5 Check that the intake and exhaust camshaft lobes for cylinder number 1 are pointed toward the outside of the cylinder head (see illustration).

6 Measure the clearance of the indicated valves with a feeler gauge (see illustrations). Record each measurement and compare your measurements with the desired valve clearance found in this Chapter's Specifications. Note which are out of specification, as this data will be

5.5 At TDC for number one cylinder, the intake and exhaust lobes for that cylinder will be pointing outward

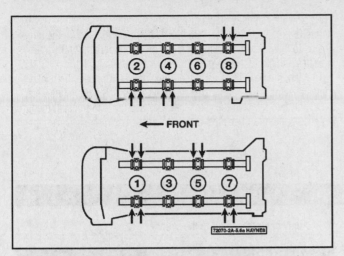

5.6a When the no. 1 piston is at TDC on the compression stroke, the intake valve clearance for the no. 1, no. 2, no. 4 and no. 5 cylinders can be measured, and the exhaust clearance for cylinders no. 1, no. 7 and no. 8 can also be measured

5.6b Measure the clearance for each valve with a feeler gauge of the specified thickness - if the clearance is correct, you should feel a slight drag on the gauge as you pull it out

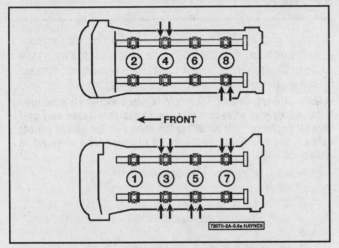

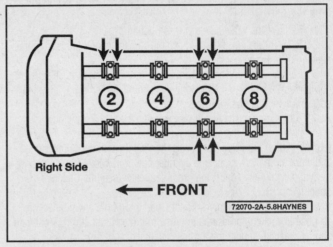

5.7 After checking the valves indicated in illustration 5.6a, turn the crankshaft 270-degrees clockwise (achieving TDC for cylinder no. 3) and check the intake valve clearances for the no. 3 , no. 7 and no. 8 cylinders; the exhaust valve clearances can be checked at cylinders no. 3, no. 4 and no. 5

5.8 After checking the valves indicated in illustration 5.7, turn the crankshaft 90-degrees (1/4-turn) clockwise and check the intake and exhaust valve clearances for cylinder no. 6, and the cylinder no. 2 exhaust valve clearances

used later to determine the required replacement lifters.

7   Turn the crankshaft 270 degrees (3/4-turn) clockwise to place cylinder number 3 at TDC. Measure and record the clearances of the indicated valves (see illustration).

8   Turn the crankshaft 90-degrees clockwise (TDC for cylinder number 6). Measure and record the clearances of the indicated valves (see illustration).

9   If a lifter is out of specification for clearance, the lifter must be replaced with a new lifter that has a different thickness head to correct the clearance. Refer to Section 8 and remove the camshafts to access the lifters.

10 Mark the lifters that are to be replaced, and record which valve they came from. Use a micrometer to measure the thickness of the lifter in the center, making sure the measurement is precise and on the center projection on the underside of the lifter (see illustration).

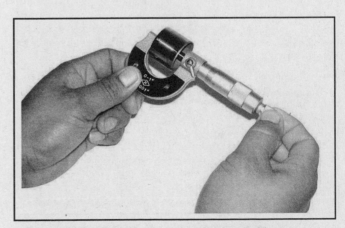

5.10 Measure the thickness of the lifter head with a micrometer

11 To calculate the correct thickness for a replacement lifter that will place the valve clearance within the specified value, use the following formula:

$$N = R + (M1 - M2)$$

N = thickness of new lifter
R = thickness of old lifter
$M1$ = measured valve clearance
$M2$ = standard valve clearance

12 New lifters are available in 25 standard thicknesses, from 0.3102 inch to 0.3291 inch (7.88 to 8.36 mm). Lifters are marked on the underside as to their size. A marking of N788 on the underside of the lifter indicates a thickness value of 0.3102 inch (7.88 mm).

13 Mark the new lifters as to their destination, lubricate them with engine assembly lube and install them. After replacing the lifters, refer to Section 8 to reinstall the camshafts and Section 7 to reinstall the timing chains, then re-check the valve clearances.

6 Valve springs, retainers and seals - replacement

◆ **Refer to illustrations 6.5, 6.7a, 6.7b, 6.13 and 6.15**

➡**Note: Broken valve springs and defective valve stem seals can be replaced without removing the cylinder heads. Two special tools and a compressed air source are normally required to perform this operation, so read through this Section carefully. The universal shaft-type valve spring compressor required for the tight valve spring pockets of this vehicle may not be available at all tool rental yards, so check on the availability before beginning the job.**

1 Remove the valve cover(s) (see Section 4).

2 Refer to Section 8 and remove the camshafts and lifters from the affected cylinder head.

3 Remove the spark plug from the cylinder that has the defective component. If all of the valve stem seals are being replaced, all of the spark plugs should be removed.

4 Turn the crankshaft until the piston in the affected cylinder is at Top Dead Center on the compression stroke (see Section 3). If you're replacing all of the valve stem seals, begin with cylinder number one and work on the valves for one cylinder at a time. Move from cylinder-to-cylinder following the firing order sequence (see this Chapter's ·Specifications).

5 Thread a long adapter into the spark plug hole and connect an air hose from a compressed air source to it (see illustration). Most auto parts stores can supply the air hose adapter.

➡**Note: Because of the length of the spark plug tubes, it will be necessary to use a long spark plug adapter with a length of hose attached (as used on many cylinder compression gauges), utilizing a quick-disconnect fitting to hook to your air source.**

6 Apply compressed air to the cylinder.

✳✳ WARNING:

The piston may be forced down by the compressed air, causing the crankshaft to turn suddenly. If the wrench used when positioning the number one piston at TDC is still attached to the bolt in the crankshaft nose, it could cause damage or injury when the crankshaft moves.

7 Stuff shop rags into the cylinder head holes around the valves to prevent parts and tools from falling into the engine, then use a valve spring compressor to compress the spring (see illustrations). Remove the keepers with small needle-nose pliers or a magnet.

➡**Note: The valves should be held in place by the air pressure. If the valve faces or seats are in poor condition, leaks may prevent air pressure from retaining the valves. If the valves cannot hold air, the cylinder head should be removed for a valve job at a machine shop.**

8 Remove the spring retainer and valve spring, then remove the valve stem seal.

9 Wrap a rubber band or tape around the top of the valve stem so the valve won't fall into the combustion chamber, then release the air pressure.

10 Inspect the valve stem for damage. Rotate the valve in the guide and check the end for eccentric movement, which would indicate that the valve is bent.

11 Move the valve up-and-down in the guide and make sure it

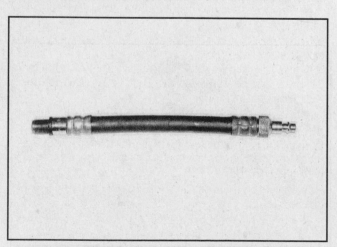

6.5 The air hose adapter threads into the spark plug hole - adapters are commonly available from auto parts stores

6.7a Compress the valve spring enough to release the valve stem keepers . . .

6.7b . . . and lift them out with a magnet or needle-nose pliers

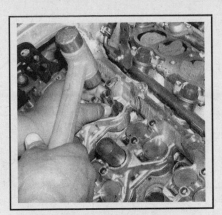

6.13 Using a deep socket and hammer, gently tap the new seals onto the valve guide (only until seated)

6.15 Apply a small dab of grease to each keeper as shown here before installation - it will hold them in place on the valve stem as the spring is released

doesn't bind. If the valve stem binds, either the valve is bent or the guide is damaged. In either case, the cylinder head will have to be removed for repair.

12 Reapply air pressure to the cylinder to retain the valve in the closed position, then remove the tape or rubber band from the valve stem.

13 Lubricate the valve stems with engine oil and install new valve stem seals. Valve stem seals can be installed with a special tool, or a deep socket and hammer - tap the seal only until seated (see illustration).

14 Install the valve spring in position over the valve, with the more closely-wound spring coils and the paint mark toward the cylinder head.

15 Install the valve spring retainer. Compress the valve springs and

carefully position the keepers in the groove. Apply a small dab of grease to the inside of each keeper to hold it in place (see illustration).

16 Remove the pressure from the spring tool and make sure the keepers are seated.

17 Disconnect the air hose and remove the adapter from the spark plug hole.

18 Refer to Section 8 and install the camshaft and lifters, then refer to Section 7 and install the timing chain.

19 Refer to Section 4 and install the valve covers.

20 Install the spark plug(s), ignition coils and the upper and lower intake plenum, referring to the appropriate Sections as necessary.

21 Start and run the engine, then check for oil leaks and unusual sounds coming from the valve cover area.

7   Timing chains and sprockets - removal, inspection and installation

➡ **Note 1: The timing chain procedure for these engines is a difficult procedure for the home mechanic. Great care must be taken to mark the relationship of all parts before disassembly, length of various bolts and their locations must be noted, and instant or digital photos should be taken for reference as you proceed.**

➡ **Note 2: The engine must be removed from the vehicle to perform this procedure (see Chapter 2B). Make sure you have all the proper equipment and tools before beginning.**

REMOVAL

◆ **Refer to illustrations 7.13 and 7.14**

❋ **CAUTION:**

The timing system is complex. Severe engine damage will occur if you make any mistakes. Do not attempt this procedure unless you are highly experienced with this type of repair. If you are at all unsure of your abilities, consult an expert. Double-check all your work and be sure everything is correct before you attempt to start the engine.

1 Relieve the system fuel pressure (see Chapter 4).

2 Remove the engine cover (see illustration 4.2).

3 Remove the spark plugs (see Chapter 1). Position the number 1 piston at TDC on the compression stroke (see Section 3).

4 Disconnect the cable from the negative terminal of the battery (see Chapter 5).

5 Remove the drivebelt and tensioner (see Chapter 1) and the idler pulley brackets.

6 Drain the cooling system and the engine oil (see Chapter 1). Remove the upper and lower radiator hoses, the engine cooling fans and the radiator (see Chapter 3).

7 Remove the engine from the vehicle (see Chapter 2B).

8 Remove the crankshaft pulley (see Section 12).

➡ **Note: Don't allow the crankshaft to rotate during removal of the pulley. If the crankshaft moves, the number one piston will no longer be at TDC.**

9 Remove the intake manifold (see Section 9) and the valve covers (see Section 4).

10 Remove the thermostat housing and the water hose (see Chapter 3).

11 Remove the upper and lower oil pans (see Section 14), and the oil pump strainer.

12 On 2007 and later models, remove the Intake Valve Timing (IVT)

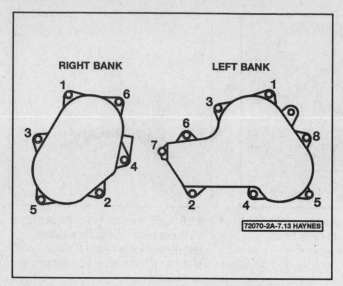

7.13 Upper timing chain covers - TIGHTENING sequence

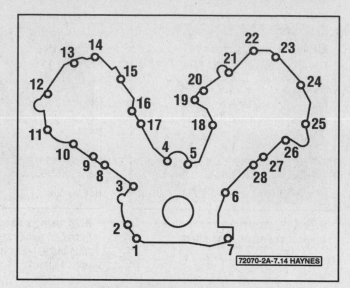

7.14 Front timing chain cover - TIGHTENING sequence

control position sensors and solenoids (see Chapter 6).

13 Remove the bolts securing the upper timing chain covers (one at the front of each cylinder head) in sequence (see illustration).

➡**Note: Use a seal cutter to cut the liquid gasket during this procedure.**

14 Remove the front timing chain cover bolts in sequence (see illustration). Note that three lengths of bolts are used. They must be reinstalled in their original locations. Mark each bolt or make a sketch to help remember where they go. Carefully pry the timing chain cover off the engine, prying only against casting protrusions or the small cutouts provided for this purpose.

➡**Note: Use a seal cutter to cut the liquid gasket during this procedure.**

15 Slide the oil pump drive spacer from the front of the crankshaft, then remove the oil pump (see Section 15).

16 Confirm that the number one piston is still at TDC on the compression stroke by verifying that the intake and exhaust camshaft lobes on the number one cylinder are pointing outward towards the edge of the cylinder head (see illustration 5.5).

17 Relieve tension on the left timing chain tensioner by squeezing the two clips on the tensioner while pushing the plunger into the tensioner body, then insert a holding pin (a large paper clip will work). Remove the tensioner.

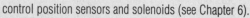

❊❊ **CAUTION:**

Use care when handling a tensioner while the plunger is secured by the pin. If the pin slips out, your fingers could be injured by the sudden release of the plunger.

18 Remove the left-hand tensioner guide and slack guide, keeping track of the bolts used.

19 Remove the left-hand timing chain and crankshaft sprocket.

20 Remove the left intake and exhaust camshaft sprockets, using a wrench to hold the hex portion of the camshaft while loosening the sprocket bolt.

❊❊ **CAUTION:**

Do not allow the camshafts to rotate at all during this procedure.

21 Repeat Steps 17 through 20 for the right-hand tensioner, chain and sprockets. Mark the camshaft sprockets with either an R or L to indicate the right or left side, and whether intake or exhaust. Don't mix the sprockets up. They must be installed on the same camshaft from which they were removed. Mark the camshaft as to their location, such as "LI" for Left-Intake and "LE" for Left-Exhaust.

INSPECTION

22 Inspect the camshaft and crankshaft sprockets for wear on the teeth and keyways. Inspect the chains for cracks or excessive wear of the rollers. Inspect the facing of the chain guides for excessive wear.

INSTALLATION

▸ **Refer to illustration 7.26**

❊❊ **CAUTION:**

Before starting the engine, carefully rotate the crankshaft by hand through at least two full revolutions (use a socket and breaker bar on the crankshaft pulley center bolt). If you feel any resistance, STOP! There is something wrong - most likely, valves are contacting the pistons. You must find the problem before proceeding. Check your work and see if any updated repair information is available.

23 Verify that you have the correct timing chains for your vehicle by counting the number of links each chain has and comparing the new chains with the old chains. Also compare the position of the colored links in the new chains with the position of the colored links in the old chains.

24 Install the crankshaft sprocket for the right timing chain, with the flange closest to the engine, followed by the crankshaft sprocket for the left timing chain, with its flange facing the end of the crankshaft. The keyway in the crankshaft should still be at a 45-degree angle from the 12 o'clock position, pointing up towards the center of the left (driver's side) cylinder head.

25 Install the camshaft sprockets, then tighten the bolts to the torque listed in this Chapter's Specifications. Hold the camshafts with a wrench placed on the hex portion of the shafts.

⁜ CAUTION:

Don't allow the camshafts to turn at all when tightening the bolts.

26 Install the timing chain for the right cylinder bank, aligning the copper-colored marks with the alignment marks on the camshaft sprockets, and the gold or yellow-colored marks with the alignment mark on the inner crankshaft sprocket (see illustration).

➡Note: It may be necessary to rotate the camshafts slightly in order to align the copper-colored chain links with the marks on the camshaft sprockets.

27 Install the right-side slack guide, tension guide and chain tensioner in their original positions. Tighten the mounting fasteners to the torque values listed in this Chapter's Specifications.

28 Make sure the colored links are still in alignment with their corresponding marks on the sprockets, then remove the holding pin from the timing chain tensioner.

29 Repeat Steps 26 through 28 to install the timing chain for the left cylinder bank.

30 Install the oil pump (see Section 15).

31 Install the oil pump drive spacer, with the front mark (a small triangle) facing out, and the keyway aligned with the crankshaft Woodruff key.

➡Note: If the spacer won't slide into place, rotate the inner rotor of the oil pump as necessary to achieve alignment.

32 Remove all traces of old sealant from the front timing chain cover, the cover bolts and the rear cover bolt holes.

33 Install new O-rings wherever they were used originally, on the block and/or the back of the timing covers. Lubricate the O-rings with clean engine oil before pushing them into their recesses.

34 Apply a 1/8-inch (3 mm) diameter bead of RTV sealant to the timing cover sealing surfaces. Place the timing chain cover in position on the engine and install the bolts in their original locations. Following the

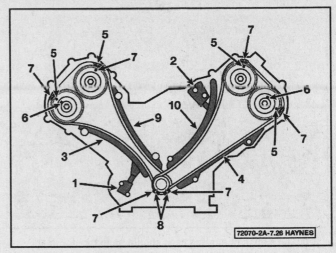

7.26 Timing chain details

1	Right chain tensioner	7	Identification marks (align
2	Left chain tensioner		with colored chain links)
3	Right chain slack guide	8	Gold or yellow colored
4	Left chain tensioner guide		chain links
5	Copper colored	9	Right chain tensioner
	chain links		guide
6	Dowel pins	10	Left chain slack guide

recommended tightening sequence, tighten the bolts to the torque listed in this Chapter's Specifications (see illustration 7.14).

➡Note: Be sure to follow the sealant manufacturer's recommendations for assembly and sealant curing times. Allow all sealant to fully cure before starting the engine.

35 Install the upper timing chain covers, tightening the bolts to the torque listed in this Chapter's Specifications, following the proper sequence (see illustration 7.13).

36 Install the crankshaft pulley, tightening the bolt to the torque listed in this Chapter's Specifications.

37 Turn the engine over by hand at least two revolutions (clockwise) to make sure the engine rotates freely. If you feel any resistance, STOP and find out why.

38 Install a new oil filter, then reinstall the engine (see Chapter 2B).

39 Refill the crankcase with oil and the cooling system with coolant (see Chapter 1).

40 Start the engine and check for leaks.

8 Camshafts and lifters - removal, inspection and installation

REMOVAL

▶ **Refer to illustrations 8.9, 8.10, 8.12a and 8.12b**

1 Disconnect the cable from the negative terminal of the battery (see Chapter 5).

2 Remove the valve covers (see Section 4).

3 Position the number 1 piston at TDC on the compression stroke (see Section 3).

4 Remove the upper timing chain covers (see Section 7).

5 Mark the relationship of the timing chains to the marks on the camshaft sprockets. The locations of the camshaft sprocket marks are shown in illustration 7.26.

6 Following the procedure in Section 7, retract and remove the left timing chain tensioner.

7 At the lower right of the main timing cover, remove the bolts and the cover providing access to remove the right chain tensioner. There isn't much room behind the cover to retract and pin this tensioner, so you may have to remove it by unbolting it and angling it out with the plunger extended.

8.9 The camshaft bearing caps should be marked with a number and letter stamp or a marker to ensure correct reinstallation

8.10 Front camshaft bearing cap details (left side shown, right side similar)

A Timing chain cover-to-front camshaft bearing cap bolts (lower bolt not visible; vicinity given)
B Front camshaft bearing cap-to-cylinder head bolts

8.12a Pull straight up to remove each lifter

8 Unbolt the camshaft sprockets from the camshafts (see Section 7).

✲✲ CAUTION:

Do not allow the camshafts to rotate at all during this procedure.

Mark each sprocket before removal so you don't mix up the sprockets. Disengage the camshaft sprockets from the timing chains and remove them.

✲✲ CAUTION:

Don't let the timing chains fall down into the timing chain cover. Support them with wire.

9 Mark the positions of the camshaft bearing caps, and with an "I" or an "E," to indicate intake or exhaust. Also mark arrows indicating the front of the engine (see illustration). Loosen the camshaft bearing caps in two or three steps, in the reverse order of the tightening sequence (see illustration 8.24).

✲✲ CAUTION:

Keep the caps in order. They must go back in the same locations from which they were removed.

10 Remove the timing chain cover-to-front camshaft bearing cap bolts (see illustration), and the front camshaft bearing cap-to-cylinder head bolts, following the reverse of the tightening sequence (see illustration 8.24). These caps will be stuck because of RTV sealant, so carefully use a plastic hammer to rock them loose.
11 Remove the camshafts. Mark them or store them separately so they can be returned to their original locations.
12 Remove the lifters from the cylinder head, keeping track of where they were installed (see illustrations).

✲✲ CAUTION:

Keep the lifters in order. They must go back into the same locations from which they were removed.

8.12b The lifters can be stored in individually marked plastic bags or a divided box as shown

8.14 Measure each journal diameter with a micrometer - if any journal measures less than the specified limit, replace the camshaft

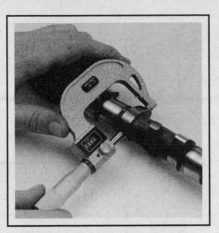

8.15 Measure the lobe heights on each camshaft - if any lobe height is less than the specified allowable minimum, replace that camshaft

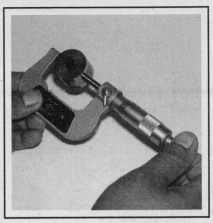

8.18 Measure the diameter of each lifter and compare it to Specifications

INSPECTION

♦ **Refer to illustrations 8.14, 8.15 and 8.18**

13 With the camshafts removed, visually check the camshaft bearing surfaces in the cylinder head for pitting, score marks, galling and abnormal wear. If the bearing surfaces are damaged, the cylinder head may have to be replaced.

14 Measure the outside diameter of each camshaft bearing journal and record your measurements (see illustration). Compare them to the journal outside diameter specified in this Chapter, then measure the inside diameter of each corresponding camshaft bearing and record the measurements. Subtract each cam journal outside diameter from its respective cam bearing bore inside diameter to determine the oil clearance for each bearing. Compare the results to the specified journal-to-bearing clearance. If any of the measurements fall outside the standard specified wear limits in this Chapter, either the camshaft or the cylinder head, or both, must be replaced.

15 Using a micrometer, measure the height of each camshaft lobe (see illustration). Compare your measurements with this Chapter's Specifications. If the height for any one lobe is less than the specified minimum, replace the camshaft.

16 Check the camshaft runout by placing the camshaft back into the cylinder head and set up a dial indicator on the center journal. Zero the dial indicator. Turn the camshaft slowly and note the dial indicator readings. If the measured runout exceeds the specified runout, replace the camshaft.

17 Also, while the camshaft is sitting in the cylinder head, check the endplay. Install the bearing caps and tighten them securely. Mount a dial indicator with the plunger of the dial indicator in line with and touching the end of the camshaft. Gently pry the camshaft fully toward the gauge, zero the gauge, then pry the camshaft fully away from the gauge and note the gauge reading. If the measured endplay is at or beyond the specified service limit, replace the camshaft and check the endplay again. If the endplay is still excessive, replace the cylinder head.

18 Inspect each lifter for scuffing and score marks. Measure the outside diameter of each lifter (see illustration) and the corresponding lifter bore inside diameter. Subtract the lifter diameter from the lifter bore diameter to determine the oil clearance. Compare it to this Chapter's Specifications. If the oil clearance is excessive, a new cylinder head and/or new lifters will be required.

INSTALLATION

♦ **Refer to illustrations 8.21 and 8.24**

19 Lubricate the lifters with clean engine oil and install them in their original locations.

20 Apply camshaft installation lubricant to the camshaft lobes and journals.

21 Install the camshafts in their original positions with the dowel pins facing up (180-degrees from the cylinder head mating surface) and in line with the cylinder bank (see illustration).

22 Apply a bead of RTV sealant to the sealing surfaces of the front camshaft bearing caps.

23 Install the bearing caps and bolts and tighten them hand tight.

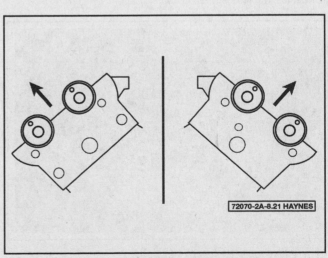

72070-2A-8.21 HAYNES

8.21 Install the camshafts with the dowel pins facing up and at a 90-degree angle to the cylinder head surface

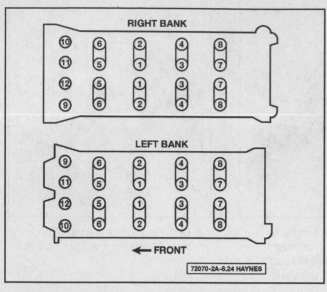

8.24 Camshaft bearing cap TIGHTENING sequence

24 Tighten the bearing cap bolts in several steps, to the torque listed in this Chapter's Specifications, using the proper tightening sequence (see illustration).

25 Engage the timing chains with the camshaft sprockets, aligning the marks made in Step 5, and being careful not to let the chain drop down into the timing chain cover. Install the camshaft sprocket bolts, tightening them to the torque listed in this Chapter's Specifications while preventing the camshafts from turning by holding them with a wrench placed on the hex portion of the shaft.

✳✳ CAUTION:

Do not allow the camshafts to rotate at all during this procedure.

26 The remainder of installation is the reverse of removal. If any part of the valve train was replaced, check and adjust the valve clearance (see Section 5).

9 Intake manifold - removal and installation

▶ **Refer to illustrations 9.5, 9.6 and 9.8**

➡ **Note: Disconnecting the electrical connector at the throttle body and later reconnecting it will cause the engine management system to require the throttle valve closed position relearn procedure to be performed (see Chapter 4, Section 10). To avoid having to perform this procedure during removal or installation of the plenum, you can unbolt the throttle body from the plenum with the connector in place and set the throttle body aside carefully.**

1   Relieve the fuel system pressure (see Chapter 4). With the engine cool, partially drain the coolant.

2   Disconnect the cable from the negative terminal of the battery (see Chapter 5).

3   Refer to Chapter 4 and remove the air intake duct. Also remove the engine cover (see illustration 4.2).

4   Remove the throttle body from the front of the intake manifold, then remove the fuel rails and fuel injectors (see Chapter 4).

✳✳ WARNING:

If you're removing the throttle body completely, wait until the engine is completely cool, then pinch-off the coolant hoses leading to the throttle body before disconnecting them.

5   Label and disconnect any hoses and harnesses that may be attached to the intake manifold (see illustration). See the **Note** at the beginning of this Section.

6   Loosen the intake manifold fasteners in the reverse order of the tightening sequence (see illustration 9.8) and remove the bolts and the manifold (see illustration).

9.5 Intake manifold mounting details:

A   EVAP purge control solenoid

B   PCV hoses

C   Hose to the intake air resonator

9.6 The intake manifold bolts are accessible after the fuel rails and injectors are removed

7   To install the manifold, clean the mounting surfaces of the intake manifold and the ports on the cylinder heads with lacquer thinner, removing all traces of the old gasket material or sealant. Install new gaskets on the intake manifold and position the manifold on the engine. There are eight individual gaskets for the manifold, one for each intake port

8   Following the recommended tightening sequence, tighten the fasteners in several steps to the torque listed in this Chapter's Specifications (see illustration).

9   The remainder of installation is the reverse of the removal procedure. If the throttle body electrical connector was disconnected, perform the relearn procedures in Chapter 4, Section 10. If the coolant hoses were disconnected from the throttle body, check the coolant level, adding if necessary (see Chapter 1). Run the engine and check for fuel, vacuum and coolant leaks.

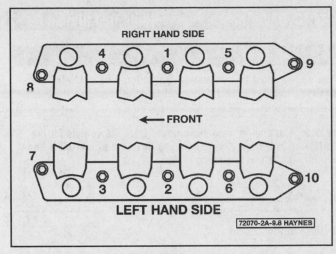

9.8 Intake manifold TIGHTENING sequence

10 Exhaust manifolds - removal and installation

❊❊ WARNING:

The engine must be completely cool before beginning this procedure.

REMOVAL

▶ **Refer to illustration 10.4**

1   Disconnect the cable from the negative terminal of the battery (see Chapter 5). Disconnect the oxygen sensor electrical connector(s), located at the rear of the valve cover(s).

2   Block the rear wheels and set the parking brake. Loosen the front wheel lug nuts.

3   Raise the front of the vehicle and support it securely on jackstands. Remove the wheels, under-vehicle splash shield and the fenderwell liners (see Chapter 11).

4   Apply penetrating oil to the exhaust fasteners and allow it to soak in. Remove the front exhaust pipe(s) (see illustration). If you can't move the center and rear exhaust pipes to the rear far enough to allow removal of the front pipes, they will have to be removed.

5   Remove the oxygen sensor(s) (see Chapter 6).

6   Support the engine from above and remove the engine mount insulators and engine mount brackets (see Section 19).

7   If you're removing the right-side exhaust manifold, remove the dipstick and dipstick tube.

8   Unbolt the exhaust heat shields from the exhaust manifolds.

9   Remove the fasteners securing the manifolds to the cylinder heads.

INSTALLATION

10   Use a scraper to remove all traces of old gasket material and carbon deposits from the manifold and cylinder head mating surfaces.

11   Position the new exhaust manifold gaskets over the studs on the cylinder head. The gaskets are marked with an arrow which should point up when installed. The marking should face the manifold side (outward, not toward the head).

12   Install the manifold and thread the mounting fasteners into place.

13   Working from the center out, tighten the nuts/bolts in several increments, to the torque listed in this Chapter's Specifications.

14   Reinstall the remaining parts in the reverse order of removal.

15   Run the engine and check for exhaust leaks.

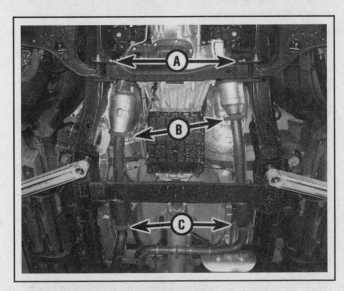

10.4 Exhaust manifold removal details

A   *Front crossmember fasteners*
B   *Front exhaust pipe-to-manifold flanges*
C   *Front exhaust pipe-to-rear exhaust pipe flanges*

11 Cylinder head - removal and installation

❊❊ WARNING:

The engine must be completely cool before beginning this procedure.

➡Note: The engine must be removed from the vehicle for the following procedure. Make sure you have the proper tools and equipment before beginning.

REMOVAL

▸ **Refer to illustration 11.7**

1   Remove the timing chains and sprockets (see Section 7).

❊❊ CAUTION:

Be careful not to disturb the crankshaft from TDC on the compression stroke of the No. 1 cylinder during the remainder of this procedure.

2   Remove the intake manifold (see Section 9) and the exhaust manifolds (see Section 10).
3   Remove the upper and lower oil pans (see Section 14).
4   Remove the timing chain (see Section 7).
5   Remove the camshafts and lifters (see Section 8).
6   Using a breaker bar and the appropriate sized Allen-head socket, loosen the cylinder head bolts in 1/4-turn increments until they can be removed by hand. Loosen the bolts in the reverse order of the tightening sequence (see illustration 11.18) to avoid warping or cracking the head. Discard the bolts and obtain new ones for reassembly.
7   Lift the cylinder head off the engine block. If it's stuck, very carefully pry up at a casting protrusion, beyond the gasket surface (see illustration).
8   Remove all external components from the head to allow for thorough cleaning and inspection.

INSTALLATION

▸ **Refer to illustrations 11.10 and 11.18**

9   The mating surfaces of the cylinder head and block must be perfectly clean when the head is installed.
10   Use a gasket scraper to remove all traces of carbon and old gasket material from the cylinder head and engine block, then clean the mating surfaces with brake system cleaner (see illustration). If there's oil on the mating surfaces when the head is installed, the gasket may not seal correctly and leaks could develop. When working on the block, stuff the cylinders with clean shop rags to keep out debris. Use a vacuum cleaner to remove material that falls into the cylinders.
11   Check the block and head mating surfaces for nicks, deep scratches and other damage. If damage is slight, it can be removed with a file; if it's excessive, machining may be the only alternative.
12   Use a tap of the correct size to chase the threads in the head bolt holes, then clean the holes with compressed air - make sure that nothing remains in the holes.

❊❊ WARNING:

Wear eye protection when using compressed air!

13   Check the head gasket surface of the head and the intake and exhaust manifold surfaces for any signs of damage, corrosion, cracks or surface irregularities.
14   Install any components that were removed from the head.
15   Position the new cylinder head gasket over the dowel pins on the block, noting which side of the gasket faces up.
16   Carefully set the head on the block without disturbing the gasket.
17   Before installing the NEW cylinder head bolts, apply a small amount of clean engine oil to the threads and the underside of the bolt heads.

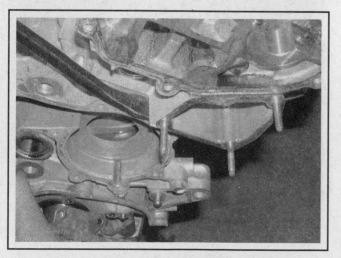

11.7 Pry on a casting protrusion to break the head loose

11.10 Carefully remove all traces of old gasket material from the sealing surfaces

18 Install the bolts and tighten them finger tight. Then tighten all the bolts in several steps, following the proper sequence (see illustration), to the torque listed in this Chapter's Specifications.

19 Remove all traces of old sealant from the rear timing chain cover and the cover bolts.

20 Apply a bead of RTV sealant to the timing chain cover sealing surfaces to the block and heads. Install new O-rings in the front of the engine block and timing chain covers.

21 Install the camshafts as described in Section 8, then install the timing chains and sprockets as described in Section 7. The remaining installation steps are the reverse of removal. If any part of the valve train was replaced, check and adjust the valve clearance (see Section 5).

22 After the engine has been installed, change the engine oil filter, then add oil and coolant (see Chapter 1).

23 Start the engine and check for oil and coolant leaks.

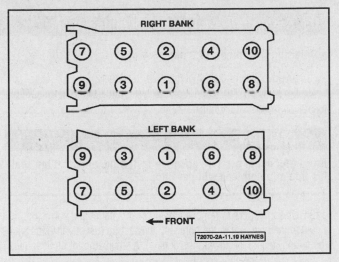

11.18 Cylinder head bolt TIGHTENING sequence

12 Crankshaft pulley - removal and installation

▶ **Refer to illustration 12.4**

1 Disconnect the cable from the negative terminal of the battery (see Chapter 5).

2 Block the rear wheels and set the parking brake. Drain the cooling system (see Chapter 1).

3 Raise the front of the vehicle and support it securely on jackstands.

4 Remove the lower splash shield if equipped (see illustration).

5 Remove the engine cooling fan and fan shroud (see Chapter 3).

6 Remove the drivebelt (see Chapter 1).

7 Remove the starter and have an assistant wedge a large screwdriver into the ring gear teeth to prevent the engine from rotating. Unscrew the crankshaft pulley bolt.

8 Remove the pulley. If the pulley is difficult to remove, use a puller that bolts to the hub of the pulley to remove it. The proper spacer should be used between the puller screw and the end of the crankshaft to prevent damage to the crankshaft.

✳✳ CAUTION:

DO NOT use a puller with jaws that grip around the outside of the crankshaft pulley or damage to the pulley will occur.

➡**Note: Depending on the length of puller you have, it may also be necessary to remove the radiator to gain sufficient clearance to use the puller.**

9 To install the crankshaft pulley, align the pulley groove with the key on the crankshaft and slide the pulley onto the crankshaft.

10 Install the crankshaft pulley retaining bolt and tighten it to the torque listed in this Chapter's Specifications.

11 The remainder of installation is the reverse of removal.

12.4 Lower splash shield mounting fasteners

13 Crankshaft front oil seal - replacement

▶ **Refer to illustrations 13.2 and 13.4**

1   Remove the crankshaft pulley (see Section 12).

2   Carefully pry the seal out of the cover with a seal removal tool or a large screwdriver (see illustration).

✺✺ CAUTION:

Be careful not to scratch, gouge or distort the area that the seal fits into or an oil leak will develop.

3   Clean the bore to remove any old seal material and corrosion. Position the new seal in the bore with the seal lip (usually the side with the spring) facing IN (toward the engine). A small amount of oil applied to the outer edge and inner lip of the new seal will make installation easier.

4   Drive the seal into the bore with a seal driver or a large socket and hammer until it's completely seated (see illustration). Select a socket that's the same outside diameter as the seal, and make sure the new seal is pressed into place until it bottoms against the cover flange.

5   Check the surface of the crankshaft pulley that the oil seal rides on. If the surface has been grooved from long-time contact with the seal, the crankshaft pulley should be replaced.

6   Lubricate the seal lips with engine oil and reinstall the crankshaft pulley. Install the crankshaft pulley retaining bolt and tighten it to the torque listed in this Chapter's Specifications.

7   The remainder of installation is the reverse of the removal. Run the engine and check for oil leaks.

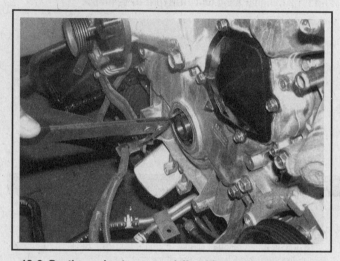

13.2 Pry the seal out very carefully with a seal removal tool or screwdriver, being careful not to nick or gouge the seal bore or the crankshaft

13.4 Use a seal driver to drive the new seal into the cover

14 Oil pans - removal and installation

✺✺ WARNING:

The engine must be completely cool before beginning this procedure.

➡**Note: The engine must be removed from the vehicle to remove the upper (cast aluminum) oil pan. If you are just removing the lower (stamped steel) oil pan, ignore the steps which don't apply.**

REMOVAL

▶ **Refer to illustration 14.11**

1   Disconnect the cable from the negative terminal of the battery (see Chapter 5).

2   Set the parking brake and block the rear wheels.

3   Raise the front of the vehicle and support it securely on jackstands.

4   Remove the splash shields under the engine (see illustration 12.4).

5   Drain the engine oil and remove the oil filter (see Chapter 1).

6   If you're just removing the lower (stamped steel) oil pan, remove the crossmember (see illustration 10.4). If you're removing the upper (cast aluminum) oil pan, remove the engine from the vehicle (see Chapter 2B).

7   Remove the mounting bolts for the lower steel pan, a little at a time and in a criss-cross pattern, then carefully pry between the upper and lower pans with a thin flat-bladed tool to separate the lower pan.

8   To remove the upper aluminum pan (also referred to as the lower block support), disconnect the hoses and remove the oil cooler (see Section 16).

9   Remove the engine oil dipstick, the dipstick tube and the oil pump screen (accessible once the lower steel pan is removed).

10   Remove the upper aluminum pan mounting bolts in the reverse of the tightening sequence (see illustration 14.15).

14.11 Insert a flat-head screwdriver or small pry bar into the notch on the side of the oil pan to break it loose - be careful not to damage the sealing surfaces!

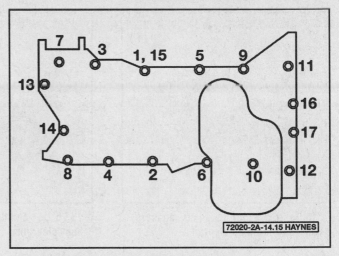

14.15 Aluminum oil pan TIGHTENING sequence

11 To loosen the upper oil pan from the block, wedge a flat head screwdriver or thin prybar into the notches on the side of the oil pan, being careful not to damage the sealing surfaces of the oil pan or engine block (see illustration).

INSTALLATION

▶ **Refer to illustration 14.15**

12 Use a scraper to remove all traces of old gasket material and sealant from the upper aluminum section of the oil pan, the lower steel pan and the engine block. Clean the mating surfaces with brake cleaner.

❊❊ CAUTION:

Be careful not to scratch or gouge the gasket surface of the block or oil pan. A leak could develop after the repairs have been completed.

13 Make sure the threaded bolt holes in the block and aluminum section of the oil pan are clean.

14 Apply a bead of RTV sealant to the ends of the timing chain cover and the rear oil seal retainer. Install new O-rings at the front cover

and oil pump, lubricated with engine oil. Apply a bead of RTV sealant around the upper aluminum oil pan flange.

➡**Note: The oil pan must be installed within 15 minutes once the sealant has been applied.**

15 Carefully position the upper aluminum oil pan on the engine block and install the bolts. Following the recommended sequence, tighten the fasteners in three or four steps to the torque listed in this Chapter's Specifications (see illustration).

16 Reinstall the oil strainer. Don't forget to reinstall any upper pan bolts that are accessible only with the steel pan removed.

17 Check the lower steel oil pan flange for distortion, particularly around the bolt holes. If necessary, place the pan on a wood block and use a hammer to flatten and restore the gasket surface.

18 Apply a bead of RTV sealant around the steel oil pan flange and install the steel oil pan.

➡**Note: The oil pan must be installed within 15 minutes once the sealant has been applied.**

Tighten the fasteners a little at a time and in a criss-cross pattern to the torque listed in this Chapter's Specifications.

19 The remainder of installation is the reverse of removal. Be sure to install a new oil filter (see Chapter 1) and wait at least one hour before adding oil.

15 Oil pump - removal, inspection and installation

➡**Note: The engine must be removed for this procedure (see Chapter 2B).**

REMOVAL

1 Remove the engine (see Chapter 2B), then refer to Section 7 and remove the timing chain covers. Refer to Section 14 and remove the oil pans.

2 Slide the oil pump drive spacer from the crankshaft.

3 If the pump is to be disassembled, use a large Phillips screw-

driver to loosen (but not remove) the oil pump cover screws.

4 Remove the oil pump mounting bolts and detach the pump from the engine.

INSPECTION

▶ **Refer to illustrations 15.7a, 15.7b, 15.7c, 15.7d and 15.7e**

5 Remove the screws and pump cover, then lift out the rotors. Clean all components with solvent, then inspect them for wear and damage.

15.7a Use feeler gauges to measure the rotor tooth tip clearance . . .

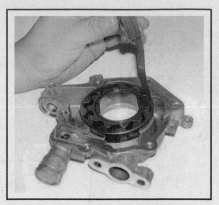

15.7b . . . and the outer rotor-to-body clearance

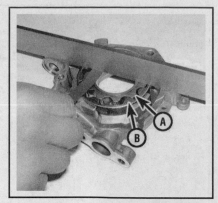

15.7c Measure the cover-to-rotor end clearance with a straightedge and feeler gauge - measure (A) above the inner rotor and (B) above the outer rotor

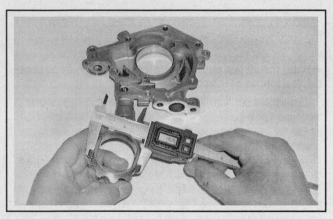

15.7d Use calipers to measure the diameter of the inner rotor ridge (the part of the inner rotor that rides in the pump body) . . .

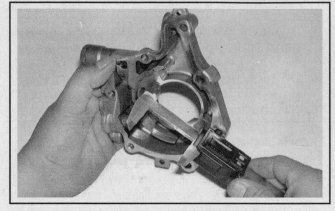

15.7e . . . and subtract the inner rotor ridge diameter from the opening in the pump body where the inner rotor rides to obtain the inner rotor ridge-tobody clearance

6 Remove the oil pressure regulator cap, washer, spring(s) and valve. Check the oil pressure regulator valve sliding surface and valve spring. If either the spring or the valve is damaged, they must be replaced as a set.

7 Check the clearance of the oil pump components (see illustrations) and compare the measurements to the clearance listed in this Chapter's Specifications. If any clearance is excessive, replace the entire oil pump as an assembly.

8 Lubricate the oil pump rotors with clean engine oil, then install them in the pump body with the marks facing out. Pack the voids in the pump with petroleum jelly to prime it. Install the cover and tighten the screws to the torque listed in this Chapter's Specifications.

9 Lubricate the pressure regulator valve with clean engine oil.

Install the valve, spring and washer, then tighten the oil pressure regulator valve cap to the torque listed in this Chapter's Specifications.

INSTALLATION

10 Install the oil pump drive spacer, with the front mark (a small triangle) facing out, and the keyway aligned with the crankshaft Woodruff key. Install the oil pump, aligning the flats on the inner rotor with the flats on the oil pump drive spacer. You may have to rotate the inner rotor slightly to align the flats. Install the oil pump bolts and tighten them to the torque listed in this Chapter's Specifications.

11 The remainder of installation is the reverse of removal.

16 Engine oil cooler - general information, removal and installation

GENERAL INFORMATION

1 These engines are provided extra cooling by an oil cooler, which

is incorporated into an adapter at the front of the oil pan, to which the oil cooler mounts. The oil cooler has two hoses connecting the cooler to the engine, where oil temperature is lowered by the engine coolant.

REMOVAL AND INSTALLATION

▶ **Refer to illustrations 16.4 and 16.5**

2   Drain the engine oil and the cooling system (see Chapter 1).

3   Detach the hose clamps and remove the inlet and outlet hoses from the oil cooler.

4   Remove the oil filter from the oil cooler assembly (see illustration).

5   Unscrew the oil cooler retaining bolt and remove the oil cooler

and O-rings (see illustration).

6   Thoroughly clean the mating surfaces of the oil pan and the oil cooler.

7   Lubricate the new oil cooler O-ring with clean engine oil. Install the O-ring in the groove on the oil cooler. Remove the relief valve from the oil pan and install a new one.

8   Position the oil cooler onto the aluminum oil pan, so that the casting tab on the cooler aligns between the two tabs on the aluminum oil pan, then install the retaining bolt.

9   Tighten the oil cooler retaining bolt to the torque listed in this Chapter's Specifications.

10   Connect the oil cooler hoses and install a new oil filter. Refill the cooling system with the proper type and mixture of antifreeze, and the engine with the proper type and amount of oil (see Chapter 1), then run the engine and check for leaks. Turn off the engine for five minutes and check the oil and coolant levels, adding fluids if necessary.

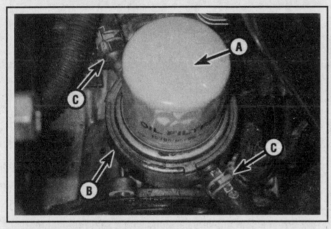

16.4 Engine oil cooler details

A   Oil filter   C   Coolant hoses
B   Oil cooler

16.5 Remove the oil cooler mounting bolt

17   Driveplate - removal and installation

▶ **Refer to illustration 17.3**

1   Raise the vehicle and support it securely on jackstands, then refer to Chapter 7 and remove the transmission.

2   Make alignment marks on the driveplate and crankshaft to ensure correct alignment during reinstallation.

3   Remove the bolts that secure the driveplate to the crankshaft (see illustration). If the crankshaft turns, hold the driveplate with a prybar or wedge a screwdriver into the ring gear teeth.

4   Remove the driveplate from the crankshaft.

5   Check for cracked and broken ring gear teeth or a loose ring gear. Lay the driveplate on a flat surface and use a straightedge to check for warpage.

17.3 Hold a lever against a casting protrusion on the engine block or place a screwdriver through a hole in the driveplate to hold the driveplate while the mounting bolts are removed - note the painted marks made at the crank and driveplate for alignment

6   Clean and inspect the mating surfaces of the driveplate and the crankshaft. If the crankshaft rear seal is leaking, replace it before reinstalling the driveplate.

7   Position the driveplate against the crankshaft. Be sure to align the marks made during removal. Note that some engines have an alignment dowel or staggered bolt holes to ensure correct installation. Before installing the bolts, apply thread locking compound to the threads.

8   Wedge a screwdriver into the ring gear teeth to keep the driveplate from turning as you tighten the bolts to the torque listed in this Chapter's Specifications.

9   The remainder of installation is the reverse of the removal.

18   Rear main oil seal - replacement

♦ **Refer to illustration 18.2**

1   The transmission must be removed from the vehicle for this procedure (see Chapter 7).

❊❊ WARNING:

The engine must be supported from above with an engine hoist or three-bar support fixture before working underneath the vehicle with the transmission removed. Remove the driveplate (see Section 17).

2   Carefully pry the old seal out with a seal removal tool or screwdriver (see illustration).

3   Apply multi-purpose grease to the crankshaft seal journal and the lip of the new seal. Preferably, a seal installation tool should be used to press the new seal into place. The lip is stiff, so carefully work it onto the seal journal of the crankshaft. Don't rush it or you may damage the seal.

➡ **Note: Install the seal squarely and only until flush with the back of the seal retainer, no further.**

4   The remaining steps are the reverse of removal.

18.2 Pry the seal out very carefully with a seal removal tool or screwdriver - if the crankshaft is damaged, the new seal will leak!

19   Engine mounts - check and replacement

1   There are two engine mounts and one transmission mount installed on the vehicles covered by this manual. The two engine mounts are located on the passenger and driver's side of the vehicle, attached to the engine block and to each frame rail. The transmission mount is mounted to the rear of the transmission and the transmission crossmember. Refer to Chapter 7A for the transmission mount replacement procedure.

CHECK

2   During the check, the engine must be raised slightly to remove the weight from the mounts.

3   Raise the vehicle and support it securely on jackstands. Support the engine/transmission from above using a hoist or three bar support fixture.

4   Check the mounts to see if the rubber is cracked, hardened or separated from the bushing in the center of the mount.

5   Check for relative movement between the mounts and the engine or frame (use a large screwdriver or prybar to attempt to move the mounts). If movement is noted, lower the engine and tighten the mount fasteners.

REPLACEMENT

♦ **Refer to illustrations 19.8, 19.9a and 19.9b**

6   Disconnect the cable from the negative terminal of the battery (see Chapter 5), set the parking brake and block the rear wheels.

7   Raise the front of the vehicle and support it securely on jackstands. Remove the splash shields from under the vehicle.

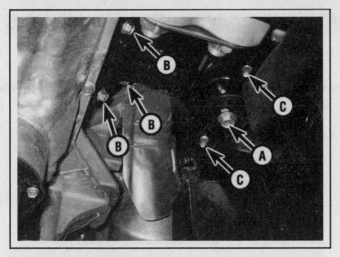

19.8 Engine mount details

A   *Engine mount insulator bolt*
B   *Mount bracket-to-engine block bolts (three of four shown here)*
C   *Mount insulator-to-frame bolts (access from above)*

19.9a Engine mount insulator-to-frame bolts - right side

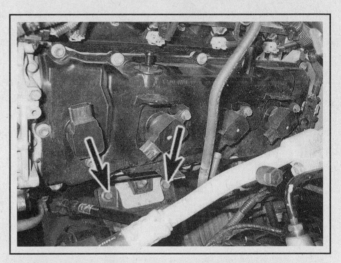

19.9b Engine mount insulator-to-frame bolts - left side

8   With the engine supported from above with a hoist or three-bar engine support, raise the engine just enough to take the weight off the mounts. Remove the engine mount insulator bolt and the engine mount bracket bolts from below (see illustration).

9   Working in the engine compartment, remove the two upper engine mount insulator-to-frame bolts (see illustrations).

➡**Note: Removing the air filter housing will make access to the left side bolts easier.**

10   Installation is the reverse of removal. Make sure the metal heat shield is in place between the insulator and the engine bracket. Apply thread locking compound to the mount nuts before installing them, then tighten them to the torque listed in this Chapter's Specifications.

Specifications

General

Engine designation	VK56DE, VK56DE FFV (flexible fuel vehicle)
Displacement	338.80 cubic inches (5.6 liters)
Bore	3.86 inches (98 mm)
Stroke	3.62 inches (92 mm)
Cylinder numbers (front to rear)	
Right (passenger side)	2-4-6-8
Left (driver side)	1-3-5-7
Firing order	1-8-7-3-6-5-4-2
Cylinder head warpage limit	0.004 inch (0.1 mm)

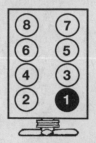

Cylinder location diagram

Camshaft and lifters

Thrust clearance (endplay)	0.0045 to 0.0074 inch (0.115 to 0.188 mm)
Camshaft runout	0.0008 inch (0.02 mm)
Camshaft bearing inside diameter	1.0236 to 1.0244 inches (26.000 to 26.0021 mm)
Journal diameter	1.0217 to 1.0224 inches (25.951 to 25.969 mm)
Journal oil clearance	
2004 through 2006	0.0012 to 0.0027 inch (0.030 to 0.068)
2007 and later	0.0012 to 0.0028 inch (0.030 to 0.071 mm)
Lobe height	
2006 and earlier models (intake and exhaust)	1.7506 to 1.7581 inches (44.465 to 44.655 mm)
2007 and later models	
Intake	1.7663 to 1.7738 inches (44.865 to 45.055 mm)
Exhaust	1.7746 to 1.7821 inches (45.075 to 45.265 mm)
Lobe wear limit (all)	0.0008 inch (0.02 mm)
Lifter outside diameter	1.3377 to 1.3381 inches (33.977 to 33.987 mm)
Lifter bore diameter	1.3386 to 1.3392 inches (34.000 to 34.016 mm)
Lifter oil clearance	0.0005 to 0.0015 inch (0.013 to 0.039 mm)

Valve clearance (cold)

Intake	0.010 to 0.013 inch (0.26 to 0.34 mm)
Exhaust	0.011 to 0.015 inch (0.29 to 0.37 mm)

Oil pump

Outer rotor-to-pump body clearance	0.0045 to 0.0079 inch (0.114 to 0.200 mm)
Inner rotor-to-outer rotor tip clearance (maximum)	0.0071 inch (0.180 mm)
Inner rotor flange-to-pump body clearance	0.0018 to 0.0036 inch (0.045 to 0.091 mm)
Inner rotor side clearance	0.0012 to 0.0028 inch (0.030 to 0.070 mm)
Outer rotor side clearance	0.0012 to 0.0035 inch (0.030 to 0.090 mm)

Torque specifications	Ft-lbs (unless otherwise indicated)	Nm

➡ **Note:** One foot-pound (ft-lb) of torque is equivalent to 12 inch-pounds (in-lbs) of torque. Torque values below approximately 15 ft-lbs are expressed in inch-pounds, since most foot-pound torque wrenches are not accurate at these smaller values.

Camshaft bearing caps		
Step 1, bolts 9 through 12	17 in-lbs	2
Step 2, bolts 1 through 8	17 in-lbs	2
Step 3, all bolts (in sequence)	52 in-lbs	6
Step 4, all bolts (in sequence)	92 in-lbs	10
Camshaft sprocket bolts		
2006 and earlier models (intake and exhaust)	112	152
2007 and later models		
Intake (VTC) valve timing control	76	103
Exhaust	112	152
Crankshaft pulley-to-crankshaft bolt		
Step 1	69	93
Step 2	Tighten an additional 90-degrees	
Cylinder head bolts (in sequence - see illustration 11.19)		
Step 1	72	98
Step 2	Loosen all bolts in the reverse order of tightening sequence	
Step 3	33	44
Step 4	Tighten an additional 60-degrees	
Step 5	Tighten an additional 60-degrees	
Drivebelt idler pulley bolt	26	35
Driveplate bolts	65	88
Engine mount		
Insulator bolt	65	88
Mount bracket-to-engine block bolts	65	88
Insulator-to-frame bolts	65	88
Exhaust manifold-to-cylinder head fasteners		
2004 models	21	28
2005 and later models	25	34
Intake manifold-to-cylinder head bolts	73 in-lbs	8
Oil cooler bolt	36	49
Oil pan bolts (steel lower pan)	80 in-lbs	9
Oil pan bolts (aluminum upper pan)		
Numbers 15 and 16	80 in-lbs	9
All remaining bolts	192 in-lbs	22
Oil pick-up tube/strainer	192 in-lbs	22
Oil pump mounting bolts	96 in-lbs	11
Oil pump cover screws	61 in-lbs	7
Oil pump pressure regulator valve cap	40	53
Timing chain tensioner bolts	61 in-lbs	7
Timing chain tension and slack guide bolts	144 in-lbs	16
Timing chain cover bolts	96 in-lbs	11
Valve cover bolts		
Step 1	17 in-lbs	2
Step 2	73 in-lbs	8

Notes

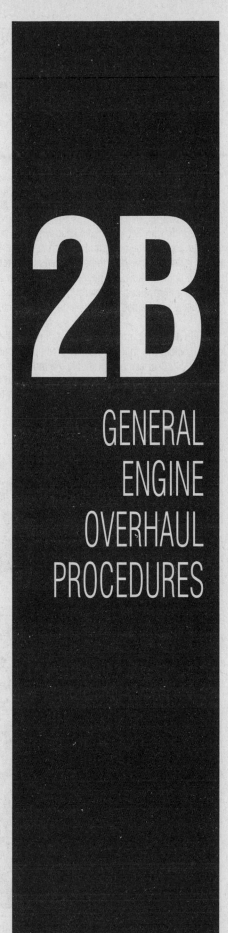

2B

GENERAL ENGINE OVERHAUL PROCEDURES

Section

1   General information - engine overhaul

▶ **Refer to illustrations 1.1, 1.2, 1.3, 1.4, 1.5 and 1.6**

Included in this portion of Chapter 2 are general information and diagnostic testing procedures for determining the overall mechanical condition of your engine.

The information ranges from advice concerning preparation for an overhaul and the purchase of replacement parts and/or components to detailed, step-by-step procedures covering removal and installation.

The following Sections have been written to help you determine whether your engine needs to be overhauled and how to remove and install it once you've determined it needs to be rebuilt. For information concerning in-vehicle engine repair, see Chapter 2A.

It's not always easy to determine when, or if, an engine should be completely overhauled, because a number of factors must be considered.

High mileage is not necessarily an indication that an overhaul is needed, while low mileage doesn't preclude the need for an overhaul. Frequency of servicing is probably the most important consideration. An engine that's had regular and frequent oil and filter changes, as well as other required maintenance, will most likely give many thousands of miles of reliable service. Conversely, a neglected engine may require an overhaul very early in its service life.

Excessive oil consumption is an indication that piston rings, valve seals and/or valve guides are in need of attention. Make sure that oil leaks aren't responsible before deciding that the rings and/or guides are bad. Perform a cylinder compression check to determine the extent of the work required (see Section 3). Also check the vacuum readings under various conditions (see Section 4).

Check the oil pressure with a gauge installed in place of the oil pressure sending unit and compare it to this Chapter's Specifications (see Section 2). If it's extremely low, the bearings and/or oil pump are probably worn out.

Loss of power, rough running, knocking or metallic engine noises, excessive valve train noise and high fuel consumption rates may also point to the need for an overhaul, especially if they're all present at the same time. If a complete tune-up doesn't remedy the situation, major mechanical work is the only solution.

An engine overhaul involves restoring the internal parts to the specifications of a new engine. During an overhaul, the piston rings are replaced and the cylinder walls are reconditioned (rebored and/or honed) (see illustrations 1.1 and 1.2). If a rebore is done by an automotive machine shop, new oversize pistons will also be installed. The main

1.1 An engine block being bored - an engine rebuilder will use special machinery to recondition the cylinder bores

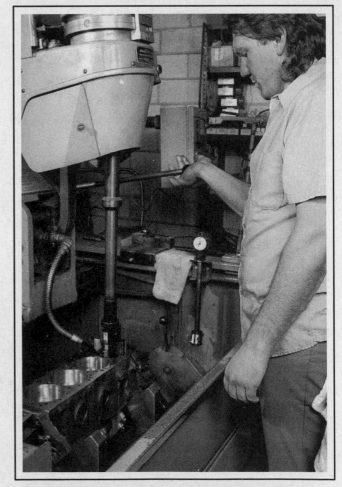

1.2 If the cylinders are bored, the machine shop will normally hone the engine on a machine like this

1.3 A crankshaft having a main bearing journal ground

1.4 A machinist checks for a bent connecting rod, using specialized equipment

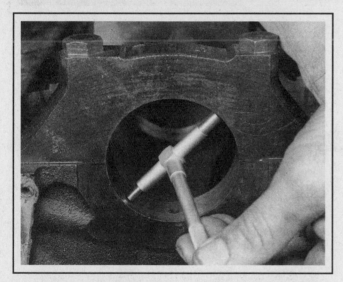

1.5 A bore gauge being used to check the main bearing bore

1.6 Uneven piston wear like this indicates a bent connecting rod

bearings and connecting rod bearings are generally replaced with new ones and, if necessary, the crankshaft may be reground to restore the journals (see illustration 1.3). Generally, the valves are serviced as well, since they're usually in less-than-perfect condition at this point. While the engine is being overhauled, other components, such as the starter and alternator, can be rebuilt as well. The end result should be a like-new engine that will give many trouble-free miles.

➡**Note: Critical cooling system components such as the hoses, drivebelts, thermostat and water pump should be replaced with new parts when an engine is overhauled. The radiator should be checked carefully to ensure that it isn't clogged or leaking (see Chapter 3). If you purchase a rebuilt engine or short block, some rebuilders will not warranty their engines unless the radiator has been professionally flushed. Also, we don't recommend overhauling the oil pump - always install a new one when an engine is rebuilt.**

Overhauling the internal components on today's engines is a difficult and time-consuming task that requires a significant amount of specialty tools and is best left to a professional engine rebuilder (see illustrations 1.4, 1.5 and 1.6). A competent engine rebuilder will handle the inspection of your old parts and offer advice concerning the reconditioning or replacement of the original engine. Never purchase parts or have machine work done on other components until the block has been thoroughly inspected by a professional machine shop. As a general rule, time is the primary cost of an overhaul, especially since the vehicle may be tied up for a minimum of two weeks or more. Be aware that some engine builders only have the capability to rebuild the engine you bring them while other rebuilders have a large inventory of rebuilt exchange engines in stock. Also be aware that many machine shops could take as much as two weeks time to completely rebuild your engine depending on shop workload. Sometimes it makes more sense to simply exchange your engine for another engine that's already rebuilt to save time.

2   Oil pressure check

♦ **Refer to illustration 2.2**

1   Low engine oil pressure can be a sign of an engine in need of rebuilding. A low oil pressure indicator (often called an "idiot light") is not a test of the oiling system. Such indicators only come on when the oil pressure is dangerously low. Even a factory oil pressure gauge in the instrument panel is only a relative indication, although much better for driver information than a warning light. A better test is with a mechanical (not electrical) oil pressure gauge.

2   Locate the oil pressure indicator sending unit - it's located in the aluminum upper oil pan, close to the block at the left-front of the engine (see illustration).

3   Disconnect the electrical connector, unscrew and remove the oil pressure sending unit and screw in the hose for your oil pressure gauge. If necessary, install an adapter fitting. Use Teflon tape or thread sealant on the threads of the adapter and/or the fitting on the end of your gauge's hose.

4   Connect an accurate tachometer to the engine, according to the tachometer manufacturer's instructions.

5   Check the oil pressure with the engine running (normal operating temperature) at the specified engine speed, and compare it to this Chapter's Specifications. If it's extremely low, the bearings and/or oil pump are probably worn out.

6   Installation is the reverse of removal. Clean the threads on the sensor and use new sealant on the threads before installation.

2.2 The oil pressure sending unit is located at the left-front of the aluminum oil pan, near the oil filter

3   Cylinder compression check

♦ **Refer to illustrations 3.5a and 3.5b**

1   A compression check will tell you what mechanical condition the upper end of your engine (pistons, rings, valves, head gaskets) is in. Specifically, it can tell you if the compression is down due to leakage caused by worn piston rings, defective valves and seats or a blown head gasket.

➡**Note: The engine must be at normal operating temperature and the battery must be fully charged for this check.**

2   Begin by cleaning the area around the spark plugs before you remove them (compressed air should be used, if available). The idea is to prevent dirt from getting into the cylinders as the compression check is being done.

3   Unplug the electrical connectors and remove the ignition coil assemblies (see Chapter 5). Also disable the fuel pump by removing the fuel pump fuse (see Chapter 4).

4   Remove all of the spark plugs (see Chapter 1).

5   Install a compression gauge in the spark plug hole (see illustrations).

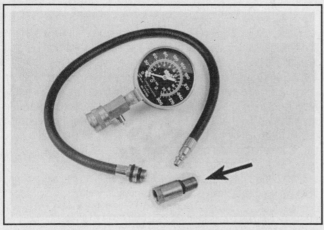

3.5a Use a compression gauge with a threaded fitting for the spark plug hole, not the type that requires hand pressure to maintain the seal

3.5b Thread the compression gauge hose into the spark plug hole, being careful not to cross-thread the fitting

6   Detach the air intake duct from the throttle body, then block the throttle wide open.

7   Crank the engine over at least seven compression strokes and watch the gauge. Stop cranking when you or a helper observe the reading stabilize on the gauge. The compression should build up quickly in a healthy engine. Low compression on the first stroke, followed by gradually increasing pressure on successive strokes, indicates worn piston rings. A low compression reading on the first stroke, which doesn't build up during successive strokes, indicates leaking valves or a blown head gasket (a cracked head could also be the cause). Deposits on the undersides of the valve heads can also cause low compression. Record the highest gauge reading obtained.

8   Repeat the procedure for the remaining cylinders and compare the results to this Chapter's Specifications.

9   Add some engine oil (about three squirts from a plunger-type oil can) to each cylinder, through the spark plug hole, and repeat the test.

10 If the compression increases after the oil is added, the piston rings are definitely worn. If the compression doesn't increase significantly, the leakage is occurring at the valves or head gasket. Leakage past the valves may be caused by burned valve seats and/or faces or warped, cracked or bent valves.

11 If two adjacent cylinders have equally low compression, there's a strong possibility that the head gasket between them is blown. The appearance of coolant in the combustion chambers or the crankcase would verify this condition.

12 If one cylinder is slightly lower than the others, and the engine has a slightly rough idle, a worn lobe on the camshaft could be the cause.

13 If the compression is unusually high, the combustion chambers are probably coated with carbon deposits. If that's the case, the cylinder head(s) should be removed and decarbonized.

14 If compression is way down or varies greatly between cylinders, it would be a good idea to have a leak-down test performed by an automotive repair shop. This test will pinpoint exactly where the leakage is occurring and how severe it is.

15 After completing the compression check, don't forget to unblock the throttle.

4   Vacuum gauge diagnostic checks

▶ **Refer to illustrations 4.4 and 4.6**

1   A vacuum gauge provides inexpensive but valuable information about what is going on in the engine. You can check for worn rings or cylinder walls, leaking head or intake manifold gaskets, restricted exhaust, stuck or burned valves, weak valve springs, improper ignition or valve timing and ignition problems.

2   Unfortunately, vacuum gauge readings are easy to misinterpret, so they should be used in conjunction with other tests to confirm the diagnosis.

3   Both the absolute readings and the rate of needle movement are important for accurate interpretation. Most gauges measure vacuum in inches of mercury (in-Hg). The following references to vacuum assume the diagnosis is being performed at sea level. As elevation increases (or atmospheric pressure decreases), the reading will decrease. For every 1,000-foot increase in elevation above approximately 2000 feet, the gauge readings will decrease about one inch of mercury.

4   Connect the vacuum gauge directly to the intake manifold vacuum, not to ported (throttle body) vacuum (see illustration). Be sure no hoses are left disconnected during the test or false readings will result.

5   Before you begin the test, allow the engine to warm up completely. Block the wheels and set the parking brake. With the transmission in Park, start the engine and allow it to run at normal idle speed.

4.4 A simple vacuum gauge can be handy in diagnosing engine condition and performance. The vacuum port behind the throttle body (for the EVAP purge hose) is a good place to connect the gauge

❊❊ WARNING:

Keep your hands and the vacuum gauge clear of the fans and drivebelts.

6   Read the vacuum gauge; an average, healthy engine should normally produce about 17 to 22 in-Hg with a fairly steady needle (see illustration). Refer to the following vacuum gauge readings and what they indicate about the engine's condition:

7   A low steady reading usually indicates a leaking gasket between the intake manifold and cylinder head(s) or throttle body, a leaky vacuum hose, late ignition timing or incorrect camshaft timing. Check ignition timing with a timing light and eliminate all other possible causes, utilizing the tests provided in this Chapter before you remove the timing belt cover to check the timing marks.

8   If the reading is three to eight inches below normal and it fluctuates at that low reading, suspect an intake manifold gasket leak at an intake port or a faulty fuel injector.

9   If the needle has regular drops of about two-to-four inches at a steady rate, the valves are probably leaking. Perform a compression check or leak-down test to confirm this.

10 An irregular drop or down-flick of the needle can be caused by a sticking valve or an ignition misfire. Perform a compression check or leak-down test and read the spark plugs.

11 A rapid vibration of about four in-Hg variation at idle combined with exhaust smoke indicates worn valve guides. Perform a leak-down test to confirm this. If the rapid vibration occurs with an increase in engine speed, check for a leaking intake manifold gasket or head gasket, weak valve springs, burned valves or ignition misfire.

12 A slight fluctuation, say one inch up and down, may mean ignition problems. Check all the usual tune-up items and, if necessary, run the engine on an ignition analyzer.

13 If there is a large fluctuation, perform a compression or leak-down test to look for a weak or dead cylinder or a blown head gasket.

14 If the needle moves slowly through a wide range, check for a clogged PCV system, incorrect idle fuel mixture, throttle body or intake manifold gasket leaks.

15 Check for a slow return after revving the engine by quickly snapping the throttle open until the engine reaches about 2,500 rpm and let it shut. Normally the reading should drop to near zero, rise above normal idle reading (about 5 in-Hg over) and then return to the previous idle reading. If the vacuum returns slowly and doesn't peak when the throttle is snapped shut, the rings may be worn. If there is a long delay, look for a restricted exhaust system (often the muffler or catalytic converter). An easy way to check this is to temporarily disconnect the exhaust ahead of the suspected part and redo the test.

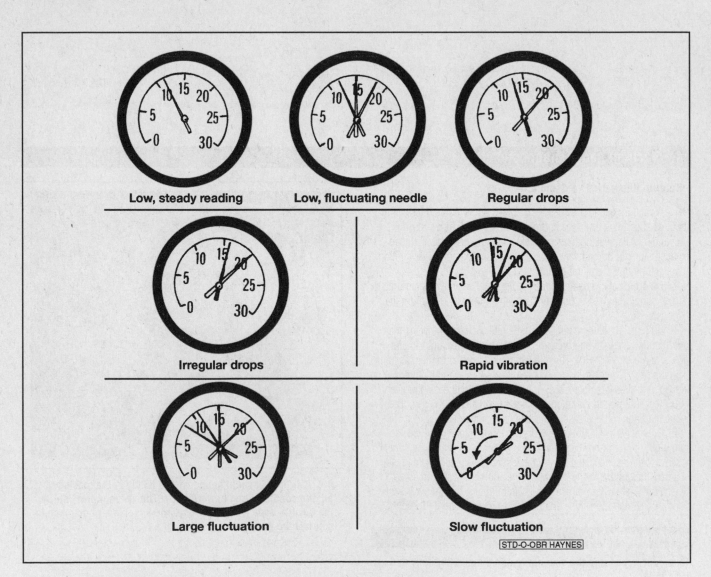

4.6 Typical vacuum gauge readings

5 Engine rebuilding alternatives

The do-it-yourselfer is faced with a number of options when purchasing a rebuilt engine. The major considerations are cost, warranty, parts availability and the time required for the rebuilder to complete the project. The decision to replace the engine block, piston/connecting rod assemblies and crankshaft depends on the final inspection results of your engine. Only then can you make a cost effective decision whether to have your engine overhauled or simply purchase an exchange engine for your vehicle.

Some of the rebuilding alternatives include:

Individual parts - If the inspection procedures reveal that the engine block and most engine components are in reusable condition, purchasing individual parts and having a rebuilder rebuild your engine may be the most economical alternative. The block, crankshaft and piston/connecting rod assemblies should all be inspected carefully by a machine shop first.

Short block - A short block consists of an engine block with a crankshaft and piston/connecting rod assemblies already installed. All new bearings are incorporated and all clearances will be correct. The existing camshafts, valve train components, cylinder head and external

parts can be bolted to the short block with little or no machine shop work necessary.

Long block - A long block consists of a short block plus an oil pump, oil pan, cylinder head, valve cover, camshaft and valve train components, timing sprockets and belt or gears and timing cover. All components are installed with new bearings, seals and gaskets incorporated throughout. The installation of manifolds and external parts is all that's necessary.

Low mileage used engines - Some companies now offer low mileage used engines that are a very cost effective way to get your vehicle up and running again. These engines often come from vehicles that have been in totaled in accidents or come from other countries that have a higher vehicle turn over rate. A low mileage used engine also usually has a similar warranty like the newly remanufactured engines.

Give careful thought to which alternative is best for you and discuss the situation with local automotive machine shops, auto parts dealers and experienced rebuilders before ordering or purchasing replacement parts.

6 Engine removal - methods and precautions

▶ Refer to illustrations 6.1, 6.2, and 6.3

If you've decided that an engine must be removed for overhaul or major repair work, several preliminary steps should be taken. Read all removal and installation procedures carefully prior to committing to this job.

Locating a suitable place to work is extremely important. Adequate work space, along with storage space for the vehicle, will be needed. If a shop or garage isn't available, at the very least a flat, level, clean work surface made of concrete or asphalt is required.

Cleaning the engine compartment and engine before beginning the

removal procedure will help keep tools clean and organized (see illustrations 6.1 and 6.2).

An engine hoist will be necessary and a transmission jack is also very helpful. Safety is of primary importance, considering the potential hazards involved in removing the engine from the vehicle.

If you're a novice at engine removal, get at least one helper. One person cannot easily do all the things you need to do to remove a big heavy engine and transmission assembly from the engine compartment. Also helpful is to seek advice and assistance from someone who's experienced in engine removal.

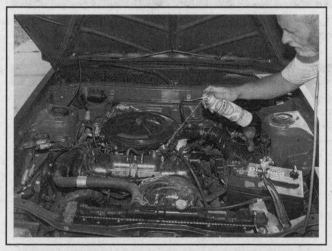

6.1 After tightly wrapping water-vulnerable components, use a spray cleaner on everything, with particular concentration on the greasiest areas, usually around the valve cover and lower edges of the block. If one section dries out, apply more cleaner

6.2 Depending on how dirty the engine is, let the cleaner soak in according to the directions and then hose off the grime and cleaner. Get the rinse water down into every area you can get at; then dry important components with a hair dryer or paper towels

6.3 Get an engine stand sturdy enough to firmly support the engine while you're working on it. Stay away from three-wheeled models; they have a tendency to tip over more easily, so get a four-wheeled unit

Plan the operation ahead of time. Arrange for or obtain all of the tools and equipment you'll need prior to beginning the job (see illustration 6.3). Some of the equipment necessary to perform engine removal and installation safely and with relative ease are (in addition to an engine hoist) a heavy duty floor jack (preferably fitted with a transmission jack head adapter), complete sets of wrenches and sockets as described in the front of this manual, wooden blocks, plenty of rags and cleaning solvent for mopping up spilled oil, coolant and gasoline.

Plan for the vehicle to be out of use for quite a while. A machine shop can do the work that is beyond the scope of the home mechanic. Machine shops often have a busy schedule, so before removing the engine, consult the shop for an estimate of how long it will take to rebuild or repair the components that may need work.

7   Engine - removal and installation

※※ WARNING:

Gasoline is extremely flammable, so take extra precautions when you work on any part of the fuel system. Don't smoke or allow open flames or bare light bulbs near the work area, and don't work in a garage where a gas-type appliance (such as a water heater or clothes dryer) is present. Since gasoline is carcinogenic, wear fuel-resistant gloves when there's a possibility of being exposed to fuel, and, if you spill any fuel on your skin, rinse it off immediately with soap and water. Mop up any spills immediately and do not store fuel-soaked rags where they could ignite. The fuel system is under constant pressure, so, if any fuel lines are to be disconnected, the fuel pressure in the system must be relieved first (see Chapter 4 for more information). When you perform any kind of work on the fuel system, wear safety glasses and have a Class B type fire extinguisher on hand.

※※ WARNING:

The air conditioning system is under high pressure. Do not loosen any hose fittings or remove any components until after the system has been discharged. Air conditioning refrigerant must be properly discharged into an EPA-approved recovery/recycling unit at a dealer service department or an automotive

air conditioning repair facility. Always wear eye protection when disconnecting air conditioning system fittings.

※※ WARNING:

The engine must be completely cool before beginning this procedure.

※※ WARNING:

Only begin this procedure if all of the necessary equipment is at hand. You will need to use an engine hoist, which can be rented at most tool rental yards.

REMOVAL

▶ **Refer to illustration 7.15**

1   Have the air conditioning system discharged by an automotive air conditioning technician.

2   Relieve the fuel system pressure (see Chapter 4), then disconnect the cables from the negative and positive battery terminals (see Chapter 5).

3   Park the vehicle squarely on a hard, level surface. Point the wheels straight ahead. Remove the hood and the cowl cover (see Chapter 11).

4   Remove the engine cover (see Chapter 2A).

5   Remove the air filter housing and the intake air duct (see Chapter 4).

6   Drain the cooling system and disconnect the heater hoses at the firewall (see Chapter 1).

7   Remove the drivebelts (see Chapter 1).

8   Remove the radiator, shroud and engine cooling fan (see Chapter 3). Also remove the heater hoses and the coolant reservoir.

9   Remove the alternator (see Chapter 5).

10   Remove the power steering reservoir and power steering pump, without disconnecting the hoses, and tie them out of the way (see Chapter 10).

11   Detach the fuel line from the fuel rail (see Chapter 4).

12   Remove the PCV hose (see Chapter 6).

➡**Note: It's important to attach tags to hoses and electrical connectors before disconnecting them.**

13   Loosen the front wheel lug nuts. If you're working on an 4x4 model, you will have to remove the front axle assembly. With the vehicle raised and safely supported high enough for you to work underneath the engine/transmission, remove the front wheels and the engine undercover.

14   Drain the automatic transmission fluid (see Chapter 1).

15   Label and disconnect all wires from the engine (see illustration). Masking tape and/or a touch-up paint applicator work well for marking items. Disconnect the main engine harness connectors at the PCM, and disconnect the engine harness from the underhood fuse/relay box. Look over the engine and engine compartment carefully to locate any ground wires attached to the engine or engine compartment.

➡**Note: Take digital photos or sketch the locations of components and brackets to help with reassembly.**

16   Label and remove all vacuum lines between the engine and the firewall (or other components in the engine compartment).

17   Detach the transmission cooler lines from the engine brackets and the transmission (see Chapter 7A).

18   Disconnect the engine block heater, if equipped.

19   Disconnect the oxygen sensors and the crankshaft position sensor connector (see Chapter 6).

20   Disconnect the catalytic converters from the exhaust manifolds and remove the pipes and exhaust manifolds.

21   Remove the starter (see Chapter 5).

22   Attach an engine lifting bracket to each cylinder head, one at the left-rear and one at the right-front.

❋❋ CAUTION:

Make sure the lifting mounts or hoist chains don't apply any force to the valve covers.

Raise the engine enough to take the weight from the engine mounts.

23   Remove the transmission (see Chapter 7).

❋❋ WARNING:

The transmission is heavy and awkward to handle. You can rent a transmission jack that allows you to secure the transmission to the jack with chains, and safely raise/lower the transmission or tilt it for alignment with the engine.

24   Drain the engine oil, remove the oil filter and disconnect the coolant hoses from the oil cooler (see Chapter 3).

25   Remove the engine mount fasteners, then raise the engine slowly out of the vehicle. An assistant to guide the engine out is very helpful.

26   Remove the driveplate and mount the engine on an engine stand.

INSTALLATION

27   Check the engine mounts. If they're worn or damaged, replace them (see Chapter 2A).

28   Inspect the front transmission fluid seal and bearing.

29   Attach the hoist to the engine, remove the engine from the engine stand and install the driveplate (see Chapter 2A).

30   Use the hoist to lower the engine into the vehicle and secure it with the engine mounts.

31   Install the transmission (see Chapter 7A), and raise the transmission enough to install the transmission mount. If you're working on a 4x4 model, install the front differential and front driveshaft, tightening the fasteners to the torque values listed in the Chapter 8 Specifications. On all models, install the crossmember and tighten the engine mount-to-engine nuts to the torque listed in the Chapter 2A Specifications.

32   Tighten all the bolts on the crossmembers and mounts, then remove the hoist and transmission jack. Refer to Chapter 10 for installation of the front suspension components.

33   Reinstall the remaining components in the reverse order of removal.

34   Add coolant, oil, power steering and transmission fluid as needed (see Chapter 1).

35   Run the engine and check for proper operation and leaks. Shut off the engine and recheck the fluid levels.

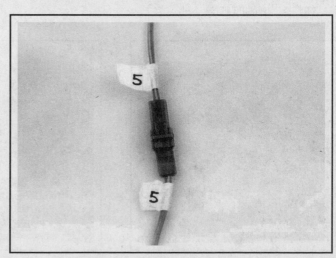

7.15 Label both ends of each wire or hose connection before disconnecting them

8 Engine overhaul - disassembly sequence

1   It's much easier to remove the external components if the engine is mounted on a portable engine stand. A stand can often be rented quite cheaply from an equipment rental yard. Before the engine is mounted on a stand, the driveplate should be removed from the engine.

2   If a stand isn't available, it's possible to remove the external engine components with it blocked up on the floor. Be extra careful not to tip or drop the engine when working without a stand.

3   If you're going to obtain a rebuilt engine, all external components must come off first, to be transferred to the replacement engine. These components include:

Driveplate
Ignition system components
Emissions-related components
Engine mounts and mount brackets
Intake/exhaust manifolds
Fuel injection components
Oil filter and oil cooler
Thermostat and housing assembly
Water pump

➡**Note: When removing the external components from the engine, pay close attention to details that may be helpful or important during installation. Note the installed position of gaskets, seals, spacers, pins, brackets, washers, bolts and other small items.**

4   If you're going to obtain a short block (assembled engine block, crankshaft, pistons and connecting rods), then remove the timing chain, cylinder heads, oil pan, oil pump pick-up tube, oil pump and water pump from your engine so that you can turn in your old short block to the rebuilder as a core. See *Engine rebuilding alternatives* for additional information regarding the different possibilities to be considered.

9 Pistons and connecting rods - removal and installation

REMOVAL

◆ **Refer to illustrations 9.1, 9.3 and 9.4**

➡**Note: Prior to removing the piston/connecting rod assemblies, remove the cylinder head and oil pan (see Chapter 2A).**

1   Use your fingernail to feel if a ridge has formed at the upper limit of ring travel (about 1/4-inch down from the top of each cylinder). If carbon deposits or cylinder wear have produced ridges, they must be completely removed with a special tool (see illustration). Follow the manufacturer's instructions provided with the tool. Failure to remove the ridges before attempting to remove the piston/connecting rod assemblies may result in piston breakage.

2   After the cylinder ridges have been removed, turn the engine so the crankshaft is facing up.

3   Before the main bearing cap assembly and connecting rods are removed, check the connecting rod endplay with feeler gauges. Slide them between the first connecting rod and the crankshaft throw until the play is removed (see illustration). Repeat this procedure for each connecting rod. The endplay is equal to the thickness of the feeler gauge(s). Check with an automotive machine shop for the endplay service limit (a typical endplay should measure from 0.005 to 0.015 inch [0.127 to 0.381 mm]). If the play exceeds the service limit, new connecting rods will be required. If new rods (or a new crankshaft) are installed, the endplay may fall under the minimum allowable. If it does, the rods will have to be machined to restore it. If necessary, consult an automotive machine shop for advice.

4   Check the connecting rods and caps for identification marks. If they aren't plainly marked, use paint or marker (see illustration) to clearly identify each rod and cap (1, 2, 3, etc., depending on the cylinder they're associated with). Do not interchange the rod caps. Install the

9.1 Before you try to remove the pistons, use a ridge reamer to remove the raised material (ridge) from the top of the cylinders

9.3 Checking the connecting rod endplay (side clearance)

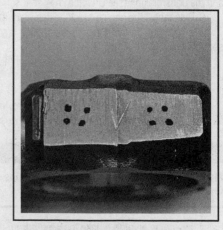

9.4 If the connecting rods or caps are not marked, use permanent ink or paint to mark the caps to the rods by cylinder number (for example, this would be number 4 cylinder connecting rod)

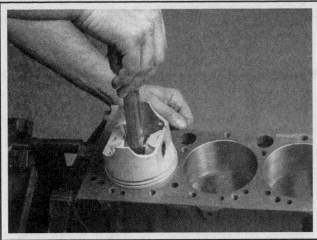

9.13 Install the piston ring into the cylinder then push it down into position using a piston so the ring will be square in the cylinder

exact same rod cap onto the same connecting rod.

⁂ CAUTION:

Do not use a punch and hammer to mark the connecting rods or they may be damaged.

5 Loosen each of the connecting rod cap bolts or nuts 1/2-turn at a time until they can be removed by hand.

6 Remove the number one connecting rod cap and bearing insert. Don't drop the bearing insert out of the cap.

7 Remove the bearing insert and push the connecting rod/piston assembly out through the top of the engine. Use a wooden or plastic hammer handle to push on the upper bearing surface in the connecting rod. If resistance is felt, double-check to make sure that all of the ridge was removed from the cylinder.

8 Repeat the procedure for the remaining cylinders.

9 After removal, reassemble the connecting rod caps and bearing inserts in their respective connecting rods and install the cap bolts finger tight. Leaving the old bearing inserts in place until reassembly will help prevent the connecting rod bearing surfaces from being accidentally nicked or gouged.

10 The pistons and connecting rods are now ready for inspection and overhaul at an automotive machine shop.

PISTON RING INSTALLATION

◆ **Refer to illustrations 9.13, 9.14, 9.15, 9.19a, 9.19b and 9.22**

11 Before installing the new piston rings, the ring end gaps must be checked. It's assumed that the piston ring side clearance has been checked and verified correct.

12 Lay out the piston/connecting rod assemblies and the new ring sets so the ring sets will be matched with the same piston and cylinder during the end gap measurement and engine assembly.

13 Insert the top (number one) ring into the first cylinder and square it up with the cylinder walls by pushing it in with the top of the piston (see illustration) The ring should be near the bottom of the cylinder, at the lower limit of ring travel.

9.14 With the ring square in the cylinder, measure the ring end gap with a feeler gauge

14 To measure the end gap, slip feeler gauges between the ends of the ring until a gauge equal to the gap width is found (see illustration). The feeler gauge should slide between the ring ends with a slight amount of drag. A typical ring gap should fall between 0.010 and 0.020 inch (0.25 to 0.50 mm) for compression rings and up to 0.030 inch (0.76 mm) for the oil ring steel rails. If the gap is larger or smaller than specified, double-check to make sure you have the correct rings before proceeding.

15 If the gap is too small, it must be enlarged or the ring ends may come in contact with each other during engine operation, which can cause serious damage to the engine. If necessary, increase the end gaps by filing the ring ends very carefully with a fine file. Mount the file in a vise equipped with soft jaws, slip the ring over the file with the ends contacting the file face and slowly move the ring to remove material from the ends. When performing this operation, file only by pushing the ring from the outside end of the file towards the vise (see illustration).

16 Excess end gap isn't critical unless it's greater than 0.040 inch (1.01 mm). Again, double-check to make sure you have the correct ring type.

9.15 If the ring end gap is too small, clamp a file in a vise as shown and file the piston ring ends - be sure to remove all raised material

9.19a Installing the spacer/expander in the oil ring groove

9.19b DO NOT use a piston ring installation tool when installing the oil control side rails

17 Repeat the procedure for each ring that will be installed in the first cylinder and for each ring in the remaining cylinders. Remember to keep rings, pistons and cylinders matched up.

18 Once the ring end gaps have been checked/corrected, the rings can be installed on the pistons.

19 The oil control ring (lowest one on the piston) is usually installed first. It's composed of three separate components. Slip the spacer/expander into the groove (see illustration). If an anti-rotation tang is used, make sure it's inserted into the drilled hole in the ring groove. Next, install the lower side rail in the same manner (see illustration). Don't use a piston ring installation tool on the oil ring side rails, as they may be damaged. Instead, place one end of the side rail into the groove between the spacer/expander and the ring land, hold it firmly in place and slide a finger around the piston while pushing the rail into the groove. Finally, install the upper side rail.

20 After the three oil ring components have been installed, check

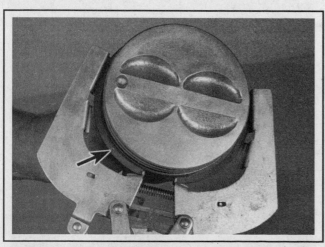

9.22 Use a piston ring installation tool to install the compression rings - on some engines the number two compression ring has a directional mark that must face toward the top of the piston

to make sure that both the upper and lower side rails can be rotated smoothly inside the ring grooves.

21 The number two (middle) ring is installed next. It's usually stamped with a mark which must face up, toward the top of the piston. Do not mix up the top and middle rings, as they have different cross-sections.

→**Note: Always follow the instructions printed on the ring package or box - different manufacturers may require different approaches.**

22 Use a piston ring installation tool and make sure the identification mark is facing the top of the piston, then slip the ring into the middle groove on the piston (see illustration). Don't expand the ring any more than necessary to slide it over the piston.

→**Note: Be careful not to confuse the number one and number two rings.**

23 Install the number one (top) ring in the same manner.

24 Repeat the procedure for the remaining pistons and rings.

INSTALLATION

25 Before installing the piston/connecting rod assemblies, the cylinder walls must be perfectly clean, the top edge of each cylinder bore must be chamfered, and the crankshaft must be in place.

26 Remove the cap from the end of the number one connecting rod (refer to the marks made during removal). Remove the original bearing inserts and wipe the bearing surfaces of the connecting rod and cap with a clean, lint-free cloth. They must be kept spotlessly clean.

Connecting rod bearing oil clearance check

▶ **Refer to illustrations 9.30, 9.35, 9.37 and 9.41**

27 Clean the back side of the new upper bearing insert, then lay it in place in the connecting rod.

28 Make sure the tab on the bearing fits into the recess in the rod. Don't hammer the bearing insert into place and be very careful not to nick or gouge the bearing face. Don't lubricate the bearing at this time.

29 Clean the back side of the other bearing insert and install it in the

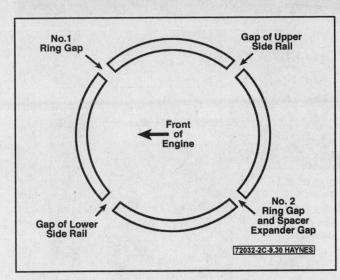

9.30 Position the piston ring end gaps as shown

No.1 Ring Gap

Gap of Upper Side Rail

Front of Engine

Gap of Lower Side Rail

No. 2 Ring Gap and Spacer Expander Gap

72032-2C-9.30 HAYNES

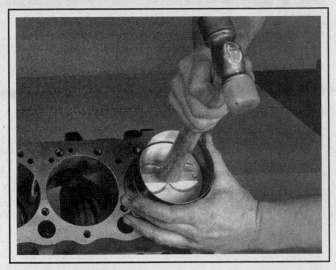

9.35 Use a plastic or wooden hammer handle to push the piston into the cylinder

rod cap. Again, make sure the tab on the bearing fits into the recess in the cap, and don't apply any lubricant. It's critically important that the mating surfaces of the bearing and connecting rod are perfectly clean and oil free when they're assembled.

30 Position the piston ring gaps at the intervals around the piston as shown (see illustration).

31 Lubricate the piston and rings with clean engine oil and attach a piston ring compressor to the piston. Leave the skirt protruding about 1/4-inch to guide the piston into the cylinder. The rings must be compressed until they're flush with the piston.

32 Rotate the crankshaft until the number one connecting rod journal is at BDC (bottom dead center) and apply a liberal coat of engine oil to the cylinder walls. Refer to the TDC locating procedure in Chapter 2A for additional information.

33 With the "front" mark (letter F, a dot or an arrow) on the piston facing the front (timing chain end) of the engine, gently insert the piston/connecting rod assembly into the number one cylinder bore and rest the bottom edge of the ring compressor on the engine block.

➡**Note: Some engines have a letter "F" marking on the side of the piston near the wrist pin, others have an arrow, an "F" or a dimple or groove on the top of the piston. All of these are marks that indicate the front of the piston.**

34 Tap the top edge of the ring compressor to make sure it's contacting the block around its entire circumference.

35 Gently tap on the top of the piston with the end of a wooden or plastic hammer handle (see illustration) while guiding the end of the connecting rod into place on the crankshaft journal. The piston rings may try to pop out of the ring compressor just before entering the cylinder bore, so keep some downward pressure on the ring compressor. Work slowly, and if any resistance is felt as the piston enters the cylinder, stop immediately. Find out what's hanging up and fix it before proceeding. Do not, for any reason, force the piston into the cylinder - you might break a ring and/or the piston.

36 Once the piston/connecting rod assembly is installed, the connecting rod bearing oil clearance must be checked before the rod cap is permanently installed.

37 Cut a piece of the appropriate size Plastigage slightly shorter than the width of the connecting rod bearing and lay it in place on the

number one connecting rod journal, parallel with the journal axis (see illustration).

38 Clean the connecting rod cap bearing face and install the rod cap. Make sure the mating mark on the cap is on the same side as the mark on the connecting rod (see illustration 9.4).

39 Install the rod bolts and tighten them to the torque listed in this Chapter's Specifications.

➡**Note: Use a thin-wall socket to avoid erroneous torque readings that can result if the socket is wedged between the rod cap and the bolt or nut. If the socket tends to wedge itself between the fastener and the cap, lift up on it slightly until it no longer contacts the cap. DO NOT rotate the crankshaft at any time during this operation.**

40 Remove the fasteners and detach the rod cap, being very careful not to disturb the Plastigage. Discard the cap bolts at this time as they should not be reused.

9.37 Place Plastigage on each connecting rod bearing journal parallel to the crankshaft centerline

ENGINE BEARING ANALYSIS

Debris

Babbitt bearing embedded with debris from machinings

Microscopic detail of debris

Microscopic detail of gouges

Overplated copper alloy bearing gouged by cast iron debris

Aluminum bearing embedded with glass beads

Microscopic detail of glass beads

Damaged lining caused by dirt left on the bearing back

Misassembly

Result of a lower half assembled as an upper - blocking the oil flow

Excessive oil clearance is indicated by a short contact arc

Polished and oil-stained backs are a result of a poor fit in the housing bore

Result of a wrong, reversed, or shifted cap

Overloading

Damage from excessive idling which resulted in an oil film unable to support the load imposed

Damaged upper connecting rod bearings caused by engine lugging; the lower main bearings (not shown) were similarly affected

The damage shown in these upper and lower connecting rod bearings was caused by engine operation at a higher-than-rated speed under load

Misalignment

A warped crankshaft caused this pattern of severe wear in the center, diminishing toward the ends

A poorly finished crankshaft caused the equally spaced scoring shown

A tapered housing bore caused the damage along one edge of this pair

A bent connecting rod led to the damage in the "V" pattern

Lubrication

Result of dry start: The bearings on the left, farthest from the oil pump, show more damage

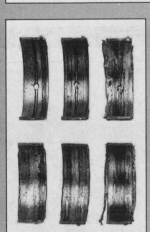

Result of a low oil supply or oil starvation

Severe wear as a result of inadequate oil clearance

Corrosion

Microscopic detail of corrosion

Corrosion is an acid attack on the bearing lining generally caused by inadequate maintenance, extremely hot or cold operation, or inferior oils or fuels

Microscopic detail of cavitation

Example of cavitation - a surface erosion caused by pressure changes in the oil film

Damage from excessive thrust or insufficient axial clearance

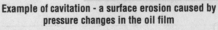

Bearing affected by oil dilution caused by excessive blow-by or a rich mixture

41 Compare the width of the crushed Plastigage to the scale printed on the Plastigage envelope to obtain the oil clearance (see illustration). The connecting rod bearing oil clearance is usually about 0.001 to 0.002 inch. Consult an automotive machine shop for the clearance specified for the rod bearings on your engine.

42 If the clearance is not as specified, the bearing inserts may be the wrong size (which means different ones will be required). Before deciding that different inserts are needed, make sure that no dirt or oil was between the bearing inserts and the connecting rod or cap when the clearance was measured. Also, recheck the journal diameter. If the Plastigage was wider at one end than the other, the journal may be tapered. If the clearance still exceeds the limit specified, the bearing will have to be replaced with an undersize bearing.

❋❋ CAUTION:

When installing a new crankshaft always use a standard size bearing.

Final installation

43 Carefully scrape all traces of the Plastigage material off the rod journal and/or bearing face. Be very careful not to scratch the bearing - use your fingernail or the edge of a plastic card.

44 Make sure the bearing faces are perfectly clean, then apply a uniform layer of clean moly-base grease or engine assembly lube to both of them. You'll have to push the piston into the cylinder to expose the face of the bearing insert in the connecting rod.

45 Slide the connecting rod back into place on the journal, install the rod cap, install the NEW bolts and tighten them to the torque listed in this Chapter's Specifications.

46 Repeat the entire procedure for the remaining pistons/connecting rods.

47 The important points to remember are:

a) Keep the back sides of the bearing inserts and the insides of the connecting rods and caps perfectly clean when assembling them.

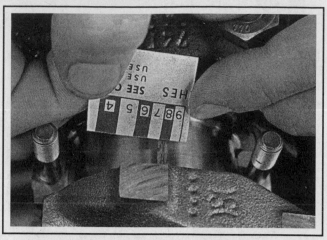

9.41 Use the scale on the Plastigage package to determine the bearing oil clearance - be sure to measure the widest part of the Plastigage and use the correct scale; it comes with both standard and metric scales

b) Make sure you have the correct piston/rod assembly for each cylinder.

c) The mark on the piston must face the front (timing chain end) of the engine.

d) Lubricate the cylinder walls liberally with clean oil.

e) Lubricate the bearing faces when installing the rod caps after the oil clearance has been checked.

48 After all the piston/connecting rod assemblies have been correctly installed, rotate the crankshaft a number of times by hand to check for any obvious binding.

49 As a final step, check the connecting rod endplay again. If it was correct before disassembly and the original crankshaft and rods were reinstalled, it should still be correct. If new rods or a new crankshaft were installed, the endplay may be inadequate. If so, the rods will have to be removed and taken to an automotive machine shop for resizing.

10 Crankshaft - removal and installation

REMOVAL

▸ **Refer to illustrations 10.1 and 10.3**

➡**Note: The crankshaft can be removed only after the engine has been removed from the vehicle. It's assumed that the driveplate, crankshaft pulley, timing chain, oil pan, oil pump, oil filter and piston/connecting rod assemblies have already been removed. The rear main oil seal retainer must be unbolted and separated from the block before proceeding with crankshaft removal.**

1 Before the crankshaft is removed, measure the endplay. Mount a dial indicator with the indicator in line with the crankshaft and touching the end of the crankshaft (see illustration).

2 Pry the crankshaft all the way to the rear and zero the dial indicator. Next, pry the crankshaft to the front as far as possible and check the reading on the dial indicator. The distance traveled is the endplay. A typical crankshaft endplay will be from 0.003 to 0.010 inch (0.076

10.1 Checking crankshaft endplay with a dial indicator

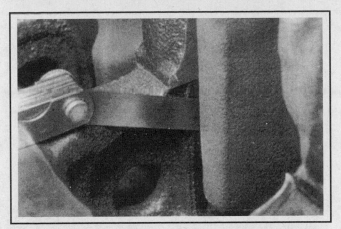

10.3 Checking crankshaft endplay with feeler gauges at the thrust bearing journal

10.14 Insert the thrust washer into the machined surface between the crankshaft and the upper bearing saddle, then rotate it down into the block until it's flush with the parting line on the main bearing saddle - make sure the oil grooves

to 0.254 mm). If it is greater than that, check the crankshaft thrust washer/bearing assembly surfaces for wear after it's removed. If no wear is evident, new main bearings should correct the endplay. Refer to Step 14 for the location of the thrust washer/bearing assembly on each engine.

3   If a dial indicator isn't available, feeler gauges can be used. Gently pry the crankshaft all the way to the front of the engine. Slip feeler gauges between the crankshaft and the front face of the thrust bearing or washer to determine the clearance (see illustration).

4   Loosen the main bearing cap and block side-bolts 1/4-turn at a time each, until they can be removed by hand, following the opposite of the tightening sequence (see illustration 10.19). Loosen bolts 30 to 21 first, then bolts 20 to 11, and lastly, bolts 10 through 1.

5   Gently tap the main bearing caps with a soft-face hammer to loosen the caps. Pull the main bearing cap straight up and off the cylinder block. Try not to drop the bearing inserts if they come out with the assembly.

6   Carefully lift the crankshaft out of the engine. It may be a good idea to have an assistant available, since the crankshaft is quite heavy and awkward to handle. With the bearing inserts in place inside the engine block and main bearing caps, reinstall the main bearing cap assembly onto the engine block and tighten the bolts finger tight. Make sure you install the main bearing cap assembly with the arrow facing the front of the engine.

INSTALLATION

7   Crankshaft installation is the first step in engine reassembly. It's assumed at this point that the engine block and crankshaft have been cleaned, inspected and repaired or reconditioned.

8   Position the engine block with the bottom facing up.

9   Remove the mounting bolts and lift off the main bearing caps.

10   If they're still in place, remove the original bearing inserts from the block and from the main bearing caps. Wipe the bearing surfaces of the block and main bearing caps with a clean, lint-free cloth. They must be kept spotlessly clean. This is critical for determining the correct bearing oil clearance.

MAIN BEARING OIL CLEARANCE CHECK

▶ **Refer to illustrations 10.14, 10.17, 10.19 and 10.21**

11   Without mixing them up, clean the back sides of the new upper main bearing inserts (with grooves and oil holes) and lay one in each main bearing saddle in the block. Each upper bearing has an oil groove and oil hole in it.

✳✳ CAUTION:

The oil holes in the block must line up with the oil holes in the upper bearing inserts.

Clean the back sides of the lower main bearing inserts and lay them in the corresponding location in the main bearing caps. Make sure the tab on the bearing insert fits into the recess in the block or main bearing caps. The upper bearings with the oil holes are installed into the engine block while the lower bearings without the oil holes are installed in the caps or bedplate.

✳✳ CAUTION:

Do not hammer the bearing insert into place and don't nick or gouge the bearing faces. DO NOT apply any lubrication at this time.

12   Clean the faces of the bearing inserts in the block and the crankshaft main bearing journals with a clean, lint-free cloth.

13   Check or clean the oil holes in the crankshaft, as any dirt here can go only one way - straight through the new bearings.

14   Once you're certain the crankshaft is clean, carefully lay it in position in the block, which should be oriented on the engine stand to have the bottom side up. Lube and insert the thrust washers on either side of journal no. 3 (see illustration). The thrust washers must be installed in the correct journal.

➡**Note: Install the thrust washers with the groove in the thrust washer facing the crankshaft with the smooth sides facing the main bearing saddle.**

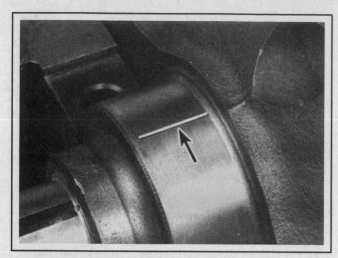

on the thrust washer face the crankshaft

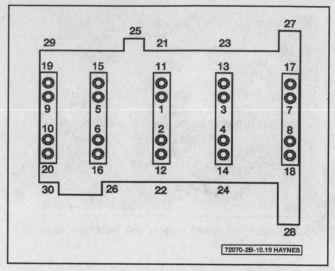

10.17 Place the Plastigage onto the crankshaft bearing journal as shown

15 Before the crankshaft can be permanently installed, the main bearing oil clearance must be checked.

16 Cut several strips of the appropriate size of Plastigage. They must be slightly shorter than the width of the main bearing journal.

17 Place one piece on each crankshaft main bearing journal, parallel with the journal axis as shown (see illustration).

18 Clean the faces of the bearing inserts in the main bearing caps. Hold the bearing inserts in place and install the caps onto the crankshaft and cylinder block. DO NOT disturb the Plastigage. Make sure you install the main bearing cap bedplate with the arrow facing the front (timing chain end) of the engine.

19 Apply clean engine oil to all bolt threads prior to installation, then install all bolts finger-tight. Tighten main bearing cap and block side-bolts (see illustration) progressing in steps and in the sequence described in this Step to the torque listed in this Chapter's Specifications. Tighten bolts 1 through 10 first, then bolts 11 through 20, and finally, side-bolts 21 through 30. DO NOT rotate the crankshaft at any time during this operation.

20 Remove the bolts in the reverse order of the tightening sequence and carefully lift the main bearing cap assembly straight up and off the block. Do not disturb the Plastigage or rotate the crankshaft. If the main bearing cap assembly is difficult to remove, tap it gently from side-to-side with a soft-face hammer to loosen it.

21 Compare the width of the crushed Plastigage on each journal to the scale printed on the Plastigage envelope to determine the main bearing oil clearance (see illustration). A typical main bearing oil clearance should fall between 0.0015 and 0.0023-inch. Check with an automotive machine shop for the clearance specified for your engine.

22 If the clearance is not as specified, the bearing inserts may be the wrong size (which means different ones will be required). Before deciding if different inserts are needed, make sure that no dirt or oil was between the bearing inserts and the cap assembly or block when the clearance was measured. If the Plastigage was wider at one end than the other, the crankshaft journal may be tapered. If the clearance still exceeds the limit specified, the bearing insert(s) will have to be replaced with an undersize bearing insert(s).

✳✳ CAUTION:

When installing a new crankshaft always install a standard bearing insert set.

23 Carefully scrape all traces of the Plastigage material off the main bearing journals and/or the bearing insert faces. Be sure to remove all residue from the oil holes. Use your fingernail or the edge of a plastic card - don't nick or scratch the bearing faces.

FINAL INSTALLATION

24 Carefully lift the crankshaft out of the cylinder block.

25 Clean the bearing insert faces in the cylinder block, then apply a thin, uniform layer of moly-base grease or engine assembly lube to each of the bearing surfaces. Be sure to coat the thrust faces as well as the journal face of the thrust washers.

➡️**Note: Install the thrust washers after the crankshaft has been installed.**

10.19 Main bearing cap and block side-bolts - tightening sequence

10.21 Use the scale on the Plastigage package to determine

26 Make sure the crankshaft journals are clean, then lay the crankshaft back in place in the cylinder block.

27 Clean the bearing insert faces and then apply the same lubricant to them. Clean the engine block thoroughly. The surfaces must be free of oil residue. Install the thrust washers.

28 Install each main bearing cap onto the crankshaft and cylinder block, noting the arrows that indicate the front of the engine.

29 Prior to installation, apply clean engine oil to all bolt threads, wiping off any excess, then install all bolts finger-tight.

30 Tighten the main bearing cap and block side-bolts to the torque listed in this Chapter's Specifications (in the proper sequence) (see illustration 10.19).

31 Recheck crankshaft endplay with a feeler gauge or a dial indicator. The endplay should be correct if the crankshaft thrust faces aren't worn or damaged and if new bearings have been installed.

32 Rotate the crankshaft a number of times by hand to check for any obvious binding. It should rotate with a running torque of 50 in-lbs or less. If the running torque is too high, identify and correct the problem at this time.

33 Install the new rear main oil seal (see Chapter 2A).

11 Engine overhaul - reassembly sequence

1 Before beginning engine reassembly, make sure you have all the necessary new parts, gaskets and seals as well as the following items on hand:

   Common hand tools
   A 1/2-inch drive torque wrench
   New engine oil
   Gasket sealant
   Thread locking compound

2 If you obtained a short block, it will be necessary to install the cylinder heads, the oil pump and pick-up tube, the oil pans, the water pump, the timing chain and timing cover, and the valve covers (see Chapter 2A). In order to save time and avoid problems, the external components must be installed in the following general order:

   Thermostat and housing cover
   Water pump
   Intake and exhaust manifolds
   Fuel injection components
   Emission control components
   Spark plugs
   Ignition coils
   Oil filter and oil cooler
   Engine mounts and mount brackets
   Driveplate

12 Initial start-up and break-in after overhaul

❋❋ WARNING:

Have a fire extinguisher handy when starting the engine for the first time.

1 Once the engine has been installed in the vehicle, double-check the engine oil and coolant levels.

2 With the spark plugs out of the engine and the ignition system and fuel pump disabled (see Chapter 4, Section 3), crank the engine until oil pressure registers on the gauge or the light goes out.

3 Install the spark plugs and ignition coils, and reinstall the fuel pump fuse.

4 Start the engine. It may take a few moments for the fuel system to build up pressure, but the engine should start without a great deal of effort.

5 After the engine starts, it should be allowed to warm up to normal operating temperature. While the engine is warming up, make a thorough check for fuel, oil and coolant leaks.

6 Shut the engine off and recheck the engine oil and coolant levels.

7 Drive the vehicle to an area with minimum traffic, accelerate from 30 to 50 mph, then allow the vehicle to slow to 30 mph with the throttle closed. Repeat the procedure 10 or 12 times. This will load the piston rings and cause them to seat properly against the cylinder walls. Check again for oil and coolant leaks.

8 Drive the vehicle gently for the first 500 miles (no sustained high speeds) and keep a constant check on the oil level. It is not unusual for an engine to use oil during the break-in period.

9 At approximately 500 to 600 miles, change the oil and filter.

10 For the next few hundred miles, drive the vehicle normally. Do not pamper it or abuse it.

11 After 2000 miles, change the oil and filter again and consider the engine broken in.

GLOSSARY

B

Backlash - The amount of play between two parts. Usually refers to how much one gear can be moved back and forth without moving the gear with which it's meshed.

Bearing Caps - The caps held in place by nuts or bolts which, in turn, hold the bearing surface. This space is for lubricating oil to enter.

Bearing clearance - The amount of space left between shaft and bearing surface. This space is for lubricating oil to enter.

Bearing crush - The additional height which is purposely manufactured into each bearing half to ensure complete contact of the bearing back with the housing bore when the engine is assembled.

Bearing knock - The noise created by movement of a part in a loose or worn bearing.

Blueprinting - Dismantling an engine and reassembling it to EXACT specifications.

Bore - An engine cylinder, or any cylindrical hole; also used to describe the process of enlarging or accurately refinishing a hole with a cutting tool, as to bore an engine cylinder. The bore size is the diameter of the hole.

Boring - Renewing the cylinders by cutting them out to a specified size. A boring bar is used to make the cut.

Bottom end - A term which refers collectively to the engine block, crankshaft, main bearings and the big ends of the connecting rods.

Break-in - The period of operation between installation of new or rebuilt parts and time in which parts are worn to the correct fit. Driving at reduced and varying speed for a specified mileage to permit parts to wear to the correct fit.

Bushing - A one-piece sleeve placed in a bore to serve as a bearing surface for shaft, piston pin, etc. Usually replaceable.

C

Camshaft - The shaft in the engine, on which a series of lobes are located for operating the valve mechanisms. The camshaft is driven by gears or sprockets and a timing chain. Usually referred to simply as the cam.

Carbon - Hard, or soft, black deposits found in combustion chamber, on plugs, under rings, on and under valve heads.

Cast iron - An alloy of iron and more than two percent carbon, used for engine blocks and heads because it's relatively inexpensive and easy to mold into complex shapes.

Chamfer - To bevel across (or a bevel on) the sharp edge of an object.

Chase - To repair damaged threads with a tap or die.

Combustion chamber - The space between the piston and the cylinder head, with the piston at top dead center, in which air-fuel mixture is burned.

Compression ratio - The relationship between cylinder volume (clearance volume) when the piston is at top dead center and cylinder volume when the piston is at bottom dead center.

Connecting rod - The rod that connects the crank on the crankshaft with the piston. Sometimes called a con rod.

Connecting rod cap - The part of the connecting rod assembly that attaches the rod to the crankpin.

Core plug - Soft metal plug used to plug the casting holes for the coolant passages in the block.

Crankcase - The lower part of the engine in which the crankshaft rotates; includes the lower section of the cylinder block and the oil pan.

Crank kit - A reground or reconditioned crankshaft and new main and connecting rod bearings.

Crankpin - The part of a crankshaft to which a connecting rod is attached.

Crankshaft - The main rotating member, or shaft, running the length of the crankcase, with offset throws to which the connecting rods are attached; changes the reciprocating motion of the pistons into rotating motion.

Cylinder sleeve - A replaceable sleeve, or liner, pressed into the cylinder block to form the cylinder bore.

D

Deburring - Removing the burrs (rough edges or areas) from a bearing.

Deglazer - A tool, rotated by an electric motor, used to remove glaze from cylinder walls so a new set of rings will seat.

E

Endplay - The amount of lengthwise movement between two parts. As applied to a crankshaft, the distance that the crankshaft can move forward and back in the cylinder block.

F

Face - A machinist's term that refers to removing metal from the end of a shaft or the face of a larger part, such as a flywheel.

Fatigue - A breakdown of material through a large number of loading and unloading cycles. The first signs are cracks followed shortly by breaks.

Feeler gauge - A thin strip of hardened steel, ground to an exact thickness, used to check clearances between parts.

Free height - The unloaded length or height of a spring.

Freeplay - The looseness in a linkage, or an assembly of parts, between the initial application of force and actual movement. Usually perceived as slop or slight delay.

Freeze plug - See Core plug.

G

Gallery - A large passage in the block that forms a reservoir for engine oil pressure.

Glaze - The very smooth, glassy finish that develops on cylinder walls while an engine is in service.

H

Heli-Coil - A rethreading device used when threads are worn or damaged. The device is installed in a retapped hole to reduce the thread size to the original size.

I

Installed height - The spring's measured length or height, as installed on the cylinder head. Installed height is measured from the spring seat to the underside of the spring retainer.

J

Journal - The surface of a rotating shaft which turns in a bearing.

K

Keeper - The split lock that holds the valve spring retainer in position on the valve stem.

Key - A small piece of metal inserted into matching grooves machined into two parts fitted together - such as a gear pressed onto a shaft - which prevents slippage between the two parts.

Knock - The heavy metallic engine sound, produced in the combustion chamber as a result of abnormal combustion - usually detonation. Knock is usually caused by a loose or worn bearing. Also referred to as detonation, pinging and spark knock. Connecting rod or main bearing knocks are created by too much oil clearance or insufficient lubrication.

L

Lands - The portions of metal between the piston ring grooves.

Lapping the valves - Grinding a valve face and its seat together with lapping compound.

Lash - The amount of free motion in a gear train, between gears, or in a mechanical assembly, that occurs before movement can begin. Usually refers to the lash in a valve train.

Lifter - The part that rides against the cam to transfer motion to the rest of the valve train.

M

Machining - The process of using a machine to remove metal from a metal part.

Main bearings - The plain, or babbitt, bearings that support the crankshaft.

Main bearing caps - The cast iron caps, bolted to the bottom of the block, that support the main bearings.

O

O.D. - Outside diameter.

Oil gallery - A pipe or drilled passageway in the engine used to carry engine oil from one area to another.

Oil ring - The lower ring, or rings, of a piston; designed to prevent excessive amounts of oil from working up the cylinder walls and into the combustion chamber. Also called an oil-control ring.

Oil seal - A seal which keeps oil from leaking out of a compartment. Usually refers to a dynamic seal around a rotating shaft or other moving part.

O-ring - A type of sealing ring made of a special rubberlike material; in use, the O-ring is compressed into a groove to provide the sealing action.

Overhaul - To completely disassemble a unit, clean and inspect all parts, reassemble it with the original or new parts and make all adjustments necessary for proper operation.

P

Pilot bearing - A small bearing installed in the center of the flywheel (or the rear end of the crankshaft) to support the front end of the input shaft of the transmission.

Pip mark - A little dot or indentation which indicates the top side of a compression ring.

Piston - The cylindrical part, attached to the connecting rod, that moves up and down in the cylinder as the crankshaft rotates. When the fuel charge is fired, the piston transfers the force of the explosion to the connecting rod, then to the crankshaft.

Piston pin (or wrist pin) - The cylindrical and usually hollow steel pin that passes through the piston. The piston pin fastens the piston to the upper end of the connecting rod.

Piston ring - The split ring fitted to the groove in a piston. The ring contacts the sides of the ring groove and also rubs against the cylinder wall, thus sealing space between piston and wall. There are two types of rings: Compression rings seal the compression pressure in the combustion chamber; oil rings scrape excessive oil off the cylinder wall.

Piston ring groove - The slots or grooves cut in piston heads to hold piston rings in position.

Piston skirt - The portion of the piston below the rings and the piston pin hole.

Plastigage - A thin strip of plastic thread, available in different sizes, used for measuring clearances. For example, a strip of plastigage is laid across a bearing journal and mashed as parts are assembled. Then parts are disassembled and the width of the strip is measured to determine clearance between journal and bearing. Commonly used to measure crankshaft main-bearing and connecting rod bearing clearances.

Press-fit - A tight fit between two parts that requires pressure to force the parts together. Also referred to as drive, or force, fit.

Prussian blue - A blue pigment; in solution, useful in determining the area of contact between two surfaces. Prussian blue is commonly used to determine the width and location of the contact area between the valve face and the valve seat.

R

Race (bearing) - The inner or outer ring that provides a contact surface for balls or rollers in bearing.

Ream - To size, enlarge or smooth a hole by using a round cutting tool with fluted edges.

Ring job - The process of reconditioning the cylinders and installing new rings.

Runout - Wobble. The amount a shaft rotates out-of-true.

S

Saddle - The upper main bearing seat.

Scored - Scratched or grooved, as a cylinder wall may be scored by abrasive particles moved up and down by the piston rings.

Scuffing - A type of wear in which there's a transfer of material between parts moving against each other; shows up as pits or grooves in the mating surfaces.

Seat - The surface upon which another part rests or seats. For example, the valve seat is the matched surface upon which the valve face rests. Also used to refer to wearing into a good fit; for example, piston rings seat after a few miles of driving.

Short block - An engine block complete with crankshaft and piston and, usually, camshaft assemblies.

Static balance - The balance of an object while it's stationary.

Step - The wear on the lower portion of a ring land caused by excessive side and back-clearance. The height of the step indicates the ring's extra side clearance and the length of the step projecting from the back wall of the groove represents the ring's back clearance.

Stroke - The distance the piston moves when traveling from top dead center to bottom dead center, or from bottom dead center to top dead center.

Stud - A metal rod with threads on both ends.

T

Tang - A lip on the end of a plain bearing used to align the bearing during assembly.

Tap - To cut threads in a hole. Also refers to the fluted tool used to cut threads.

Taper - A gradual reduction in the width of a shaft or hole; in an engine cylinder, taper usually takes the form of uneven wear, more pronounced at the top than at the bottom.

Throws - The offset portions of the crankshaft to which the connecting rods are affixed.

Thrust bearing - The main bearing that has thrust faces to prevent excessive endplay, or forward and backward movement of the crankshaft.

Thrust washer - A bronze or hardened steel washer placed between two moving parts. The washer prevents longitudinal movement and provides a bearing surface for thrust surfaces of parts.

Tolerance - The amount of variation permitted from an exact size of measurement. Actual amount from smallest acceptable dimension to largest acceptable dimension.

U

Umbrella - An oil deflector placed near the valve tip to throw oil from the valve stem area.

Undercut - A machined groove below the normal surface.

Undersize bearings - Smaller diameter bearings used with re-ground crankshaft journals.

V

Valve grinding - Refacing a valve in a valve-refacing machine.

Valve train - The valve-operating mechanism of an engine; includes all components from the camshaft to the valve.

Vibration damper - A cylindrical weight attached to the front of the crankshaft to minimize torsional vibration (the twist-untwist actions of the crankshaft caused by the cylinder firing impulses). Also called a harmonic balancer.

W

Water jacket - The spaces around the cylinders, between the inner and outer shells of the cylinder block or head, through which coolant circulates.

Web - A supporting structure across a cavity.

Woodruff key - A key with a radiused backside (viewed from the side).

Specifications

General

Engine designation	VK56DE
Displacement	338.80 cubic inches (5.6 liters)
Compression ratio	9.8:1
Cylinder compression pressure	
Minimum	192 psi at 200 rpm
Maximum variation between cylinders	14 psi at 300 rpm
Oil pressure (minimum, warm engine)	
Idle	14 psi
2,000 rpm	43 psi

Torque specifications	Ft-lbs (unless otherwise indicated)	Nm

➡ **Note: One foot-pound (ft-lb) of torque is equivalent to 12 inch-pounds (in-lbs) of torque. Torque values below approximately 15 ft-lbs are expressed in inch-pounds, since most foot-pound torque wrenches are not accurate at these smaller values.**

	Ft-lbs (unless otherwise indicated)	Nm
Connecting rod cap bolts (bolts must be replaced with new ones)		
5.6L V8 engine		
Step 1	132 in-lbs	15
Step 2	Tighten an additional 90 degrees	
Main bearing cap bolts (bolts must be replaced with new ones)		
Step 1, bolts 1 through 10	29	39
Step 2, bolts 11 through 20	22	30
Step 3, bolts 1 through 10	Tighten an additional 40 degrees	
Step 4, bolts 11 through 20	Tighten an additional 30 degrees	
Step 5, Side bolts 21 through 30	36	49

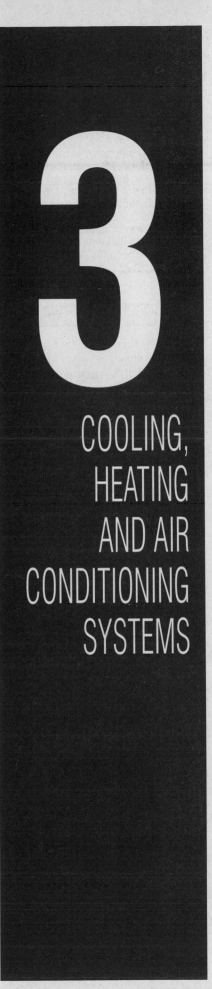

3

COOLING, HEATING AND AIR CONDITIONING SYSTEMS

1 General information

ENGINE COOLING SYSTEM

All modern vehicles employ a pressurized engine cooling system with thermostatically controlled coolant circulation. The cooling system consists of a radiator, an expansion tank or coolant reservoir, a pressure cap (located on the expansion tank or radiator), a thermostat, a cooling fan, and a water pump.

The water pump circulates coolant through the engine. The coolant flows around each cylinder and around the intake and exhaust ports, near the spark plug areas and in close proximity to the exhaust valve guides.

A thermostat controls engine coolant temperature. During warm up, the closed thermostat prevents coolant from circulating through the radiator. As the engine nears normal operating temperature, the thermostat opens and allows hot coolant to travel through the radiator, where it's cooled before returning to the engine.

HEATING SYSTEM

The heating system consists of a blower fan and heater core located in a housing under the dash, the hoses connecting the heater core to the engine cooling system and the heater/air conditioning control head on the dashboard. Hot engine coolant is circulated through the heater core. When the heater mode is activated, a flap door in the housing opens to expose the heater core to the passenger compartment through air ducts. A fan switch on the control head activates the blower motor, which forces air through the core, heating the air.

Armada models are also equipped with a rear heating and air conditioning system, mounted behind the right rear quarter trim panel in the luggage compartment area.

AIR CONDITIONING SYSTEM

The air conditioning system consists of a condenser mounted in front of the radiator, an evaporator mounted adjacent to the heater core, a compressor mounted on the engine, a receiver-drier (integral with the condenser) and the plumbing connecting all of the above components.

A blower fan forces the warmer air of the passenger compartment through the evaporator core (sort of a radiator-in-reverse), transferring the heat from the air to the refrigerant. The liquid refrigerant boils off into low pressure vapor, taking the heat with it when it leaves the evaporator.

2 Troubleshooting

COOLANT LEAKS

▶ Refer to illustration 2.2

1 A coolant leak can develop anywhere in the cooling system, but the most common causes are:

a) A loose or weak hose clamp
b) A defective hose
c) A faulty pressure cap
d) A damaged radiator
e) A bad heater core
f) A faulty water pump
g) A leaking gasket at any joint that carries coolant

2 Coolant leaks aren't always easy to find. Sometimes they can only be detected when the cooling system is under pressure. Here's where a cooling system pressure tester comes in handy. After the engine has cooled completely, the tester is attached in place of the pressure cap, then pumped up to the pressure value equal to that of the pressure cap rating (see illustration). Now, leaks that only exist when the engine is fully warmed up will become apparent. The tester can be left connected to locate a nagging slow leak.

2.2 The cooling system pressure tester is connected in place of the pressure cap or radiator cap, then pumped up to pressurize the system

2.5a The combustion leak detector consists of a bulb, syringe and test fluid

2.5b Place the tester over the cooling system filler neck and use the bulb to draw a sample into the tester

2.8 Checking the cooling system pressure cap with a cooling system pressure tester

COOLANT LEVEL DROPS, BUT NO EXTERNAL LEAKS

▶ **Refer to illustrations 2.5a and 2.5b**

3   If you find it necessary to keep adding coolant, but there are no external leaks, the probable causes include:

   a) A blown head gasket
   b) A leaking intake manifold gasket (only on engines that have cool-ant passages in the manifold)
   c) A cracked cylinder head or cylinder block

4   Any of the above problems will also usually result in contamination of the engine oil, which will cause it to take on a milkshake-like appearance. A bad head gasket or cracked head or block can also result in engine oil contaminating the cooling system.

5   Combustion leak detectors (also known as block testers) are available at most auto parts stores. These work by detecting exhaust gases in the cooling system, which indicates a compression leak from a cylinder into the coolant. The tester consists of a large bulb-type syringe and bottle of test fluid (see illustration). Fluid is added to the syringe, then the syringe is placed over the cooling system filler neck and, with the engine running, the bulb is squeezed and a sample of the gases present in the cooling system are drawn up through the test fluid (see illustration). If any combustion gases are present in the sample taken, the test fluid will change color.

6   If the test indicates combustion gas is present in the cooling system, you can be sure that the engine has a blown head gasket or a crack in the cylinder head or block, and will require disassembly to repair.

PRESSURE CAP

▶ **Refer to illustration 2.8**

✳✳ WARNING:

Wait until the engine is completely cool before beginning this check.

7   The cooling system is sealed by a spring-loaded cap, which raises the boiling point of the coolant. If the cap's seal or spring are worn out, the coolant can boil and escape past the cap. With the engine completely cool, remove the cap and check the seal; if it's cracked, hardened or deteriorated in any way, replace it with a new one.

8   Even if the seal is good, the spring might not be; this can be checked with a cooling system pressure tester (see illustration). If the cap can't hold a pressure within approximately 1-1/2 lbs of its rated pressure (which is marked on the cap), replace it with a new one.

9   The cap is also equipped with a vacuum relief spring. When the engine cools off, a vacuum is created in the cooling system. The vacuum relief spring allows air back into the system, which will equalize the pressure and prevent damage to the radiator (the radiator tanks could collapse if the vacuum is great enough). If, after turning the engine off and allowing it to cool down you notice any of the cooling system hoses collapsing, replace the pressure cap with a new one.

THERMOSTAT

▶ **Refer to illustration 2.10**

10   Before assuming the thermostat (see illustration) is responsible for a cooling system problem, check the coolant level (see Chapter 1), drive-belt tension (see Chapter 1) and temperature gauge (or light) operation.

11   If the engine takes a long time to warm up (as indicated by the temperature gauge or heater operation), the thermostat is probably stuck

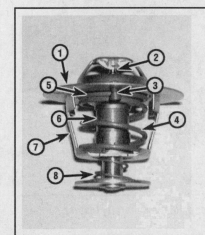

2.10 Typical thermostat:

1   Flange
2   Piston
3   Jiggle valve
4   Main coil spring
5   Valve seat
6   Valve
7   Frame
8   Secondary coil spring

open. Replace the thermostat with a new one.

12 If the engine runs hot or overheats, a thorough test of the thermostat should be performed.

13 Definitive testing of the thermostat can only be made when it is removed from the vehicle. If the thermostat is stuck in the open position at room temperature, it is faulty and must be replaced.

> **✳✳ CAUTION:**
>
> **Do not drive the vehicle without a thermostat. The computer may stay in open loop and emissions and fuel economy will suffer.**

14 To test a thermostat, suspend the (closed) thermostat on a length of string or wire in a pot of cold water.

15 Heat the water on a stove while observing thermostat. The thermostat should fully open before the water boils.

16 If the thermostat doesn't open and close as specified, or sticks in any position, replace it.

COOLING FAN

Electric cooling fan

17 If the engine is overheating and the cooling fan is not coming on when the engine temperature rises to an excessive level, unplug the fan motor electrical connector(s) and connect the motor directly to the battery with fused jumper wires. If the fan motor doesn't come on, replace the motor.

18 If the radiator fan motor is okay, but it isn't coming on when the engine gets hot, the fan relay might be defective. A relay is used to control a circuit by turning it on and off in response to a control decision by the Powertrain Control Module (PCM). These control circuits are fairly complex, and checking them should be left to a qualified automotive technician. Sometimes, the control system can be fixed by simply identifying and replacing a bad relay.

19 Locate the fan relays in the engine compartment fuse/relay box.

20 Test the relay (see Chapter 12).

21 If the relay is okay, check all wiring and connections to the fan motor. Refer to the wiring diagrams at the end of Chapter 12. If no obvious problems are found, the problem could be the Engine Coolant

2.28 The water pump weep hole is generally located on the underside of the pump

Temperature (ECT) sensor or the Powertrain Control Module (PCM). Have the cooling fan system and circuit diagnosed by a dealer service department or repair shop with the proper diagnostic equipment.

➡**Note: These models are equipped with a cooling fan motor resistor. Have the resistor checked if the fan motor does not respond to the speed variations signaled by the PCM.**

Belt-driven cooling fan

22 Disconnect the cable from the negative terminal of the battery and rock the fan back and forth by hand to check for excessive bearing play.

23 With the engine cold (and not running), turn the fan blades by hand. The fan should turn freely.

24 Visually inspect for substantial fluid leakage from the clutch assembly. If problems are noted, replace the clutch assembly.

25 With the engine completely warmed up, turn off the ignition switch and disconnect the negative battery cable from the battery. Turn the fan by hand. Some drag should be evident. If the fan turns easily, replace the fan clutch.

WATER PUMP

26 A failure in the water pump can cause serious engine damage due to overheating.

Drivebelt-driven water pump

▶ **Refer to illustration 2.28**

27 There are two ways to check the operation of the water pump while it's installed on the engine. If the pump is found to be defective, it should be replaced with a new or rebuilt unit.

28 Water pumps are equipped with weep (or vent) holes (see illustration). If a failure occurs in the pump seal, coolant will leak from the hole.

29 If the water pump shaft bearings fail, there may be a howling sound at the pump while it's running. Shaft wear can be felt with the drivebelt removed if the water pump pulley is rocked up and down (with the engine off). Don't mistake drivebelt slippage, which causes a squealing sound, for water pump bearing failure.

Timing chain or timing belt-driven water pump

30 Water pumps driven by the timing chain or timing belt are located underneath the timing chain or timing belt cover.

31 Checking the water pump is limited because of where it is located. However, some basic checks can be made before deciding to remove the water pump. If the pump is found to be defective, it should be replaced with a new or rebuilt unit.

32 One sign that the water pump may be failing is that the heater (climate control) may not work well. Warm the engine to normal operating temperature, confirm that the coolant level is correct, then run the heater and check for hot air coming from the ducts.

33 Check for noises coming from the water pump area. If the water pump impeller shaft or bearings are failing, there may be a howling sound at the pump while the engine is running.

➡**Note: Be careful not to mistake drivebelt noise (squealing) for water pump bearing or shaft failure.**

34 It you suspect water pump failure due to noise, wear can be confirmed by feeling for play at the pump shaft. This can be done by rocking the drive sprocket on the pump shaft up and down. To do this you will need to remove the tension on the timing chain or belt as well as access the water pump.

All water pumps

35 In rare cases or on high-mileage vehicles, another sign of water pump failure may be the presence of coolant in the engine oil. This condition will adversely affect the engine in varying degrees.

➡**Note: Finding coolant in the engine oil could indicate other serious issues besides a failed water pump, such as a blown head gasket or a cracked cylinder head or block.**

36 Even a pump that exhibits no outward signs of a problem, such as noise or leakage, can still be due for replacement. Removal for close examination is the only sure way to tell. Sometimes the fins on the back of the impeller can corrode to the point that cooling efficiency is diminished significantly.

HEATER SYSTEM

37 Little can go wrong with a heater. If the fan motor will run at all speeds, the electrical part of the system is okay. The three basic heater problems fall into the following general categories:

a) Not enough heat
b) Heat all the time
c) No heat

38 If there's not enough heat, the control valve or door is stuck in a partially open position, the coolant coming from the engine isn't hot enough, or the heater core is restricted. If the coolant isn't hot enough, the thermostat in the engine cooling system is stuck open, allowing coolant to pass through the engine so rapidly that it doesn't heat up quickly enough. If the vehicle is equipped with a temperature gauge instead of a warning light, watch to see if the engine temperature rises to the normal operating range after driving for a reasonable distance.

39 If there's heat all the time, the control valve or the door is stuck wide open.

40 If there's no heat, coolant is probably not reaching the heater core, or the heater core is plugged. The likely cause is a collapsed or plugged hose, core, or a frozen heater control valve. If the heater is the type that flows coolant all the time, the cause is a stuck door or a broken or kinked control cable.

AIR CONDITIONING SYSTEM

41 If the cool air output is inadequate:

a) Inspect the condenser coils and fins to make sure they're clear
b) Check the compressor clutch for slippage.
c) Check the blower motor for proper operation.
d) Inspect the blower discharge passage for obstructions.

e) Check the system air intake filter for clogging.

42 If the system provides intermittent cooling air:

a) Check the circuit breaker, blower switch and blower motor for a malfunction.
b) Make sure the compressor clutch isn't slipping.
c) Inspect the plenum door to make sure it's operating properly.
d) Inspect the evaporator to make sure it isn't clogged.
e) If the unit is icing up, it may be caused by excessive moisture in the system, incorrect super heat switch adjustment or low thermostat adjustment.

43 If the system provides no cooling air:

a) Inspect the compressor drivebelt. Make sure it's not loose or broken.
b) Make sure the compressor clutch engages. If it doesn't, check for a blown fuse.
c) Inspect the wire harness for broken or disconnected wires.
d) If the compressor clutch doesn't engage, bridge the terminals of the A/C pressure switch(es) with a jumper wire; if the clutch now engages, and the system is properly charged, the pressure switch is bad.
e) Make sure the blower motor is not disconnected or burned out.
f) Make sure the compressor isn't partially or completely seized.
g) Inspect the refrigerant lines for leaks.
h) Check the components for leaks.
i) Inspect the receiver-drier/accumulator or expansion valve/tube for clogged screens.

44 If the system is noisy:

a) Look for loose panels in the passenger compartment.
b) Inspect the compressor drivebelt. It may be loose or worn.
c) Check the compressor mounting bolts. They should be tight.
d) Listen carefully to the compressor. It may be worn out.
e) Listen to the idler pulley and bearing and the clutch. Either may be defective.
f) The winding in the compressor clutch coil or solenoid may be defective.
g) The compressor oil level may be low.
h) The blower motor fan bushing or the motor itself may be worn out.
i) If there is an excessive charge in the system, you'll hear a rumbling noise in the high pressure line, a thumping noise in the compressor or see bubbles or cloudiness in the sight glass.
j) If there's a low charge in the system, you might hear hissing in the evaporator case at the expansion valve, or see bubbles or cloudiness in the sight glass.

---

3 Air conditioning and heating system - check and maintenance

AIR CONDITIONING SYSTEM

▸ **Refer to illustration 3.1**

✳ WARNING:

The air conditioning system is under high pressure. Do not loosen any hose fittings or remove any components until after the system has been discharged. Air conditioning refrigerant should be properly discharged into an EPA-approved recovery/recycling unit at a dealer service department or an automotive air conditioning repair facility. Always wear eye protection when disconnecting air conditioning system fittings.

✳ CAUTION:

All models covered by this manual use environmentally friendly R-134a. This refrigerant (and its appropriate refrigerant oils) are not compatible with R-12 refrigerant system components and must never be mixed or the components will be damaged.

3.1 The evaporator drain hose is located on the passenger's side of the firewall

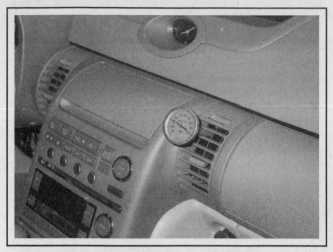

3.9 Insert a thermometer in the center vent, turn on the air conditioning system and wait for it to cool down; depending on the humidity, the output air should be 30 to 40 degrees cooler than the ambient air temperature

✳✳ CAUTION:

When replacing entire components, additional refrigerant oil should be added equal to the amount that is removed with the component being replaced. Be sure to read the can before adding any oil to the system, to make sure it is compatible with the R-134a system.

1   The following maintenance checks should be performed on a regular basis to ensure that the air conditioning continues to operate at peak efficiency.

   a) *Inspect the condition of the compressor drivebelt. If it is worn or deteriorated, replace it (see Chapter 1).*
   b) *Check the drivebelt tension (see Chapter 1).*
   c) *Inspect the system hoses. Look for cracks, bubbles, hardening and deterioration. Inspect the hoses and all fittings for oil bubbles or seepage. If there is any evidence of wear, damage or leakage, replace the hose(s).*
   d) *Inspect the condenser fins for leaves, bugs and any other foreign material that may have embedded itself in the fins. Use a fin comb or compressed air to remove debris from the condenser.*
   e) *Make sure the system has the correct refrigerant charge.*
   f) *If you hear water sloshing around in the dash area or have water dripping on the carpet, check the evaporator housing drain tube (see illustration) and insert a piece of wire into the opening to check for blockage.*

2   It's a good idea to operate the system for about ten minutes at least once a month. This is particularly important during the winter months because long term non-use can cause hardening, and subsequent failure, of the seals. Note that using the Defrost function operates the compressor.

3   If the air conditioning system is not working properly, proceed to Step 6 and perform the general checks outlined below.

4   Because of the complexity of the air conditioning system and the special equipment necessary to service it, in-depth troubleshooting and repairs beyond checking the refrigerant charge and the compressor clutch operation are not included in this manual. However, simple checks and component replacement procedures are provided in this Chapter.

5   The most common cause of poor cooling is simply a low system refrigerant charge. If a noticeable drop in system cooling ability occurs, one of the following quick checks will help you determine if the refrigerant level is low.

Checking the refrigerant charge
▶ **Refer to illustration 3.9**

6   Warm the engine up to normal operating temperature.

7   Place the air conditioning temperature selector at the coldest setting and put the blower at the highest setting.

8   After the system reaches operating temperature, feel the larger pipe exiting the evaporator at the firewall. The outlet pipe should be cold (the tubing that leads back to the compressor). If the evaporator outlet pipe is warm, the system probably needs a charge.

9   Insert a thermometer in the center air distribution duct (see illustration) while operating the air conditioning system at its maximum setting - the temperature of the output air should be 35 to 40 degrees F below the ambient air temperature (down to approximately 40 degrees F). If the ambient (outside) air temperature is very high, say 110 degrees F, the duct air temperature may be as high as 60 degrees F, but generally the air conditioning is 35 to 40 degrees F cooler than the ambient air.

10   Further inspection or testing of the system requires special tools and techniques and is beyond the scope of the home mechanic.

Adding refrigerant
▶ **Refer to illustrations 3.11 and 3.13**

✳✳ CAUTION:

Make sure any refrigerant, refrigerant oil or replacement component you purchase is designated as compatible with R-134a systems.

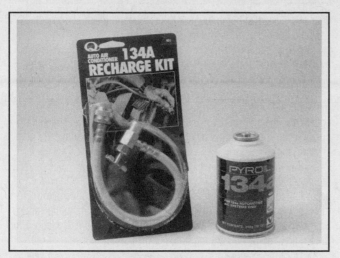

3.11 R-134a automotive air conditioning charging kit

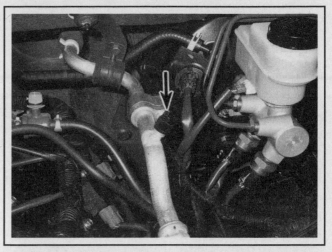

3.13 Location of the low-side charging port

11 Purchase an R-134a automotive charging kit at an auto parts store (see illustration). A charging kit includes a can of refrigerant, a tap valve and a short section of hose that can be attached between the tap valve and the system low side service valve.

❊❊ CAUTION:

Never add more than one can of refrigerant to the system. If more refrigerant than that is required, the system should be evacuated and leak tested.

12 Back off the valve handle on the charging kit and screw the kit onto the refrigerant can, making sure first that the O-ring or rubber seal inside the threaded portion of the kit is in place.

❊❊ WARNING:

Wear protective eyewear when dealing with pressurized refrigerant cans.

13 Remove the dust cap from the low-side charging port and attach the hose's quick-connect fitting to the port (see illustration).

❊❊ WARNING:

DO NOT hook the charging kit hose to the system high side! The fittings on the charging kit are designed to fit only on the low side of the system.

14 Warm up the engine and turn on the air conditioning. Keep the charging kit hose away from the fan and other moving parts.

➡**Note: The charging process requires the compressor to be running. If the clutch cycles off, you can put the air conditioning switch on High and leave the car doors open to keep the clutch on and compressor working. The compressor can be kept on during the charging by removing the connector from the pressure switch and bridging it with a paper clip or jumper wire during the procedure.**

15 Turn the valve handle on the kit until the stem pierces the can, then back the handle out to release the refrigerant. You should be able to hear the rush of gas. Keep the can upright at all times, but shake it occasionally. Allow stabilization time between each addition.

➡**Note: The charging process will go faster if you wrap the can with a hot-water-soaked rag to keep the can from freezing up.**

16 If you have an accurate thermometer, you can place it in the center air conditioning duct inside the vehicle and keep track of the output air temperature. A charged system that is working properly should cool down to approximately 40 degrees F. If the ambient (outside) air temperature is very high, say 110 degrees F, the duct air temperature may be as high as 60 degrees F, but generally the air conditioning is 35 to 40 degrees F cooler than the ambient air.

17 When the can is empty, turn the valve handle to the closed position and release the connection from the low-side port. Reinstall the dust cap.

18 Remove the charging kit from the can and store the kit for future use with the piercing valve in the UP position, to prevent inadvertently piercing the can on the next use.

HEATING SYSTEMS

19 If the carpet under the heater core is damp, or if antifreeze vapor or steam is coming through the vents, the heater core is leaking. Remove it (see Section 11) and install a new unit (most radiator shops will not repair a leaking heater core).

20 If the air coming out of the heater vents isn't hot, the problem could stem from any of the following causes:

a) *The thermostat is stuck open, preventing the engine coolant from warming up enough to carry heat to the heater core. Replace the thermostat (see Section 4).*

b) *There is a blockage in the system, preventing the flow of coolant through the heater core. Feel both heater hoses at the firewall. They should be hot. If one of them is cold, there is an obstruction in one of the hoses or in the heater core, or the heater control valve is shut. Detach the hoses and back flush the heater core with a water hose. If the heater core is clear but circulation is impeded, remove the two hoses and flush them out with a water hose.*

c) *If flushing fails to remove the blockage from the heater core, the core must be replaced (see Section 11).*

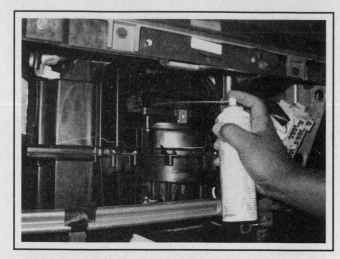

3.24 Insert the nozzle of the disinfectant can into the air recirculation intake behind the glove box

ELIMINATING AIR CONDITIONING ODORS

▶ **Refer to illustration 3.24**

21 Unpleasant odors that often develop in air conditioning systems are caused by the growth of a fungus, usually on the surface of the evaporator core. The warm, humid environment there is a perfect breeding ground for mildew to develop.

22 The evaporator core on most vehicles is difficult to access, and factory dealerships have a lengthy, expensive process for eliminating the fungus by opening up the evaporator case and using a powerful disinfectant and rinse on the core until the fungus is gone. You can service your own system at home, but it takes something much stronger than basic household germ-killers or deodorizers.

23 Aerosol disinfectants for automotive air conditioning systems are available in most auto parts stores, but remember when shopping for them that the most effective treatments are also the most expensive. The basic procedure for using these sprays is to start by running the system in the RECIRC mode for ten minutes with the blower on its highest speed. Use the highest heat mode to dry out the system and keep the compressor from engaging by disconnecting the wiring connector at the compressor.

24 The disinfectant can usually comes with a long spray hose. Insert the nozzle into the air recirculation port inside the cabin, and spray according to the manufacturer's recommendations (see illustration). Try to cover the whole surface of the evaporator core, by aiming the spray up, down and sideways. Follow the manufacturer's recommendations for the length of spray and waiting time between applications.

25 Once the evaporator has been cleaned, the best way to prevent the mildew from coming back again is to make sure your evaporator housing drain tube is clear (see illustration 3.1).

AUTOMATIC HEATING AND AIR CONDITIONING SYSTEMS

26 Some vehicles are equipped with an optional automatic climate control system. This system has its own computer that receives inputs from various sensors in the heating and air conditioning system. This computer, like the PCM, has self-diagnostic capabilities to help pinpoint problems or faults within the system. Vehicles equipped with automatic heating and air conditioning systems are very complex and considered beyond the scope of the home mechanic. Vehicles equipped with automatic heating and air conditioning systems should be taken to a dealer service department or other qualified facility for repair.

4 Thermostat - replacement

▶ **Refer to illustrations 4.2, 4.4 and 4.5**

❊❊ WARNING:

Do not attempt to remove the radiator cap, reservoir/expansion tank pressure cap, or thermostat until the engine has cooled completely.

1 Drain the engine cooling system (see Chapter 1). See the **Warning** in Section 1.

2 Remove the engine cover (see illustration).

3 Remove the air intake duct between the throttle body and the air filter housing (see Chapter 4).

4 Remove the thermostat housing cover mounting bolts, then separate the cover from the housing (see illustration).

➡**Note: Leave the radiator hose attached to the housing cover unless the hose is going to be replaced.**

4.2 Engine cover fasteners

4.4 Thermostat housing cover bolts

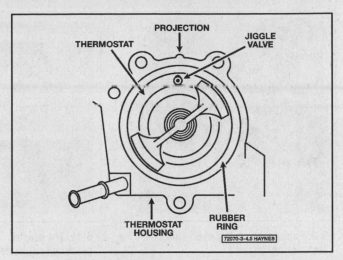

4.5 The thermostat's installed position and details

5   Note the position of the thermostat, then pull the thermostat out of the housing (see illustration).

6   Clean off any part of the seal that may have stuck to the housing or cover.

7   Installation is the reverse of removal. Use a new seal during installation. Position the thermostat with the jiggle valve up (matching the index on the thermostat housing) (see illustration 4.5). Tighten the thermostat housing cover fasteners to the torque listed in this Chapter's Specifications.

8   Refill and bleed the cooling system (see Chapter 1). Run the engine and check for leaks and for proper thermostat operation.

5   Engine cooling fans - replacement

❄❄ WARNING:

To avoid possible injury or damage, DO NOT operate the engine with a damaged fan. Do not attempt to repair fan blades. Always replace a damaged fan with a new one.

BELT-DRIVEN FAN

▶ **Refer to illustration 5.3**

1   Remove the air intake duct between the throttle body and the air filter housing (see Chapter 4).

2   Remove the engine splash shield beneath the front of the vehicle.

3   Disconnect the automatic transmission fluid cooler hoses (see illustration).

4   Remove the lower radiator shroud (see illustration 5.3).

2010 Armada models

▶ **Refer to illustration 5.7**

5   Drain the engine cooling system (see Chapter 1). See **Warning** in Section 1.

6   Disconnect the upper radiator hose from the radiator.

7   Remove the upper radiator shroud mounting bolts, then remove the shroud (see illustration).

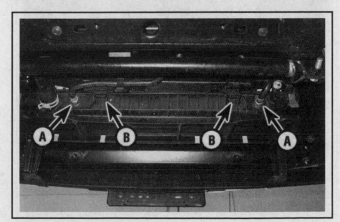

5.3 Automatic transmission fluid cooler hose connections (A) and the mounting tabs for the lower shroud (B)

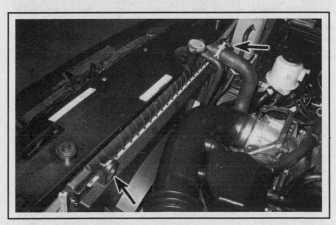

5.7 Fan shroud upper fasteners

5.8 Fan mounting fasteners (one fastener not shown)

5.15 The electric fan electrical connector

5.16 The electric fan assembly mounting bolt (beneath the wire harness)

All models

▸ **Refer to illustration 5.8**

8 Loosen, but do not remove, the mounting fasteners on the fan pulley (see illustration).

9 Remove the drivebelt (see Chapter 1).

10 Remove the fan mounting fasteners, then remove the fan and fan clutch and lower it out from the bottom (see illustration 5.8). If necessary, raise the vehicle and securely support it on jackstands.

➡**Note 1: On Armada models equipped with a rear auto-leveling suspension, turn the ignition key to the OFF position before raising the vehicle.**

➡**Note 2: On 2010 Armada models, the cooling fan is removed out the top of the engine compartment.**

11 Carefully inspect the fan blades for any damage. Replace if necessary. Inspect the fan clutch for signs of fluid leakage or roughness when rotating the assembly. Inspect the fan bracket on the engine by spinning the bearing, checking for any signs of roughness or play. Replace the fan bracket/bearing assembly if necessary.

12 At this point, the fan may be unbolted from the clutch, if necessary. Be sure to re-install the fan blade with the "F" mark on the fan hub facing towards the front of the vehicle.

13 Installation is the reverse of removal. Be sure to tighten the fan and clutch mounting nuts evenly and securely.

ELECTRIC FAN

▸ **Refer to illustrations 5.15 and 5.16**

14 Remove the radiator grille and the front bumper (see Chapter 11).

15 Disconnect the fan electrical connector (see illustration).

16 Remove the mounting bolt for the fan assembly, then remove assembly (see illustration).

17 Installation is the reverse of removal. Be sure to tighten the fan assembly fasteners securely.

---

6   Radiator and coolant expansion tank - removal and installation

✳✳ **WARNING:**

Wait until the engine is completely cool before beginning this procedure.

COOLANT EXPANSION TANK

▸ **Refer to illustrations 6.2a and 6.2b**

1 Partially drain the cooling system (see Chapter 1).

2 Remove the reservoir mounting screws and detach the hoses (see illustrations). Lift the reservoir from the engine compartment.

3 Be careful not to spill coolant on painted surfaces. Clean spills immediately with soapy water and rinse the area thoroughly. See **Warning** in Section 1.

4 After washing the reservoir inside and out (use a household bottle

6.2a Expansion tank mounting fasteners

6.2b Expansion tank hose connections

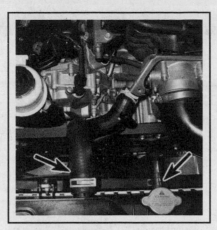

6.11a Upper radiator hose and filler neck hose fittings

6.11b Lower radiator hose fitting

brush to clean inside), inspect the reservoir for cracks or other damage and replace it as necessary.

❊❊ WARNING:

If you use a brush to clean the coolant reservoir, never again use it for cleaning drinking glasses or bottles.

5 Installation is the reverse of removal.

RADIATOR

▶ **Refer to illustrations 6.11a, 6.11b and 6.13**

6 Remove the engine cover (see illustration 4.2).

7 Remove the air intake duct and the air filter housing (see Chapter 4).

8 Raise the front of the vehicle and support it securely on jackstands. Set the parking brake and block the rear wheels.

➡**Note: On Armada models equipped with a rear auto-leveling suspension, turn the ignition key to the OFF position before raising the vehicle.**

9 Disconnect the automatic transmission cooler hoses (see illustration 5.3). Use a drain pan to catch spilled fluid and plug the hoses and fittings.

10 Drain the cooling system (see Chapter 1). See **Warning** in Section 1. If the coolant is relatively new or in good condition, save it and reuse it.

11 Squeeze the hose clamps and move them away from the fittings (see illustrations), then detach the radiator hoses from the radiator. If they're stuck, grasp each hose near the end with a pair of slip joint pliers and twist it to break the seal, then pull it off - be careful not to damage the radiator fittings! If the hoses are old or deteriorated, cut them off and install new ones. Also, disconnect the small hose to the coolant reservoir at the radiator filler neck.

12 Refer to Section 5 and remove both radiator shrouds.

13 Remove the mounting bolts at the top of the radiator, then remove the two small bolts that secure the air conditioning condenser to the radiator (see illustration).

14 Detach the power steering fluid cooler from the radiator and move it aside.

15 Carefully lift the condenser up and slightly forward to separate it from the radiator; do not put stress on the line fittings at the condenser. Lift the radiator out. Once the radiator is removed, support the condenser to prevent strain on the refrigerant line fittings. Take care not to spill coolant on the vehicle.

➡**Note: The fins on the radiator and condenser can easily become damaged. Be careful during radiator removal.**

16 Inspect the radiator for leaks and damage. If it needs repair, have a radiator shop or dealer service department perform the work, as special tools and techniques are required.

17 Bugs and dirt can be removed from the radiator by spraying it with a garden hose nozzle from the back side. The radiator should be flushed out with a garden hose before reinstallation.

18 Check the radiator mounts for deterioration and replace if necessary.

19 Installation is the reverse of the removal procedure. Guide the radiator into the lower mounts until they seat properly.

20 Refill and bleed the cooling system (see Chapter 1).

21 Start the engine and allow it to reach normal operating temperature while checking for leaks. Let the engine cool completely, then recheck and adjust the coolant level.

22 Check and adjust the automatic transmission fluid level as needed (see Chapter 1).

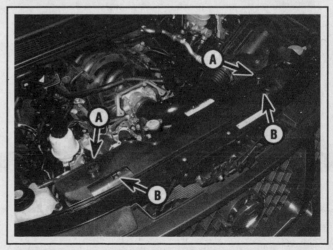

6.13 Mounting fasteners for the radiator (A) and condenser (B)

7 Water pump - replacement

▶ Refer to illustration 7.4

✳✳ WARNING:

Wait until the engine is completely cool before beginning this procedure.

1 Drain the cooling system (see Chapter 1). See **Warning** in Section 1. If the coolant is relatively new or in good condition, save it and reuse it.
2 Remove the engine cover (see illustration 4.2).
3 Remove the air intake duct between the throttle body and the air filter housing (see Chapter 4).
4 Loosen, but do not remove, the mounting fasteners on the water pump pulley (see illustration).

2010 ARMADA MODELS

5 Remove the belt-driven engine cooling fan (see Section 5).
6 Remove the lower radiator hose.

ALL MODELS

▶ Refer to illustration 7.9

7 Remove the drivebelt (see Chapter 1).
8 Remove the water pump pulley mounting fasteners, then remove the pulley (see illustration 7.4).
9 Remove the water pump mounting bolts, then detach the water pump from the engine (see illustration). Check the impeller on the backside for evidence of corrosion or missing fins.
10 Compare the new pump to the old one to make sure they're identical.
11 Remove all traces of the old gasket from the engine as necessary.
12 Carefully attach the pump to the engine and thread the bolts into the holes finger tight.
13 Tighten the bolts, a little at a time, to the torque listed in this Chapter's Specifications. Don't overtighten the bolts or the pump may be distorted.
14 Reinstall all parts removed for access to the pump.
15 Refill and bleed the cooling system (see Chapter 1). Run the engine and check for leaks and proper operation.

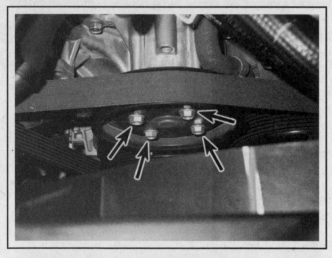

7.4 Water pump pulley mounting fasteners

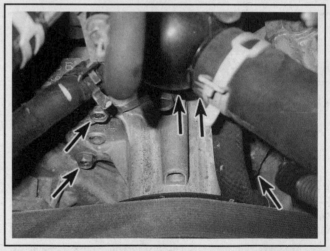

7.9 Water pump mounting bolts (some bolts not visible in this photo)

8 Coolant temperature gauge sending unit

All models covered in this manual utilize a variety of electronic sensors and an onboard computer to monitor various engine parameters, engine temperature being one of them. The Powertrain Control Module (PCM) controls the temperature gauge on the instrument cluster. An individual sending unit for the temperature gauge is not necessary with the use of this technology. See Chapter 6 for information on the Engine Coolant Temperature (ECT) sensor.

11.6a Location of the water valve

11.6b The heater hoses at the firewall

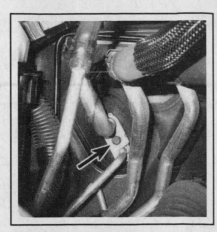

11.7 The refrigerant lines at the firewall

11.11a The driver's side and center cowl support bar fasteners

11.11b The passenger's side and center cowl support bar fasteners

11.11c Fuse box fasteners (A) and the cowl support fasteners on the passenger's side (B)

6 Working in the engine compartment, move the water valve for clearance (see illustration), then disconnect the heater hoses at the firewall (see illustration).

➡**Note: If the heater hoses are stuck to the tubes, place a small blunt tool in between the tubes and hoses. Work the tool around the tubes completely to break the bond. If the hoses are old and due for replacement, simply cut them off.**

7 Disconnect the air conditioning refrigerant lines from the expansion valve at the firewall (see illustration).

❊❊ **WARNING:**

Always wear eye protection when disconnecting air conditioning system fittings.

8 Remove the steering column (see Chapter 10).

9 Remove the instrument panel and floor console, as equipped (see Chapter 11).

10 Disconnect the instrument panel wiring harness at each end of the cowl support bar and from the fuse box.

11 Remove the floor heating ducts. Remove the cowl support bar

mounting bolts and carefully pull the bar away from the firewall with the heating/air conditioning unit attached (see illustrations).

➡**Note: Take your time and don't use excessive force - there may be fasteners you haven't found and removed yet.**

12 Remove the heater core pipe bracket from the top of the unit, then remove the screws and the heater core cover. Slide the heater core and its pipes upward out of the heating/air conditioning unit.

13 Reassemble the heating/air conditioning unit and check the operation of the control flaps. If any parts bind, correct the problem before installation.

14 Reinstall the remaining parts in the reverse order of removal. When attaching the steering column to the support bracket, tighten the fasteners to the torque listed in the Chapter 10 Specifications.

REAR

♦ **Refer to illustration 11.16**

15 Remove the lower right-rear interior trim panel in the luggage compartment (see Section 9, Step 6).

---

9   Blower motor and blower motor resistor - removal and installation

❊❊ **WARNING:**

The models covered by this manual are equipped with Supplemental Restraint Systems (SRS), more commonly known as airbags. Always disable the airbag system before working in the vicinity of any airbag system components to avoid the possibility of accidental deployment of the airbag(s), which could cause personal injury (see Chapter 12).

1 Disconnect the cable from the negative battery terminal (see Chapter 5).

BLOWER MOTOR

Front

♦ **Refer to illustration 9.3**

2 Remove the glove compartment and lower dash trim (see Chapter 11).

3 Disconnect the electrical connector from the blower motor (see illustration).

4 Detach the harness from the blower motor housing and remove the blower motor mounting screws. Pull the blower motor carefully out of the housing.

5 If you are replacing the motor, detach the fan and transfer it to the new motor.

Rear

6 Remove the upper and lower right-rear interior trim panels in the luggage compartment (see Chapter 11).

2008 and later models

♦ **Refer to illustrations 9.7a, 9.7b, 9.7c and 9.8**

❊❊ **WARNING:**

The air conditioning system is under high pressure. Do not loosen any hose fittings or remove any components until after the system has been discharged. Air conditioning refrigerant must be properly discharged into an EPA-approved recovery/recycling unit at a dealer service department or an automotive air conditioning repair facility. Always wear eye protection when disconnecting air conditioning system fittings.

❊❊ **WARNING:**

Wait until the engine is completely cool before beginning this procedure.

7 Remove the rear heating/air conditioning unit:

a) Have the air conditioning system discharged at a dealer service department or service station.

b) Drain the cooling system (see Chapter 1). See **Warning** in Section 1. If the coolant is relatively new or in good condition, save it and reuse it.

c) Remove the upper and lower right-rear interior trim panels in the luggage compartment (see Chapter 11).

d) Disconnect the heater hoses from the heater core (see illustration).

➡**Note: If the heater hoses are stuck to the tubes, place a small blunt tool in between the tubes and the hoses. Work the tool around the tubes completely to break the bond. If the hoses are old and due for replacement, simply cut them off.**

e) Disconnect the air conditioning refrigerant lines from the expansion valve.

❊❊ **WARNING:**

Always wear eye protection when disconnecting air conditioning system fittings.

f) Disconnect all of the electrical connectors from the heating/air conditioning unit (see illustration).

g) Detach the ducts and the drain hose for the evaporator.

h) Remove the mounting fasteners, then lift the unit out (see illustration).

i) Installation is the reverse of removal.

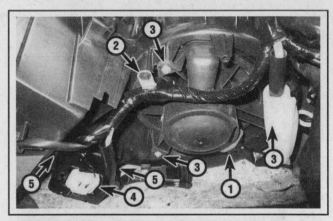

9.3 Front blower motor and resistor mounting details

1   Blower motor electrical connector
2   Harness fastener at blower motor housing
3   Blower motor mounting screws (one fastener not visible - vicinity given)
4   Blower motor resistor electrical connector
5   Blower motor resistor mounting fasteners (vicinity given)

9.7a Rear heating/air conditioning unit mounting details (1 of 2)

1   Refrigerant line fitting retaining bolt at expansion valve
2   Heater core hoses
3   Condenser drain hose

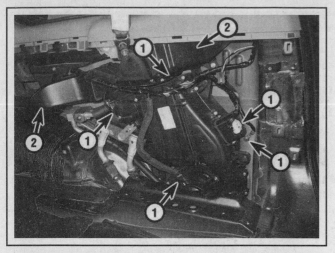

9.7c Rear heating/air conditioning unit mounting fasteners (one fastener hidden - vicinity given)

9.7b Rear heating/air conditioning unit mounting details (2 of 2)

1 Electrical connectors (one hidden on back - vicinity given)
2 Air ducts

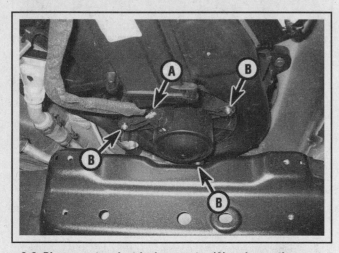

9.8 Blower motor electrical connector (A) and mounting screws (B) (2008 model shown, other models similar)

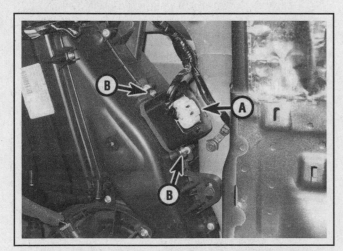

9.18 Rear blower motor resistor electrical connector (A) and mounting screws (B)

8 Remove the blower motor mounting screws (see illustration), then pull the blower motor out of the housing.

9 If you are replacing the motor, detach the fan and transfer it to the new motor.

2007 and earlier models

10 Disconnect the electrical connector from the blower motor (see illustration 9.8).

11 Remove the blower motor mounting screws, then pull the blower motor carefully out of the housing.

12 If you are replacing the motor, detach the fan and transfer it to the new motor.

Front and rear

13 Installation is the reverse of removal. Run the blower and check for proper operation.

BLOWER MOTOR RESISTOR

➡Note: The manufacturer refers to this component as a "variable blower motor control" for some model years.

Front

14 Remove the glove compartment and lower dash trim (see Chapter 11).

15 Disconnect the electrical connector for the blower motor resistor (see illustration 9.3).

16 Remove the blower motor resistor mounting screws, then carefully pull the resistor out of the housing.

Rear

♦ Refer to illustration 9.18

17 Remove the lower right-rear interior trim panel in the luggage compartment (see Step 6).

18 Disconnect the electrical connector for the blower motor resistor (see illustration).

19 Remove the blower motor resistor mounting screws, then carefully pull the resistor out of the housing (see illustration 9.18).

Front and rear

20 Installation is the reverse of removal. Run the blower and check for proper operation.

10 Heater and air conditioning control assembly - removal and installation

✳ **WARNING:**

The models covered by this manual are equipped with Supplemental Restraint Systems (SRS), more commonly known as airbags. Always disable the airbag system before working in the vicinity of any airbag system components to avoid the possibility of accidental deployment of the airbag(s), which could cause personal injury (see Chapter 12).

1 Disconnect the cable from the negative battery terminal (see Chapter 5).

FRONT

2 Refer to Chapter 11 for removal of the center instrument panel bezel.

2009 and later models

3 Remove the display unit from the center instrument panel bezel.

4 Remove the mounting fasteners for the control assembly, then detach it from the back of the display unit.

2008 and earlier models

5 Pull off the knobs from the front of the assembly, then disconnect the electrical connectors on the back.

6 Remove the control assembly mounting screws, then remove the assembly.

All models

7 Installation is the reverse of the removal procedure.

REAR

2009 and later models

8 Pry the trim from the overhead console that contains the control assembly.

9 Remove the control assembly mounting screws from the rear, then remove the assembly.

2008 and earlier models

10 Remove the rear overhead console.

11 Remove the control assembly mounting screws from the rear, then remove the assembly.

All models

12 Installation is the reverse of the removal procedure.

11 Heater core - replacement

✳ **WARNING 1:**

The models covered by this manual are equipped with a Supplemental Restraint System (SRS), more commonly known as airbags. Always disarm the airbag system before working in the vicinity of any airbag system component to avoid the possibility of accidental deployment of the airbag, which could cause personal injury (see Chapter 12). Do not use a memory saving device to preserve the PCM's memory when working on or near airbag system components.

✳ **WARNING 2:**

The air conditioning system is under high pressure. Do not loosen any hose fittings or remove any components until after the system has been discharged. Air conditioning refrigerant must be properly discharged into an EPA-approved recovery/recycling unit at a dealer service department or an automotive air conditioning repair facility. Always wear eye protection when disconnecting air conditioning system fittings.

✳ **WARNING 3:**

Wait until the engine is completely cool before beginning this procedure.

➡Note: Replacing a front heater core is difficult for the home mechanic. It involves removal of the entire dashboard, floor console and many wiring connectors. If you attempt this procedure at home, keep track of the assemblies by taking notes and keeping screws and other hardware in small, marked plastic bags for reassembly.

1 Have the air conditioning system discharged at a dealer service department or service station.

2 Drain the cooling system (see Chapter 1). See **Warning** in Section 1. If the coolant is relatively new or in good condition, save it and reuse it.

FRONT

♦ Refer to illustrations 11.6a, 11.6b, 11.7, 11.11a, 11.11b, 11.11c, 11.11d and 11.11e

3 Move the front seats to the rearmost position.

4 Turn the ignition key to the ON position, then set the heater control to HOT. Remove the ignition key. Drain the cooling system (see Chapter 1). If the coolant is relatively new, or in good condition, save it and re-use it.

5 Disconnect the cable from the negative battery terminal (see Chapter 5).

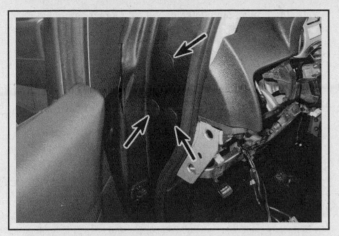

11.11d Cowl support fastener covers on the driver's side

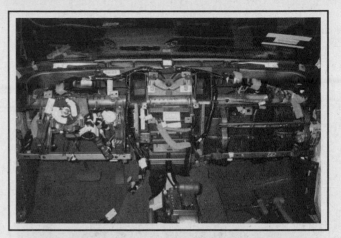

11.11e Cowl support beam with the instrument panel removed (typical)

16 Disconnect the heater hoses from the heater core (see illustration).

➡**Note: If the heater hoses are stuck to the tubes, place a small blunt tool in between the tubes and hoses. Work the tool around the tubes completely to break the bond. If the hoses are old and due for replacement, simply cut them off.**

17 Remove the small bracket over the heater core (see illustration 11.16), then pull heater core directly out of the housing.

18 Installation is the reverse of the removal procedure.

FRONT AND REAR

19 Refill the cooling system (see Chapter 1), reconnect the battery and run the engine. Check for leaks and proper operation of the system. Have the air conditioning system evacuated, recharged and leak tested by the shop that discharged it.

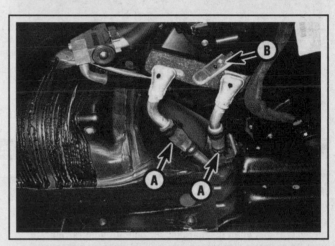

11.16 Heater core hoses (A) and retaining bracket (B)

12 Air conditioning compressor - removal and installation

✳✳ **WARNING:**

The air conditioning system is under high pressure. Do not loosen any hose fittings or remove any components until after the system has been discharged. Air conditioning refrigerant must be properly discharged into an EPA-approved recovery/recycling unit at a dealer service department or an automotive air conditioning repair facility. Always wear eye protection when disconnecting air conditioning system fittings.

➡**Note: Whenever the compressor is replaced due to an internal failure, the receiver-drier should also be replaced. This component is integrated with the condenser (see Section 14).**

REMOVAL

▶ **Refer to illustrations 12.4 and 12.7**

1 Have the air conditioning system refrigerant discharged by an air conditioning technician (see **Warning** above).

2 Remove the air intake duct and the air filter housing (see Chapter 4).

3 Remove the drivebelt (see Chapter 1).

4 Disconnect the compressor clutch electrical connector (see illustration).

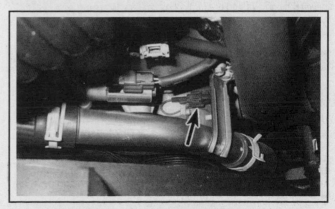

12.4 Compressor clutch electrical connector

5 Loosen the left front wheel lug nuts. Raise the front of the vehicle and support it securely on jackstands, then remove the left front wheel.

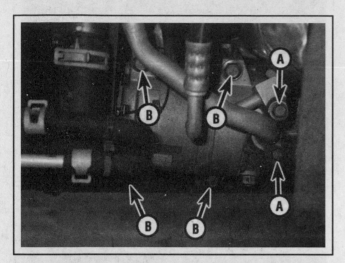

12.7 Air conditioning compressor mounting details

A   *Refrigerant line fitting bolts*
B   *Compressor mounting fasteners*

➡**Note: On Armada models equipped with a rear auto-leveling suspension, turn the ignition key to the OFF position before raising the vehicle.**

6 Remove the engine splash shield beneath the front of the vehicle. Also remove the inner fender splash shield (see Chapter 11).
7 Disconnect the refrigerant lines from the compressor (see illustration). Plug all open fittings to prevent entry of dirt and moisture.
8 Remove the compressor mounting fasteners, then remove the compressor from the vehicle.

INSTALLATION

9 If a new compressor is being installed, follow the directions with the compressor regarding the draining of excess oil prior to installation. Any refrigerant oil added must be compatible with R-134a refrigerant.
10 The clutch may have to be transferred from the original compressor to the new one.
11 Installation is the reverse of removal. Replace the O-rings with the appropriate type and lubricate them with refrigerant oil. Tighten the mounting and line fitting fasteners to the torque values listed in this Chapter's Specifications.
12 Have the system evacuated, recharged and leak-tested by the shop that discharged it.

13 Air conditioning receiver-drier - removal and installation

✳✳ WARNING:

The air conditioning system is under high pressure. Do not loosen any hose fittings or remove any components until after the system has been discharged. Air conditioning refrigerant must be properly discharged into an EPA-approved recovery/recycling unit at a dealer service department or an automotive air conditioning repair facility. Always wear eye protection when disconnecting air conditioning system fittings.

➡**Note: The receiver-drier is integrated with the condenser and replaced as an assembly according to the manufacturer. It is possible, however, that the desiccant and filter (the main components) will become available as aftermarket (non-OEM) replacement parts; but this could not be confirmed at the time of this manual's writing.**

1 Have the air conditioning system refrigerant discharged and recycled by an air conditioning technician (see **Warning** above).

2 Remove the condenser (see Section 14).
3 Remove the cap from the condenser.
4 Remove the filter from the condenser.
5 Remove the receiver-drier desiccant.
6 Installation is the reverse of removal. Be sure to install new O-rings (of the correct type) onto the receiver-drier cap. Apply a thin layer of refrigerant oil to the desiccant before installing it. Add 5 ml of the appropriate oil to the condenser.

✳✳ CAUTION:

Be sure to read the label on the container before adding any oil to the system to make sure it is compatible with R-134a type systems.

7 Have the system evacuated, recharged and leak-tested by the shop that discharged it.

14 Air conditioning condenser - removal and installation

✳✳ WARNING:

The air conditioning system is under high pressure. Do not loosen any hose fittings or remove any components until after the system has been discharged. Air conditioning refrigerant must be properly discharged into an EPA-approved recovery/recycling unit at a dealer service department or an automotive air conditioning repair facility. Always wear eye protection when disconnecting air conditioning system fittings.

➡**Note: The condenser and the receiver-drier (on the side) are manufactured as an assembly and cannot be separated**

REMOVAL

◗ **Refer to illustrations 14.3a, 14.3b and 14.4**

1 Have the refrigerant discharged and recycled by an air conditioning technician (see **Warning** above).

14.3a Right-side line fitting connection at the condenser

14.3b Left-side line fitting connection at the condenser

2   Remove the radiator (see Section 6).

3   Disconnect the refrigerant lines from the condenser and discard the O-ring seals (see illustrations). Cap the fittings on the condenser and lines to prevent entry of dirt or moisture.

4   Disconnect the refrigerant pressure sensor electrical connector (see illustration).

5   Carefully tilt the condenser back and remove it from the vehicle.

INSTALLATION

6   If the original condenser will be reinstalled, store it in a manner that will help prevent any oil spillage.

7   If a new condenser will be installed, pour 2.5 oz (75 ml) of the appropriate refrigerant oil into it prior to installation.

8   Install new R-134a compatible O-ring seals onto the refrigerant line fittings. Lubricate the O-rings with the appropriate refrigerant oil.

9   Reinstall the components in the reverse order of removal. Tighten the line fitting fasteners to the torque values listed in this Chapter's Specifications.

10 Have the system evacuated, recharged and leak-tested by the shop that discharged it.

14.4 Refrigerant pressure sensor electrical connector

Specifications

General

Coolant capacity	See Chapter 1
Drivebelt tension	See Chapter 1
Cooling system pressure cap pressure rating	14 to 18 psi
Refrigerant	R-134a
Refrigerant capacity	Refer to HVAC label under the hood

Torque specifications	Ft-lbs (unless otherwise indicated)	Nm

➡ **Note: One foot-pound (ft-lb) of torque is equivalent to 12 inch-pounds (in-lbs) of torque. Torque values below approximately 15 ft-lbs are expressed in inch-pounds, since most foot-pound torque wrenches are not accurate at these smaller values.**

Thermostat housing cover bolts	15 (180 in-lbs)	20
Water pump retaining bolts	18	24
Compressor line fitting bolts	7 (82 in-lbs)	9
Condenser line fitting bolts	7 (82 in-lbs)	9

Section

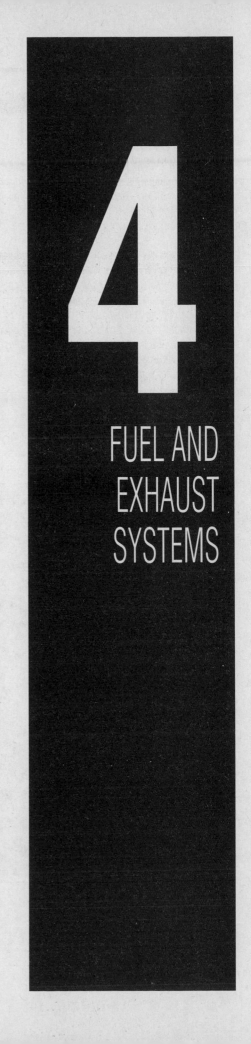

4

FUEL AND EXHAUST SYSTEMS

1 General information

FUEL SYSTEM WARNINGS

Gasoline is extremely flammable and repairing fuel system components can be dangerous. Consider your automotive repair knowledge and experience before attempting repairs which may be better suited for a professional mechanic.

- *Don't smoke or allow open flames or bare light bulbs near the work area*
- *Don't work in a garage with a gas-type appliance (water heater, clothes dryer)*
- *Use fuel-resistant gloves. If any fuel spills on your skin, wash it off immediately with soap and water*
- *Clean up spills immediately*
- *Do not store fuel-soaked rags where they could ignite*
- *Prior to disconnecting any fuel line, you must relieve the fuel pressure (see Section 3)*
- *Wear safety glasses*
- *Have a proper fire extinguisher on hand*

FUEL SYSTEM

The fuel system consists of the fuel tank, electric fuel pump/fuel level sending unit (located in the fuel tank), fuel rail and fuel injectors. The fuel injection system is a multi-port system; multi-port fuel injection uses timed impulses to inject the fuel directly into the intake port of each cylinder. The Powertrain Control Module (PCM) controls the injectors. The PCM monitors various engine parameters and delivers the exact amount of fuel required into the intake ports.

Fuel is circulated from the fuel pump to the fuel rail through fuel lines running along the underside of the vehicle. Various sections of the fuel line are either rigid metal or nylon, or flexible fuel hose. The various sections of the fuel hose are connected either by quick-connect fittings or threaded metal fittings.

EXHAUST SYSTEM

The exhaust system consists of the exhaust manifold(s), catalytic converter(s), muffler(s), tailpipe and all connecting pipes, flanges and clamps. The catalytic converters are an emission control device added to the exhaust system to reduce pollutants.

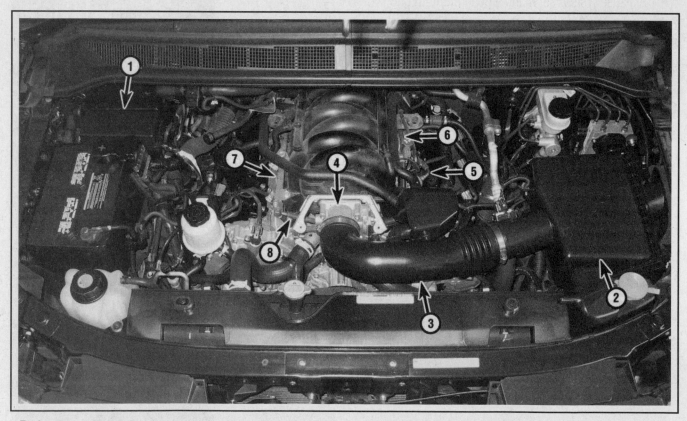

Fuel system components:

1	Engine compartment fuse and relay box	4	Throttle body	6	Left fuel rail and injectors
2	Air filter housing	5	Fuel supply line/fuel rail quick-connect	7	Right fuel rail and injectors
3	Air intake duct		fitting	8	Fuel rail crossover pipe

2 Troubleshooting

FUEL PUMP

▶ **Refer to illustration 2.2**

1 The fuel pump is located inside the fuel tank. Sit inside the vehicle with the windows closed, turn the ignition key to ON (not START) and listen for the sound of the fuel pump as it's briefly activated. You will only hear the sound for a second or two, but that sound tells you that the pump is working. Alternatively, have an assistant listen at the fuel filler cap.

2 If the pump does not come on, check the fuel pump fuse (see illustration). If the fuse is okay, check the wiring back to the fuel pump. If the fuse and wiring are okay, the pump might be defective. Other possibilities include: a faulty fuel pump relay, which is part of the Intelligent Power Distribution Module (which is part of the underhood fuse/relay box); a faulty fuel pump control module (2006 and later models only), which is located under the right side of the instrument panel, to the right of the blower motor; or a faulty Powertrain Control Module (PCM). If the pump runs continuously with the ignition key in the ON position, the Powertrain Control Module (PCM) is probably defective. Have the PCM checked by a professional mechanic.

FUEL INJECTION SYSTEM

▶ **Refer to illustration 2.9**

➡**Note: The following procedure is based on the assumption that the fuel pump is working and the fuel pressure is adequate (see Section 4).**

3 Check all electrical connectors that are related to the system. Check the ground wire connections for tightness.

4 Verify that the battery is fully charged (see Chapter 5).

5 Inspect the air filter element (see Chapter 1).

6 Check all fuses related to the fuel system (see Chapter 12).

7 Check the air induction system between the throttle body and the intake manifold for air leaks. Also inspect the condition of all vacuum hoses connected to the intake manifold and to the throttle body.

8 Remove the air intake duct from the throttle body and look for dirt, carbon, varnish, or other residue in the throttle body, particularly around the throttle plate. If it's dirty, clean it with carb cleaner, a toothbrush and a clean shop towel.

9 With the engine running, place an automotive stethoscope against each injector, one at a time, and listen for a clicking sound that indicates operation (see illustration).

✸✸ WARNING:

Stay clear of the drivebelt and any rotating or hot components.

10 If you can hear the injectors operating, but the engine is misfiring, the electrical circuits are functioning correctly, but the injectors might be dirty or clogged. Try a commercial injector cleaning product (available at auto parts stores). If cleaning the injectors doesn't help, replace the injectors.

11 If an injector is not operating (it makes no sound), disconnect the injector electrical connector and measure the resistance across the injector terminals with an ohmmeter. Compare this measurement to the other injectors. If the resistance of the non-operational injector is quite different from the other injectors, replace it.

12 If the injector is not operating, but the resistance reading is within the range of resistance of the other injectors, the PCM or the circuit between the PCM and the injector might be faulty.

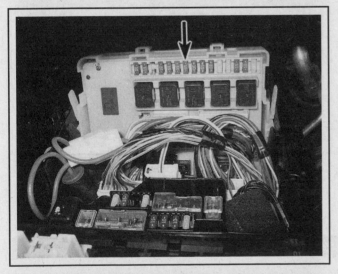

2.2 The fuel pump fuse is located in the engine compartment fuse and relay box

2.9 An automotive stethoscope is used to listen to the fuel injectors in operation

3 Fuel pressure relief procedure

1 Remove the fuel pump fuse from the underhood fuse/relay box (see illustration 2.2).

2 Attempt to start the engine; it should immediately stall. Crank the engine several more times to ensure the fuel system has been completely relieved. Disconnect the cable from the negative terminal of the battery before working on the fuel system.

3 It's a good idea to cover any fuel connection to be disassembled with rags to absorb the residual fuel that may leak out.

4 Fuel pressure - check

♦ **Refer to illustrations 4.1a and 4.1b**

➡ **Note: The following procedure assumes that the fuel pump is receiving voltage and runs.**

1 Disconnect the quick connect fitting at the left fuel rail (see illustration 4.1b), then use a T-fitting adapter to connect the fuel pressure gauge between the fuel line and the fuel rail.

2 Start the engine and allow it to idle. Note the gauge reading as soon as the pressure stabilizes, and compare it with the pressure listed in this Chapter's Specifications.

3 If the fuel pressure is not within specifications, check the following:

   a) *Check for a restriction in the fuel system (kinked fuel line, plugged fuel pump inlet strainer or clogged fuel filter). If no restrictions are found, replace the fuel pump module (see Section 7).*

   b) *If the fuel pressure is higher than specified, replace the fuel pump module (see Section 7).*

4 Turn off the engine. Fuel pressure should not fall more than 8 psi over five minutes. If it does, the problem could be a leaky fuel injector, fuel line leak, or faulty fuel pump module.

5 Disconnect the fuel pressure gauge. Wipe up any spilled gasoline.

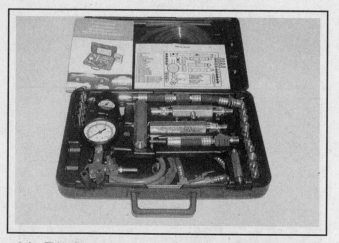

4.1a This aftermarket fuel pressure testing kit contains all the necessary fittings and adapters, along with the fuel pressure gauge, to test most automotive fuel systems

4.1b Tee into the fuel system at this quick-connect fitting between the fuel supply line and the left fuel rail

5 Fuel lines and fittings - general information and disconnection

1 Relieve the fuel pressure before servicing fuel lines or fittings (see Section 3), then disconnect the cable from the negative battery terminal (see Chapter 5) before proceeding.

2 The fuel supply line connects the fuel pump in the fuel tank to the fuel rail on the engine. The Evaporative Emission (EVAP) system lines connect the fuel tank to the EVAP canister and connect the canister to the intake manifold.

3 Whenever you're working under the vehicle, be sure to inspect

all fuel and evaporative emission lines for leaks, kinks, dents and other damage. Always replace a damaged fuel or EVAP line immediately.

4   If you find signs of dirt in the lines during disassembly, disconnect all lines and blow them out with compressed air. Inspect the fuel strainer on the fuel pump pick-up unit for damage and deterioration.

STEEL TUBING

5   It is critical that the fuel lines be replaced with lines of equivalent type and specification.

6   Some steel fuel lines have threaded fittings. When loosening these fittings, hold the stationary fitting with a wrench while turning the tube nut.

PLASTIC TUBING

7   When replacing fuel system plastic tubing, use only original equipment replacement plastic tubing.

❋❋ CAUTION:

When removing or installing plastic fuel line tubing, be careful not to bend or twist it too much, which can damage it. Also, plastic fuel tubing is NOT heat resistant, so keep it away from excessive heat.

FLEXIBLE HOSES

8   When replacing fuel system flexible hoses, use only original equipment replacements.

9   Don't route fuel hoses (or metal lines) within four inches of the exhaust system or within ten inches of the catalytic converter. Make sure that no rubber hoses are installed directly against the vehicle, particularly in places where there is any vibration. If allowed to touch some vibrating part of the vehicle, a hose can easily become chafed and it might start leaking. A good rule of thumb is to maintain a minimum of 1/4-inch clearance around a hose (or metal line) to prevent contact with the vehicle underbody.

---

6   Exhaust system servicing - general information

♦ **Refer to illustration 6.1**

❋❋ WARNING:

Allow exhaust system components to cool before inspection or repair. Also, when working under the vehicle, make sure it is securely supported on jackstands.

1   The exhaust system consists of the exhaust manifolds, catalytic converter, muffler, tailpipe and all connecting pipes, flanges and clamps. The exhaust system is isolated from the vehicle body and from chassis components by a series of rubber hangers (see illustration). Periodically inspect these hangers for cracks or other signs of deterioration, replacing them as necessary.

2   Conduct regular inspections of the exhaust system to keep it safe and quiet. Look for any damaged or bent parts, open seams, holes, loose connections, excessive corrosion or other defects which could allow exhaust fumes to enter the vehicle. Do not repair deteriorated exhaust system components; replace them with new parts.

3   If the exhaust system components are extremely corroded, or rusted together, a cutting torch is the most convenient tool for removal. Consult a properly-equipped repair shop. If a cutting torch is not available, you can use a hacksaw, or if you have compressed air, there are special pneumatic cutting chisels that can also be used. Wear safety goggles to protect your eyes from metal chips and wear work gloves to protect your hands.

4   Here are some simple guidelines to follow when repairing the exhaust system:

a) Work from the back to the front when removing exhaust system components.

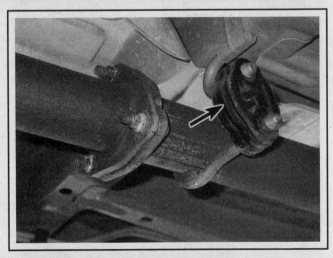

6.1 A typical exhaust system hanger. Inspect regularly and replace at the first sign of damage or deterioration

b) Apply penetrating oil to the exhaust system component fasteners to make them easier to remove.

c) Use new gaskets, hangers and clamps.

d) Apply anti-seize compound to the threads of all exhaust system fasteners during reassembly.

e) Be sure to allow sufficient clearance between newly installed parts and all points on the underbody to avoid overheating the floor pan and possibly damaging the interior carpet and insulation. Pay particularly close attention to the catalytic converter and heat shield.

Disconnecting Fuel Line Fittings

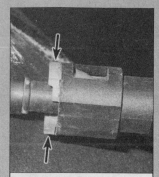

Two-tab type fitting; depress both tabs with your fingers, then pull the fuel line and the fitting apart

On this type of fitting, depress the two buttons on opposite sides of the fitting, then pull it off the fuel line

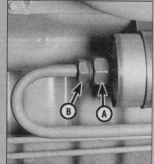

Threaded fuel line fitting; hold the stationary portion of the line or component (A) while loosening the tube nut (B) with a flare-nut wrench

Plastic collar-type fitting; rotate the outer part of the fitting

Metal collar quick-connect fitting; pull the end of the retainer off the fuel line, and disengage the other end from the female side of the fitting . . .

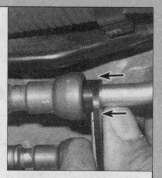

. . . insert a fuel line separator tool into the female side of the fitting, push it into the fitting until it releases the locking tabs inside the fitting, and pull the two halves of the fitting apart

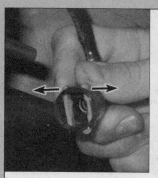

Hairpin-type clip; spread the two legs of the clip apart . . .

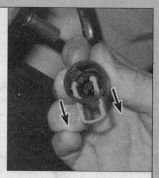

. . . pull the clip out and detach the coupling from the component (fitting detached for clarity)

Spring-lock coupling; remove the safety cover . . .

. . . install a coupling release tool and close the clamshell halves of the tool around the coupling . . .

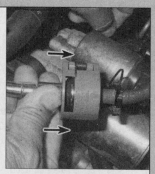

. . . push the tool into the fitting, then pull the two lines apart

7   Fuel pump/fuel level sensor module - removal and installation

♦ Refer to illustrations 7.3, 7.5, 7.6 and 7.9

✴✴ WARNING:

Gasoline is extremely flammable, so take extra precautions when you work on any part of the fuel system. See the Warning in Section 1.

1   Disconnect the cable from the negative battery terminal (see Chapter 5).

2   Relieve the fuel system pressure (see Section 3).

3   Armada models: To access the fuel pump inspection hole cover, disconnect or remove the following components (see Chapter 11): Remove the second-row left seat, the second-row center seat or center console and base, then remove the third-row rear seats. Disconnect the second and third-row seatbelts from the floor. Remove the left B-pillar trim, the left rear trim panel (behind the second-row left seat) and the left rear door sill plate. Peel back the carpeting to access the inspection hole cover. To remove the inspection hole cover, rotate the retainers clockwise 1/4-turn (see illustration), then pull off the cover.

4   Titan models: There is no fuel pump inspection hole on Titan models; remove the fuel tank (see Section 8).

5   Disconnect the fuel pump electrical connector and lines (see illustration).

6   Mark the position of the fuel pump module in relation to the fuel tank, then unscrew the pump module lock ring. On Armada models, use large water pump pliers to loosen the lock ring (see illustration). On Titan models, a special tool available at most auto parts stores can be used to loosen the lock ring, but a large pair of pliers will also work.

7   Carefully pull the fuel pump module out of the tank. Angle the module as necessary to protect the fuel level sensor float arm. On some models, you might have to detach the fuel level sensor from the pump module before you can remove the pump module from the fuel tank (see Step 9).

8   Remove and inspect the fuel pump/fuel level sensor O-ring. If the O-ring is damaged, replace it.

9   To swap a fuel level sensor to another fuel pump module, trace the sensor harness to its electrical connector and disconnect it. To disengage the sensor from the pump module, depress the locks on each side of the sensor with needle-nose pliers (see illustration) and slide the sensor up. When installing the sensor module, make sure that the locks snap into place.

10 Installation is the reverse of removal.

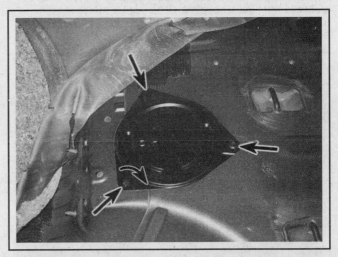

7.3 Fuel pump/fuel level sensor inspection hole cover (Armada models). Turn the retainers clockwise 1/4-turn to release them

7.5 Fuel pump/fuel level sensor module:

1   *Fuel pump/fuel level sensor electrical connector*
2   *Fuel supply line quick-connect fitting*
3   *EVAP line quick-connect fitting*

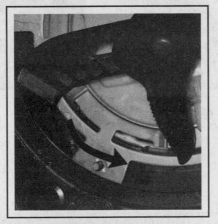

7.6 Use large water pump pliers to loosen the fuel pump/fuel level sensor module lock ring (Armada models)

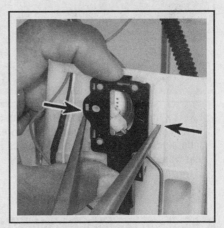

7.9 The release tabs for the fuel level sensor are located on each side of the sensor module

8 Fuel tank - removal and installation

▶ Refer to illustrations 8.8 and 8.9

✳✳ WARNING 1:

Gasoline is extremely flammable, so take extra precautions when you work on any part of the fuel system. See the Warning in Section 1.

✳✳ WARNING 2:

The following procedure is much easier to perform if the fuel tank is empty. The tank has no drain plug, so the fuel must be siphoned from the tank with a siphoning kit, which is available at most auto parts stores. NEVER try to start the siphoning action with your mouth!

1   Remove the fuel tank filler cap to relieve fuel tank pressure.
2   Relieve the fuel system pressure (see Section 3).
3   Disconnect the cable from the negative battery terminal (see Chapter 5).
4   If there is still a lot of fuel in the tank, obtain a siphon kit at an auto parts store and siphon out the remaining fuel.

✳✳ WARNING:

Always siphon fuel into an approved gasoline container.

5   Raise the rear of the vehicle and support it securely on jackstands. Remove the fuel tank shield, if equipped.
6   On Armada models, remove the access cover, then disconnect the electrical connector and the lines from the fuel pump/fuel level sensor module (see Section 7).
7   On Titan models, there is no access cover. Working in the gap between the top of the fuel tank and the underside of the vehicle, remove the fasteners that secure the fuel pump/fuel line protector and remove the protector. Then disconnect the electrical connector and the fuel line from the fuel pump module.
8   Disconnect the fuel tank filler neck hose and the EVAP breather line quick-connect fitting (see illustration).
9   Support the fuel tank securely. Remove the fuel tank retaining strap fasteners (see illustration), remove the straps and carefully lower the fuel tank.
10 Installation is the reverse of removal. Be sure to tighten the fuel tank strap bolts securely.

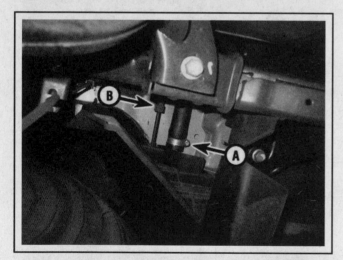

8.8 The fuel tank filler neck hose clamp (A) and the EVAP breather line quick-connect fitting (B) are located on the left underside of the vehicle, just ahead and inboard of the left rear wheel well

8.9 Fuel tank strap fastener locations

9 Air filter housing - removal and installation

AIR INTAKE DUCT

▶ Refer to illustration 9.1

1   Disconnect the PCV fresh air inlet hoses from the air intake duct resonator (see illustration).
2   Loosen the clamps that secure the air intake duct to the air filter housing and the throttle body, then lift off the intake duct.

3   Installation is the reverse of removal.

AIR FILTER HOUSING

▶ Refer to illustration 9.7

4   Loosen the hose clamp and disconnect the air intake duct from the air filter housing (see illustration 9.1).

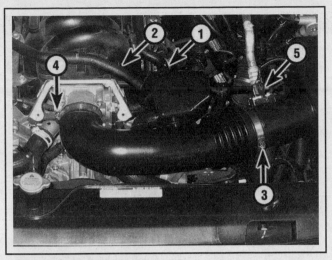

9.1 Air intake duct details

1 PCV fresh air hose-to-left valve cover
2 PCV fresh air hose-to-right valve cover
3 Hose clamp at air filter housing
4 Hose clamp at throttle body
5 Mass Air Flow (MAF) sensor electrical connector

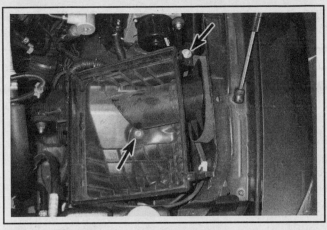

9.7 Air filter housing fastener locations

5   Disconnect the electrical connector from the MAF sensor (see illustration 9.1).
6   Remove the air filter housing cover and the filter element (see Chapter 1).
7   Remove the air filter housing mounting fasteners (see illustration) and lift out the housing.
8   Installation is the reverse of removal.

10 Throttle body - removal and installation

♦ **Refer to illustration 10.3**

❈❈ **WARNING:**

Wait until the engine is completely cool before beginning this procedure.

❈❈ **CAUTION:**

After removing and installing the throttle body, be sure to do the throttle valve closed position relearn procedure and, if you replace the throttle body, the idle-learn procedure as well, both of which are included below, to ensure that the idle is stable and that no Diagnostic Trouble Codes (DTCs) are set by the PCM.

1   Disconnect the cable from the negative terminal of the battery (see Chapter 5).
2   Remove the air intake duct (see Section 9).
3   Disconnect the electrical connector from the throttle body (see illustration).
4   Disconnect the two coolant hoses from the throttle body. Plug the hoses to prevent coolant from leaking onto the engine.
5   Remove the throttle body mounting fasteners and carefully lift off the throttle body.
6   Remove and discard the gasket. Always use a new gasket
7   Cover the intake manifold opening with a clean shop towel.
8   Installation is the reverse of removal. Be sure to use a new gasket

and tighten the throttle body fasteners to the torque listed in this Chapter's Specifications. Check the coolant level, adding some if necessary (see Chapter 1).
9   When you're done, be sure to perform the throttle valve closed position relearn and, if you replaced the throttle body, the idle air volume relearn procedure as well, both of which are described below.

10.3 Throttle body details

1   Electrical connector
2   Coolant hoses
3   Throttle body mounting fasteners

THROTTLE VALVE CLOSED POSITION RELEARN PROCEDURE

➡Note: This procedure must be performed whenever the throttle body electrical connector is disconnected.

10 Make sure that the accelerator pedal is fully released, then turn the ignition switch to ON.

11 Turn the ignition switch to OFF and wait at least 10 seconds.

12 During this 10-second phase, verify that the throttle valve moves by confirming the audible sound of the solenoid motor that opens and closes the throttle valve. The solenoid motor is inside the throttle body housing, so place your ear close enough to the throttle body to listen for the sound of the solenoid motor operating.

IDLE AIR VOLUME RELEARN PROCEDURE

➡Note: This procedure must be performed whenever the throttle body is replaced.

13 Before performing the idle air volume relearn procedure, make sure that all of the following conditions are met:

a) *Battery voltage must be more than 12.9 volts at idle*
b) *Engine coolant temperature must be 158 to 212-degrees F*
c) *The Transmission Range (TR) switch or Park Neutral Position (PNP) switch must be functioning*
d) *The air conditioning system, headlights and rear window defogger must be turned off*
e) *The front wheels must be in the straight-ahead position*
f) *The vehicle must be stationary*
g) *The transmission must be warmed up (drive the vehicle for 10 minutes)*

14 Perform the accelerator pedal release position relearn procedure (see Section 4 in Chapter 6).

15 Perform the throttle valve closed position relearn procedure (see Steps 10 through 12).

16 Start the engine and warm it up to normal operating temperature.

17 Verify that all conditions listed in Step 13 are present.

18 Turn the ignition switch to OFF and wait at least 10 seconds.

19 Verify that the accelerator pedal is fully released, then turn the ignition switch to ON and wait three seconds.

20 Quickly repeat the following procedure five times within five seconds:

a) *Fully depress the accelerator pedal*
b) *Fully release the accelerator pedal*

21 After depressing and releasing the accelerator pedal five times in five seconds, wait seven seconds, then fully depress the accelerator pedal and keep it down for about 20 seconds, until the CHECK ENGINE light stops blinking (but is still illuminated).

22 Fully release the accelerator pedal within three seconds after the CHECK ENGINE light changes from blinking to constantly illuminated.

23 Start the engine and allow it to idle for 20 seconds.

24 Rev up the engine two or three times and verify that the idle speed and ignition timing are within specifications (600 to 700 rpm and 10 to 20-degrees Before Top Dead Center [BTDC], in PARK or NEUTRAL).

25 If the idle air volume relearn procedure is unsuccessful, verify that none of the following three issues is a problem:

a) *Verify that the throttle valve is fully closed*
b) *Check PCV valve operation (see Chapter 6)*
c) *Verify that there is no air leak downstream from the throttle valve*

If none of these three issues is a problem, you have probably incorrectly installed some component. Check your work and correct any assembly mistake.

26 If the engine stalls or has an incorrect idle, correct the problem and perform the idle air volume relearn procedure again.

---

11 Fuel rail and injectors - removal and installation

REMOVAL

▶ **Refer to illustrations 11.8 and 11.11**

❋❋ **WARNING:**

Gasoline is extremely flammable, so take extra precautions when you work on any part of the fuel system. See the Warning in Section 1.

1 Relieve the fuel system pressure (see Section 3).

2 Disconnect the cable from the negative terminal of the battery (see Chapter 5).

3 Remove the engine cover (see Chapter 2A).

4 Remove the air intake duct (see Section 9).

5 Disconnect the fuel supply line from the fuel rail (see illustration 4.1b).

6 Disconnect all electrical connectors and hoses that are in the way.

7 Disconnect the electrical connector from each fuel injector. If you're removing the right fuel rail, you'll also have to detach the injector harness from two brackets on the fuel rail, then set the harness aside.

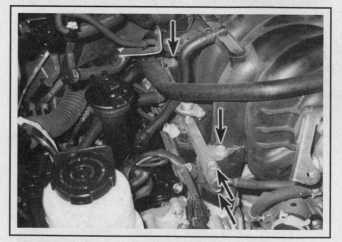

11.8 Right-side crossover hose mounting flange bolts and the right fuel rail mounting bolts (left-side similar)

8 Remove the fasteners (see illustration) that secure the fuel rail crossover hose flanges to the left and right fuel rails and remove the fuel rail crossover hose.

11.11 The injectors are secured to the fuel rails by removable clips that must be discarded

11.14 When installing new retainer clips on each injector, the lug on the injector body must be properly aligned with the upper notch in the clip

9   Remove and discard the old fuel rail crossover hose O-rings.

10 Remove the fuel rail mounting fasteners, then remove each fuel rail and its injectors as a single assembly.

11 Using needle-nose pliers pull off each fuel injector retaining clip (see illustration) and remove each injector from its bore in the fuel rail. Discard the old injector clips.

12 Remove and discard the old upper and lower O-rings from each injector

→**Note: Even if you only removed the fuel rail assembly to replace a single injector or a leaking O-ring, it's a good idea to remove all of the injectors from the fuel rails and replace all of the O-rings at the same time.**

INSTALLATION

▶ **Refer to illustrations 11.14 and 11.15**

13 Coat the new upper and lower O-rings with clean engine oil and slide them into place on the fuel injectors.

14 Install a new retaining clip on each injector. Make sure the lug on the injector is properly aligned with the clip (see illustration), then push the clip onto the injector until it snaps into place.

15 Coat each upper O-ring with clean engine oil, then align the lower notch in the clip with the tang on the fuel rail (see illustration), insert the injector into its bore in the fuel rail and push it into the bore until the clip snaps into place.

16 Coat the lower injector O-rings with clean engine oil, then install the fuel rail assemblies on the intake manifold. Tighten the fuel rail mounting fasteners securely. Using new O-rings, install the fuel rail

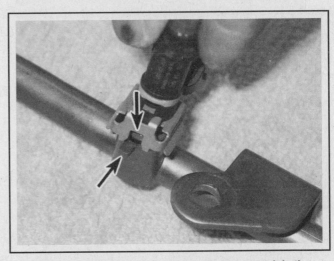

11.15 When installing each injector, the lower notch in the clip must be aligned with the tang on the fuel rail

crossover hose and tighten the crossover hose flange fasteners to the torque listed in this Chapter's Specifications.

17 The remainder of installation is the reverse of removal.

18 When you're done, reconnect the battery, then turn the ignition switch to ON (but don't operate the starter). This activates the fuel pump for about two seconds, which builds up fuel pressure in the fuel lines and the fuel rail. Repeat this step two or three times, then check the fuel lines, fuel rails and injectors for fuel leaks.

Specifications

Fuel system pressure (approximate)	51 psi (350 kPa)

Torque specifications	Ft-lbs (unless otherwise indicated)	Nm

➡ **Note: One foot-pound (ft-lb) of torque is equivalent to 12 inch-pounds (in-lbs) of torque. Torque values below approximately 15 foot-pounds are expressed in inch-pounds, because most foot-pound torque wrenches are not accurate at these smaller values.**

Throttle body mounting fasteners	6 ft-lbs (72 in-lbs)	8 Nm
Fuel rail crossover hose flange bolts	8 ft-lbs (96 in-lbs)	11 Nm

Section

5

ENGINE ELECTRICAL SYSTEMS

1   General information and precautions

GENERAL INFORMATION

Ignition system

The electronic ignition system consists of the Crankshaft Position (CKP) sensor, the Camshaft Position (CMP) sensor, the Knock Sensor (KS), the Powertrain Control Module (PCM), the ignition switch, the battery, the individual ignition coils or a coil pack, and the spark plugs. For more information on the CKP, CMP and KS sensors, as well as the PCM, refer to Chapter 6.

Charging system

The charging system includes the alternator (with an integral voltage regulator), the Powertrain Control Module (PCM), the Body Control Module (BCM), a charge indicator light on the dash, the battery, a fuse or fusible link and the wiring connecting all of these components. The charging system supplies electrical power for the ignition system, the lights, the radio, etc. The alternator is driven by a drivebelt.

Starting system

The starting system consists of the battery, the ignition switch, the starter relay, the Powertrain Control Module (PCM), the Body Control Module (BCM), the Transmission Range (TR) switch, the starter motor

and solenoid assembly, and the wiring connecting all of the components.

PRECAUTIONS

Always observe the following precautions when working on the electrical system:

a) *Be extremely careful when servicing engine electrical components. They are easily damaged if checked, connected or handled improperly.*

b) *Never leave the ignition switched on for long periods of time when the engine is not running.*

c) *Never disconnect the battery cables while the engine is running.*

d) *Maintain correct polarity when connecting battery cables from another vehicle during jump starting - see the "Booster battery (jump) starting" Section at the front of this manual.*

e) *Always disconnect the cable from the negative battery terminal before working on the electrical system, but read the battery disconnection procedure first (see Section 3).*

It's also a good idea to review the safety-related information regarding the engine electrical systems located in the *Safety first!* Section at the front of this manual before beginning any operation included in this Chapter.

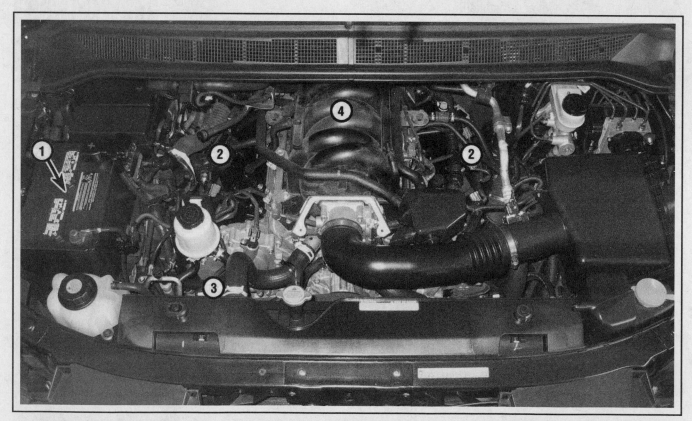

Engine electrical system details:

1   *Battery*
2   *Ignition coils (four coils on top of each valve cover)*

3   *Alternator (lower right front corner of engine block)*

4   *Starter motor (under the intake manifold)*

2 Troubleshooting

IGNITION SYSTEM

1   If a malfunction occurs in the ignition system, do not immediately assume that any particular part is causing the problem. First, check the following items:

   a) *Make sure that the cable clamps at the battery terminals are clean and tight.*
   b) *Test the condition of the battery (see Steps 21 through 24). If it doesn't pass all the tests, replace it.*
   c) *Check the ignition coil or coil pack connections.*
   d) *Check any relevant fuses in the engine compartment fuse and relay box (see Chapter 12). If they're burned, determine the cause and repair the circuit.*

Check

▶ **Refer to illustration 2.3**

> ☀ **WARNING:**
>
> **Because of the high voltage generated by the ignition system, use extreme care when performing a procedure involving ignition components.**

➡ **Note 1: The ignition system components on these vehicles are difficult to diagnose. In the event of ignition system failure that you can't diagnose, have the vehicle tested at a dealer service department or other qualified auto repair facility.**

➡ **Note 2: You'll need a spark tester for the following test. Spark testers are available at most auto supply stores.**

2   If the engine turns over but won't start, verify that there is sufficient ignition voltage to fire the spark plugs as follows.

3   On models with a coil-over-plug type ignition system, remove a coil and install the tester between the boot at the lower end of the coil and the spark plug (see illustration). On models with spark plug wires, disconnect a spark plug wire from a spark plug and install the tester between the spark plug wire boot and the spark plug.

4   Crank the engine and note whether or not the tester flashes.

> ☀ **CAUTION:**
>
> **Do NOT crank the engine or allow it to run for more than five seconds; running the engine for more than five seconds may set a Diagnostic Trouble Code (DTC) for a cylinder misfire.**

Models with a coil-over-plug type ignition system

5   If the tester flashes during cranking, the coil is delivering sufficient voltage to the spark plug to fire it. Repeat this test for each cylinder to verify that the other coils are OK.

6   If the tester doesn't flash, remove a coil from another cylinder and swap it for the one being tested. If the tester now flashes, you know that the original coil is bad. If the tester still doesn't flash, the PCM or wiring harness is probably defective. Have the PCM checked out by a dealer service department or other qualified repair shop (testing the PCM is beyond the scope of the do-it-yourselfer because it requires expensive special tools).

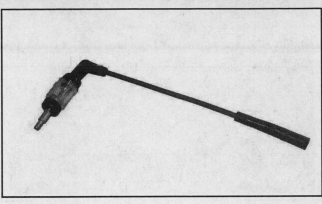

2.3 Spark tester

7   If the tester flashes during cranking but a misfire code (related to the cylinder being tested) has been stored, the spark plug could be fouled or defective.

Models with spark plug wires

8   If the tester flashes during cranking, sufficient voltage is reaching the spark plug to fire it.

9   Repeat this test on the remaining cylinders.

10   Proceed on this basis until you have verified that there's a good spark from each spark plug wire. If there is, then you have verified that the coils in the coil pack are functioning correctly and that the spark plug wires are OK.

11   If there is no spark from a spark plug wire, then either the coil is bad, the plug wire is bad or a connection at one end of the plug wire is loose. Assuming that you're using new plug wires or known good wires, then the coil is probably defective. Also inspect the coil pack electrical connector. Make sure that it's clean, tight and in good condition.

12   If all the coils are firing correctly, but the engine misfires, then one or more of the plugs might be fouled. Remove and check the spark plugs or install new ones (see Chapter 1).

13   No further testing of the ignition system is possible without special tools. If the problem persists, have the ignition system tested by a dealer service department or other qualified repair shop.

CHARGING SYSTEM

14   If a malfunction occurs in the charging system, do not automatically assume the alternator is causing the problem. First check the following items:

   a) *Check the drivebelt tension and condition, as described in Chapter 1. Replace it if it's worn or deteriorated.*
   b) *Make sure the alternator mounting bolts are tight.*
   c) *Inspect the alternator wiring harness and the connectors at the alternator and voltage regulator. They must be in good condition, tight and have no corrosion.*
   d) *Check the fusible link (if equipped) or main fuse in the underhood fuse/relay box. If it is burned, determine the cause, repair the circuit and replace the link or fuse (the vehicle will not start and/ or the accessories will not work if the fusible link or main fuse is blown).*
   e) *Start the engine and check the alternator for abnormal noises (a shrieking or squealing sound indicates a bad bearing).*

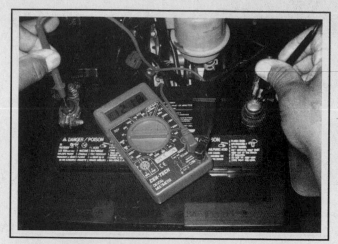

2.21 To test the open circuit voltage of the battery, touch the black probe of the voltmeter to the negative terminal and the red probe to the positive terminal of the battery; a fully charged battery should be at least 12.6 volts

f) *Check the battery. Make sure it's fully charged and in good condition (one bad cell in a battery can cause overcharging by the alternator).*

g) *Disconnect the battery cables (negative first, then positive). Inspect the battery posts and the cable clamps for corrosion. Clean them thoroughly if necessary (see Chapter 1). Reconnect the cables (positive first, negative last).*

Alternator - check

15 Use a voltmeter to check the battery voltage with the engine off. It should be at least 12.6 volts (see illustration 2.21).

16 Start the engine and check the battery voltage again. It should now be approximately 13.5 to 15 volts.

17 If the voltage reading is more or less than the specified charging voltage, the voltage regulator is probably defective, which will require replacement of the alternator (the voltage regulator is not replaceable separately). Remove the alternator and have it bench tested (most auto parts stores will do this for you).

18 The charging system (battery) light on the instrument cluster lights up when the ignition key is turned to ON, but it should go out when the engine starts.

19 If the charging system light stays on after the engine has been started, there is a problem with the charging system. Before replacing the alternator, check the battery condition, alternator belt tension and electrical cable connections.

20 If replacing the alternator doesn't restore voltage to the specified range, have the charging system tested by a dealer service department or other qualified repair shop.

Battery - check

♦ **Refer to illustrations 2.21 and 2.23**

21 Check the battery state of charge. Visually inspect the indicator eye on the top of the battery (if equipped with one); if the indicator eye is black in color, charge the battery as described in Chapter 1. Next perform an open circuit voltage test using a digital voltmeter.

➡**Note: The battery's surface charge must be removed before accurate voltage measurements can be made. Turn on the high beams for ten seconds, then turn them off and let the vehicle stand for two minutes.**

2.23 Connect a battery load tester to the battery and check the battery condition under load following the tool manufacturer's instructions

With the engine and all accessories Off, touch the negative probe of the voltmeter to the negative terminal of the battery and the positive probe to the positive terminal of the battery (see illustration). The battery voltage should be 12.6 volts or slightly above. If the battery is less than the specified voltage, charge the battery before proceeding to the next test. Do not proceed with the battery load test unless the battery charge is correct.

22 Disconnect the negative battery cable, then the positive cable from the battery.

23 Perform a battery load test. An accurate check of the battery condition can only be performed with a load tester (see illustration). This test evaluates the ability of the battery to operate the starter and other accessories during periods of high current draw. Connect the load tester to the battery terminals. Load test the battery according to the tool manufacturer's instructions. This tool increases the load demand (current draw) on the battery.

24 Maintain the load on the battery for 15 seconds and observe that the battery voltage does not drop below 9.6 volts. If the battery condition is weak or defective, the tool will indicate this condition immediately.

➡**Note: Cold temperatures will cause the minimum voltage reading to drop slightly. Follow the chart given in the manufacturer's instructions to compensate for cold climates. Minimum load voltage for freezing temperatures (32 degrees F) should be approximately 9.1 volts.**

STARTING SYSTEM

The starter rotates, but the engine doesn't

25 Remove the starter (see Section 8). Check the overrunning clutch and bench test the starter to make sure the drive mechanism extends fully for proper engagement with the flywheel ring gear. If it doesn't, replace the starter.

26 Check the flywheel ring gear for missing teeth and other damage. With the ignition turned off, rotate the flywheel so you can check the entire ring gear.

The starter is noisy

27 If the solenoid is making a chattering noise, first check the battery (see Steps 21 through 24). If the battery is okay, check the cables and connections.

28 If you hear a grinding, crashing metallic sound when you turn the key to Start, check for loose starter mounting bolts. If they're tight, remove the starter and inspect the teeth on the starter pinion gear and flywheel ring gear. Look for missing or damaged teeth.

29 If the starter sounds fine when you first turn the key to Start, but then stops rotating the engine and emits a zinging sound, the problem is probably a defective starter drive that's not staying engaged with the ring gear. Replace the starter.

The starter rotates slowly

30 Check the battery (see Steps 21 through 24).

31 If the battery is okay, verify all connections (at the battery, the starter solenoid and motor) are clean, corrosion-free and tight. Make sure the cables aren't frayed or damaged.

32 Check that the starter mounting bolts are tight so it grounds properly. Also check the pinion gear and flywheel ring gear for evidence of a mechanical bind (galling, deformed gear teeth or other damage).

The starter does not rotate at all

33 Check the battery (see Steps 21 through 24).

34 If the battery is okay, verify all connections (at the battery, the starter solenoid and motor) are clean, corrosion-free and tight. Make sure the cables aren't frayed or damaged.

35 Check all of the fuses in the underhood fuse/relay box.

36 Check that the starter mounting bolts are tight so it grounds properly.

37 Check for voltage at the starter solenoid "S" terminal when the ignition key is turned to the start position. If voltage is present, replace the starter/solenoid assembly. If no voltage is present, the problem could be the starter relay, the Transmission Range (TR) switch (see Chapter 6) or clutch start switch (see Chapter 8), or with an electrical connector somewhere in the circuit (see the wiring diagrams at the end of Chapter 12). Also, on many modern vehicles, the Powertrain Control Module (PCM) and the Body Control Module (BCM) control the voltage signal to the starter solenoid; on such vehicles a special scan tool is required for diagnosis.

3 Battery - disconnection

※※ CAUTION:

Always disconnect the cable from the negative battery terminal FIRST and hook it up LAST or the battery may be shorted by the tool being used to loosen the cable clamps.

→Note: On models equipped with the Nissan Anti-Theft System (NATS) and the Intelligent Key system, the steering column will lock when the battery is disconnected (or discharged). If it will be necessary to turn the steering wheel (or disc/hub assembly) during the course of a repair on one of these models, turn the ignition key to the ACC position before disconnecting the battery. After the repair is performed, turn the ignition key to the LOCK position before reconnecting the battery.

Some systems on the vehicle require battery power to be available at all times, either to maintain continuous operation (alarm system, power door locks, etc.), or to maintain control unit memory (radio station presets, Powertrain Control Module and other control units). When the battery is disconnected, the power that maintains these systems is cut. So, before you disconnect the battery, please note that on a vehicle with power door locks, it's a wise precaution to remove the key from the ignition and to keep it with you, so that it does not get locked inside if the power door locks should engage accidentally when the battery is reconnected!

Devices known as "memory-savers" can be used to avoid some of these problems. Precise details vary according to the device used. The typical memory saver is plugged into the cigarette lighter and is connected to a spare battery. Then the vehicle battery can be disconnected from the electrical system. The memory saver will provide sufficient current to maintain audio unit security codes, PCM memory, etc. and will provide power to always hot circuits such as the clock and radio memory circuits.

※※ WARNING:

Some memory savers deliver a considerable amount of current in order to keep vehicle systems operational after the main battery is disconnected. If you're using a memory saver, make sure that the circuit concerned is actually open before servicing it.

※※ WARNING:

If you're going to work near any of the airbag system components, the battery MUST be disconnected and a memory saver must NOT be used. If a memory saver is used, power will be supplied to the airbag, which means that it could accidentally deploy and cause serious personal injury.

To disconnect the battery for service procedures requiring power to be cut from the vehicle, loosen the cable end bolt and disconnect the cable from the negative battery terminal. Isolate the cable end to prevent it from coming into accidental contact with the battery terminal.

4   Battery - removal and installation

▶ **Refer to illustration 4.1**

1   Disconnect the cable from the negative battery terminal first, then disconnect the cable from the positive battery terminal (see illustration).
2   Remove the battery cover, if equipped.
3   Remove the battery hold-down clamp bolt and clamp.
4   Lift out the battery. Be careful - it's heavy.

➡**Note: Battery straps and handlers are available at most auto parts stores for reasonable prices. They make it easier to remove and carry the battery.**

5   If you are replacing the battery, make sure you get one that's identical, with the same dimensions, amperage rating, cold cranking rating, etc.
6   Installation is the reverse of removal. Be sure to connect the positive cable first and the negative cable last.

4.1 Battery details:

1   *Negative battery cable*
2   *Positive battery cable*
3   *Battery hold-down clamp*

5   Battery cables - replacement

1   When removing the cables, always disconnect the cable from the negative battery terminal first and hook it up last, or you might accidentally short out the battery with the tool you're using to loosen the cable clamps. Even if you're only replacing the cable for the positive terminal, be sure to disconnect the negative cable from the battery first.
2   Disconnect the old cables from the battery, then trace each of them to their opposite ends and disconnect them. Be sure to note the routing of each cable before disconnecting it to ensure correct installation.
3   If you are replacing any of the old cables, take them with you when buying new cables. It is vitally important that you replace the cables with identical parts.
4   Clean the threads of the solenoid or ground connection with a wire brush to remove rust and corrosion. Apply a light coat of battery terminal corrosion inhibitor or petroleum jelly to the threads to prevent future corrosion.
5   Attach the cable to the solenoid or ground connection and tighten the mounting nut/bolt securely.
6   Before connecting a new cable to the battery, make sure that it reaches the battery post without having to be stretched.
7   Connect the cable to the positive battery terminal first, then connect the ground cable to the negative battery terminal.

6   Ignition coils - removal and installation

▶ **Refer to illustration 6.3**

➡**Note: This procedure applies to all eight ignition coils.**

1   Disconnect the cable from the negative battery terminal (see Section 3).
2   If you're removing a coil from the left valve cover, you might have to move the engine harness out of the way. To do so, disconnect the electrical connectors and harness clips for the harness, then set the harness aside.
3   Disconnect the electrical connector from the ignition coil (see illustration).
4   Remove the coil mounting fastener and remove the ignition coil by pulling it off the spark plug.
5   Apply a little silicone dielectric compound to the inside of the spark plug boot before installing the coil. Installation is otherwise the reverse of removal.

6.3 The ignition coils are located on the valve covers (right side shown, forward-most coil not visible in this photo)

7 Alternator - removal and installation

▶ **Refer to illustrations 7.4 and 7.5**

1 Disconnect the cable from the negative terminal of the battery (see Section 3).

2 Remove the fan shroud (see Chapter 3).

3 Remove the drivebelt (see Chapter 1).

4 Disconnect the electrical connector from the alternator, then remove the nut that secures the battery cable to the alternator's B+ terminal (see illustration) and remove the alternator.

5 Remove the upper and lower alternator mounting fasteners (see illustration) and remove the alternator.

6 If you're replacing the alternator, take the old one with you when purchasing the replacement unit. Make sure that the new/rebuilt unit looks identical to the old alternator. Look at the electrical terminals on the backside of the alternator. They should be the same in number, size and location as the terminals on the old alternator.

7 Some new/rebuilt alternators DO NOT have a pulley installed, so you might have to swap the pulley from the old unit to the new/rebuilt one. When buying an alternator, find out the store's policy regarding pulley swaps. Some stores perform this service free of charge. If your local auto parts store doesn't offer this service, you'll have to purchase a puller for removing the pulley and do it yourself.

8 Installation is the reverse of removal. Be sure to tighten the alternator mounting fasteners securely.

9 Reconnect the cable to the negative terminal of the battery (see Section 3).

10 Check the charging voltage (see Section 2) to verify that the alternator is operating correctly.

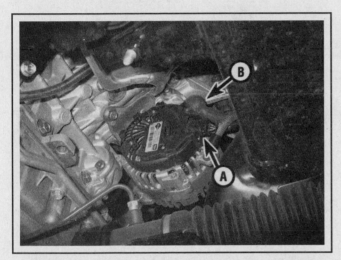

7.4 Alternator electrical connector (A) and battery cable terminal (B) (under rubber cover)

7.5 Upper and lower alternator mounting fasteners

8 Starter motor - removal and installation

1 Disconnect the cable from the negative terminal of the battery (see Section 3).

2 Remove the intake manifold (see Chapter 2A).

3 Disconnect the starter motor electrical connectors.

4 Remove the starter motor mounting bolts and remove the starter motor.

5 Installation is the reverse of removal. Be sure to tighten the starter mounting bolts securely.

Notes

6

EMISSIONS
AND ENGINE
CONTROL
SYSTEMS

Section

1 General information

To prevent pollution of the atmosphere from incompletely burned and evaporating gases, and to maintain good driveability and fuel economy, a number of emission control systems are incorporated. They include the:

CATALYTIC CONVERTER

A catalytic converter is an emission control device in the exhaust system that reduces certain pollutants in the exhaust gas stream. There are two types of converters: oxidation converters and reduction converters.

Oxidation converters contain a monolithic substrate (a ceramic honeycomb) coated with the semi-precious metals platinum and palladium. An oxidation catalyst reduces unburned hydrocarbons (HC) and carbon monoxide (CO) by adding oxygen to the exhaust stream as it passes through the substrate, which, in the presence of high temperature and the catalyst materials, converts the HC and CO to water vapor (H_2O) and carbon dioxide (CO_2).

Reduction converters contain a monolithic substrate coated with platinum and rhodium. A reduction catalyst reduces oxides of nitrogen (NOx) by removing oxygen, which in the presence of high temperature and the catalyst material produces nitrogen (N) and carbon dioxide (CO_2).

Catalytic converters that combine both types of catalysts in one assembly are known as "three-way catalysts" or TWCs. A TWC can reduce all three pollutants.

EVAPORATIVE EMISSIONS CONTROL (EVAP) SYSTEM

The Evaporative Emissions Control (EVAP) system prevents fuel system vapors (which contain unburned hydrocarbons) from escaping into the atmosphere. On warm days, vapors trapped inside the fuel tank expand until the pressure reaches a certain threshold. Then the fuel vapors are routed from the fuel tank through the fuel vapor vent valve and the fuel vapor control valve to the EVAP canister, where they're stored temporarily until the next time the vehicle is operated. When the

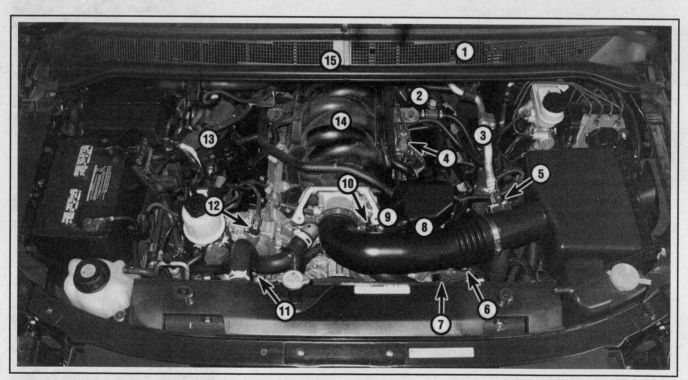

Emissions and engine control system components

1. Accelerator Pedal Position (APP) sensor (located at the top of the accelerator pedal assembly)
2. Camshaft Position (CMP) sensor - 2006 and earlier models (at the rear of the left cylinder head)
3. Left bank upstream oxygen sensor (threaded into theexhaust manifold)
4. EVAP purge control solenoid valve
5. Mass Air Flow/Intake Air Temperature (MAF/IAT) sensor
6. Camshaft Position (CMP) sensor - 2007 and later models

7. Intake valve timing control position solenoid (2007 and later models) - left side
8. Intake valve timing control position sensor (2007 and later models) - left side (not visible)
9. Engine Coolant Temperature (ECT) sensor (located on the inner side of the left cylinder head, at the front corner of the head)
10. Throttle Position (TP) sensor
11. Intake valve timing control position solenoid (2007 and later models) - right side

12. Intake valve timing control position sensor (2007 and later models) - right side
13. Right bank upstream oxygen sensor (threaded into theexhaust manifold)
14. Knock sensors (located underneath the intake manifold, on top of the engine block)
15. Crankshaft Position (CKP) sensor (located on the bottom of the transmission bellhousing)

Information Sensors

Accelerator Pedal Position (APP) sensor - As you press the accelerator pedal, the APP sensor alters its voltage signal to the PCM in proportion to the angle of the pedal, and the PCM commands a motor inside the throttle body to open or close the throttle plate accordingly

Camshaft Position (CMP) sensor - produces a signal that the PCM uses to identify the number 1 cylinder and to time the firing sequence of the fuel injectors

Crankshaft Position (CKP) sensor - produces a signal that the PCM uses to calculate engine speed and crankshaft position, which enables it to synchronize ignition timing with fuel injector timing, and to detect misfires

Engine Coolant Temperature (ECT) sensor - a thermistor (temperature-sensitive variable resistor) that sends a voltage signal to the PCM, which uses this data to determine the temperature of the engine coolant

Fuel tank pressure sensor - measures the fuel tank pressure and controls fuel tank pressure by signaling the EVAP system to purge the fuel tank vapors when the pressure becomes excessive

Intake Air Temperature (IAT) sensor - monitors the temperature of the air entering the engine and sends a signal to the PCM to determine injector pulse-width (the duration of each injector's on-time) and to adjust spark timing (to prevent spark knock)

Knock sensor - a piezoelectric crystal that oscillates in proportion to engine vibration which produces a voltage output that is monitored by the PCM. This retards the ignition timing when the oscillation exceeds a certain threshold

Manifold Absolute Pressure (MAP) sensor - monitors the pressure or vacuum inside the intake manifold. The PCM uses this data to determine engine load so that it can alter the ignition advance and fuel enrichment

Mass Air Flow (MAF) sensor - measures the amount of intake air drawn into the engine. It uses a hot-wire sensing element to measure the amount of air entering the engine

Oxygen sensors - generates a small variable voltage signal in proportion to the difference between the oxygen content in the exhaust stream and the oxygen content in the ambient air. The PCM uses this information to maintain the proper air/fuel ratio. A second oxygen sensor monitors the efficiency of the catalytic converter

Throttle Position (TP) sensor - a potentiometer that generates a voltage signal that varies in relation to the opening angle of the throttle plate inside the throttle body. Works with the PCM and other sensors to calculate injector pulse width (the duration of each injector's on-time)

Photos courtesy of Wells Manufacturing, except APP and MAF sensors.

conditions are right (engine warmed up, vehicle up to speed, moderate or heavy load on the engine, etc.) the PCM opens the canister purge valve, which allows fuel vapors to be drawn from the canister into the intake manifold. Once in the intake manifold, the fuel vapors mix with incoming air before being drawn through the intake ports into the combustion chambers where they're burned up with the rest of the air/fuel mixture. The EVAP system is complex and virtually impossible to troubleshoot without the right tools and training.

POWERTRAIN CONTROL MODULE (PCM)

The Powertrain Control Module (PCM) is the brain of the engine management system. It also controls a wide variety of other vehicle systems. In order to program the new PCM, the dealer needs the vehicle as well as the new PCM. If you're planning to replace the PCM with a new one, there is no point in trying to do so at home because you won't be able to program it yourself.

POSITIVE CRANKCASE VENTILATION (PCV) SYSTEM

The Positive Crankcase Ventilation (PCV) system reduces hydrocarbon emissions by scavenging crankcase vapors, which are rich in unburned hydrocarbons. A PCV valve or orifice regulates the flow of gases into the intake manifold in proportion to the amount of intake vacuum available.

The PCV system generally consists of the fresh air inlet hose, the PCV valve or orifice and the crankcase ventilation hose (or PCV hose). The fresh air inlet hose connects the air intake duct to a pipe on the valve cover. The crankcase ventilation hose (or PCV hose) connects the PCV valve or orifice in the valve cover to the intake manifold.

2   On Board Diagnosis (OBD) system

GENERAL DESCRIPTION

1   All models are equipped with the second generation OBD-II system. This system consists of an on-board computer known as the Powertrain Control Module (PCM), and information sensors, which monitor various functions of the engine and send data to the PCM. This system incorporates a series of diagnostic monitors that detect and identify fuel injection and emissions control system faults and store the information in the computer memory. This system also tests sensors and output actuators, diagnoses drive cycles, freezes data and clears codes.

2   The PCM is the brain of the electronically controlled fuel and emissions system. It receives data from a number of sensors and other electronic components (switches, relays, etc.). Based on the information it receives, the PCM generates output signals to control various relays, solenoids (fuel injectors) and other actuators. The PCM is specifically calibrated to optimize the emissions, fuel economy and driveability of the vehicle.

3   It isn't a good idea to attempt diagnosis or replacement of the PCM or emission control components at home while the vehicle is under warranty. Because of a federally-mandated warranty which covers the emissions system components and because any owner-induced damage to the PCM, the sensors and/or the control devices may void this warranty, take the vehicle to a dealer service department if the PCM or a system component malfunctions.

SCAN TOOL INFORMATION

▶ **Refer to illustrations 2.4a and 2.4b**

4   Because extracting the Diagnostic Trouble Codes (DTCs) from an engine management system is now the first step in troubleshooting many computer-controlled systems and components, a code reader, at the very least, will be required (see illustration). More powerful scan tools can also perform many of the diagnostics once associated with expensive factory scan tools (see illustration). If you're planning to obtain a generic scan tool for your vehicle, make sure that it's compatible with OBD-II systems. If you don't plan to purchase a code reader or scan tool and don't have access to one, you can have the codes extracted by a dealer service department or an independent repair shop.

2.4a Simple code readers are an economical way to extract trouble codes when the CHECK ENGINE light comes on

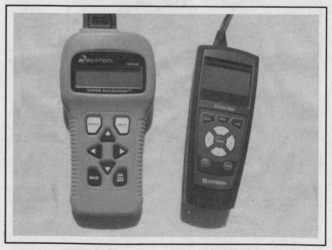

2.4b Hand-held scan tools like these can extract computer codes and also perform diagnostics

OBD-II DIAGNOSTIC TROUBLE CODES (DTCS) (CONTINUED)

➡Note: Not all trouble codes apply to all models.

Code	Possible cause
P0304	Cylinder 4 misfire
P0305	Cylinder 5 misfire
P0306	Cylinder 6 misfire
P0307	Cylinder 7 misfire
P0308	Cylinder 8 misfire
P0327	Knock sensor circuit (Bank 1), excessively low voltage signal
P0328	Knock sensor circuit (Bank 1), excessively high voltage signal
P0332	Knock sensor circuit (Bank 2), low input voltage to PCM
P0333	Knock sensor circuit (Bank 2), high input voltage to PCM
P0335	Crankshaft Position (CKP) sensor circuit, no voltage signal, incorrect signal or signal with irregular pattern
P0340	Camshaft Position (CMP) sensor circuit (Bank 1), no voltage signal first few seconds during cranking, no signal while engine running or signal with irregular pattern
P0420	Three-way catalyst function (Bank 1), catalyst doesn't operate correctly or has insufficient oxygen storage capacity
P0430	Three-way catalyst function (Bank 2), catalyst doesn't operate correctly or has insufficient oxygen storage capacity
P0441	Evaporative Emissions (EVAP) control system, incorrect purge flow
P0442	Evaporative Emissions (EVAP) control system, small leak detected
P0443	Evaporative Emissions (EVAP) control system, canister purge flow occurs when EVAP canister purge volume control solenoid valve is completely closed
P0444	Evaporative Emissions (EVAP) control system, purge volume control solenoid valve, low voltage signal
P0445	Evaporative Emissions (EVAP) control system, purge volume control solenoid valve, high voltage signal
P0447	Evaporative Emissions (EVAP) control system, vent control valve, incorrect voltage signal
P0448	EVAP canister vent control valve, valve stays closed under conditions during which it's supposed to open
P0451	Evaporative Emissions (EVAP) control system, pressure sensor, incorrect voltage signal
P0452	Evaporative Emissions (EVAP) control system, pressure sensor, low voltage signal
P0453	Evaporative Emissions (EVAP) control system, pressure sensor, high voltage signal
P0455	Evaporative Emissions (EVAP) control system, large leak detected

3   Obtaining and clearing Diagnostic Trouble Codes (DTCs)

All models covered by this manual are equipped with on-board diagnostics. When the PCM recognizes a malfunction in a monitored emission or engine control system, component or circuit, it turns on the Malfunction Indicator Light (MIL) on the dash. The PCM will continue to display the MIL until the problem is fixed and the Diagnostic Trouble Code (DTC) is cleared from the PCM's memory. You'll need a scan tool to access any DTCs stored in the PCM.

Before outputting any DTCs stored in the PCM, thoroughly inspect ALL electrical connectors and hoses. Make sure that all electrical connections are tight, clean and free of corrosion. And make sure that all hoses are correctly connected, fit tightly and are in good condition (no cracks or tears).

ACCESSING THE DTCS

♦ Refer to illustration 3.1

1   The Diagnostic Trouble Codes (DTCs) can only be accessed with a code reader or scan tool. Professional scan tools are expensive, but relatively inexpensive generic code readers or scan tools (see illustrations 2.4a and 2.4b) are available at most auto parts stores. Simply plug the connector of the scan tool into the diagnostic connector (see illustration). Then follow the instructions included with the scan tool to extract the DTCs.

2   Once you have outputted all of the stored DTCs, look them up on the accompanying DTC chart.

3   After troubleshooting the source of each DTC, make any necessary repairs or replace the defective component(s).

Clearing the DTCs

4   Clear the DTCs with the code reader or scan tool in accordance with the instructions provided by the tool's manufacturer.

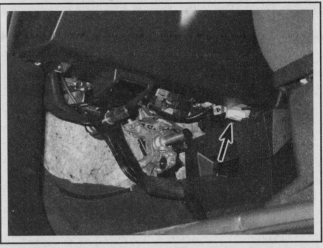

3.1 The Data Link Connector (DLC) is located under the lower edge of the dash

DIAGNOSTIC TROUBLE CODES

5   The accompanying tables are a list of the Diagnostic Trouble Codes (DTCs) that can be accessed by a do-it-yourselfer working at home (there are many, many more DTCs available to professional mechanics with proprietary scan tools and software, but those codes cannot be accessed by a generic scan tool). If, after you have checked and repaired the connectors, wire harness and vacuum hoses (if applicable) for an emission-related system, component or circuit, the problem persists, have the vehicle checked by a dealer service department or other qualified repair shop.

OBD-II DIAGNOSTIC TROUBLE CODES (DTCS)

➡Note: Not all trouble codes apply to all models.

Code	Possible cause
P0011	Intake Valve Timing (IVT) control (Bank 1), gap between target angle and phase-control angle
P0014	Exhaust Valve Timing (EVT) control (Bank 1), gap between target angle and phase-control angle
P0021	Intake Valve Timing (IVT) control (Bank 2), gap between target angle and phase-control angle
P0024	Exhaust Valve Timing (EVT) control (Bank 2), gap between target angle and phase-control angle
P0031	Upstream oxygen sensor heater control circuit (Bank 1), excessively low voltage signal
P0032	Upstream oxygen sensor heater control circuit (Bank 1), excessively high voltage signal
P0037	Downstream oxygen sensor heater control circuit (Bank 1), excessively low voltage signal
P0038	Downstream oxygen sensor heater control circuit (Bank 1), excessively high voltage signal

OBD-II DIAGNOSTIC TROUBLE CODES (DTCS) (CONTINUED)

➡Note: Not all trouble codes apply to all models.

Code	Possible cause
P0043	Downstream (No. 3) oxygen sensor heater (Bank 1)
P0051	Upstream oxygen sensor heater control circuit (Bank 2), excessively low voltage signal
P0052	Upstream oxygen sensor heater control circuit (Bank 2), excessively high voltage signal
P0057	Downstream oxygen sensor heater control circuit (Bank 2), excessively low voltage signal
P0058	Downstream oxygen sensor heater control circuit (Bank 2), excessively high voltage signal
P0075	Intake Valve Timing (IVT) control solenoid valve (Bank 1), incorrect voltage signal
P0078	Exhaust Valve Timing (EVT) control magnet retarder (Bank 1), incorrect voltage signal
P0081	Intake Valve Timing (IVT) control solenoid valve (Bank 2), incorrect voltage signal
P0084	Exhaust Valve Timing (EVT) control magnet retarder (Bank 2), incorrect voltage signal
P0101	Mass Air Flow (MAF) sensor circuit, high voltage signal with light load or low voltage signal with heavy load
P0102	Mass Air Flow (MAF) sensor circuit, excessively low voltage signal
P0103	Mass Air Flow (MAF) sensor circuit, excessively high voltage signal
P0112	Intake Air Temperature (IAT) sensor circuit, excessively low voltage signal
P0113	Intake Air Temperature (IAT) sensor circuit, excessively high voltage signal
P0116	Engine Coolant Temperature (ECT) sensor circuit
P0117	Engine Coolant Temperature (ECT) sensor circuit, excessively low voltage signal
P0118	Engine Coolant Temperature (ECT) sensor circuit, excessively high voltage signal
P0122	Throttle Position (TP) sensor circuit, low voltage input
P0123	Throttle Position (TP) sensor circuit, high voltage input
P0125	Engine Coolant Temperature (ECT) sensor circuit, voltage signal not rational or coolant temperature insufficient for closed loop fuel control
P0127	Intake Air Temperature (IAT) sensor circuit, voltage signal irrational compared to ECT sensor signal
P0128	Thermostat malfunction, engine coolant temperature doesn't reach specified temperature after warm-up
P0130	Upstream oxygen sensor circuit (Bank 1), voltage signal is constantly about 1.5 volts
P0131	Upstream oxygen sensor circuit (Bank 1), voltage signal is constantly zero

Code	Possible cause
P0132	Upstream oxygen sensor circuit (Bank 1), excessively high voltage signal
P0133	Upstream oxygen sensor circuit (Bank 1), response of voltage signal takes more than specified time
P0134	Upstream oxygen sensor circuit (Bank 1), no activity detected, voltage signal is constantly about 0.3 volts
P0137	Downstream oxygen sensor circuit (Bank 1), sensor signal voltage doesn't reach specified voltage
P0138	Downstream oxygen sensor circuit (Bank 1), excessively high voltage signal
P0139	Downstream oxygen sensor circuit (Bank 1), excessive time for response interval between rich and lean
P0150	Upstream oxygen sensor circuit (Bank 2), voltage signal is constantly about 1.5 volts
P0151	Upstream oxygen sensor circuit (Bank 2), voltage signal is constantly zero
P0152	Upstream oxygen sensor circuit (Bank 2), excessively high voltage signal
P0153	Upstream oxygen sensor circuit (Bank 2), response of voltage signal takes more than specified time
P0154	Upstream oxygen sensor circuit (Bank 2), no activity detected, voltage signal is constantly about 0.3 volts
P0157	Downstream oxygen sensor circuit (Bank 2), sensor signal voltage doesn't reach specified voltage
P0158	Downstream oxygen sensor circuit (Bank 2), excessively high voltage signal
P0159	Downstream oxygen sensor circuit (Bank 2), excessive time for response interval between rich and lean
P0171	Fuel system mixture ratio too lean or fuel injection system malfunction (Bank 1)
P0172	Fuel system mixture ratio too rich or fuel injection system malfunction (Bank 1)
P0174	Fuel system mixture ratio too lean or fuel injection system malfunction (Bank 2)
P0175	Fuel system mixture ratio too rich or fuel injection system malfunction (Bank 2)
P0181	Fuel Tank Temperature (FTT) sensor circuit range/performance problem, rationally incorrect voltage signal compared to signals from ECT and IAT sensors
P0182	Fuel Tank Temperature (FTT) sensor circuit, excessively low voltage signal
P0183	Fuel Tank Temperature (FTT) sensor circuit, excessively high voltage signal
P0222	Throttle Position (TP) sensor 1 circuit, excessively low voltage signal
P0223	Throttle Position (TP) sensor 1 circuit, excessively high voltage signal
P0300	Multiple cylinder misfire
P0301	Cylinder 1 misfire
P0302	Cylinder 2 misfire
P0303	Cylinder 3 misfire

Code	Possible cause
P0456	Evaporative Emissions (EVAP) control system, very small leak detected
P0460	Fuel level sensor, sloshing voltage signal from sensor while vehicle is stationary
P0461	Fuel level sensor, no change in voltage signal
P0462	Fuel level sensor circuit, excessively low voltage signal
P0463	Fuel level sensor circuit, excessively high voltage signal
P0500	Vehicle Speed Sensor (VSS) circuit, 0 mph signal sent to PCM when vehicle is moving
P0506	Idle Speed Control (ISC) system, idle speed less than target idle speed by 100 rpm or more
P0507	Idle Speed Control (ISC) system, idle speed more than target idle speed by 200 rpm or more
P0550	Power steering pressure sensor circuit, excessively high or low voltage signal
P0603	Powertrain Control Module (PCM) back-up Random Access Memory (RAM) system not functioning correctly
P0605	Powertrain Control Module (PCM), calculation, EEPROM or self shut-off malfunction
P0643	Sensor power supply, PCM detects excessively high or low voltage to APP, EVAP control system pressure, PSP or refrigerant pressure sensor
P0700	Transmission Control Module (TCM), defective TCM
P0705	Park Neutral Position (PNP) switch circuit, incorrect or missing voltage signal
P0710	Automatic Transmission Fluid (ATF) temperature sensor circuit, excessively high or low voltage signal
P0717	Input speed sensor A, Transmission Control Module (TCM) not receiving correct voltage from sensor
P0720	Vehicle Speed Sensor (VSS) circuit, incorrect voltage signal
P0731	Automatic transmission first gear function
P0732	Automatic transmission second gear function
P0733	Automatic transmission third gear function
P0734	Automatic transmission fourth gear function
P0735	Automatic transmission fifth gear function
P0740	Torque Converter Clutch (TCC) solenoid circuit, incorrect or irregular voltage signal
P0744	Torque Converter Clutch (TCC) solenoid valve, incorrect or irregular voltage signal
P0745	Line pressure solenoid circuit, incorrect or irregular voltage signal
P0850	Park Neutral Position (PNP) position switch circuit, PNP switch signal doesn't change when starting and driving

4   Accelerator Pedal Position (APP) sensor - replacement

▶ **Refer to illustration 4.4**

1   On vehicles with the optional adjustable accelerator and brake pedal feature, move the pedal assembly to its forward position.

2   Disconnect the cable from the negative terminal of the battery (see Chapter 5, Section 3).

3   On vehicles with the optional adjustable accelerator and brake

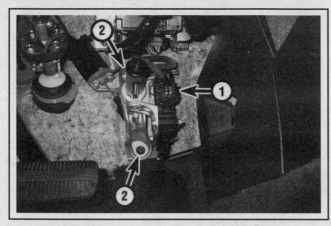

4.4 The APP sensor is located at the top of (and is an integral component of) the accelerator pedal assembly

1	*Electrical connector*	*2*	*Mounting nuts*

pedal feature, disconnect the adjustable brake pedal cable from the pedal. Trace the cable from the adjustable pedal electric motor over to the brake pedal assembly and unscrew the threaded collar that secures the cable to the pedal, then pull on the cable to disconnect it from the brake pedal assembly.

4   Disconnect the electrical connector from the APP sensor (see illustration).

5   Remove the accelerator pedal assembly mounting fasteners and remove the assembly.

6   Installation is the reverse of removal.

7   When you're done, perform the following relearn procedure or the APP sensor will not function correctly.

ACCELERATOR PEDAL RELEASE POSITION RELEARN PROCEDURE

➡**Note: The Accelerator Pedal Release Position Learning procedure must be performed any time that the APP sensor electrical connector OR the Powertrain Control Module (PCM) is disconnected.**

8   Make sure that the accelerator pedal is fully released.

9   Turn the ignition switch to ON and wait at least two seconds.

10 Turn the ignition switch to OFF and wait at least 10 seconds.

11 Turn the ignition switch to ON and wait at least two seconds.

12 Turn the ignition switch to OFF and wait at least 10 seconds.

5   Camshaft Position (CMP) sensor - replacement

2006 AND EARLIER MODELS

▶ **Refer to illustration 5.1**

1   Locate the CMP sensor at the rear of the left (driver's side) cylinder head (see illustration).

2   Disconnect the CMP sensor electrical connector.

➡**Note: It might be easier to disconnect the connector after the sensor has been removed from the head.**

3   Remove the CMP sensor mounting fastener and remove the CMP sensor.

4   Installation is the reverse of removal.

2007 AND LATER MODELS

▶ **Refer to illustration 5.6**

5   Remove the air intake duct (see *Air filter housing - removal and installation* in Chapter 4).

6   Disconnect the CMP sensor electrical connector (see illustration).

7   Remove the CMP sensor mounting fastener and remove the CMP sensor.

8   Installation is the reverse of removal.

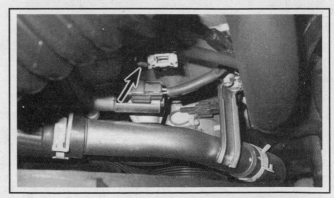

5.1 On 2006 and earlier models, the CMP sensor is located at the rear of the left (driver's side) cylinder head. It's reflection is shown in a shop mirror here

5.6 On 2007 and later models, the CMP sensor is located on the front of the left (driver's side) intake valve timing control solenoid valve cover

6   Crankshaft Position (CKP) sensor - replacement

▶ **Refer to illustration 6.2**

1 Raise the front of the vehicle and support it securely on jackstands.

2 Disconnect the electrical connector from the CKP sensor (see illustration).

3 Remove the CKP sensor mounting fastener and remove the CKP sensor.

4 Installation is the reverse of removal.

6.2 **The CKP sensor is located on the underside of the transmission bellhousing**

7   Engine Coolant Temperature (ECT) sensor - replacement

▶ **Refer to illustration 7.4**

✵ WARNING:

Wait until the engine has cooled completely before beginning this procedure.

1 Remove the engine cover (see Chapter 2A).

2 Remove the air intake duct (see *Air filter housing – removal and installation* in Chapter 4).

3 Drain the engine coolant (see Chapter 1).

4 Disconnect the electrical connector from the ECT sensor (see illustration).

5 Unscrew the ECT sensor from the cylinder head. Discard the sealing washer (a new one should be used).

6 Using a new sealing washer, install the ECT sensor and tighten it to the torque listed in this Chapter's Specifications.

7 Refill the cooling system (see Chapter 1).

7.4 **The ECT sensor is located on the inner side of the left cylinder head, near the front upper corner of the head**

8   Knock sensor - replacement

➡ **Note: This procedure applies to either knock sensor.**

1 Disconnect the cable from the negative battery terminal (see Chapter 5).

2 Remove the intake manifold (see Chapter 2A).

3 Disconnect the knock sensor electrical connector.

4 Unscrew the knock sensor retaining bolt and remove the sensor.

5 Installation is the reverse of removal. Be sure to tighten the knock sensor bolt to the torque listed in this Chapter's Specifications.

9   Mass Air Flow (MAF)/Intake Air Temperature (IAT) sensor - replacement

▶ **Refer to illustration 9.1**

1   Disconnect the electrical connector from the MAF/IAT sensor (see illustration).

2   Remove the MAF/IAT sensor fasteners and remove the sensor from the air filter housing.

3   Installation is the reverse of removal.

9.1 Location of the MAF/IAT sensor

10   Oxygen sensors - replacement

➡**Note: Because it is installed in the exhaust manifold or pipe, both of which contract when cool, an oxygen sensor might be very difficult to loosen when the engine is cold. Rather than risk damage to the sensor or its mounting threads, start and run the engine for a minute or two, then shut it off. Be careful not to burn yourself during the following procedure.**

1   Be particularly careful when servicing an oxygen sensor:

a) *Oxygen sensors have a permanently attached pigtail and an electrical connector that cannot be removed. Damaging or removing the pigtail or electrical connector will render the sensor useless.*

b) *Keep grease, dirt and other contaminants away from the electrical connector and the louvered end of the sensor.*

c) *Do not use cleaning solvents of any kind on an oxygen sensor.*

d) *Oxygen sensors are extremely delicate. Do not drop a sensor, throw it around or handle it roughly.*

e) *Make sure that the silicone boot on the sensor is installed in the correct position. Otherwise, the boot might melt and it might prevent the sensor from operating correctly.*

UPSTREAM OXYGEN SENSORS

▶ **Refer to illustration 10.3**

2   Locate the upstream oxygen sensor electrical connector at the rear of the valve cover and disconnect the connector. Disengage the sensor harness from any harness clips.

3   Unscrew the upstream oxygen sensor with an oxygen sensor socket, if available (see illustration). It can be reached from above, but is more easily accessed from under the vehicle.

4   If you're going to install the old sensor, apply anti-seize compound to the threads of the sensor to facilitate future removal. If you're going to install a new oxygen sensor, it's not necessary to apply anti-seize compound to the threads; the threads on new sensors already have anti-seize compound on them.

5   Installation is the reverse of removal. Be sure to tighten the oxygen sensor to the torque listed in this Chapter's Specifications.

10.3 The upstream oxygen sensors are located on the exhaust manifolds, directly above the catalytic converters (left upstream sensor shown, as seen from underneath)

DOWNSTREAM OXYGEN SENSORS

▶ **Refer to illustration 10.7**

6   Raise the vehicle and support it securely on jackstands.

7   Locate the downstream oxygen sensor (see illustration), then trace the lead up to the electrical connector and disconnect the connector.

8   Unscrew the downstream oxygen sensor, using an oxygen sensor socket if one is available.

9   If you're going to install the old sensor, apply anti-seize compound to the threads of the sensor to facilitate future removal. If you're going to install a new oxygen sensor, it's not necessary to apply anti-seize compound to the threads. The threads on new sensors already have anti-seize compound on them.

10   Installation is the reverse of removal. Be sure to tighten the oxygen sensor to the torque listed in this Chapter's Specifications.

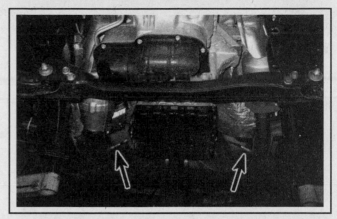

10.7 The downstream oxygen sensors are located in the exhaust pipes below the outlet ends of the catalysts

11 Transmission speed sensors - replacement

The transmission speed sensors are integral components of the valve body/Transmission Control Module (TCM) assembly, which is located inside the transmission. Replacing one of these sensors is beyond the scope of the home mechanic.

12 Powertrain Control Module (PCM) - removal and installation

The Powertrain Control Module (PCM) cannot be replaced at home because the new unit must be reprogrammed with the Vehicle Identification Number (VIN) and other data. Doing so is impossible without a factory scan tool. Do not disconnect or remove the PCM.

13 Catalytic converter - replacement

The catalytic converters are integral components of the exhaust manifolds. If you need to replace an upstream catalyst, you must replace the exhaust manifold (see Chapter 2A).

14 Evaporative Emissions Control (EVAP) system - component replacement

EVAP PURGE CONTROL SOLENOID VALVE

▶ **Refer to illustration 14.2**

1   Remove the engine cover.

2   Disconnect the electrical connector from the purge control solenoid valve (see illustration).

3   Loosen the hose clamps and disconnect the hoses from the purge control solenoid valve.

4   Remove the purge control valve mounting fasteners and remove the purge valve from its mounting bracket.

5   Installation is the reverse of removal.

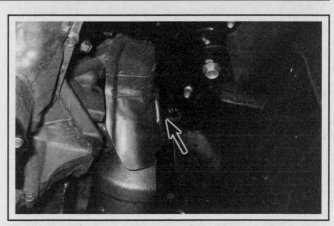

14.2 The EVAP purge control solenoid valve is located on the left side of the intake manifold

EVAP CANISTER

♦ **Refer to illustration 14.6**

6   Raise the vehicle and support it securely on jackstands.

➡**Note: The EVAP canister is located underneath the vehicle (see illustration).**

7   Disconnect the EVAP hoses from the EVAP canister. See Chapter 4 for information on quick-connect fittings.

8   Disconnect the electrical connector from the canister.

9   Remove the fastener that secures the EVAP canister and remove the canister.

10   Installation is the reverse of removal.

14.6 The EVAP canister is located under the vehicle, to the rear of the fuel tank

15 Intake Valve Timing (IVT) control position sensors and solenoids - replacement

SENSORS

♦ **Refer to illustration 15.2**

1   If you're replacing the IVT control position sensor for the left intake cam, remove the air intake duct (see *Air filter housing - removal and installation* in Chapter 4).

2   Disconnect the electrical connector from the sensor (see illustration).

3   Unscrew the mounting fastener and remove the sensor from the IVT control solenoid valve cover.

4   Installation is the reverse of removal. Be sure to use a new O-ring on the sensor.

SOLENOIDS

5   If you're replacing the IVT control position solenoid for the left intake cam, remove the air intake duct (see *Air filter housing - removal and installation* in Chapter 4).

6   Disconnect the IVT control position solenoid electrical connector (see illustration 15.2).

7   Remove the IVT solenoid mounting fastener and remove the solenoid.

8   Installation is the reverse of removal.

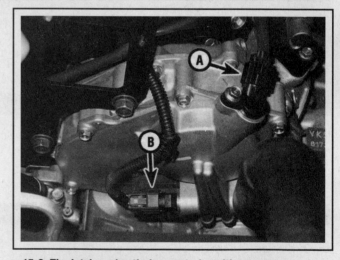

15.2 The intake valve timing control position sensors (A) are located on top of the intake valve timing control position solenoid covers, at the front of each cylinder head. The Intake Valve Timing (IVT) solenoids (B) are below the sensors (right cylinder bank shown)

16 Throttle Position (TP) sensor - replacement

The Throttle Position sensor on these vehicles is an integral part of the throttle body and is not serviceable separately. Refer to Chapter 4 for the throttle body replacement procedure.

Torque specifications

Engine Coolant Temperature (ECT) sensor	18 ft-lbs	24 Nm
Knock sensor retaining bolts	16 ft-lbs	22 Nm
Oxygen sensors (all sensors, upstream and downstream)	37 ft-lbs	50 Nm

Notes

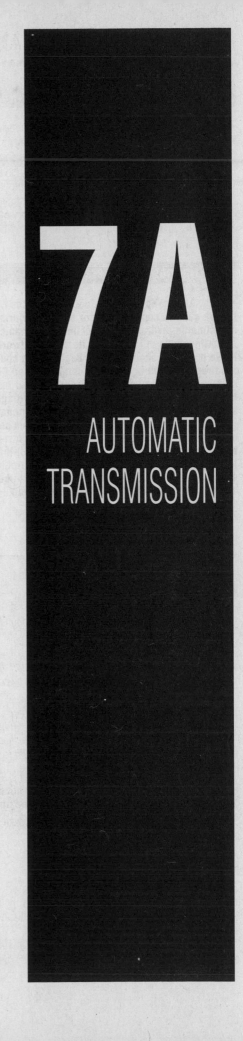

7A
AUTOMATIC TRANSMISSION

Section

1 General information

The automatic transmission used in these models is known as the RE5R05A. It is an electronic-shift five-speed transmission with three planetary gears and three one-way clutches. The shifting is controlled by the Transmission Control Module (TCM) using information from various engine and transmission sensors and output actuators through communication with the vehicle's PCM and BCM (see Chapter 6). The TCM is mounted inside the valve body of the transmission.

Because of the complexity of the clutches and the electronic and hydraulic control systems, and because of the special tools and expertise needed to overhaul an automatic transmission, diagnosis and repair of this transmission should be handled by a dealer service department or a transmission repair shop. But if the transmission must be rebuilt or replaced, you can save money by removing and installing it yourself, so instructions for that procedure are included as well.

2 Diagnosis - general

➡**Note: Automatic transmission malfunctions may be caused by five general conditions: poor engine performance, improper adjustments, hydraulic malfunctions, mechanical malfunctions or malfunctions in the TCM or its signal network. Diagnosis of these problems should always begin with a check of the easily repaired items: fluid level and condition (see Chapter 1), and shift cable adjustment. Next, perform a road test to determine if the problem has been corrected or if more diagnosis is necessary. If the problem persists after the preliminary tests and corrections are completed, additional diagnosis should be done by a dealer service department or transmission repair shop. Refer to the Troubleshooting section at the front of this manual for information on symptoms of transmission problems. Problems with the electronic transmission controls can be diagnosed with a scan tool to retrieve DTC's (Diagnostic Trouble Codes) (see Chapter 6).**

PRELIMINARY CHECKS

1   Drive the vehicle to warm the transmission to normal operating temperature.

2   Check the fluid level as described in Chapter 1:

a) *If the fluid level is unusually low, add enough fluid to bring the level within the designated area of the dipstick, then check for external leaks (see below).*

b) *If the fluid level is abnormally high, drain off the excess, then check the drained fluid for contamination by coolant. The presence of engine coolant in the automatic transmission fluid indicates that a failure has occurred in the internal radiator walls that separate the coolant from the transmission fluid (see Chapter 3).*

c) *If the fluid is foaming, drain it and refill the transmission, then check for coolant in the fluid or a high fluid level.*

3   Check for any stored trouble codes (see Chapter 6).

➡**Note: If the engine is malfunctioning, do not proceed with the preliminary checks until it has been repaired and runs normally.**

4   Inspect the shift linkage (see Section 4). Make sure it's properly adjusted and operates smoothly.

FLUID LEAK DIAGNOSIS

5   Most fluid leaks are easy to locate visually. Repair usually consists of replacing a seal or gasket. If a leak is difficult to find, the following procedure may help.

6   Identify the fluid. Make sure it's transmission fluid and not engine oil or brake fluid (automatic transmission fluid is a deep red color).

7   Try to pinpoint the source of the leak. Drive the vehicle several miles, then park it over a large sheet of cardboard. After a minute or two, you should be able to locate the leak by determining the source of the fluid dripping onto the cardboard.

8   Make a careful visual inspection of the suspected component and the area immediately around it. Pay particular attention to gasket mating surfaces. A mirror is often helpful for finding leaks in areas that are hard to see.

9   If the leak still cannot be found, clean the suspected area thoroughly with a degreaser or solvent, then dry it.

10 Drive the vehicle for several miles at normal operating temperature and varying speeds. After driving the vehicle, visually inspect the suspected component again.

11 Once the leak has been located, the cause must be determined before it can be properly repaired. If a gasket is replaced but the sealing flange is bent, the new gasket will not stop the leak. The bent flange must be straightened.

12 Before attempting to repair a leak, check to make sure the following conditions are corrected or they may cause another leak.

➡**Note: Some of the following conditions cannot be fixed without highly specialized tools and expertise. Such problems must be referred to a transmission repair shop or a dealer service department.**

Gasket leaks

13 Check the pan periodically. Make sure the bolts are tight, no bolts are missing, the gasket is in good condition and the pan is flat (dents in the pan may indicate damage to the valve body inside).

14 If the pan gasket is leaking, the fluid level or the fluid pressure may be too high, the vent may be plugged, the pan bolts may be too tight, the pan sealing flange may be warped, the sealing surface of the transmission housing may be damaged, the gasket may be damaged or the transmission casting may be cracked or porous. If sealant instead of gasket material has been used to form a seal between the pan and the transmission housing, it may be the wrong sealant.

Seal leaks

15 If a transmission seal is leaking, the fluid level or pressure may be too high, the vent may be plugged, the seal bore may be damaged, the seal itself may be damaged or improperly installed, the surface of the shaft protruding through the seal may be damaged or a loose bearing may be causing excessive shaft movement.

16 Make sure the dipstick tube seal is in good condition and the tube is properly seated. Periodically check for leakage in the area around the rear seal or the transmission control electrical harness where it enters the case. If transmission fluid is evident, replace the rear seal (see Section 7) or the O-ring around the control harness sealing nut for damage.

Case leaks

17 If the case itself appears to be leaking, the casting is porous and will have to be repaired or replaced.

18 Make sure the oil cooler hose fittings are tight and in good condition.

Fluid comes out vent pipe or fill tube

19 If this condition occurs, the transmission is overfilled, there is coolant in the fluid, the case is porous, the dipstick is incorrect, the vent is plugged or the drain-back holes are plugged.

3 Shift cable - adjustment

♦ **Refer to illustration 3.3**

➡Note: This procedure applies to both steering column and console type shifters.

1 Place the shift lever in the "P" position.
2 Raise the vehicle and support it securely on jackstands.

➡Note: On Armada models equipped with a rear auto-leveling suspension, turn the ignition key to the OFF position before raising the vehicle.

3 Loosen the shift cable-to-manual lever locknut (see illustration). Place the manual shift lever in the "P" position.

4 Push the cable into the casing with a force of about 2.2 pounds (9.8 Nm), then release the cable and let it find its relaxed position. Tighten the nut on the cable at the manual lever.

5 Move the shifter through its range, making sure that the engine can be started only in Park or Neutral, and that the backup lights illuminate only when the shifter is in Reverse.

6 Remove the jackstands and lower the vehicle.

3.3 The shift cable and locknut are located on the right side of the transmission

4 Shift lever assembly - removal and installation

※※ **WARNING:**

The models covered by this manual are equipped with airbags. Always disable the airbag system when working in the vicinity of airbag system components (see Chapter 12).

1 Disconnect the cable from the negative battery terminal (see Chapter 5).

FLOOR TYPE

♦ **Refer to illustrations 4.2 and 4.5**

2 Unscrew the knob from the shift lever (see illustration).
3 Remove the center console (see Chapter 11).
4 Unplug the shifter assembly electrical connectors.
5 Remove the shifter assembly mounting fasteners (see illustration), then detach the shifter assembly from the floor.

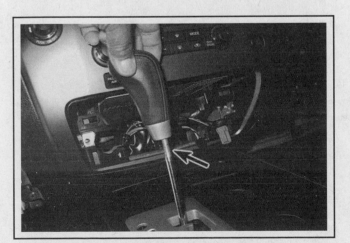

4.2 The shift knob is threaded onto the shift lever

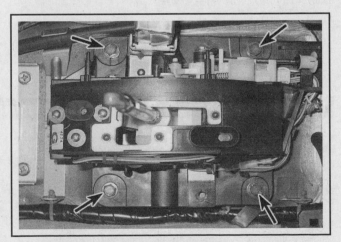

4.5 Shift lever assembly mounting bolts

COLUMN TYPE

6 Remove the knee bolster and steering column covers (see Chapter 11).
7 Detach the shift cable.
8 Unplug any electrical connectors that would inhibit the shifter assembly removal.

9 Remove the shifter assembly mounting fasteners, then detach the shifter assembly from the steering column.

BOTH TYPES

10 Installation is the reverse of removal. Be sure to adjust the shift cable (see Section 3).

---

5 Shift interlock system - description and override

✳✳ WARNING:

The models covered by this manual are equipped with airbags. Always disable the airbag system when working in the vicinity of airbag system components (see Chapter 12).

DESCRIPTION

1 The shift interlock system prevents the shift lever from being shifted out of Park or Neutral unless the ignition key (or knob, on models with the Intelligent Key system) is in the ON position and the brake pedal is depressed. A solenoid is used at the shift lever mechanism to lock the shift lever when the above conditions are not met. Diagnosis of the shift interlock system should be left to a dealer service department or other qualified repair shop. In the event that this system malfunctions, an override procedure can be used to release the shift lever (see below).

➡Note: The shift interlock system will not release the shift lever if the battery is completely discharged.

OVERRIDE

▶ Refer to illustration 5.2

2 Set the parking brake and remove the ignition key. Pry off the small cover (see illustration).

5.2 Remove the small cover, then depress the shift override button and move the shifter out of Park

➡Note: On column shift models, the cover and release button are behind the steering wheel near the shift lever. Place the steering wheel in the lowest position for access.

3 Insert a small tool to press the release button.
4 Hold the release button down while moving the shift lever out of Park.

---

6 Transmission Range (TR) sensor - general information

➡Note: The Transmission Range sensor includes all of the functions of a Park/Neutral Position (PNP) switch, but the PNP switch term is still widely used amongst various manufacturers.

1 The Transmission Range (TR) sensor prevents the engine from starting in any gear position other than PARK or NEUTRAL. The TR sensor also monitors the selector lever position and sends a signal to the Transmission Control Module (TCM). The TCM uses this information to determine the correct pressure for the electronic pressure control sys-

tem of the transmission. The TR sensor is housed inside the transmission at the valve body. If diagnostic trouble codes indicate a problem with this component (or related components), it is suggested that these repairs are performed at a dealership service department or a qualified transmission repair shop.

2 If the engine will start when the shift lever is in any position other than Park or Neutral, consider shift cable adjustment (see Section 3) before involving professional repair services.

7 Extension housing oil seal (2WD models) - replacement

▶ **Refer to illustrations 7.4 and 7.5**

1 Oil leaks frequently occur due to wear of the extension housing oil seal. Replacement of this seal is relatively easy, since it can be performed without removing the transmission from the vehicle.

2 The extension housing oil seal is located at the extreme rear of the transmission, where the driveshaft is attached. If leakage at the seal is suspected, raise the vehicle and support it securely on jackstands. If the seal is leaking, transmission lubricant will be built up on the front of the driveshaft and may be dripping from the rear of the transmission.

➡ **Note: On Armada models equipped with a rear auto-leveling suspension, turn the ignition key to the OFF position before raising the vehicle.**

3 Remove the driveshaft (see Chapter 8).

4 Using a seal removal tool or a large screwdriver, carefully pry the oil seal out of the rear of the transmission (see illustration). Do not damage the splines on the transmission output shaft.

5 Using a seal driver or a very large deep socket as a drift, install the new oil seal (see illustration). Drive it into the bore squarely and make sure it's completely seated.

6 Lubricate the splines of the transmission output shaft and the outside of the driveshaft yoke with lightweight grease, then install the driveshaft (see Chapter 8). Be careful not to damage the lip of the new seal.

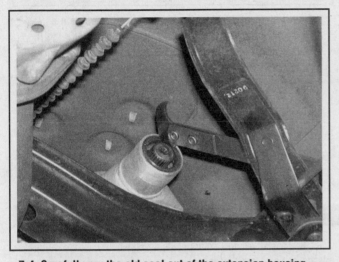

7.4 Carefully pry the old seal out of the extension housing - don't damage the splines on the output shaft

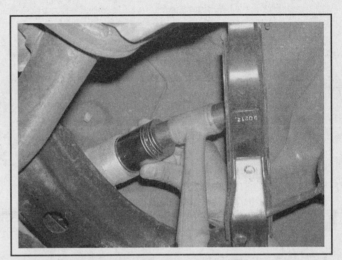

7.5 Drive the new seal into place with a hammer and a seal driver or a large socket

8 Transmission mount - check and replacement

CHECK

▶ **Refer to illustration 8.2**

1 Raise the vehicle and support it securely on jackstands.

➡ **Note: On Armada models equipped with a rear auto-leveling suspension, turn the ignition key to the OFF position before raising the vehicle.**

2 Insert a large screwdriver or prybar into the space between the transmission extension housing and the crossmember and try to pry the transmission up slightly (see illustration).

3 The transmission should not move much at all - if the mount is cracked or torn, replace it.

8.2 To check the transmission mount, insert a large screwdriver or prybar between the crossmember and the transmission and try to pry the transmission up - it should move very little

REPLACEMENT

♦ Refer to illustration 8.5

4   Support the transmission with a floor jack. Place a block of wood on the jack head to act as a cushion.

5   Remove the fasteners attaching the mount to the crossmember and transmission (see illustration).

6   Raise the transmission slightly with the jack and remove the mount.

7   Installation is the reverse of the removal procedure. Be sure to tighten all nuts and bolts securely.

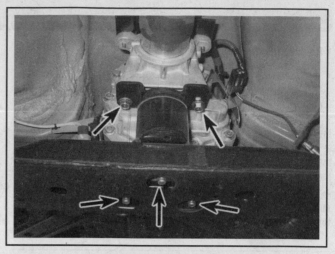

8.5 With the weight of the transmission supported on a jack, remove the mount-to-transmission bolts (upper two), then remove the mount-to-crossmember bolts and raise the transmission to allow room for mount removal

9   Automatic transmission - removal and installation

REMOVAL

♦ Refer to illustrations 9.10, 9.11a, 9.11b, 9.11c and 9.14

✳✳ CAUTION:

Remove the transmission and torque converter together as a single assembly. If you try to leave the torque converter attached to the driveplate, the driveplate will be damaged along with the pump bushing and oil seal.

1   Disconnect the cable from the negative battery terminal (see Chapter 5).

2   Remove the engine cover (see illustration 4.2 in Chapter 3).

3   Raise the vehicle and support it securely on jackstands. Remove the skid plate and skid plate crossmember, if equipped.

➥Note: On Armada models equipped with a rear auto-leveling suspension, turn the ignition key to the OFF position before raising the vehicle.

4   Remove the engine splash shield from under the vehicle, as equipped.

5   Drain the transmission fluid (see Chapter 1).

6   Detach the shift cable from the manual lever and from the bracket on the transmission.

7   Mark the yokes and remove the driveshaft (see Chapter 8). On 4WD models, remove both driveshafts.

8   Remove all exhaust components which would interfere with transmission removal (see Chapter 4).

9   Remove the Crankshaft Position sensor (see Chapter 6).

10 Follow the wiring harnesses from the transmission up to their electrical connectors, then unplug the connectors (see illustration). Mark and disconnect any other electrical connectors that would interfere with transmission removal.

9.10 The location of an electrical connector

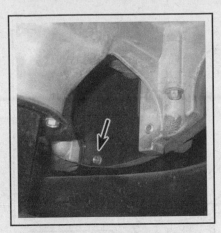

9.11a Driveplate inspection cover bolt

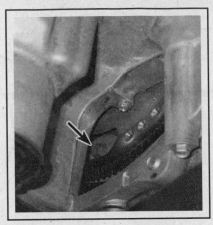

9.11b Remove one of the torque converter bolts . . .

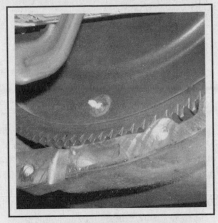

9.11c . . . and mark the relationship of the driveplate to the torque converter (typical shown)

11 Remove the inspection cover and mark the relationship of the torque converter to the driveplate so they can be installed in the same position (see illustrations).

12 Remove the torque converter-to-driveplate bolts. Turn the crankshaft for access to each bolt.

✳✳ **CAUTION:**

Turn the crankshaft in a clockwise direction only (as viewed from the front).

13 Remove the fill/dipstick tube brackets and bolts and pull the tube out of the transmission. Don't lose the tube seal (it can be reused if it's still in good shape).

14 Remove the fitting bolts and detach the fluid cooler lines from the transmission (see illustration). Discard the sealing washers that are present on either side of the fittings; new ones must be used when reconnecting the fittings.

15 On 4WD models, remove the transfer case (see Chapter 7B).

➡**Note: If you are not planning to replace the transmission, but are removing it in order to gain access to other components such as the torque converter, it isn't really necessary to remove the transfer case. However, the transmission and transfer case are awkward and heavy when removed and installed as a single assembly; they're much easier to maneuver off and on as separate units. If you decide to leave the transfer case attached, disconnect the electrical connectors from the transfer case speed sensors and detach the transfer case vent tube (see Chapter 7B).**

✳✳ **WARNING:**

If you decide to leave the transfer case attached to the transmission, be sure to use safety chains to help stabilize the transmission and transfer case assembly and to prevent it from falling off the jack head, which could cause serious damage to the transmission and/or transfer case and serious bodily injury to you.

16 Support the engine with an engine hoist or support fixture from above, or with a jack placed under the oil pan. If you use a floor jack, place a block of wood on the jack head to spread the load.

17 Support the transmission with a jack - preferably a jack made for this purpose (available at most tool rental yards). Safety chains will help steady the transmission on the jack.

18 Remove the fasteners securing the transmission mount to the crossmember. Then raise the transmission slightly and remove the crossmember.

19 Lower the engine and transmission slightly and remove the bolts securing the transmission to the engine. A long extension and a U-joint socket will greatly simplify this step.

➡**Note: Different length bolts are used - be sure to note the location of each bolt so they can be returned to their original positions when the transmission is installed.**

20 Move the transmission to the rear to disengage it from the engine block dowel pins and make sure the torque converter is detached from the driveplate. Lower the transmission with the jack. Clamp a pair of locking pliers on the bellhousing case. The pliers will prevent the torque converter from falling out while you're removing the transmission.

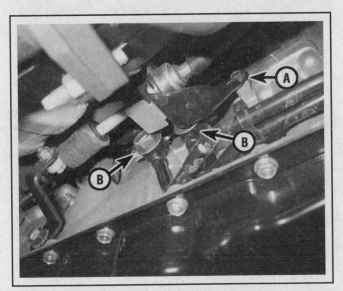

9.14 Location of the shift cable bracket (A) and the transmission fluid line fittings at the transmission (B)

INSTALLATION

▶ **Refer to illustration 9.25**

21 Prior to installation, make sure the torque converter is securely engaged in the pump. If you've removed the converter, apply a small amount of transmission fluid on the torque converter rear hub, where the transmission front seal rides. Install the torque converter onto the front input shaft of the transmission while rotating the converter back and forth. It should engage into the transmission front pump in stages. To make sure the converter is fully engaged, lay a straightedge across the transmission-to-engine mating surface and measure the distance from the straightedge and the converter lugs. The converter lugs must be at least 0.94-inch (24 mm) below the straightedge.

22 With the transmission secured to the jack, raise it into position.

23 Turn the torque converter to line up the holes with the holes in the driveplate. The marks on the torque converter and driveplate made in Step 11 must line up.

24 Move the transmission forward carefully until the dowel pins engage with the holes in the bellhousing. Make sure the transmission mates with the engine with no gap. If there's a gap, make sure there are no wires or other objects pinched between the engine and transmission and also make sure the torque converter is completely engaged in the transmission front pump. Try to rotate the converter - if it doesn't rotate easily, it's probably not fully engaged in the pump. If necessary, lower the transmission and install the converter fully.

25 Install the transmission-to-engine bolts and tighten them to the torque values listed in this Chapter's Specifications (see illustration). As you're tightening the bolts, make sure that the engine and transmission mate completely at all points. If not, find out why. Never try to force the engine and transmission together with the bolts or you'll break the transmission case!

26 Raise the rear of the transmission and install the transmission crossmember.

27 Remove the jacks supporting the transmission and the engine.

28 Install the torque converter-to-driveplate bolts. Once all the bolts have been installed, tighten them to the torque listed in this Chapter's Specifications.

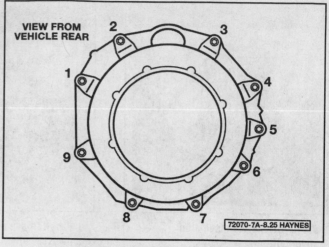

9.25 Transmission-to-engine mounting bolt tightening sequence

29 Install the transmission dipstick tube and seal into the transmission housing, then install the bolt and tighten it securely.

30 Install the torque converter inspection cover.

31 Using new sealing washers, connect the transmission fluid cooler lines to the transmission, tightening the fitting bolts securely.

32 Plug in the transmission electrical connectors.

33 Connect the shift cable (see Section 4).

34 On 4WD models, install the transfer case, if removed (see Chapter 7B).

35 Install the driveshaft(s) (see Chapter 8).

36 Adjust the shift cable (see Section 4).

37 Install any exhaust system components that were removed or disconnected (see Chapter 4).

38 Remove the jackstands and lower the vehicle.

39 Fill the transmission with the specified fluid (see Chapter 1), run the engine and check for fluid leaks.

10 Transmission Control Module (TCM) - removal and installation

The Transmission Control Module (TCM) is a microprocessor that controls many aspects of automatic transmission performance. It is located inside of the transmission at the valve body, along with the transmission fluid temperature sensor. The harness from these two electronic devices extends to a plug secured to the transmission case, sealed with an O-ring and an external lock-ring.

Other than with a Nissan Consult-II or other professional-grade scan tool, there is no way for the home mechanic to troubleshoot or diagnose the TCM, and removal or installation of the TCM should be performed at a dealership service department or a qualified transmission repair shop.

Specifications

General

Transmission fluid type	See Chapter 1

Torque Specifications	Ft-lbs (unless otherwise indicated)	Nm

➡ **Note: One foot-pound (ft-lb) of torque is equivalent to 12 inch-pounds (in-lbs) of torque. Torque values below approximately 15 ft-lbs are expressed in inch-pounds, since most foot-pound torque wrenches are not accurate at these smaller values.**

Transmission fluid pan bolts	70 in-lbs	8
Torque converter-to-driveplate bolts	38	52
Transmission-to-engine bolts	83	113

Notes

Section

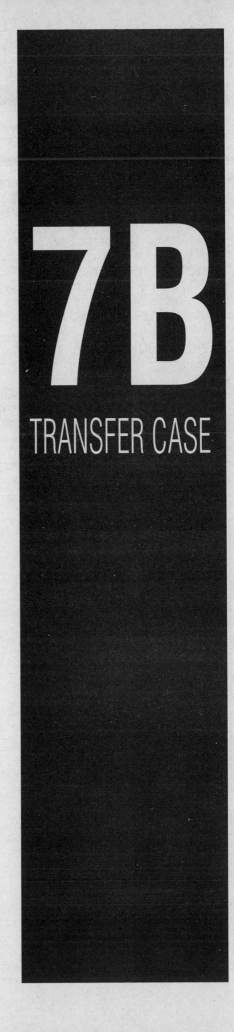

7B
TRANSFER CASE

1 General information

1 Four-Wheel Drive (4WD) models are equipped with an electronically-controlled transfer case that distributes power to both front and rear axles when the system is engaged. A switch on the instrument panel allows a choice of 2WD, 4WD High or 4WD Low.

2 Input from the switch goes to the Transfer Control Unit, which communicates with the transfer case actuator, the automatic transmission, and other devices. The actuator consists of an electric shift motor and a Transfer Case Position Switch. The motor actually does the mechanical shifting of the transfer case, when directed by the Transfer Control Unit. The Transfer Case Position Switch communicates the actual position of the electric shift motor to the Control Unit at all times.

3 We don't recommend trying to rebuild this transfer case. They're difficult to overhaul without special tools, and rebuilt units may be available that represent a savings of time and money.

TROUBLESHOOTING

▶ **Refer to illustration 1.11**

4 Problems with the transfer case system will make the 4WD warning light illuminate on the instrument panel when the engine is started. Although the transfer case control system is electronic and a scan tool is the best diagnostic device, you can output a number of diagnostic codes through the 4WD warning light.

5 Begin with the engine at normal operating temperature. Turn the ignition key On and Off twice, ending with the key Off. Apply the vehicle parking brake.

6 Move the transmission shift lever to Park. With the 4WD switch turned to the 2WD position, turn the key On. The 4WD warning light should come on for a second or two, then go off, indicating the 4WD system is OK.

7 Move the transmission shifter to Reverse.

8 In sequence, turn the 4WD selector switch from 2WD to 4High and back to 2WD.

9 Move the transmission shift lever to Park and turn the shift switch from 4High to 2WD and back to 4High.

10 Move the transmission shifter to Neutral and turn the 4WD selector switch to 2WD.

11 Move the transmission shift lever to Park. You can now read the trouble codes as a series of blinks on the 4WD warning light. Two blinks would be code 2, 10 blinks would be code 10. Refer to the chart (see illustration) for a list of codes.

➡**Note: When the light first comes on, it will be on for 2.5 seconds, off for 1 second, then the code blinks will begin.**

1.11 Diagnostic chart for reading codes through the blinks of the 4WD warning light on the instrument panel

Blinks	Problem with Transfer Case control system
2	Output shaft revolution sensor signal
3	Vehicle Speed Sensor (ABS system)
4	CAN network communication error
5	Transfer Control Unit
6	4Low switch, open or short
7	Improper engine speed signal from PCM
8	Power supply voltage low
9	4WD shift switch, short circuit
10	Improper signal from wait detection switch
11	Malfunction in actuator motor
12	Actuator position switch
13	Transfer shutoff relays
14	PNP switch signal
constant, four times per second	Memory backup power supply drained
none	PNP of 4WD switches, shorted or open

2 Transfer control unit - replacement

1   With the transfer case in 2WD, turn off the engine and disconnect the cable from the negative battery terminal.

2   Remove the glove compartment (see Chapter 11).

3   Disconnect the two electrical connectors at the Transfer Control Unit.

4   Remove the bolts and take the Transfer Control Unit out.

5   Installation is the reverse of the removal procedure, with the following exception. Check for correct positions of the transfer case system by moving the 4WD selector switch through its range. If the position on the switch does not correspond to the position of the shift actuator on the transfer case, perform the following Steps.

6   With the vehicle warmed to operating temperature, move the 4WD selector switch from 2WD to 4High to 4Low to 4High and back to 2WD. Keep the selector in each of these positions for at least two seconds.

7   Observe the 4WD shift indicator light on the instrument panel and the 4Low indicator light. The 4Low light should come on only when in 4Low, and it will flash for a few seconds while waiting for the shift actuator to complete a move to 4Low. Move the vehicle enough to ascertain that the transfer case is in 4Low when the selector switch is in that position and the dash light is on. If the 4WD indicator light or 4Low light are blinking for more than a few seconds, return to 2WD and have the relationship between the 4WD switch and the shift actuator corrected at a dealership with a scan tool.

3 Shift actuator and position switch - replacement

1   Position the 4WD selector switch to 2WD and turn off the vehicle. Raise the vehicle and support it securely on jackstands.

➡**Note: On Armada models equipped with a rear auto-leveling suspension, turn the ignition key to the OFF position before raising the vehicle.**

2   From below, disconnect the electrical connector at the shift actuator assembly. The shift position switch is an integral part of the shift actuator assembly.

3   Disconnect the breather hose from the actuator, then remove the mounting bolts and pull the actuator assembly from the transfer case.

4   Before reinstalling the actuator assembly, turn the flat-sided end of the shift rod on the transfer case as far as it can go counterclockwise and make a mark on the end of the rod.

5   Turn the notch in the shift actuator rod to align with the mark on the rod and, with a new O-ring in place on the actuator (lubricated with petroleum jelly), install the shift actuator assembly.

6   The remainder of the installation is the reverse of the removal procedure.

4 Oil seals - replacement

➡**Note: This procedure applies to both the front and rear output shaft seals.**

1   Raise the vehicle and support it securely on jackstands.

➡**Note: On Armada models equipped with a rear auto-leveling suspension, turn the ignition key to the OFF position before raising the vehicle.**

2   If you're replacing the front seal, remove the front driveshaft; if you're replacing the rear seal, remove the rear driveshaft (see Chapter 8).

➡**Note: It may be helpful to drain some of the fluid from the transfer case. Otherwise be prepared for some spillage.**

FRONT SEAL

▶ **Refer to illustrations 4.3 and 4.4**

3   A flange holding tool will be required to keep the companion flange from moving while the nut is loosened. A chain wrench will also work (see illustration). Remove the flange nut, then make index marks matching the relationship of the shaft (that the nut was removed from) to the flange.

4   Withdraw the flange. It may be necessary to use a two-jaw puller engaged behind the flange to draw it off (see illustration). Do not attempt to pry or hammer behind the flange or hammer on the end of the shaft.

4.3 A chain wrench can be used to prevent the flange from turning while the nut is removed

4.4 A two-jaw puller will be required to remove the flange if it won't come off by hand

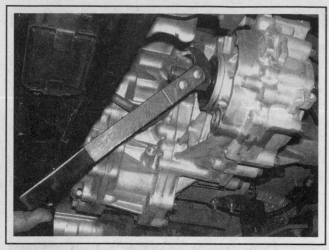

4.5 Use a seal removal tool or a large screwdriver to pry the seal out

4.6 Drive the new seal into place with a seal driver or a socket with an outside diameter slightly smaller than that of the seal

FRONT OR REAR SEAL

◆ **Refer to illustrations 4.5 and 4.6**

5   Pry out the old seal and discard it (see illustration). On rear seals, pry the dust cover off of the case that's near the shaft to expose the seal.

6   Lubricate the lips of the new seal and the seal case with petroleum jelly, then tap it evenly into position with a seal installation tool or a large socket (see illustration). Make sure it enters the housing squarely and is tapped in to its full depth.

7   Install a new dust cover with the index mark at the 12 o'clock position. Lubricate the inner circumference of the dust cover with petroleum jelly.

FRONT SEAL

→**Note: When installing the companion flange, use a new self-locking nut.**

8   Install the companion flange by using the matchmarks made in Step 3. If necessary, tighten the nut to draw the flange into place. Do not try to hammer the flange into position.

9   Apply a bead of RTV sealant to the ends of the splines visible in the center of the flange so oil will be sealed in.

10   Install the nut. Tighten the nut to the torque listed in this Chapter's Specifications.

FRONT OR REAR SEAL

11   Install the driveshaft (see Chapter 8). Check and, if necessary, add the recommended type of lubricant to bring the level up to the bottom of the filler hole (see Chapter 1).

5   Transfer case - removal and installation

REMOVAL

→**Note: Be sure to set the transfer assembly to 2WD before performing the following procedure.**

1   Position the 4WD selector switch to 2WD and turn off the vehicle. Disconnect the cable from the negative battery terminal (see Chapter 5).

2   Raise the vehicle and support it securely on jackstands. Remove the skid plate, if equipped.

Note: On Armada models equipped with a rear auto-leveling suspension, turn the ignition key to the OFF position before raising the vehicle.

3   Remove the main muffler and related exhaust pipes (see Chapter 4).

4   Disconnect the two vent tubes, one from the shift actuator and one from the transfer case.

5   Drain the transfer case lubricant (see Chapter 1).

6   Remove the front and rear driveshafts (see Chapter 8).

7   Insert a rubber plug into the rear seal after the rear driveshaft has been removed.

8   Unplug all electrical connectors and detach the vent hose from the top of the transfer case.

9   Support the transmission with a floor jack. Place a block of wood on the jack head to spread the load.

10   Support the transfer case with a jack - preferably a special jack made for this purpose. Safety chains will help steady the transfer case on the jack.

11   Remove the crossmember used to support the transmission.

12   Lower the jacks supporting the transmission and transfer case just enough for access to the upper mounting fasteners.

13 Remove the transmission-to-transfer case bolts.

➡**Note: On some models, there may be two different lengths of bolts securing the transfer case to the transmission. Mark their positions or keep them in order when removed so they can be returned to their proper locations.**

14 Make a final check that all wires and hoses have been disconnected from the transfer case, then move the transfer case and jack toward the rear of the vehicle until the transfer case is clear of the transmission. Keep the transfer case level as this is done. Once the input shaft is clear, lower the transfer case and remove it from under the vehicle.

INSTALLATION

15 Installation is the reverse of removal, noting the following points:

a) *Apply anaerobic liquid gasket sealant (not RTV sealant) to the transfer case-to-transmission mating surface.*

b) *Be sure to install the transmission-to-transfer case bolts in their proper locations and tighten them to the torque listed in this Chapter's Specifications.*

c) *Refill the transfer case with the proper type and quantity of lubricant (see Chapter 1).*

d) *Check that the 4WD shift indicator corresponds to the position of the transfer case (see Section 2)*

6   Transfer case overhaul - general information

Overhauling a transfer case is a difficult job for the do-it-yourselfer. It involves the disassembly and reassembly of many small parts. Numerous clearances must be precisely measured and, if necessary, changed with select-fit spacers and snap-rings. As a result, if transfer case problems arise, it can be removed and installed by a competent do-it-yourselfer, but overhaul should be left to a transmission repair shop. Rebuilt transfer cases may be available - check with your dealer parts department and auto parts stores. At any rate, the time and money involved in an overhaul is almost sure to exceed the cost of a rebuilt unit.

Nevertheless, it's not impossible for an inexperienced mechanic to rebuild a transfer case if the special tools are available and the job is done in a deliberate step-by-step manner so nothing is overlooked.

The tools necessary for an overhaul include internal and external snap-ring pliers, a bearing puller, a slide hammer, a set of pin punches, a dial indicator and possibly a hydraulic press. In addition, a large, sturdy workbench will be required.

During disassembly of the transfer case, make careful notes of how each piece comes off, where it fits in relation to other pieces and what holds it in place. Note how parts are installed when you remove them; this will make it much easier to get the transfer case back together.

Before taking the transfer case apart for repair, it will help if you have some idea what area of the transfer case is malfunctioning. Certain problems can be closely tied to specific areas in the transfer case, which can make component examination and replacement easier. Refer to the *Troubleshooting* section at the front of this manual for information regarding possible sources of trouble. Check for trouble codes for the transfer case system with the procedure outlined in Section 1.

Torque specifications	Ft-lbs	Nm
Actuator assembly-to-transfer case bolts	16	22
Companion flange nut	203	275
Oil drain or fill plugs	26	35
Transfer case-to-transmission mounting bolts	27	37

8

DRIVELINE

Section

1 Driveshaft and universal joints - general information and inspection

GENERAL INFORMATION

1 A driveshaft is a tube, or a pair of tubes, that transmits power between the transmission (or transfer case on 4WD models) and the differential. Universal joints are located at either end of the driveshaft and in the center on two-piece driveshafts.

2 Single-piece rear driveshafts employ a splined yoke at the front, which slips into the extension housing of the transfer case or transmission. The rear portion of a two-piece rear driveshaft has a splined yoke that slips onto the rear of the front portion of the driveshaft. This arrangement allows the driveshaft to slide back-and-forth during vehicle operation to compensate for changes in length due to suspension movement.

3 Models with a two-piece rear driveshaft are equipped with a center support bearing attached to a frame crossmember.

4 The front driveshaft on 4WD models is equipped with a slip joint in the center of the shaft to allow for changes in driveshaft length due to suspension movement.

5 The driveshaft assembly requires very little service. The universal joints are lubricated for life and must be replaced if problems develop. The driveshaft must be removed from the vehicle for this procedure.

6 Since the driveshaft is a balanced unit, it's important that no undercoating, mud, etc. be allowed to stay on it. When the vehicle is raised for service it's a good idea to clean the driveshaft and inspect it for any obvious damage. Also, make sure the small weights used to originally balance the driveshaft are in place and securely attached. Whenever the driveshaft is removed it must be reinstalled in the same relative position to preserve the balance.

7 Problems with the driveshaft are usually indicated by a noise or vibration while driving the vehicle. A road test should verify if the problem is the driveshaft or another vehicle component. Refer to the *Troubleshooting* Section at the front of this manual. If you suspect trouble, inspect the driveline.

INSPECTION

8 Raise the vehicle and support it securely on jackstands. Block the wheels at the opposite end to keep the vehicle from rolling off the stands. Release the parking brake (if you're inspecting the rear driveshaft) and place the transmission in Neutral.

9 Crawl under the vehicle and visually inspect the driveshaft. Look for any dents or cracks in the tubing. If any are found, the driveshaft must be replaced.

10 Check for oil leakage at the front and rear of the driveshaft. Leakage where the driveshaft enters the transmission or transfer case indicates a defective transmission/transfer case seal (see Chapter 7). If you're working on an Armada, also check for looseness of the joints of the rear driveaxles. Grease leakage at the CV joint boots means a damaged rubber boot.

11 While under the vehicle, have an assistant rotate a wheel so the driveshaft will rotate. As it does, make sure the universal joints are operating properly without binding, noise or looseness. Listen for any noise from the center bearing (two-piece driveshafts), indicating it's worn or damaged. Also check the rubber portion of the center bearing for cracking or separation, which will necessitate replacement.

12 The universal joint can also be checked with the driveshaft motionless, by gripping your hands on either side of the joint and attempting to twist the joint. Any movement at all in the joint is a sign of considerable wear. Lifting up on the shaft will also indicate movement in the universal joints.

13 Finally, check the driveshaft mounting bolts at the ends to make sure they're tight.

14 On 4WD models, the above driveshaft checks should be repeated on the front driveshaft, as well. In addition, check for leakage around the slip yoke, indicating failure of the yoke seal.

15 Check for leakage where the driveshafts connect to the transfer case and front differential. Leakage indicates worn oil seals.

16 At the same time, check for looseness in the joints of the front driveaxles. Also check for grease or oil leakage from around the driveaxles by inspecting the rubber boots and both ends of each axle. Oil leakage around the axle flanges indicates a defective axleshaft oil seal. Grease leakage at the CV joint boots means a damaged rubber boot. For servicing of these components, see the appropriate Sections.

2 Driveshaft(s) - removal and installation

❉❉ WARNING:

The manufacturer recommends replacing the universal joint flange nuts and bolts whenever they are removed.

REAR DRIVESHAFT

Removal

♦ **Refer to illustration 2.2**

1 Raise the vehicle and support it securely on jackstands. Place the transmission in Neutral with the parking brake off.

2 Make reference marks on the driveshaft flange and the pinion flange in line with each other (see illustration).

3 Remove the rear universal joint nuts and bolts. Turn the driveshaft (or wheels) as necessary to bring the bolts into the most accessible position.

4 If you're working on a model with a two-piece driveshaft, unbolt the center support bearing from the crossmember.

5 Lower the rear of the driveshaft, then slide the front yoke out of the transmission or transfer case.

6 Wrap a plastic bag over the transmission or transfer case housing and hold it in place with a rubber band. This will prevent loss of fluid and protect against contamination while the driveshaft is out.

Installation

7   Remove the plastic bag from the transmission or transfer case and wipe the area clean. Inspect the oil seal carefully. Procedures for replacement of this seal can be found in Chapter 7.

8   Slide the front yoke of the driveshaft into the transmission or transfer case, being careful not to damage the seal in the process.

9   If you're working on model with a two-piece driveshaft, raise the center support bearing into position, install the fasteners and tighten them securely.

10 Raise the rear of the driveshaft into position, checking to be sure the marks are in alignment. If not, turn the rear wheels to match the pinion flange and the driveshaft.

11 Install the new bolts and nuts, tightening them securely.

FRONT DRIVESHAFT (4WD MODELS)

Removal

12 Raise the front of the vehicle and place it securely on jackstands. Remove the skid plate, if equipped.

13 Mark the relationship of the driveshaft to the front differential companion flange and to the transfer case companion flange.

14 Remove the bolts and nuts from the flanges, then lower the shaft from the vehicle.

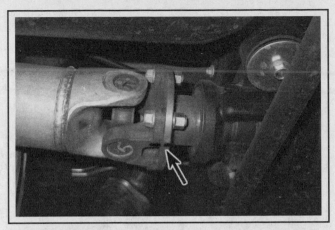

2.2 Mark the relationship of the driveshaft flange to the pinion flange

Installation

15 Attach the ends of the shaft to the differential and transfer case companion flanges (be sure to line up the marks), install the new bolts and nuts and tighten them securely.

16 Install the skid plate (if equipped).

---

3   Driveshaft center support bearing - replacement

1   Remove the driveshaft (see Section 2).

2   Mark the relationship of the front portion of the driveshaft to the rear portion of the driveshaft (it's best to make the mark on the slip yoke). Slide the rear shaft off the front shaft.

3   If you have access to a hydraulic press (one tall enough to accommodate the shaft) and the necessary fixtures, press the shaft out

of the center support bearing. Reverse this operation to install the new bearing.

4   If you do not have the necessary equipment, take the shaft to an automotive machine shop or other qualified repair facility to have the old bearing pressed off and the new one pressed on.

---

4   Universal joints - replacement

▶ **Refer to illustrations 4.3, 4.4, 4.5, 4.6 and 4.16**

➡**Note 1: Always purchase a universal joint service kit for your model vehicle before beginning this procedure. Also, read through the entire procedure before beginning work.**

➡**Note 2: On all models, select-fit snap-rings are available to adjust the universal joint endplay, which should be 0.0008-inch (0.02 mm) or less. Check with your local auto parts store or dealer service department if the endplay is greater than specified after the joint is assembled (or if the joint is extremely tight and won't free-up).**

1   Remove the driveshaft (see Section 2).

2   Place the driveshaft on a bench equipped with a vise.

3   Remove the snap-rings with a small pair of pliers (see illustration).

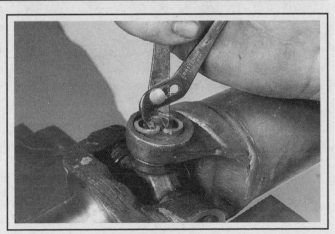

4.3 Use a small pair of pliers to remove the snap-rings from the ends of the universal joint yokes

4.4 To remove the U-joint from the driveshaft, use a vise as a press - the small socket will push the cross and bearing cap into the large socket

4.5 Locking pliers can be used to remove the bearing caps from the yoke

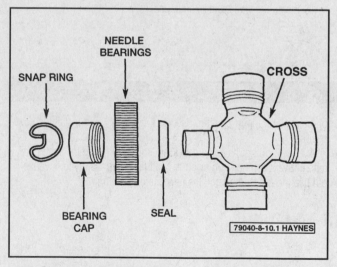

4.6 Outer snap-ring type U-joint

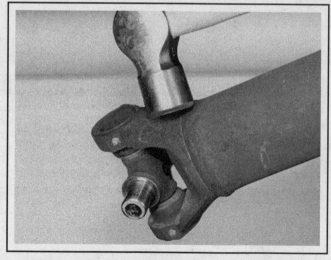

4.16 Strike the yoke sharply with a hammer to spring the yoke ears, which will free-up the joint

4 Support the cross (also called a spider) on a short piece of pipe or a large socket and use another socket to press out the cross by closing the vise (see illustration).

5 Press the cross through as far as possible, then grip the bearing cap with pliers and remove it (see illustration).

6 A universal joint repair kit will contain a new cross, seals, bearings, caps and snap-rings (see illustration).

7 Inspect the bearing cap bores in the yokes for wear and damage.

8 If the bearing cap bores in the yoke are so worn that the caps are a loose fit, the driveshaft will have to be replaced with a new one.

9 Make sure the dust seals are properly located on the cross.

10 Using a vise, press one bearing cap into the yoke approximately 1/4-inch.

11 Use chassis grease to hold the needle rollers in place in the caps.

12 Insert the cross into the partially installed bearing cap, taking care not to dislodge the needle rollers.

13 Hold the cross in correct alignment and press both caps into place by slowly and carefully closing the jaws of the vise.

14 Use a socket slightly smaller in diameter than the caps to press them into the yoke. Press in one side, install the snap-ring, then press the other side to shift the cross assembly tight against the installed snap-ring and install the other snap-ring.

15 Repeat the operations for the remaining two bearing caps.

16 If the joint is stiff after assembly, strike the yoke sharply with a hammer (see illustration). This will spring the yoke ears slightly and free up the joint.

5 Rear axleshaft, bearing and oil seals (Titan models only) - removal, bearing/seal replacement and installation

❋❋ WARNING:

The manufacturer recommends replacing the axle retaining plate nuts with new ones whenever they are removed.

REMOVAL

▶ **Refer to illustration 5.3**

1 Loosen the wheel lug nuts, raise the rear of the vehicle and support it securely on jackstands. Chock the front wheels to prevent the vehicle from rolling. Remove the wheel.

2 Remove the brake caliper and wire it to the chassis so it doesn't hang by the brake hose (see Chapter 9). Remove the brake disc and disconnect the ABS wheel speed sensor and position it out of the way.

3 Remove the nuts securing the axle retaining plate to the axle housing (see illustration).

4 Connect a slide hammer and adapter to the axle flange and pull the axle from the housing. The disc brake dust shield will come out with the axle.

5 The manufacturer suggests that any time an axle is pulled, the axle bearing and the axle seal should be replaced. The axle should be taken to a machine shop, where the old bearing and axle seal can be removed and a new bearing pressed on. In the process of removing the bearing, inspect the ABS wheel sensor rotor and replace if necessary. If the sensor rotor is removed, it must be replaced with a new ABS sensor rotor.

INSTALLATION

6 Wipe the bore in the axle housing clean and apply a thin coat of

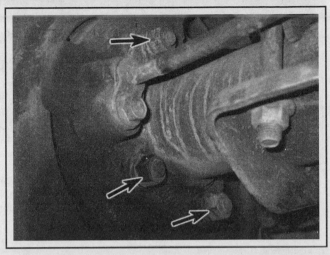

5.3 Rear axle retaining plate nuts (three of four shown)

grease to the outer surface of the axle bearing.

7 Guide the axleshaft straight into the axle housing. Rotate the shaft slightly to engage the splines on the shaft with the splines in the differential side gear.

8 Install new axle retaining plate nuts and tighten them to the torque listed in this Chapter's Specifications.

9 The remainder of installation is the reverse of removal. Check the differential lubricant level and add some, if necessary.

10 Install the wheel and lug nuts. Lower the vehicle and tighten the lug nuts to the torque listed in the Chapter 1 Specifications.

6 Pinion oil seal (front and rear) - replacement

▶ **Refer to illustrations 6.4, 6.5, 6.6, 6.8 and 6.10**

1 Loosen the wheel lug nuts. Raise the front (for front differential) or rear (for rear differential) of the vehicle and support it securely on jackstands. Block the opposite set of wheels to keep the vehicle from rolling off the stands. Remove the wheels.

2 Disconnect the driveshaft from the differential companion flange and fasten it out of the way (see Section 2).

3 Remove the rear brake discs.

4 Rotate the pinion a few times by hand. Use a beam-type or dial-type inch-pound torque wrench to check the torque required to rotate the pinion (see illustration). Record it for use later.

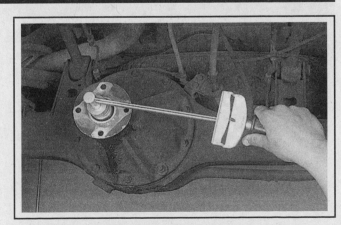

6.4 Use an inch-pound torque wrench to check the torque necessary to rotate the pinion shaft

6.5 Mark the position of the flange to the shaft and count the number of exposed threads above the nut

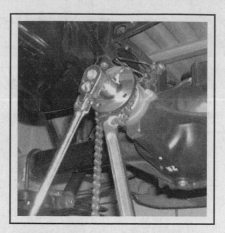

6.6 A chain wrench is being used here to prevent the pinion flange from turning while the nut is loosened

6.8 If you can't pull the pinion flange off by hand, remove it with a puller

6.10 Lubricate the lips of the new seal and seat it squarely in the bore, then drive it into the carrier with a seal driver or a large socket

5   Mark the relationship of the pinion flange to the shaft (see illustration), then count and write down the number of exposed threads on the shaft.

6   A flange holding tool will be required to keep the companion flange from moving while the self-locking pinion nut is loosened. A chain wrench will also work (see illustration).

7   Remove the pinion nut.

8   Withdraw the flange. It may be necessary to use a two-jaw puller engaged behind the flange to draw it off (see illustration). Do not attempt to pry or hammer behind the flange or hammer on the end of the pinion shaft.

9   Pry out the old seal and discard it.

10 Lubricate the lips of the new seal and fill the space between the seal lips with wheel bearing grease, then tap it evenly into position with a seal installation tool or a large socket (see illustration). Make sure it enters the housing squarely and is tapped in to its full depth.

11 Install the pinion flange, lining up the marks made in Step 5. If necessary, tighten the pinion nut to draw the flange into place. Do not try to hammer the flange into position.

12 Apply a bead of RTV sealant to the ends of the splines visible in the center of the flange so oil will be sealed in.

13 Install a new pinion nut and pinion nut lockwasher. Do not reuse the old nut or lockwasher. Tighten the nut until the number of threads exposed in Step 5 is showing.

14 Measure the torque required to rotate the pinion and tighten the nut in small increments (no more than 5 ft-lbs) until it matches the figure recorded in Step 4. To compensate for the drag of the new oil seal, the nut should be tightened a little more until the rotational torque of the pinion exceeds the earlier recording by 5 in-lbs.

✳✳ CAUTION:

If the maximum nut torque is reached before the desired preload is obtained, the differential must be disassembled and a new collapsible spacer must be installed.

15 Reinstall all components removed previously by reversing the removal Steps and tightening all fasteners to their specified torque values.

7 Axle assembly (rear) - removal and installation

TITAN MODELS

1 Loosen the rear wheel lug nuts, raise the rear of the vehicle and support it securely on jackstands placed under the frame rails. Block the front wheels to keep the vehicle from rolling off the stands. Remove the rear wheels.

2 Position a jack under the rear axle differential housing. If you have two floor jacks, position one under each axle tube.

3 Disconnect the driveshaft from the differential companion flange (see Section 2). Secure the driveshaft out of the way with a piece of wire from the underbody.

4 Disconnect the vent hose from the fitting on the axle housing and fasten it out of the way.

5 Drain the differential lubricant (see Chapter 1).

6 Remove the brake calipers and set them aside (see Chapter 9). Wire the calipers to the chassis so they don't hang by the brake hoses (see Chapter 9). Remove the brake discs. Disconnect and set aside the ABS wheel sensor harness connectors at the axle ends.

7 Disconnect the parking brake cables, the brake lines and the ABS wheel speed sensor harnesses from the axle assembly, being careful to plug the open brake line fittings to prevent entry of dirt.

8 Remove the nuts from the bottom of the leaf-spring U-bolts and remove the spring plates (see Chapter 10).

9 Make sure nothing is still connected, then lower the jack(s) and remove the rear axle from under the vehicle.

10 Installation is the reverse of removal. Tighten all suspension fasteners to the torque values listed in the Chapter 10 Specifications. Tighten the U-joint bolts to the torque listed in this Chapter's Specifications.

ARMADA MODELS

▶ **Refer to illustration 7.14**

11 Loosen the rear wheel lug nuts, raise the rear of the vehicle and support it securely on jackstands placed under the frame rails. Block the front wheels to keep the vehicle from rolling off the stands. Remove the rear wheels.

12 Remove the spare tire.

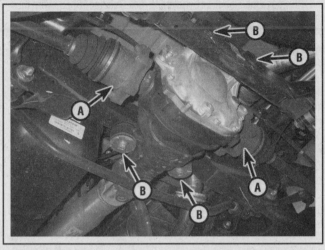

7.14 Rear differential assembly details - Armada models

A   *Rear driveaxle and flange bolts*
B   *Rear differential mounting fasteners*

13 Remove the rear stabilizer bar (see Chapter 10).

14 Unbolt the end of the driveaxles (see illustration) from the differential flanges and support the driveaxles with pieces of wire from the underbody.

15 Disconnect the driveshaft (see Section 2). Secure the driveshaft out of the way with a piece of wire from the underbody.

16 Drain the differential lubricant (see Chapter 1).

17 Position a jack under the rear differential housing.

18 Disconnect the vent hose from the fitting on the differential housing and fasten it out of the way.

19 Remove the rear differential mounting fasteners, then the fasteners at the front of the differential assembly and slowly lower the assembly down.

20 Installation is the reverse of removal. Tighten the U-joint bolts, the driveaxle flange bolts and the rear differential mounting bolts to the torque listed in this Chapter's Specifications. Tighten the stabilizer bar fasteners to the torque values listed in the Chapter 10 Specifications.

8 Driveaxle (4WD and Armada models) - removal and installation

FRONT DRIVEAXLE (4WD MODELS)

1 Loosen the wheel lug nuts, pry off the hub cover and remove the cotter pin from the driveaxle/hub nut, then use a breaker bar and a socket to loosen the driveaxle/hub nut. Raise the front of the vehicle and support it securely on jackstands. Remove the front wheel(s).

2 Remove the screws and the engine undercover.

3 Disconnect the ABS wheel sensor harness at the hub and wire it out of the way.

4 Remove the driveaxle/hub nut.

5 Remove the coil spring/shock absorber assembly (see Chapter 10).

6 Disconnect the upper balljoint from the upper control arm (see Chapter 10).

7 Pull the steering knuckle outward enough for the splines of the

driveaxle to clear the knuckle.

8 Unbolt the end of the driveaxle from the front differential flange.

9 Installation is the reverse of removal. Tighten the driveaxle flange bolts to the torque listed in this Chapter's Specifications.

10 Install the wheel and lug nuts. Lower the vehicle and tighten the lug nuts to the torque listed in the Chapter 1 Specifications. Tighten the driveaxle/hub nut to the torque listed in this Chapters Specifications.

REAR DRIVEAXLE (ARMADA MODELS)

▶ **Refer to illustration 8.14**

11 Loosen the wheel lug nuts, pry off the hub cover and remove the cotter pin from the driveaxle/hub nut, then use a breaker bar and a

socket to loosen the driveaxle/hub nut. Raise the rear of the vehicle and support it securely on jackstands. Remove the rear wheel(s).

12 Remove the stabilizer bar clamps (see Chapter 10) and wire the bar out of the way.

13 Remove the driveaxle/hub nut.

14 Unbolt the end (see illustration) of the driveaxle from the rear differential flange.

15 To loosen the driveaxle from the hub splines, tap the end of the driveaxle with a hammer and brass punch. If the driveaxle is stuck in the hub splines and won't move, it may be necessary to push the driveaxle with a suitable puller.

16 Installation is the reverse of removal. Tighten the driveaxle flange bolts to the torque listed in this Chapter's Specifications. Tighten the stabilizer bar clamp bolts to the torque listed in the Chapter 10 Specifications.

17 Install the wheel and lug nuts. Lower the vehicle and tighten the lug nuts to the torque listed in the Chapter 1 Specifications. Tighten the driveaxle/hub nut to the torque listed in this Chapters Specifications.

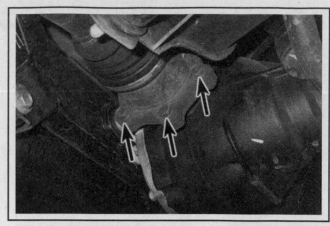

8.14 Remove the driveaxle mounting bolts and separate the driveaxle from the differential assembly - three of six bolts shown

9 Driveaxle boot - replacement

➡**Note 1: If the CV joints are worn, indicating the need for an overhaul (usually due to torn boots), explore all options before beginning the job. Complete rebuilt driveaxles are available on an exchange basis, which eliminates much time and work.**

➡**Note 2: Some auto parts stores carry split type replacement boots, which can be installed without removing the driveaxle from the vehicle. This is a convenient alternative; however, the driveaxle should be removed and the CV joint disassembled and cleaned to ensure the joint is free from contaminants such as moisture and dirt which will accelerate CV joint wear.**

1 Remove the driveaxle from the vehicle (see Section 8).

2 Mount the driveaxle in a vise. The jaws of the vise should be lined with wood or rags to prevent damage to the driveaxle.

INNER CV JOINT

Disassembly

▶ **Refer to illustrations 9.3, 9.4, 9.5, 9.7, 9.9, 9.10 and 9.11**

3 Pry open the locking tabs on the boot clamps, remove the clamps from the boot and discard them (see illustration).

4 Slide the boot back on the axleshaft and pry the wire ring ball retainer from the outer race (see illustration).

5 Pull the outer race off the inner bearing assembly (see illustration).

6 Wipe as much grease as possible off the inner bearing.

7 Remove the snap-ring from the end of the axleshaft (see illustration).

8 Slide the inner bearing assembly off the axleshaft. If it won't slide off, tap it off using a hammer and brass punch placed against the inner race.

9 Mark the inner race and cage to ensure that they are reassembled with the correct sides facing out (see illustration).

10 Using a screwdriver or piece of wood, pry the balls from the cage (see illustration). Be careful not to scratch the inner race, the balls or the cage.

11 Rotate the inner race 90-degrees, align the inner race lands with the cage windows and rotate the race out of the cage (see illustration).

9.3 To remove the boot clamps, pry open the locking tabs

9.4 Pry the wire retainer ring from the CV joint housing with a small screwdriver

9.5 With the retainer removed, the outer race can be pulled off the bearing assembly

9.7 Remove the snap-ring from the end of the axleshaft

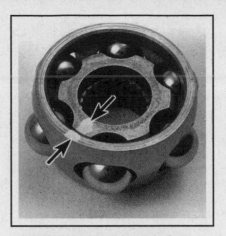

9.9 Make index marks on the inner race and cage so they'll both be facing the same direction when reassembled

9.10 Pry the balls from the cage with a screwdriver (be careful not to nick or scratch them)

9.11 Tilt the inner race 90-degrees and rotate it out of the cage

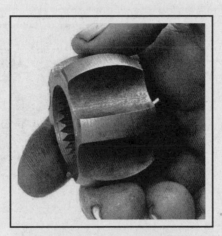

9.12a Inspect the inner race lands and grooves for pitting and score marks

9.12b Inspect the cage for cracks, pitting and score marks (shiny spots are normal and don't affect operation)

Inspection

‣ **Refer to illustrations 9.12a and 9.12b**

12 Clean the components with solvent to remove all traces of grease. Inspect the cage and races for pitting, score marks, cracks and other signs of wear and damage. Shiny, polished spots are normal and will not adversely affect CV joint performance (see illustrations). If the outer CV joint boot is torn or damaged, now is the time to set aside the inner CV joint parts, remove the outer boot, and clean and inspect the outer CV joint.

Reassembly

‣ **Refer to illustrations 9.14, 9.15, 9.17, 9.20, 9.23a, 9.23b, 9.24a and 9.24b**

13 Insert the inner race into the cage. Verify that the matchmarks are on the same side. However, it's not necessary for them to be in direct alignment with each other.

14 Press the balls into the cage windows with your thumbs (see illustration).

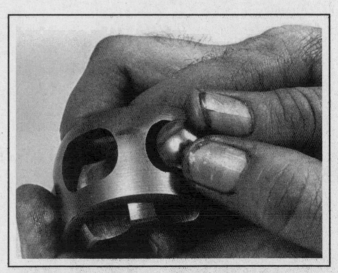

9.14 Press the balls into the cage through the windows

9.15 Wrap the splined area of the axleshaft with tape to prevent damage to the boot(s) when installing it

9.17 Install the inner race and cage assembly with the large diameter end toward the splined end of the axleshaft

9.20 Pack grease into the bearing until it's completely full

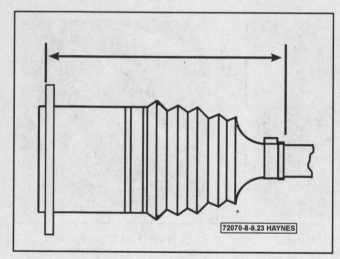

9.23a Before tightening the boot clamps, adjust the CV joint to the proper length . . .

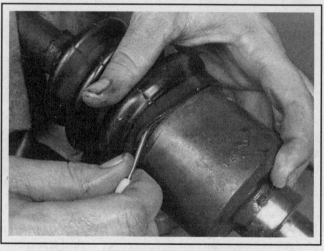

9.23b . . . then equalize the pressure inside the boot by inserting a small, dull screwdriver between the boot and the outer race

15 Wrap the axleshaft splines with tape to avoid damaging the boot (see illustration).

16 Slide the small boot clamp and boot onto the axleshaft, then remove the tape.

17 Install the inner race and cage assembly on the axleshaft with the larger diameter side, or bulge, of the cage facing the axleshaft end (see illustration).

18 Install the snap-ring.

19 Fill the boot with CV joint grease (normally included with the new boot kit).

20 Pack the inner race and cage assembly with grease, by hand, until grease is worked completely into the assembly (see illustration).

21 Slide the outer race down onto the inner race and install the wire ring retainer.

22 Wipe any excess grease from the axle boot groove on the outer race. Seat the small diameter of the boot in the recessed area on the axleshaft and install the clamp. Push the other end of the boot onto the outer CV joint housing and seat it into the recessed area on the housing.

23 Adjust the CV joint to the proper length, then equalize the pressure in the boot by inserting a dull screwdriver between the boot and the outer race (see illustrations). Don't damage the boot with the tool.

24 Install the boot clamps (see illustrations).

25 Install the driveaxle assembly (see Section 8).

OUTER CV JOINT

▶ **Refer to illustrations 9.27a through 9.27k**

26 Remove the driveaxle (see Section 8), then remove the boot clamps (see illustration 9.3).

27 Refer to the accompanying illustrations and perform the outer CV joint boot replacement procedure (see illustrations 9.27a through 9.27k).

9.24a To install new fold-over type clamps, bend the tang down . . .

9.24b . . . and flatten the tabs to hold it in place

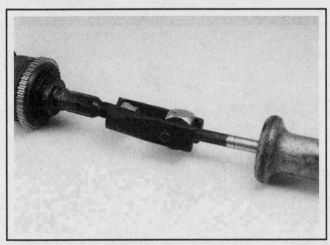

9.27a Outer CV joints can be removed with a slide hammer; you'll need an adapter and a slide hammer setup such as the one shown here

9.27b With the axleshaft firmly clamped down in a bench vise and the adapter gripping the driveaxle/hub nut, carefully extract the outer CV joint from the axleshaft. If it won't come off after five or six attempts, replace the driveaxle assembly

9.27c After the old grease has been rinsed away, move the inner race through its full range of motion and inspect the bearing surfaces for wear or damage

9.27d Apply CV joint grease through the splined hole, then insert a wooden dowel (slightly smaller in diameter than the hole) into the hole and push down - the dowel will force the grease into the joint. Repeat this until the joint is packed

9.27e Wrap the splined area of the axleshaft with tape to prevent damage to the boot when installing it

9.27f Install the small clamp and the boot on the driveaxle and apply grease to the inside of the axle boot . . .

9.27g . . . until the level is up to the end of the axle

9.27h Install a new circlip into the groove at the end of the driveaxle. Position the CV joint assembly on the driveaxle, aligning the splines . . .

9.27i . . . then use a hammer and brass punch to carefully drive the joint onto the driveaxle

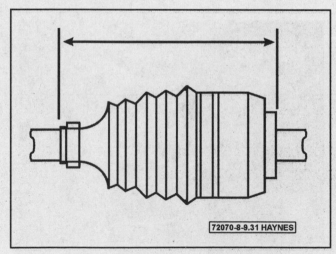

72070-8-9.31 HAYNES

9.27j Seat the boot in its grooves, measure the length of the joint at the indicated points to make sure it has been installed properly, then equalize the pressure inside the boot (see illustration 9.23b)

9.27k Install the new clamps and crimp them into place (the tool shown is available at most auto parts stores)

0 Axle assembly (front) - removal and installation

1   Raise the vehicle and support it securely on jackstands. Remove the skid plate, then detach the vent hose from the differential housing.

2   Mark the relationship of the driveshaft to the differential companion flange, then unbolt the driveshaft from the flange (see Section 2). Support the driveshaft with a piece of wire from the underbody.

3   Unbolt the end of the driveaxles from the front differential assembly and support the driveaxles with pieces of wire from the underbody.

4   Drain the differential lubricant (see Chapter 1).

5   Remove the front crossmember.

6   Support the front axle assembly with a floor jack placed under the differential.

7   Remove the differential and axle tube mounting bolts, then maneuver the axle/differential assembly out from under the vehicle.

8   Installation is the reverse of the removal procedure.

Specifications

General

Driveaxle boot length

Front (all 4WD models)

Inner boot	5.71 inches (145 mm)
Outer boot	6.63 inches (168.4 mm)

Rear (Armada models)

Inner boot	5.82 inches (147.9 mm)
Outer boot	5.30 inches (134.5 mm)

Torque specifications

	Ft-lbs	Nm
Driveaxles		
Front (4WD models)		
Driveaxle/hub nut	101	137
Driveaxle flange bolts	54	74
Rear (Armada models)		
Driveaxle/hub nut	170	230
Driveaxle flange bolts	87	118
Front differential (4WD)		
Differential housing-to-chassis mounting bolts	135	183
Rear axle		
Armada		
Rear axle assembly mounting bolts	81	110
Rear axle assembly mounting nut	129	175
Titan		
Rear axle bearing flange mounting nuts	87	118
Leaf spring U-bolt nuts	See Chapter 10	

Notes

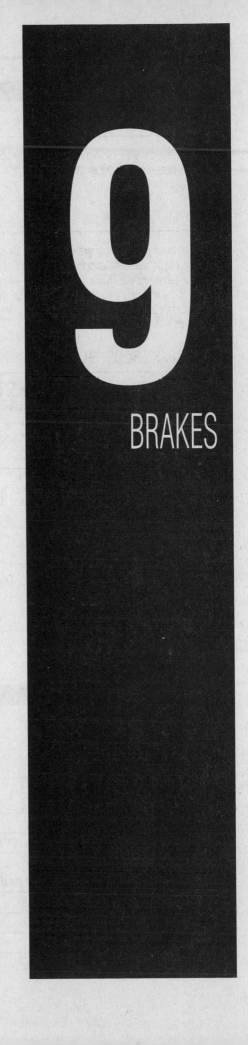

9

BRAKES

Section

1 General information

GENERAL

The vehicles covered by this manual are equipped with hydraulically operated front and rear brake systems. Both front and rear brakes are disc-type and are self-adjusting.

HYDRAULIC SYSTEM

The hydraulic system consists of two separate circuits. The master cylinder has separate reservoirs for the two circuits, and, in the event of a leak or failure in one hydraulic circuit, the other circuit will remain operative and a warning indicator will light up on the instrument panel when a substantial amount of brake fluid is lost, showing that a failure has occurred.

POWER BRAKE BOOSTER

The power brake booster uses engine manifold vacuum to provide assistance to the brakes. It is mounted on the firewall in the engine compartment, directly behind the master cylinder.

PARKING BRAKE

Control cables are routed to the rear axle, where they operate small drum brake shoes that apply pressure to the inner diameter of the rear brake discs.

SERVICE

After completing any operation involving disassembly of any part of the brake system, always test drive the vehicle to check for proper braking performance before resuming normal driving. When testing the brakes, perform the tests on a clean, dry, flat surface. Conditions other than these can lead to inaccurate test results.

Test the brakes at various speeds with both light and heavy pedal pressure. The vehicle should stop evenly without pulling to one side or the other. Under hard braking, the ABS system may engage, resulting in brake pedal pulsation. This is considered normal operation.

Tires, vehicle load and wheel alignment are factors which also affect braking performance.

PRECAUTIONS

There are some general cautions and warnings involving the brake system on this vehicle:

a) *Use only brake fluid conforming to DOT 3 specifications.*
b) *The brake pads and linings contain fibers which are hazardous to your health if inhaled. Whenever you work on brake system components, clean all parts with brake system cleaner. Do not allow the fine dust to become airborne. Also, wear an approved filtering mask.*
c) *Safety should be paramount whenever any servicing of the brake components is performed. Do not use parts or fasteners which are not in perfect condition, and be sure that all clearances and torque specifications are adhered to. If you are at all unsure about a certain procedure, seek professional advice. Upon completion of any brake system work, test the brakes carefully in a controlled area before putting the vehicle into normal service. If a problem is suspected in the brake system, don't drive the vehicle until it's fixed.*
d) *Used brake fluid is considered a hazardous waste and it must be disposed of in accordance with federal, state and local laws. DO NOT pour it down the sink, into septic tanks or storm drains, or on the ground.*
e) *Clean up any spilled brake fluid immediately and then wash the area with large amounts of water. This is especially true for any finished or painted surfaces.*

2 Troubleshooting

PROBABLE CAUSE	CORRECTIVE ACTION

No brakes - pedal travels to floor

PROBABLE CAUSE	CORRECTIVE ACTION
1 Low fluid level 2 Air in system	1 and 2 Low fluid level and air in the system are symptoms of another problem - a leak somewhere in the hydraulic system. Locate and repair the leak
3 Defective seals in master cylinder	3 Replace master cylinder
4 Fluid overheated and vaporized due to heavy braking	4 Bleed hydraulic system (temporary fix). Replace brake fluid (proper fix)

Brake pedal slowly travels to floor under braking or at a stop

PROBABLE CAUSE	CORRECTIVE ACTION
1 Defective seals in master cylinder	1 Replace master cylinder
2 Leak in a hose, line, caliper or wheel cylinder	2 Locate and repair leak
3 Air in hydraulic system	3 Bleed the system, inspect system for a leak

PROBABLE CAUSE

CORRECTIVE ACTION

Brake pedal feels spongy when depressed

1 Air in hydraulic system	1 Bleed the system, inspect system for a leak
2 Master cylinder or power booster loose	2 Tighten fasteners
3 Brake fluid overheated (beginning to boil)	3 Bleed the system (temporary fix). Replace the brake fluid (proper fix)
4 Deteriorated brake hoses (ballooning under pressure)	4 Inspect hoses, replace as necessary (it's a good idea to replace all of them if one hose shows signs of deterioration)

Brake pedal feels hard when depressed and/or excessive effort required to stop vehicle

1 Power booster faulty	1 Replace booster
2 Engine not producing sufficient vacuum, or hose to booster clogged, collapsed or cracked	2 Check vacuum to booster with a vacuum gauge. Replace hose if cracked or clogged, repair engine if vacuum is extremely low
3 Brake linings contaminated by grease or brake fluid	3 Locate and repair source of contamination, replace brake pads or shoes
4 Brake linings glazed	4 Replace brake pads or shoes, check discs and drums for glazing, service as necessary
5 Caliper piston(s) or wheel cylinder(s) binding or frozen	5 Replace calipers or wheel cylinders
6 Brakes wet	6 Apply pedal to boil-off water (this should only be a momentary problem)
7 Kinked, clogged or internally split brake hose or line	7 Inspect lines and hoses, replace as necessary

Excessive brake pedal travel (but will pump up)

1 Drum brakes out of adjustment	1 Adjust brakes
2 Air in hydraulic system	2 Bleed system, inspect system for a leak

Excessive brake pedal travel (but will not pump up)

1 Master cylinder pushrod misadjusted	1 Adjust pushrod
2 Master cylinder seals defective	2 Replace master cylinder
3 Brake linings worn out	3 Inspect brakes, replace pads and/or shoes
4 Hydraulic system leak	4 Locate and repair leak

Brake pedal doesn't return

1 Brake pedal binding	1 Inspect pivot bushing and pushrod, repair or lubricate
2 Defective master cylinder	2 Replace master cylinder

Brake pedal pulsates during brake application

1 Brake drums out-of-round	1 Have drums machined by an automotive machine shop
2 Excessive brake disc runout or disc surfaces out-of-parallel	2 Have discs machined by an automotive machine shop
3 Loose or worn wheel bearings	3 Adjust or replace wheel bearings
4 Loose lug nuts	4 Tighten lug nuts

Brakes slow to release

1 Malfunctioning power booster	1 Replace booster
2 Pedal linkage binding	2 Inspect pedal pivot bushing and pushrod, repair/lubricate
3 Malfunctioning proportioning valve	3 Replace proportioning valve
4 Sticking caliper or wheel cylinder	4 Repair or replace calipers or wheel cylinders
5 Kinked or internally split brake hose	5 Locate and replace faulty brake hose

PROBABLE CAUSE	CORRECTIVE ACTION

Brakes grab (one or more wheels)

1 Grease or brake fluid on brake lining	1 Locate and repair cause of contamination, replace lining
2 Brake lining glazed	2 Replace lining, deglaze disc or drum

Vehicle pulls to one side during braking

1 Grease or brake fluid on brake lining	1 Locate and repair cause of contamination, replace lining
2 Brake lining glazed	2 Deglaze or replace lining, deglaze disc or drum
3 Restricted brake line or hose	3 Repair line or replace hose
4 Tire pressures incorrect	4 Adjust tire pressures
5 Caliper or wheel cylinder sticking	5 Repair or replace calipers or wheel cylinders
6 Wheels out of alignment	6 Have wheels aligned
7 Weak suspension spring	7 Replace springs
8 Weak or broken shock absorber	8 Replace shock absorbers

Brakes drag (indicated by sluggish engine performance or wheels being very hot after driving)

1 Brake pedal pushrod incorrectly adjusted	1 Adjust pushrod
2 Master cylinder pushrod (between booster and master cylinder)	2 Adjust pushrod incorrectly adjusted
3 Obstructed compensating port in master cylinder	3 Replace master cylinder
4 Master cylinder piston seized in bore	4 Replace master cylinder
5 Contaminated fluid causing swollen seals throughout system	5 Flush system, replace all hydraulic components
6 Clogged brake lines or internally split brake hose(s)	6 Flush hydraulic system, replace defective hose(s)
7 Sticking caliper(s) or wheel cylinder(s)	7 Replace calipers or wheel cylinders
8 Parking brake not releasing	8 Inspect parking brake linkage and parking brake mechanism, repair as required
9 Improper shoe-to-drum clearance	9 Adjust brake shoes
10 Faulty proportioning valve	10 Replace proportioning valve

Brakes fade (due to excessive heat)

1 Brake linings excessively worn or glazed	1 Deglaze or replace brake pads and/or shoes
2 Excessive use of brakes	2 Downshift into a lower gear, maintain a constant slower speed (going down hills)
3 Vehicle overloaded	3 Reduce load
4 Brake drums or discs worn too thin	4 Measure drum diameter and disc thickness, replace drums or discs as required
5 Contaminated brake fluid	5 Flush system, replace fluid
6 Brakes drag	6 Repair cause of dragging brakes
7 Driver resting left foot on brake pedal	7 Don't ride the brakes

Brakes noisy (high-pitched squeal)

1 Glazed lining	1 Deglaze or replace lining
2 Contaminated lining (brake fluid, grease, etc.)	2 Repair source of contamination, replace linings
3 Weak or broken brake shoe hold-down or return spring	3 Replace springs
4 Rivets securing lining to shoe or backing plate loose	4 Replace shoes or pads
5 Excessive dust buildup on brake linings	5 Wash brakes off with brake system cleaner
6 Brake drums worn too thin	6 Measure diameter of drums, replace if necessary

PROBABLE CAUSE	CORRECTIVE ACTION

Brakes noisy (high-pitched squeal) (contiued)

7 Wear indicator on disc brake pads contacting disc	7 Replace brake pads
8 Anti-squeal shims missing or installed improperly	8 Install shims correctly

➡Note: Other remedies for quieting squealing brakes include the application of an anti-squeal compound to the backing plates of the brake pads, and lightly chamfering the edges of the brake pads with a file. The latter method should only be performed with the brake pads thoroughly wetted with brake system cleaner, so as not to allow any brake dust to become airborne.

Brakes noisy (scraping sound)

1 Brake pads or shoes worn out; rivets, backing plate or brake shoe metal contacting disc or drum	1 Replace linings, have discs and/or drums machined (or replace)

Brakes chatter

1 Worn brake lining	1 Inspect brakes, replace shoes or pads as necessary
2 Glazed or scored discs or drums	2 Deglaze discs or drums with sandpaper (if glazing is severe, machining will be required)
3 Drums or discs heat checked	3 Check discs and/or drums for hard spots, heat checking, etc. Have discs/drums machined or replace them
4 Disc runout or drum out-of-round excessive	4 Measure disc runout and/or drum out-of-round, have discs or drums machined or replace them
5 Loose or worn wheel bearings	5 Adjust or replace wheel bearings
6 Loose or bent brake backing plate (drum brakes)	6 Tighten or replace backing plate
7 Grooves worn in discs or drums	7 Have discs or drums machined, if within limits (if not, replace them)
8 Brake linings contaminated (brake fluid, grease, etc.)	8 Locate and repair source of contamination, replace pads or shoes
9 Excessive dust buildup on linings	9 Wash brakes with brake system cleaner
10 Surface finish on discs or drums too rough after machining	10 Have discs or drums properly machined(especially on vehicles with sliding calipers)
11 Brake pads or shoes glazed	11 Deglaze or replace brake pads or shoes

Brake pads or shoes click

1 Shoe support pads on brake backing plate grooved or	1 Replace brake backing plateexcessively worn
2 Brake pads loose in caliper	2 Loose pad retainers or anti-rattle clips
3 Also see items listed under Brakes chatter	

Brakes make groaning noise at end of stop

1 Brake pads and/or shoes worn out	1 Replace pads and/or shoes
2 Brake linings contaminated (brake fluid, grease, etc.)	2 Locate and repair cause of contamination, replace brake pads or shoes
3 Brake linings glazed	3 Deglaze or replace brake pads or shoes
4 Excessive dust buildup on linings	4 Wash brakes with brake system cleaner
5 Scored or heat-checked discs or drums	5 Inspect discs/drums, have machined if within limits (if not, replace discs or drums)
6 Broken or missing brake shoe attaching hardware	6 Inspect drum brakes, replace missing hardware

Rear brakes lock up under light brake application

1 Tire pressures too high	1 Adjust tire pressures
2 Tires excessively worn	2 Replace tires
3 Defective proportioning valve	3 Replace proportioning valve

PROBABLE CAUSE	CORRECTIVE ACTION

Brake warning light on instrument panel comes on (or stays on)

1 Low fluid level in master cylinder reservoir (reservoirs with fluid level sensor)	1 Add fluid, inspect system for leak, check the thickness of the brake pads and shoes
2 Failure in one half of the hydraulic system	2 Inspect hydraulic system for a leak
3 Piston in pressure differential warning valve not centered	3 Center piston by bleeding one circuit or the other (close bleeder valve as soon as the light goes out)
4 Defective pressure differential valve or warning switch	4 Replace valve or switch
5 Air in the hydraulic system	5 Bleed the system, check for leaks
6 Brake pads worn out (vehicles with electric wear sensors - small probes that fit into the brake pads and ground out on the disc when the pads get thin)	6 Replace brake pads (and sensors)

Brakes do not self adjust

Disc brakes

1 Defective caliper piston seals	1 Replace calipers. Also, possible contaminated fluid causing soft or swollen seals (flush system and fill with new fluid if in doubt)
2 Corroded caliper piston(s)	2 Same as above

Drum brakes

1 Adjuster screw frozen	1 Remove adjuster, disassemble, clean and lubricate with high-temperature grease
2 Adjuster lever does not contact star wheel or is binding	2 Inspect drum brakes, assemble correctly or clean or replace parts as required
3 Adjusters mixed up (installed on wrong wheels after brake job)	3 Reassemble correctly
4 Adjuster cable broken or installed incorrectly (cable-type adjusters)	4 Install new cable or assemble correctly

Rapid brake lining wear

1 Driver resting left foot on brake pedal	1 Don't ride the brakes
2 Surface finish on discs or drums too rough	2 Have discs or drums properly machined
3 Also see Brakes drag	

---

3   Anti-lock Brake System (ABS) - general information

GENERAL INFORMATION

♦ **Refer to illustration 3.2**

1   The anti-lock brake system is designed to maintain vehicle steerability, directional stability and optimum deceleration under severe braking conditions on most road surfaces. It does so by monitoring the rotational speed of each wheel and controlling the brake line pressure to each wheel during braking. This prevents the wheels from locking up.

2   The ABS system has three main components - the wheel speed sensors, the electronic control unit (ECU) and the hydraulic unit (see illustration). Four wheel speed sensors - one at each wheel - send a variable voltage signal to the control unit, which monitors these signals, compares them to its program and determines whether a wheel is about to lock up. When a wheel is about to lock up, the control unit signals the hydraulic unit to reduce hydraulic pressure (or not increase it further) at that wheel's brake caliper. Pressure modulation is handled by electrically-operated solenoid valves.

3   If a problem develops within the system, an "ABS" warning light will glow on the dashboard. Sometimes, a visual inspection of the ABS system can help you locate the problem. Carefully inspect the ABS wiring harness. Pay particularly close attention to the harness and connections near each wheel. Look for signs of chafing and other damage caused by incorrectly routed wires. If a wheel sensor harness is damaged, the sensor must be replaced.

✳ WARNING:

Do NOT try to repair an ABS wiring harness. The ABS system is sensitive to even the smallest changes in resistance. Repairing the harness could alter resistance values and cause the system to malfunction. If the ABS wiring harness is damaged in any way, it must be replaced.

✳ CAUTION:

Make sure the ignition is turned off before unplugging or reattaching any electrical connections.

3.2 The ABS hydraulic unit

3.6a Front wheel ABS sensor location

3.6b Rear wheel ABS sensor location (Armada)

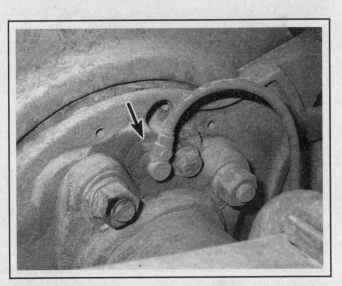

3.6c Rear wheel ABS sensor location (Titan)

DIAGNOSIS AND REPAIR

4   If a dashboard warning light comes on and stays on while the vehicle is in operation, the ABS system requires attention. Although special electronic ABS diagnostic testing tools are necessary to properly diagnose the system, you can perform a few preliminary checks before taking the vehicle to a dealer service department.

a) *Check the brake fluid level in the reservoir.*
b) *Verify that the computer electrical connectors are securely connected.*
c) *Check the electrical connectors at the hydraulic control unit.*
d) *Check the fuses.*
e) *Follow the wiring harness to each wheel and verify that all connections are secure and that the wiring is undamaged.*

If the above preliminary checks do not rectify the problem, the vehicle should be diagnosed by a dealer service department or other qualified repair shop. Due to the complex nature of this system, all actual repair work must be done by a qualified automotive technician.

WHEEL SPEED SENSOR - REPLACEMENT

▶ **Refer to illustrations 3.6a, 3.6b and 3.6c**

5   Front and rear wheel speed sensors can be replaced if determined to be faulty or damaged.

6   Disconnect the ABS sensor's electrical harness, then remove the mounting bolt (see illustrations).

7   Remove the sensors straight out and do not use a pry tool or pull them by the wire harness. If the sensor is being removed to perform other brake or suspension work (not for replacement), be sure to clean it before installing it. Use brake cleaner to clean the sensor and the hole.

8   When reinstalling an ABS sensor, replace the O-ring with a new one, lubricated with suitable grease. Tighten the mounting bolt to the torque listed in this Chapter's Specifications.

4 Disc brake pads - replacement

▶ Refer to illustrations 4.3, 4.5, 4.6a through 4.6q and 4.7a through 4.7o

✳✳ WARNING:

Disc brake pads must be replaced on both front or both rear wheels at the same time - never replace the pads on only one side. Also, the dust created by the brake system is harmful to your health. Never blow it out with compressed air and don't inhale any of it. An approved filtering mask should be worn when working on the brakes. Do not, under any circumstances, use petroleum-based solvents to clean brake parts. Use brake system cleaner only!

➡Note 1: On Armada models equipped with a rear auto-leveling suspension, turn the ignition key to the OFF position before raising the vehicle.

➡Note 2: This procedure applies to front and rear disc brakes.

1   Remove the cap from the brake fluid reservoir and remove about two-thirds of the fluid. Discard the used brake fluid properly (see Section 1).

2   Loosen the wheel lug nuts, raise the front or rear of the vehicle and support it securely on jackstands. Remove the front or rear wheels.

3   Position a drain pan under the brake caliper assembly and thoroughly clean it with brake system cleaner (see illustration).

4   Inspect the brake disc carefully as outlined in Section 6. If machining is necessary, follow the information in that Section to remove the disc, at which time the calipers and pads can be removed as well.

5   Push the piston(s) completely back into the bore(s) using a C-clamp (see illustration). This is necessary to provide space for the new brake pads. When a piston is depressed to the bottom of the caliper bore, the fluid in the master cylinder will rise. Make sure that it doesn't overflow by removing more fluid as necessary.

6   For front pad replacement, follow illustrations 4.6a through 4.6q for the actual pad replacement procedure. Be sure to stay in order and read the caption under each illustration. Work on one brake assembly at a time using the assembled brake for reference if necessary.

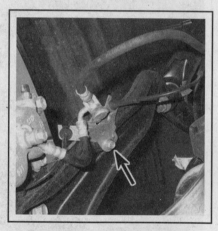

4.3 Always wash the brakes with brake cleaner before disassembling anything

4.5 Before removing the caliper, slowly depress the piston into the caliper bore by using a large C-clamp between the outer brake pad and the back of the caliper

4.6a Remove the brake hose/wire harness bracket from the steering knuckle

4.6b Remove the lower caliper mounting bolt

4.6c Pivot the caliper up and secure it with wire; do not allow the caliper to hang by the flexible brake hose. Be careful not to damage the upper guide pin boot while rotating the caliper

4.6d Remove the outer pad with the shim(s) . . .

4.6e . . . and the inner pad with the shim(s)

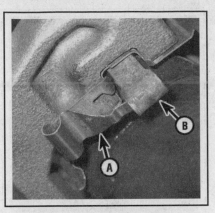

4.6f Some designs will utilize a return spring (A) on the pad retainer that engages with the pad's wear sensor (B)

4.6g Remove the upper and lower pad retainers. If they are loose or worn, replace them

4.6h Install clean or new pad retainers

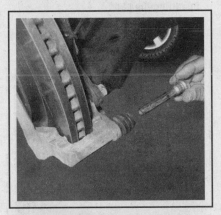

4.6i Carefully pull out the lower guide pin while separating the guide pin boot from the caliper bracket. Clean the guide pin and inspect it for wear or damage

4.6j Apply a coat of high-temperature grease to the guide pin and reinstall it. Seat the guide pin into the boot. Replace any guide pins or boots that are worn or damaged

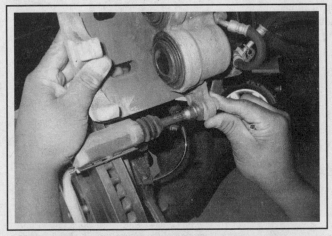

4.6k Unhook the caliper, then carefully pull it away from the mounting bracket with the upper guide pin. Be careful not to tear the guide pin boot. Clean and lubricate the upper guide pin, then place the caliper back in position. Seat the guide pin boot securely around the guide pin. Replace any guide pins or boots that are worn or damaged

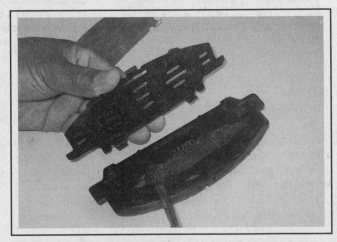

4.6l Lubricate the back of each pad and related shims with high-temperature grease. DO NOT allow grease to get onto the pad lining. Note: The manufacturer recommends using new shims when replacing the brake pads. Some aftermarket brake pads may have shims that are permanently attached

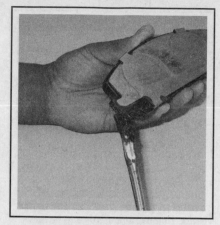

4.6m Lubricate the ends of each pad with high-temperature grease. DO NOT allow grease to get onto the pad lining

4.6n Install the inboard brake pad with the shim(s). Note: On some models, refer to illustration 4.6f and engage the pad return spring when installing the pads

4.6o Install the outboard brake pad with the shim(s). Note: On some models, refer to illustration 4.6f and engage the pad return spring when installing the pads

4.6p Carefully pivot the caliper down onto the mounting bracket and over the new brake pads while noting the position guide pin's end in relation to the caliper

4.6q Install the lower mounting bolt and tighten it to the torque listed in this Chapter's Specifications. Reattach the brake hose/wire harness bracket to the steering knuckle

4.7a Remove the caliper mounting bolts

7 For rear pad replacement, follow illustrations 4.7a through 4.7o, for the actual pad replacement procedure. Be sure to stay in order and read the caption under each illustration. Work on one brake assembly at a time using the assembled brake for reference if necessary.

8 When reinstalling the caliper, be sure to tighten the mounting bolt to the torque listed in this Chapter's Specifications.

9 After the job has been completed, perform the following:

a) Slowly depress the brake pedal about two-thirds of its travel a few times until the pedal is firm. This will bring the pads into contact with the brake disc.

b) Install the wheels and lug nuts. Lower the vehicle to the ground and tighten the lug nuts to the torque listed in the Chapter 1 Specifications.

c) Check the level of the brake fluid, adding some if necessary.

d) In an isolated area, drive the vehicle and make a few hard stops to seat the pads to the disc. Allow the brakes to cool by driving the vehicle at least one minute in between stops.

e) Continue making stops until the brakes feel responsive and normal. Remember to cool the brakes in between stops.

f) Finally, check the operation of the brakes carefully before placing the vehicle into normal service.

4.7b Press the small spring down and pull the top of the caliper rearward to remove it

4.7c Secure the caliper with wire; do not allow the caliper to hang by the flexible brake hose

4.7d Remove the outboard brake pad by pulling it off of the caliper

4.7e Remove the inboard brake pad by pushing its retainers out of the caliper piston

4.7f Clean the outside of the upper and lower slippers, then remove them and clean the mounting surface on the rear knuckle. Inspect them for damage or wear and replace them if necessary

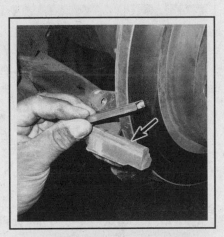

4.7g Lubricate the mounting surface with a small amount of disc brake grease, then reinstall the slippers

4.7h Carefully lubricate the area where the brake pads sit on the slippers with a very small amount of disc brake grease. DO NOT allow grease to get onto the brake disc or any other parts. Clean the brake disc with brake parts cleaner if necessary

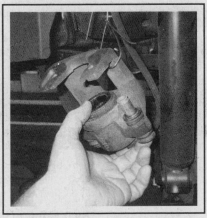

4.7i Push both caliper sleeves out of the sleeve boots to clean and inspect them

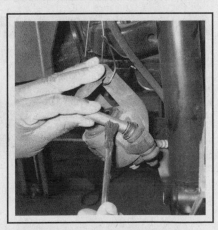

4.7j Apply a coat of high-temperature grease to the sleeves, then reinstall them into the sleeve boots

4.7k Install the inboard brake pad

4.7l Install the outboard brake pad

4.7m Place the bottom of the caliper into position making sure the ends of the pads sit correctly on the slippers

4.7n Push the top of the caliper into position

4.7o Install the caliper mounting bolts and tighten them to the torque listed in this Chapter's Specifications

5 Brake caliper - removal and installation

✳✳ WARNING:

The dust created by the brake system is harmful to your health. Never blow it out with compressed air and don't inhale any of it. An approved filtering mask should be worn when working on the brakes. Do not, under any circumstances, use petroleum-based solvents to clean brake parts. Use brake system cleaner only!

➡Note 1: On Armada models equipped with a rear auto-leveling suspension, turn the ignition key to the OFF position before raising the vehicle.

➡Note 2: This procedure applies to the front and rear disc brake calipers.

REMOVAL

▶ Refer to illustrations 5.2a and 5.2b

1   Loosen the wheel lug nuts, raise the vehicle and place it securely on jackstands. Block the wheels at the opposite end. Remove the wheel.

Front caliper (all models) and rear caliper (Armada models)

2   Disconnect the brake hose from the caliper (see illustrations). Discard the old sealing washers. Plug the brake hose immediately to keep contaminants and air out of the brake system and to prevent losing any more brake fluid than is necessary.

➡Note: If you are simply removing the caliper for access to other components, leave the brake hose connected.

3   Remove the caliper mounting bolts and detach the caliper. If the hose is still connected, secure the caliper with wire and don't let it hang by the hose.

Rear caliper (Titan models)

4   Break loose the brake hose fitting, but don't unscrew it yet.

➡Note: If you're just removing the caliper for access to other components, don't loosen the hose.

5   Remove the caliper mounting bolts, detach the caliper, then

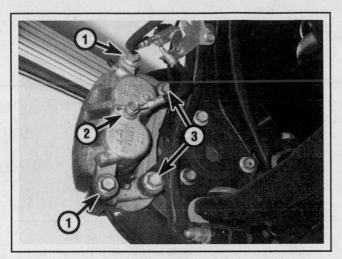

5.2a Front caliper mounting details

1 *Caliper mounting bolts*
2 *Inlet fitting bolt*

3 *Caliper mounting bracket bolts*

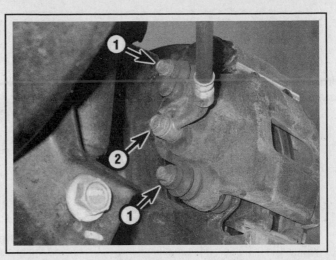

5.2b Rear caliper mounting details (Armada model shown - Titan models are similar)

1 *Mounting bolts*
2 *Inlet fitting bolt (Armada only)*

unscrew the caliper from the brake hose. If you intend to leave the hose connected, secure the caliper with wire and don't let it hang by the brake hose.

INSTALLATION

Front caliper (all models) and rear caliper (Armada models)

6 Installation is the reverse of removal. Don't forget to use new sealing washers on each side of the brake hose inlet fitting and be sure to tighten the fitting bolt and the caliper mounting bolts to the torque values listed in this Chapter's Specifications.

Rear caliper (Titan models)

7 Install a new sealing washer on the brake hose. Thread the caliper onto the brake hose as far as possible, but don't tighten the hose with a wrench yet.

8 Install the caliper and mounting bolts, tightening the bolts to the torque listed in this Chapter's Specifications.

9 Tighten the brake hose securely. Make sure the hose isn't twisted.

All models

10 Bleed the brake system (see Section 10).

➡**Note: If the brake hose was not disconnected, bleeding won't be required.**

Make sure there are no leaks from the hose connections. Test the brakes carefully before returning the vehicle to normal service.

6 Brake disc - inspection, removal and installation

➡**Note: On Armada models equipped with a rear auto-leveling suspension, turn the ignition key to the OFF position before raising the vehicle.**

INSPECTION

▸ **Refer to illustrations 6.4, 6.5a, 6.5b, 6.6a and 6.6b**

1 Loosen the wheel lug nuts, raise the vehicle and support it securely on jackstands. Remove the wheel.

2 Remove the brake caliper as outlined in Section 5. It's not necessary to disconnect the brake line or hose for this procedure, but detach the hose/line bracket from the steering knuckle on front brakes, if necessary.

3 Reinstall the lug nuts with washers (for spacing) to hold the disc securely against the hub.

4 Visually check the disc surface for score marks, cracks and other damage. Light scratches and shallow grooves are normal after use and may not always be detrimental to brake operation. Deep score marks or cracks may require disc refinishing by an automotive machine shop or

6.4 The brake pads on this vehicle were obviously neglected - they wore out completely and cut deep grooves into the disc; if the disc is worn this severely, replace it

disc replacement (see illustration). Be sure to check both sides of the disc. If the brake pedal pulsates during brake application, suspect disc runout.

6.5a Measure the brake disc runout with a dial indicator; if the reading exceeds the maximum allowable runout limit, the disc must be resurfaced or replaced

6.5b Using a swirling motion, remove the glaze from the disc surface with sandpaper or emery cloth

6.6a Measure the brake disc thickness at several points with a micrometer (typical)

6.6b The minimum allowable thickness dimension is usually cast into the back side of the disc (typical shown)

6.9a Clean any rust and corrosion from the areas of the hub flange that contact the disc. A wire brush or sanding tool, designed to be used with a power drill, can make the job a lot easier (typical)

6.9b Clean any rust or corrosion from the inside of the disc that contacts the hub flange. Again, power tools are very useful for this job

➡Note: The most common symptoms of damaged or worn brake discs are pulsation in the brake pedal when the brakes are applied or loud grinding noises caused from severely worn brake pads. If these symptoms are extreme, it is very likely that the disc(s) will need replacing.

5   To check disc runout, place a dial indicator at a point about 1/2-inch from the outer edge of the disc (see illustration). Set the indicator to zero and turn the disc. An indicator reading that exceeds 0.003 of an inch could cause pulsation upon brake application and will require disc refinishing by an automotive machine shop or disc replacement.

➡Note: If disc refinishing or replacement is not necessary, you can deglaze the brake pad surface on the disc with emery cloth or sandpaper (use a swirling motion to ensure a non-directional finish) (see illustration).

6   The disc must not be machined to a thickness less than the specified minimum refinish thickness. The minimum (or discard) thick-ness is cast into the front or backside of the disc (see illustration). The disc thickness can be checked with a micrometer (see illustration).

REMOVAL AND INSTALLATION

▶ Refer to illustrations 6.9a and 6.9b

7   Remove the brake caliper as outlined in Section 5. If you're removing a front disc, also remove the caliper mounting bracket. It's not necessary to disconnect the brake hose for this procedure, but detach the hose bracket from the steering knuckle on front brakes, if necessary.

8   Mark the disc in relation to the hub so that it can be installed in its original position on the hub, then remove the disc. If it's stuck, you can use a mallet or equivalent to free it from the hub.

➡Note: On rear discs, make sure the parking brake is released.

9   Clean the hub flange and the inside of the brake disc thoroughly, removing any rust or corrosion, then install the disc onto the hub assembly (see illustrations).

10   On front calipers, install the caliper mounting bracket (using new bolts). On all calipers, install the brake pads and caliper. Tighten all mounting bolts to the torque values listed in this Chapter's Specifications.

11   Install the wheels and lug nuts, then lower the vehicle to the ground. Tighten the wheel lug nuts to the torque listed in the Chapter 1 Specifications. Depress the brake pedal a few times to bring the brake pads into contact with the disc. Bleeding of the system will not be necessary unless the brake hose/line was disconnected from the caliper. Check the operation of the brakes carefully before placing the vehicle into normal service.

7   Parking brake shoes - replacement

▶ **Refer to illustrations 7.5a through 7.5n**

❊❊ WARNING 1:

Dust created by the brake system is hazardous to your health. Never blow it out with compressed air and don't inhale any of it. An approved filtering mask should be worn when working on the brakes. Do not, under any circumstances, use petroleum-based solvents to clean brake parts. Use brake system cleaner only!

❊❊ WARNING 2:

Parking brake shoes must be replaced on both wheels at the same time - never replace the shoes on only one wheel.

1   Remove the rear brake discs (see Section 6).

2   Measure the thickness of the lining material on the shoes. If the lining has worn down to 0.5 mm or less, replace the shoes.

3   Inspect the drum portion of the disc for scoring, grooves or cracks due to heat. If any of these conditions exist or there is significant wear to the drum, the disc must be replaced.

4   Wash off the brake parts with brake system cleaner.

5   Follow the accompanying illustrations for the brake shoe replacement procedure (see illustrations 7.5a through 7.5n). Be sure to stay in order and read the caption under each illustration.

➡ **Note: Work on one side at a time using the opposite side for reference as necessary.**

6   Adjust the rear parking brake shoes (see Section 12).

7   Install the brake disc and caliper. Be sure to tighten the bolts to the torque values listed in this Chapter's Specifications.

8   Install the wheels and lug nuts, then lower the vehicle to the ground. Tighten the wheel lug nuts to the torque listed in the Chapter 1 Specifications.

9   Check the parking brake for proper operation and adjust it again if necessary (see Section 12).

7.5a Turn the adjuster until it's at its shortest setting (the threads disappear into the adjuster)

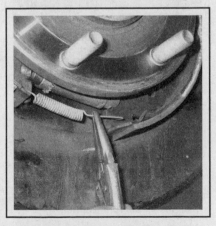

7.5b Remove the adjuster spring

7.5c Remove the adjuster

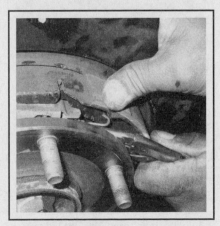

7.5d Remove the return spring

7.5e Remove the rear shoe retaining spring, pin and shoe

7.5f Remove the front shoe retaining spring, pin and shoe

7.5g Detach the actuator from the cable (if necessary)

7.5h Clean the adjuster, then lubricate the threads with a thin film of high-temperature brake grease

7.5i Clean the backing plate thoroughly, then lubricate the brake shoe contact areas on the plate with high-temperature grease

7.5j Place the front shoe in position and install the retaining spring and pin

7.5k Place the rear shoe in position and install the retaining spring and pin

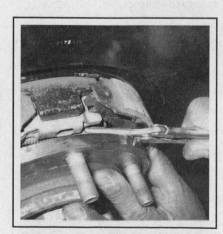

7.5l Install the return spring

7.5m Install the adjuster

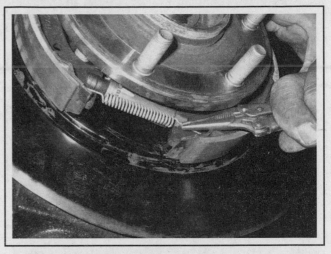

7.5n Install the adjuster spring

8   Master cylinder - removal, installation and reservoir/seal replacement

REMOVAL

▶ **Refer to illustration 8.2**

1   Disconnect the cable from the negative battery terminal (see Chapter 5).

2   Disconnect the electrical connectors for the brake fluid level warning light and the brake fluid pressure sensor (see illustration).

3   Remove as much fluid as possible from the reservoir with a suction gun, large syringe or a poultry baster.

✳✳ WARNING:

If a poultry baster is used, never again use it for the preparation of food.

4   Place rags under the fittings and prepare caps or plastic bags to cover the ends of the lines once they're disconnected.

✳✳ CAUTION:

Brake fluid will damage paint. Cover all body parts and be careful not to spill fluid during this procedure. Loosen the fittings at the ends of the brake lines where they enter the master cylinder. To prevent rounding off the flats, use a flare-nut wrench, which wraps around the fitting hex.

5   Pull the brake lines away from the master cylinder and plug the ends to prevent contamination.

6   Remove the nuts attaching the master cylinder to the power booster (see illustration 8.2). Pull the master cylinder off the studs to remove it. Again, be careful not to spill the fluid as this is done.

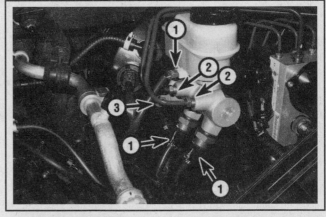

8.2 Master cylinder details

1   Electrical connector
2   Brake line fittings

3   Mounting nuts (one seen here)

➡**Note: If necessary, remove the pin on the left side of the master cylinder that retains the reservoir and pull it from the master cylinder. Lubricate the reservoir seals with clean brake fluid, then press the reservoir into place on the master cylinder body. Install the pin that retains the reservoir.**

INSTALLATION

▶ **Refer to illustrations 8.8 and 8.16**

7   Bench bleed the new master cylinder before installing it. Mount the master cylinder in a vise, with the jaws of the vise clamping on the mounting flange.

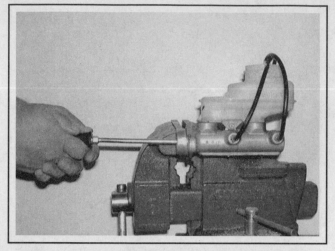

8.8 The best way to bleed air from the master cylinder before installing it on the vehicle is with a pair of bleeder tubes that direct brake fluid into the reservoir during bleeding

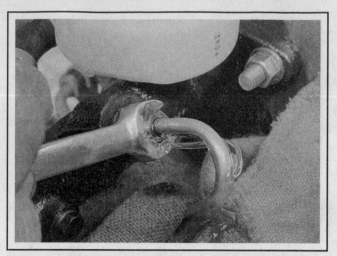

8.16 Have an assistant depress the brake pedal and hold it down, then loosen the fitting nut, allowing air and fluid to escape; repeat this procedure on both fittings until the fluid is clear of air bubbles

8 Attach a pair of master cylinder bleeder tubes to the outlet ports of the master cylinder (see illustration).

9 Fill the reservoir with brake fluid of the recommended type (see Chapter 1).

10 Slowly push the pistons into the master cylinder (a large Phillips screwdriver can be used for this) - air will be expelled from the pressure chambers and into the reservoir. Because the tubes are submerged in fluid, air can't be drawn back into the master cylinder when you release the pistons.

11 Repeat the procedure until no more air bubbles are present.

12 Remove the bleed tubes, one at a time, and install plugs in the open ports to prevent fluid leakage and air from entering. Install the reservoir cap.

13 Install the master cylinder over the studs on the power brake booster and tighten the attaching nuts only finger tight at this time. Don't forget to use a new O-ring.

14 Thread the brake line fittings into the master cylinder. Since the master cylinder is still a bit loose, it can be moved slightly so the fittings thread in easily. Don't strip the threads as the fittings are tightened.

15 Tighten the mounting nuts to the torque listed in this Chapter's

Specifications. Tighten the brake line fittings securely.

16 Fill the master cylinder reservoir with fluid, then bleed the lines at the master cylinder, followed by bleeding the remainder of the brake system (see Section 10). To bleed the lines at the master cylinder, have an assistant depress the brake pedal and hold it down. Loosen the fitting to allow air and fluid to escape (see illustration). Tighten the fitting, then allow your assistant to return the pedal to its rest position. Repeat this procedure on both fittings until the fluid is free of air bubbles, then bleed the rest of the system.

17 Check the brake pedal height and adjust if necessary (see Section 14).

18 Check the operation of the brake system carefully before driving the vehicle.

✳✳ WARNING:

If you do not have a firm brake pedal at the end of the bleeding procedure, or have any doubts as to the effectiveness of the brake system, DO NOT drive the vehicle. Have it towed to a dealer service department or other qualified repair shop for diagnosis.

9 Brake hoses and lines - inspection and replacement

INSPECTION

1 About every six months, with the vehicle raised and supported securely on jackstands, the rubber hoses which connect the steel brake lines with the front and rear brake assemblies should be inspected for cracks, chafing of the outer cover, leaks, blisters and other damage. These are important and vulnerable parts of the brake system and inspection should be complete. A light and mirror will be helpful for a thorough check. If a hose exhibits any of the above conditions, replace it with a new one.

REPLACEMENT

Flexible brake hose

Front

▶ **Refer to illustrations 9.3a and 9.3b**

2 There are two flexible front brake hoses and two rear flexible brake hoses. The procedure is similar for all flexible hoses. Loosen the

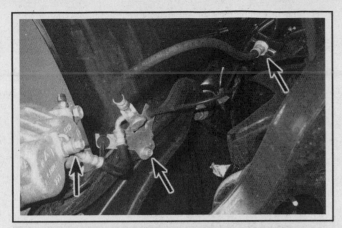

9.3a Front brake hose connections and brackets

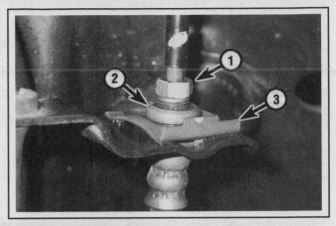

9.3b Brake hose fitting details

1   Metal tube nut (use a flare-nut wrench here)
2   Brake hose fitting
3   Retaining clip (pull straight out with pliers)

9.11a Rear brake hose connections and bracket (Armada models)

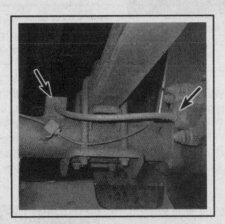

9.11b Rear brake hose connections and bracket (Titan models)

9.14 Brake hoses and connections between the rear axle and the chassis (Titan models)

wheel lug nuts, raise the vehicle and support it securely on jackstands. Remove the wheel.

3   At the frame bracket, unscrew the brake line fitting from the hose (see illustrations). Use a flare-nut wrench to prevent rounding off the corners of the fitting nut, and support the frame bracket with a wrench to keep if from twisting, if necessary. Remove the brake hose bracket from the steering knuckle

4   Remove the U-clip from the female fitting at the bracket (see illustration 9.3b), then pass the hose through the bracket.

5   At the caliper end of the hose, remove the inlet fitting bolt, then separate the hose from the caliper. Discard the two copper sealing washers on each side of the inlet fitting.

6   Connect the fitting to the caliper with the inlet fitting bolt and new sealing washers. Tighten the inlet fitting bolt to the torque listed in this Chapter's Specifications.

7   Route the hose into the frame bracket, making sure it isn't twisted. Connect the brake line fitting, starting the threads by hand. Install the U-clip, then tighten the fitting securely.

8   Bleed the caliper (see Section 10).

9   Install the wheel and lug nuts, lower the vehicle and tighten the lug nuts to the torque listed in the Chapter 1 Specifications.

Rear

▶ **Refer to illustrations 9.11a, 9.11b and 9.14**

10   Raise the rear of the vehicle and support it securely on jackstands. Block the front wheels to prevent the vehicle from rolling.

11   On Armada models, there is a bracket at the chassis (see illustration). On Titan models, there is a bracket on the rear axle housing (tube) (see illustration). Unscrew the brake line fitting from the hose (see illustration 9.3b). Use a flare-nut wrench to prevent rounding off the corners of the fitting nut.

12   Remove the U-clip from the female fitting at the bracket (see illustration 9.3b), then pass the hose through the bracket.

13   If you're working on a Titan, unscrew the brake hose from the caliper. If you're working on an Armada, unscrew the inlet fitting bolt and detach the fitting from the caliper. Discard the sealing washers; new ones should be used during installation.

14   Titan models have two hoses connecting the rigid lines on the rear axle housing to the rigid lines on the chassis (see illustration). Unscrew the brake line fittings with a flare-nut wrench, then remove the bolt securing the hose to the bracket on the axle housing. Installation is the reverse the removal procedure. Always use new sealing washers when connecting hose fittings. Bleed both rear brakes (see Section 10).

Metal brake lines

15 When replacing brake lines, be sure to use the correct parts. Don't use copper tubing for any brake system components. Purchase steel brake lines from a dealer or auto parts store.

16 Prefabricated brake line, with the tube ends already flared and fittings installed, is available at auto parts stores and dealer parts departments. These lines must be bent to the proper shapes using a tubing bender.

17 When installing the new line, make sure it's securely supported in the brackets and has plenty of clearance between moving or hot components.

18 After installation, check the master cylinder fluid level and add fluid as necessary. Bleed the brake system (see Section 9) and test the brakes carefully before driving the vehicle in traffic.

10 Brake hydraulic system - bleeding

◆ Refer to illustration 10.9

❋❋ **WARNING:**

Wear eye protection when bleeding the brake system. If the fluid comes in contact with your eyes, immediately rinse them with water and seek medical attention.

➡ **Note: Bleeding the hydraulic system is necessary to remove any air that manages to find its way into the system when it's been opened during removal and installation of a hose, line, caliper or master cylinder.**

1 You'll probably have to bleed the system at all four brakes if air has entered it due to low fluid level, or if the brake lines have been disconnected at the master cylinder.

2 If a brake line was disconnected only at a wheel, then only that caliper must be bled. If a brake line is disconnected at a fitting located between the master cylinder and any of the brakes, that part of the system served by the disconnected line must be bled.

3 Remove any residual vacuum from the brake power booster by applying the brake several times with the engine off.

4 Disconnect the cable from the negative battery terminal (see Chapter 5).

➡ **Note: Battery disconnection is necessary to disable the ABS system.**

5 Remove the master cylinder reservoir cap and fill the reservoir with brake fluid. Reinstall the cap.

➡ **Note: Check the fluid level often during the bleeding operation and add fluid as necessary to prevent the fluid level from falling low enough to allow air bubbles into the master cylinder.**

6 If air has entered the master cylinder, bleed the master cylinder as described in Section 7.

7 Have an assistant on hand, as well as a supply of new brake fluid, a clear container partially filled with clean brake fluid, a length of clear tubing to fit over the bleeder valve and a wrench to open and close the bleeder valve.

8 Working at the right rear wheel, loosen the bleeder valve slightly, then tighten it to a point where it's snug but can still be loosened quickly and easily.

9 Place one end of the tubing over the bleeder valve and submerge the other end in brake fluid in the container (see illustration).

10 Have the assistant depress the brake pedal slowly and hold it in the depressed position.

11 While the pedal is held down, open the bleeder valve just enough to allow a flow of fluid to leave the valve. Watch for air bubbles to exit the submerged end of the tube. When the fluid flow slows after a couple of seconds, close the valve and have your assistant release the pedal.

12 Repeat Steps 10 and 11 until no more air is seen leaving the tube, then tighten the bleeder valve and proceed to the left front wheel, the left rear wheel and the right front wheel, in that order, and perform the same procedure. Be sure to check the fluid in the master cylinder reservoir frequently.

13 Never use old brake fluid. It contains moisture which can cause the fluid to boil, rendering the brake system inoperative.

14 Refill the master cylinder with fluid at the end of the operation.

15 Check the operation of the brakes. The pedal should feel solid when depressed, with no sponginess. If necessary, repeat the entire process.

❋❋ **WARNING:**

Do not operate the vehicle if you're in doubt about the effectiveness of the brake system.

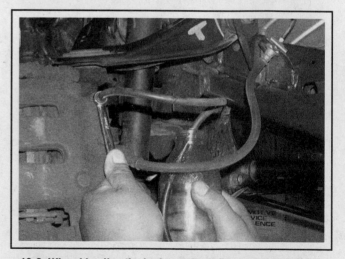

10.9 When bleeding the brakes, a hose is connected to the bleed screw at the component to be bled, then submerged in brake fluid - air will be seen as bubbles in the tube and container (all air must be expelled before moving to the next component)

11 Power brake booster - check, replacement and adjustment

CHECK

Operating check

1 Depress the brake pedal several times with the engine off and make sure there's no change in the pedal reserve distance.

2 Depress the pedal and start the engine. If the pedal goes down slightly, operation is normal.

Airtightness check

3 Start the engine and turn it off after one or two minutes. Depress the brake pedal slowly several times. If the pedal depresses less each time, the booster is airtight.

4 Depress the brake pedal while the engine is running, then stop the engine with the pedal depressed. If there's no change in the pedal reserve travel after holding the pedal for 30 seconds, the booster is airtight.

REPLACEMENT

⯈ **Refer to illustrations 11.8 and 11.9**

➡**Note: Power brake booster units shouldn't be disassembled; if a problem with the booster develops, replace it with a new or rebuilt one.**

5 Remove the brake master cylinder, if you haven't already done so (see Section 8).

6 Carefully disconnect the vacuum hose and the electrical connectors (if equipped) from the booster.

7 Locate the pushrod clevis connecting the booster to the brake pedal.

8 Remove the retaining clip for the clevis pin, then remove the pin (see illustration). Detach the pushrod clevis from the brake pedal.

9 Remove the four nuts holding the brake booster to the firewall (see illustration).

10 Slide the booster straight out from the firewall until the studs clear the holes. It may be necessary to tilt the booster slightly during removal.

11 Installation is the reverse of removal. But be sure to measure the following dimensions before installing the power brake booster assembly. Replace the sealing gaskets. Also, check the brake pedal height and adjust if necessary (see Section 14).

ADJUSTMENT

⯈ **Refer to illustrations 11.12, 11.13a and 11.13b**

12 Measure the distance between the power brake booster spacer block and the hole in the clevis (see illustration) and compare it to the dimension listed in this Chapter's Specifications. If it isn't the same, loosen the lock nut and turn the clevis in or out to the specified length, then tighten the nut.

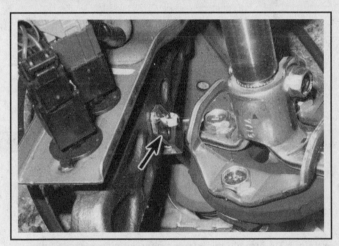

11.8 Booster pushrod clevis pin and retaining clip

11.9 Power brake booster mounting fasteners

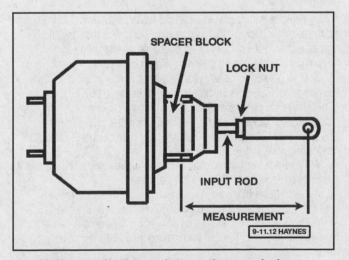

11.12 Measure the distance between the power brake booster and the hole in the clevis and compare your measurement to the dimension listed in this Chapter's Specifications; if necessary, adjust the clevis before installing the booster

11.13a With vacuum applied to the booster, measure the distance between the booster output rod and the face of the power booster (typical)

11.13b To adjust the length of the booster output rod, hold the serrated portion of the rod with a pair of pliers and turn the adjusting screw (typical)

13 Using a vacuum pump, apply 20 in-Hg to the booster and measure the distance between the end of the output rod and the master cylinder flange mounting surface of the booster (see illustration). Compare the measurement with the one listed in this Chapter's Specifications and adjust it if necessary (see illustration).

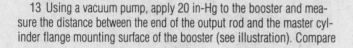

12 Parking brake - adjustment

Refer to illustration 12.6

➡ **Note 1:** If the parking brake shoe clearance or cable adjusting nut require a significant amount of adjustment, it is advisable to inspect the brake shoe lining thickness (see Section 10).

➡ **Note 2:** On Armada models equipped with a rear auto-leveling suspension, turn the ignition key to the OFF position before raising the vehicle.

1 Vehicles equipped with a parking brake pedal should fully engage in three to four clicks. If the number of clicks is less than specified, there's a chance the parking brake might not be releasing completely and might be dragging on the drum portion of the disc. If the number of clicks is greater than specified, the parking brake may not hold the vehicle adequately on an incline, allowing the car to roll.

2 There are two areas of adjustment for the parking brake: the star-wheel adjuster at the shoes for each wheel and the adjusting nut on the brake cable at the parking brake pedal. Adjustment at the shoes is performed first.

3 Block the front wheels, raise the rear of the vehicle and support it securely on jackstands. Remove the rear wheels.

4 Remove the brake disc (see Section 6). Turn the star-wheel adjuster a couple of notches to expand the shoes (see illustration 7.5a). Adjust both wheels. Put the discs back on and secure each one with a couple of lug nuts. Turn the hub making sure that the disc does not drag.

5 Set the parking brake fully and compare the number of clicks to those specified in Step 1. If more adjustment is necessary, repeat Step 4. If the brake discs start to drag, then move on to the next adjustment at the parking brake pedal assembly.

6 Locate the adjusting nut at the pedal assembly and either tighten or loosen it to achieve the proper number of clicks when the parking brake is set (see illustration). Tightening the nut (turning it clockwise) decreases the number of clicks, while the opposite is achieved by loosening the nut (turning it counterclockwise).

7 Confirm that the parking brake is fully engaged within the number of clicks stated in Step 1.

8 Release the parking brake and confirm that the brakes don't drag when the rear wheels are turned.

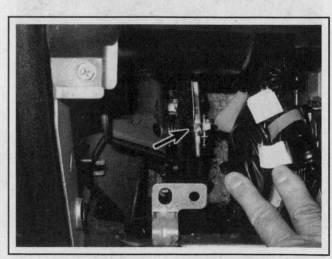

12.6 Parking brake cable adjusting nut (panel removed for clarity)

13 Brake light switch - replacement

◗ **Refer to illustration 13.2**

➡**Note: There is an additional switch mounted above the brake light switch that is used for the speed control feature. This switch is very similar to the brake light switch and can be removed in the same manner.**

1   Remove the lower instrument panel insulator below the driver's side knee bolster for access if equipped (see Chapter 11).
2   The brake light switch is mounted to a bracket attached near the top of the brake pedal assembly (see illustration).
3   Depress and hold the brake pedal.
4   Rotate the switch about 45 degrees counterclockwise and remove it from its bracket.

➡**Note: If you need to remove the switch for the speed control, use the same procedure.**

5   Disconnect the electrical connector for the brake light switch.
6   To install the switch, lightly pull up on the brake pedal, place the switch into the bracket fitting until it touches the brake pedal arm, then turn the switch 45 degrees clockwise to lock it in place.
7   Press and release the brake pedal and make sure that there is a

13.2 Brake light switch location

small gap between the threaded portion of the switch and the pedal arm. Measure the gap and compare it to the dimension listed in this Chapter's Specifications.

8   Test the brake lights for proper operation.

14 Brake pedal - adjustment

➡**Note: On vehicles equipped with electrically adjustable pedals, move the pedals to their lowest position (closest to the floor) before checking or adjusting the brake pedal height.**

BRAKE PEDAL RELEASED HEIGHT

◗ **Refer to illustrations 14.2 and 14.4**

1   Remove the brake light and speed control switches (see Section 13).
2   Peel back the carpet and insulator pad. With the brake pedal fully

released, measure the distance from the top of the pedal to the floor (see illustration).
3   If the height is not as listed this Chapter's Specifications, it must be adjusted.
4   Loosen the pushrod locknut just in front of the power brake booster clevis (see illustration).
5   Turn the booster pushrod until the pedal height is correct.
6   Tighten the locknut and reinstall the brake light and speed control switches (see Section 13).
7   After adjusting the pedal height, check the freeplay.

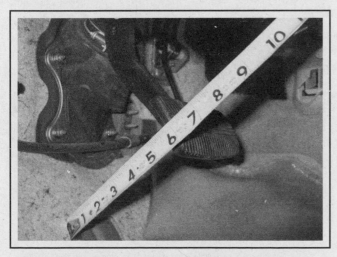

14.2 With the brake pedal fully released, measure the distance from the top of the pedal pad to the floor

14.4 Brake pedal adjustment details

1	*Booster pushrod clevis*	*3* *Booster pushrod*
2	*Locknut*	

BRAKE PEDAL FREEPLAY

8   Press down lightly on the brake pedal and measure the distance that it moves freely before resistance is felt. The freeplay should be within the measurements listed in this Chapter's Specifications. If it isn't, check and adjust the pedal height.

BRAKE PEDAL DEPRESSED HEIGHT

9   Check the pedal depressed height only after the brake pedal released height and freeplay are within specification.
10   With the engine running, press the brake pedal fully and measure the pedal pad-to-floor distance.
11   If the height is less than specified in this Chapter's Specifications, check the brake system for fluid leaks or other damage.

Specifications

General

Brake fluid type	See Chapter 1

Brake light switch

Plunger-to-pedal stopper clearance	0.029 to 0.077 inch (0.74 to 1.96 mm)

Brake pedal

Brake pedal freeplay	0.12 to 0.43 inch (3 to 11 mm)
Brake pedal depressed height	More than 3.55 inches (90 mm)
Brake pedal released height	7.18 to 7.57 inches (182 to 192 mm)

Disc brakes (front and rear)

Minimum pad lining thickness	See Chapter 1
Brake disc minimum thickness	Cast into disc
Maximum disc runout	
Front	0.001 inch (0.03 mm)
Rear	0.002 inch (0.05 mm)
Maximum disc thickness variation	0.0006 inch (0.015 mm)

Power brake booster

Booster spacer block-to-center of clevis hole dimension	5.94 inches (151 mm)
Booster output rod-to-outer surface (vacuum applied)	0.614 to 0.626 inch (15.6 to 15.9 mm)

Torque specifications	Ft-lbs (unless otherwise indicated)	Nm
Note: One foot-pound (ft-lb) of torque is equivalent to 12 inch-pounds (in-lbs) of torque. Torque values below approximately 15 ft-lbs are expressed in inch-pounds, since most foot-pound torque wrenches are not accurate at these smaller values.		
ABS wheel speed sensor mounting bolts	6 (73 in-lbs)	8
Brake booster-to-body mounting nuts	18	24
Caliper mounting bolts		
Front	32	43
Rear	24	32
Caliper mounting bracket bolts (front)	155	210
Brake hose-to-caliper bolt or fitting	13 (156 in-lbs)	18
Master cylinder-to-brake booster retaining nuts	20	27
Wheel lug nuts	See Chapter 1	

Section

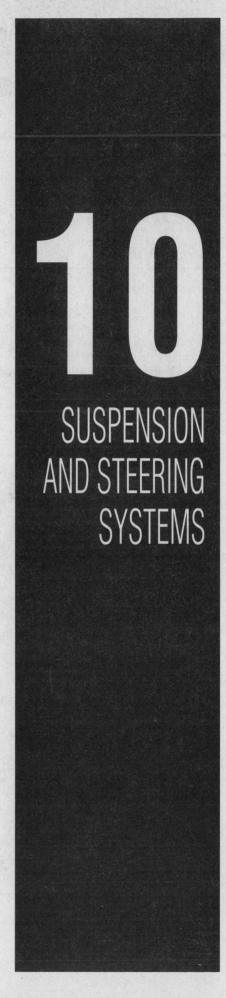

10

SUSPENSION AND STEERING SYSTEMS

1 General information

FRONT SUSPENSION

▶ **Refer to illustration 1.1**

The front suspension (see illustration) is fully independent. All models use upper and lower control arms and shock absorber/coil spring assemblies. On all models, a stabilizer bar connected to the frame and to the two lower control arms reduces body roll during cornering.

REAR SUSPENSION

▶ **Refer to illustrations 1.2 and 1.3**

On Titan models, the rear suspension consists of a pair of multi-leaf springs and two shock absorbers (see illustration). The rear axle assembly is attached to the leaf springs by U-bolts. The front ends of the springs are attached to the frame at the front hangers, through rubber bushings. The rear ends of the springs are attached to the frame by shackles which allow the springs to alter their length as they compress and rebound.

On Armada models, the rear suspension consists of an independent

multi-link suspension consisting of shock absorbers, coil springs, a few specialized links and knuckles (see illustration). Additionally, all Armada models incorporate a stabilizer bar to control body roll.

Some Armada models are equipped with a rear auto-leveling suspension that maintains the rear height of the vehicle. This system is best described as an automatic "air-shock" system. It includes an air compressor, various controls and other components.

✳✳ WARNING:

Special tools are required to service this system. Also, removal and installation of some components that are not part of this system may be limited. Refer to a dealership service department or other qualified repair shop regarding repairs on this system or related components.

STEERING SYSTEM

The steering system on all models consists of a rack-and-pinion steering gear and two adjustable tie-rods. Power assist is standard.

1.1 Front suspension components:

| 1 | Stabilizer bar | 3 | Steering knuckles | 5 | Lower control arms |
| 2 | Tie-rod ends | 4 | Lower balljoints | | |

1.2 Rear suspension components (Titan models):

1   *Leaf spring*   3   *Spring plate*   4   *Shackle*
2   *Shock absorber*

1.3 Rear suspension components (Armada models):

1   *Stabilizer bar*   3   *Lower balljoints*   5   *Rear lower links*
2   *Front lower links*   4   *Rear knuckles*   6   *Coil springs*

PRECAUTIONS

Frequently, when working on the suspension or steering system components, you may come across fasteners which seem impossible to loosen. These fasteners on the underside of the vehicle are continually subjected to water, road grime, mud, etc., and can become rusted or frozen, making them extremely difficult to remove. In order to unscrew these stubborn fasteners without damaging them (or other components), be sure to use lots of penetrating oil and allow it to soak in for a while. Using a wire brush to clean exposed threads will also ease removal of the nut or bolt and prevent damage to the threads. Sometimes a sharp blow with a hammer and punch is effective in breaking the bond between a nut and bolt threads, but care must be taken to prevent the punch from slipping off the fastener and ruining the threads. Heating the stuck fastener and surrounding area with a torch sometimes helps too, but isn't recommended because of the obvious dangers associated with fire. Long breaker bars and extension, or cheater, pipes will increase leverage, but never use an extension pipe on a ratchet - the ratcheting mechanism could be damaged. Sometimes, turning the nut or bolt in the tightening (clockwise) direction first will help to break it loose. Fasteners that require drastic measures to unscrew should always be replaced with new ones.

Since most of the procedures that are dealt with in this Chapter involve jacking up the vehicle and working underneath it, a good pair of jackstands will be needed. A hydraulic floor jack is the preferred type of jack to lift the vehicle, and it can also be used to support certain components during various operations.

✳✳ WARNING:

Never, under any circumstances, rely on a jack to support the vehicle while working on it. Also, whenever any of the suspension or steering fasteners are loosened or removed they must be inspected and, if necessary, replaced with new ones of the same part number or of original equipment quality and design. Torque specifications must be followed for proper reassembly and component retention. Never attempt to heat or straighten suspension or steering components. Instead, replace bent or damaged parts with new ones.

➡Note: On Armada models equipped with a rear auto-leveling suspension, turn the ignition key to the OFF position before raising the vehicle.

---

2 Shock absorber/coil spring assembly (front) - removal and installation

✳✳ WARNING:

Always replace shock absorbers in pairs - never replace just one of them.

➡Note 1: On Armada models equipped with a rear auto-leveling suspension, turn the ignition key to the OFF position before raising the vehicle.

➡Note 2: It is possible to replace the shocks or springs individually, but the unit will have to be disassembled by a qualified repair shop with the proper equipment. This will add considerable cost to the project. You can compare the cost of replacing the complete assemblies yourself to the cost of replacing individual components (with the help of a shop).

REMOVAL

▶ **Refer to illustrations 2.2 and 2.3**

1 Loosen the front wheel lug nuts. Raise the vehicle and support it securely on jackstands. Remove the front wheels.
2 Remove the shock absorber lower mounting bolt (see illustration).
3 Remove the fasteners that attach the upper end of the shock to the frame (see illustration).
4 Turn the steering knuckle outward for clearance, then remove the shock absorber.
5 Inspect the shock absorber for leaking fluid, dents, cracks and other damage. Inspect the coil spring for chips and cracks which could cause premature failure. Inspect the spring seats for hardness and general deterioration. If any of the components of the assembly are worn or damaged, have the unit serviced by a qualified repair shop or replace it.

2.2 The lower shock assembly mounting bolt (A) and the spring end facing outward (B)

2.3 The upper shock assembly mounting nuts. DO NOT remove the nut from the damper shaft (the nut in the center)

INSTALLATION

6   Installation is the reverse of removal, making sure the spring end is facing outward (see illustration 2.2). Be sure to tighten the fasteners to the torque listed in this Chapter's Specifications.

7   Tighten the wheel lug nuts to the torque listed in the Chapter 1 Specifications.

---

3   Stabilizer bar, bushings and links (front) - removal and installation

◆ **Refer to illustrations 3.2 and 3.3**

❋❋ WARNING:

The manufacturer recommends replacing the stabilizer bar link nuts with new ones whenever they are removed.

➡**Note: On Armada models equipped with a rear auto-leveling suspension, turn the ignition key to the OFF position before raising the vehicle.**

1   Raise the vehicle and support it securely on jackstands. Remove the engine splash shield as necessary.

2   Remove the nuts from the links and detach the links from the bar (see illustration).

➡**Note: Be sure to keep the parts for the left and right sides separate.**

3   Remove the stabilizer bar bracket bolts (see illustration).
4   Remove the stabilizer bar.
5   Remove the rubber bushings.
6   Inspect all parts for wear and damage, replacing them as necessary.
7   Installation is the reverse of removal. Be sure to tighten all fasteners to the torque listed in this Chapter's Specifications.

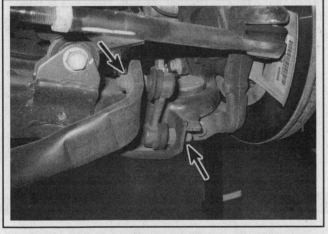

3.2 Front stabilizer bar link nuts

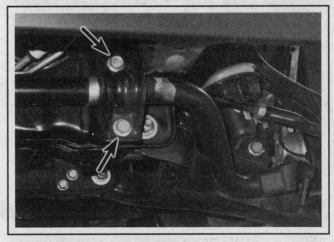

3.3 Front stabilizer bar bracket bolts

---

4   Upper control arm - removal and installation

➡**Note 1: On Armada models equipped with a rear auto-leveling suspension, turn the ignition key to the OFF position before raising the vehicle.**

➡**Note 2: The manufacturer recommends using new locknuts on the control arm pivot bolts during installation.**

REMOVAL

◆ **Refer to Illustrations 4.3 and 4.4**

1   Loosen the wheel lug nuts, raise the front of the vehicle and support it securely on jackstands. Remove the wheel.

2   Remove the fenderwell liner (see Chapter 11).

➡**Note: It may be possible to simply move the liner aside to gain access to the upper control arm mounting fasteners.**

4.3 The upper balljoint with a puller tool installed

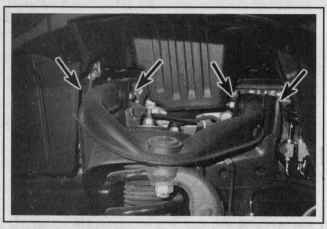

4.4 Upper control arm pivot bolts and nuts

3   To disconnect the upper control arm from the steering knuckle, remove the cotter pin, loosen the upper balljoint nut a few turns (don't remove it), install a balljoint separator and break the balljoint loose from the knuckle (see illustration). Remove the nut.

➡**Note 1: If you don't have a press-type balljoint removal tool, a picklefork type balljoint separator can be used, but keep in mind that this type of tool will probably destroy the balljoint boot.**

➡**Note 2: It's a good idea to secure the steering knuckle with wire so that it does not fall outward and cause damage to the brake lines or other components.**

4   Remove the upper control arm pivot bolts and nuts, noting which way the bolts are installed (see illustration). Remove the control arm.

INSTALLATION

5   Position the arm in the frame brackets and install the bolts and nuts, but don't tighten them yet.

6   Attach the balljoint to the steering knuckle and tighten the ballstud nut to the torque listed in this Chapter's Specifications. Install a new cotter pin.

➡**Note: If necessary, tighten the nut a little more to align the slots in the nut with the hole in the ballstud; don't loosen the nut to insert the cotter pin.**

7   Tighten the control arm pivot bolts/nuts to the torque listed in this Chapter's Specifications.

➡**Note: Raise the lower control arm with a floor jack to simulate normal ride height before tightening the upper control arm mounting fasteners, or tighten them when the wheel is installed and the vehicle is resting on the ground.**

8   The remainder of installation is the reverse of removal. Tighten the wheel lug nuts to the torque listed in the Chapter 1 Specifications.

9   Have the front end alignment checked and, if necessary, adjusted.

5	Lower control arm - removal and installation

➡**Note 1: On Armada models equipped with a rear auto-leveling suspension, turn the ignition key to the OFF position before raising the vehicle.**

➡**Note 2: The manufacturer recommends using new locknuts on the control arm pivot bolts and the balljoint pinch bolt during installation.**

REMOVAL

◆ **Refer to illustrations 5.5 and 5.6**

1   Loosen the wheel lug nuts, raise the vehicle and support it securely on jackstands placed under the frame rails. Remove the wheel.

2   If you're working on a 4WD model, remove the driveaxle (see Chapter 8).

3   Detach the stabilizer bar link from the lower control arm (see Section 3).

4   Remove the shock absorber lower mounting bolt (see Section 2).

5   To remove the lower control arm, remove the pinch-bolt securing the lower balljoint (see illustration), then use a small puller, or equivalent, to push the ballstud out of the control arm. It's also possible to pry the control arm from the steering knuckle to separate them.

6   Mark the positions of the lower control arm pivot fasteners on both sides relative to the frame, then hold the bolts and remove the locknuts and discard them (see illustration 5.5 and the accompanying illustration).

➡**Note: In most cases, the pivot bolts are cam adjuster type bolts and marking helps preserve the alignment angle during installation.**

7   Carefully inspect the control arm bushings for hardening, excessive wear and cracks. If they appear to be worn or deteriorated, replace the control arm.

➡**Note: It may be possible to have the bushing pressed out of the arm by an automotive machine shop or a repair shop that specializes in suspension work. A replacement part may be available as an aftermarket (non-OEM) part, but this could not be confirmed at the time of this manual's writing.**

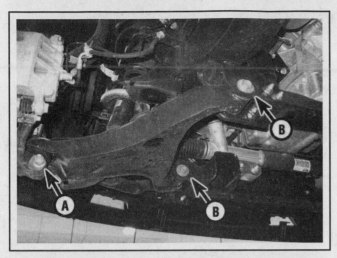

5.5 Lower control arm balljoint pinch bolt/nut (A) and pivot fasteners (B)

5.6 Index marks on the lower control arm pivot/adjuster bolts

INSTALLATION

8   Installation is the reverse of removal. Use new locknuts for the balljoint pinch-bolt and the control arm pivot bolts. Align the marks made in Step 6, then tighten all fasteners to the torque listed in this Chapter's Specifications.

➡**Note: Raise the lower control arm with a floor jack to simulate normal ride height before tightening the control arm pivot fasteners, or tighten them when the wheel is installed and the vehicle is resting on the ground.**

Be sure to tighten the wheel lug nuts to the torque listed in the Chapter 1 Specifications.

9   Have the front wheel alignment checked and, if necessary, adjusted.

6   Balljoints - check and replacement

CHECK

➡**Note: On Armada models equipped with a rear auto-leveling suspension, turn the ignition key to the OFF position before raising the vehicle.**

1   Inspect the control arm balljoint(s) for looseness anytime a balljoint is separated from the steering knuckle. See if you can turn the ballstud in its socket with your fingers. If the balljoint is loose, or if the ballstud can be turned, replace the balljoint. You can also check the balljoints with the suspension assembled as follows.

Upper balljoint

2   Raise the front of the vehicle and support it securely on jackstands placed under the frame rails. Place a floor jack under the lower control arm and raise it far enough to lift the upper control arm off its stop.

3   Attempt to move the control arm up and down; a prybar may be helpful. If any play is felt, replace the upper control arm and balljoint as an assembly (the balljoint is not replaceable separately according to the manufacturer).

4   Also try to move the steering knuckle in-and-out. If any play is felt, replace the upper control arm/balljoint assembly.

5   Check the balljoint boot for cracks and tears. If any are present, replace the control arm.

Lower balljoint

6   Raise the front of the vehicle and support it securely on jackstands placed under the frame rails.

7   Place a floor jack under the lower control arm and raise it slightly. Attempt to move the steering knuckle up and down; a large prybar underneath the tire, or a prybar placed between the end of the control arm and the steering knuckle will be helpful. If any play is felt, replace the control arm and balljoint as an assembly (the balljoint is not replaceable separately according to the manufacturer).

8   Also try to move the steering knuckle in-and-out. If any play is felt, replace the control arm/balljoint assembly.

9   Check the balljoint boot for cracks and tears. If any are present, replace the control arm.

REPLACEMENT

10   The balljoints on these models are integrated with the control arm as an assembly. In the event the balljoint fails, the arm must be replaced according to the manufacturer.

➡**Note: It may be possible to have the balljoint pressed out of the arm by an automotive machine shop or a repair shop that specializes in suspension work. A replacement part may be available as an aftermarket (non-OEM) part, but this could not be confirmed at the time of this manual's writing.**

7 Steering knuckle - removal and installation

➡Note: On Armada models equipped with a rear auto-leveling suspension, turn the ignition key to the OFF position before raising the vehicle.

1 Loosen the wheel lug nuts, raise the vehicle and support it securely on jackstands placed underneath the frame (or subframe) rails. Remove the wheel.

2 Remove the wheel speed sensor, brake caliper and brake disc (see Chapter 9). Hang the caliper out of the way with a piece of wire (don't disconnect the brake hose).

3 Remove the wheel bearing and hub assembly (see Section 8).

4 Disconnect the tie-rod end from the steering knuckle (see Section 17).

5 Disconnect the balljoints from the steering knuckle (see Sections 4 and 5) and remove the steering knuckle.

6 Installation is the reverse of removal. Be sure to tighten the balljoint and tie-rod end fasteners to the torque values listed in this Chapter's Specifications and use new cotter pins.

➡Note: If necessary, tighten the nuts a little more to align the slots in the nut with the hole in the ballstud; don't loosen the nut to insert the cotter pin.

Tighten the caliper mounting bolts to the torque values listed in the Chapter 9 Specifications. On 4WD models, tighten the driveaxle hub nut to the torque values listed in the Chapter 8 Specifications and use a new cotter pin. Tighten the wheel lug nuts to the torque listed in the Chapter 1 Specifications.

8 Hub and bearing assembly - removal and installation

✷✷ WARNING:

The dust created by the brake system is harmful to your health. Never blow it out with compressed air and don't inhale any of it. Do not, under any circumstances, use petroleum-based solvents to clean brake parts. Use brake system cleaner only.

✷✷ WARNING:

The manufacturer recommends replacing the hub-to-knuckle bolts with new ones whenever they are removed.

➡Note: The hub and bearing assembly is sealed-for-life. If worn or damaged, it must be replaced as a unit.

➡Note: This procedure applies to the front hub and bearing assembly on all models, and the rear hub and bearing assembly on Armada models.

REMOVAL

▸ Refer to illustration 8.5

1 If you're removing the front hub and bearing assembly on a 4WD model or the rear hub and bearing assembly on an Armada, remove the cotter pin and loosen the driveaxle/hub nut (see Chapter 8).

2 Loosen the wheel lug nuts, raise the vehicle and support it securely on jackstands. Remove the wheel.

3 Remove the brake disc (see Chapter 9).

4 Remove the wheel speed sensor from the hub (see Chapter 9).

5 Working from the back side of the knuckle, remove the hub retaining bolts (see illustration).

➡Note: This can usually be done without removing the driveaxle, provided you have a swivel socket and a long extension. If you do not have a tool setup that can unscrew the bolts with the driveaxle in place, the driveaxle will have to be removed.

6 Remove the hub and disc shield from the knuckle. If you're removing the front hub and bearing assembly on a 4WD model or the rear hub and bearing assembly on an Armada, pull the assembly off the driveaxle splines.

✷✷ CAUTION:

Be careful not to pull outward on the driveaxle, as this could separate the inner CV joint components. If the driveaxle splines stick in the hub, attach a two-jaw puller to the hub flange and push the stub axle out of the hub. The hub assembly should come right out of the knuckle, but if it doesn't, tap it from side-to-side to free it.

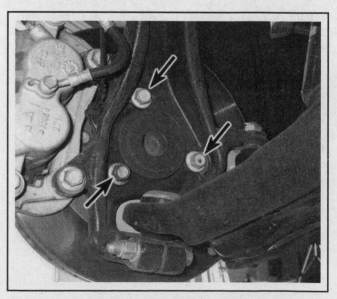

8.5 Front hub and bearing assembly-to-steering knuckle bolts (2WD model)

INSTALLATION

7   Clean the mating surfaces on the knuckle, bearing flange and knuckle bore.

8   Insert the hub and bearing assembly into the knuckle and, on 4WD models or the rear hub on Armada models, onto the end of the driveaxle.

➡**Note: On 4WD models or the rear hub on Armada models, lubricate the splines of the driveaxle with multi-purpose grease before installing the hub.**

Position the disc shield and install the NEW bolts, tightening them to the torque listed in this Chapter's Specifications.

9   Install the wheel speed sensor (see Chapter 9).

10 Install the brake disc, caliper mounting bracket and caliper (see Chapter 9).

11 On the front hub and bearing on 4WD models or the rear hub and bearing assembly on an Armada, install the driveaxle/hub nut and tighten it to the torque listed in the Chapter 8 Specifications. Install a new cotter pin.

12 Install the wheel, lower the vehicle and tighten the lug nuts to the torque listed in the Chapter 1 Specifications.

9 Shock absorber (rear) - removal and installation

▸ **Refer to illustrations 9.4a and 9.4b**

✳✳ **WARNING:**

Always replace shock absorbers in pairs - never replace just one of them.

➡**Note: This procedure does not apply to Armada models equipped with a rear auto-leveling suspension (see Section 1).**

1   Raise the rear of the vehicle and support it securely on jackstands placed underneath the frame rails. Block the front wheels so the vehicle doesn't roll off the stands.

2   On Armada models, remove the fenderwell liner (see Chapter 11).

3   If you're working on a Titan, support the rear axle with a floor jack placed under the axle tube closest to the shock absorber being removed. If you're working on an Armada, support the rear lower link with a floor jack placed under the outer end of the lower link.

4   Remove the shock absorber upper and lower mounting fasteners (see illustrations).

5   Remove the shock absorber.

6   Installation is the reverse of removal. Tighten all fasteners to the torque values listed in this Chapter's Specifications.

9.4a Rear shock absorber mounting fasteners - Titan

9.4b Rear shock absorber mounting fasteners - Armada

10 Stabilizer bar, bushings and links (rear) - removal and installation

▶ Refer to illustrations 10.2 and 10.3

➡Note: On Armada models equipped with a rear auto-leveling suspension, turn the ignition key to the OFF position before raising the vehicle.

1 Loosen the rear wheel lug nuts, raise the rear of the vehicle and support it securely on jackstands. Block the front wheels to keep the vehicle from rolling off the stands. Remove the rear wheels.

2 Remove the nuts from the upper ends of the stabilizer bar links, then separate the links from the bar (see illustration).

3 Remove the stabilizer bar clamp bolts (see illustration) and remove the stabilizer bar.

4 Inspect the stabilizer bar bushings for cracks, tears and other signs of deterioration. Replace as necessary. Also check the ballstuds on the ends of the links for looseness. Replace the links if necessary.

5 Installation is the reverse of removal. Be sure to tighten all fasteners to the torque values listed in this Chapter's Specifications.

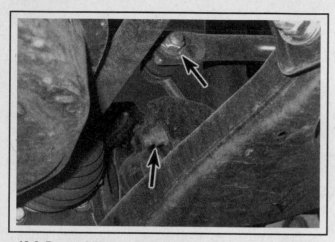

10.2 Rear stabilizer bar link nuts

10.3 Rear stabilizer bar clamp bolts

11 Leaf spring - removal and installation

REMOVAL

▶ Refer to illustrations 11.3a, 11.3b, 11.3c, 11.3d, 11.4 and 11.5

1 Loosen the rear wheel lug nuts, raise the rear of the vehicle and support it securely on jackstands placed underneath the frame rails. Block the front wheels to keep the vehicle from rolling off the stands. Remove the rear wheels.

2 Support the axle with a floor jack placed under the axle tube and raise it slightly to take the weight of the axle. Remove the shock absorber lower mounting bolt.

3 Remove the four U-bolt nuts (see illustration), the spring plate, the two U-bolts and the small bumper on top of the spring. Lower the jack just enough to relieve spring tension. If you're working on the left side leaf spring, remove the rear storage box:

a) *Remove the mudguard fasteners, then remove the mudguard (see illustration).*

b) *Remove the bracket-to-body bolts while supporting the storage box, then remove it (see illustrations).*

4 Remove the front spring fasteners (see illustration).

5 Remove the shackle-to-frame fasteners (see illustration).

6 Remove the spring assembly. Remove the shackle as necessary.

7 If the bushings at the ends of the spring are worn or deteriorated,

an automotive machine shop or dealer service department can press the old ones out and press new ones in.

➡Note: It's possible that the upper shackle bushings can be replaced without the use of special tools.

INSTALLATION

➡Note: The manufacturer recommends using new nuts for U-bolt installation.

8 Place the spring in position and install the front mounting fasteners, but don't tighten them yet.

9 Raise the rear of the spring and shackle into position and install the mounting fasteners but don't tighten them yet.

10 Raise the axle on the jack until it mates properly with the spring. Install the small bumper and U-bolts, the spring plate, then install new nuts. Tighten the U-bolt nuts, in a criss-cross pattern, to the torque listed in this Chapter's Specifications.

11 Install the storage box and tighten the bracket mounting fasteners securely.

12 Install the wheel, lower the vehicle to the ground and bounce it a few times, then tighten the front, rear and shackle mounting fasteners to the torque values listed in this Chapter's Specifications. Tighten the lug nuts to the torque listed in the Chapter 1 Specifications.

11.3a The U-bolt nuts, spring plate and U-bolts

11.3b Mudguard fasteners

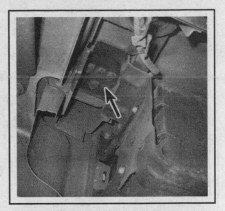

11.3c Storage box mounting bracket bolts (rear)

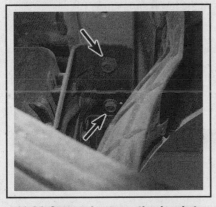

11.3d Storage box mounting bracket bolts (front)

11.4 Leaf spring front mounting bolt

11.5 Rear leaf spring/shackle fasteners

12 Suspension links (rear, Armada models) - removal and installation

➡**Note: On Armada models equipped with a rear auto-leveling suspension, turn the ignition key to the OFF position before raising the vehicle.**

1   Loosen the wheel lug nuts, raise the rear of the vehicle and support it securely on jackstands placed under the frame rails. Remove the wheel.

➡**Note: When removing the upper arm link, place the jackstands away from the subframe.**

UPPER ARM LINK

▸ **Refer to illustrations 12.4, 12.5, 12.10 and 12.11**

➡**Note 1: This procedure does not apply to Armada models equipped with a rear auto-leveling suspension (see Section 1).**

➡**Note 2: This procedure requires lowering the rear subframe for clearance to remove the forward upper arm link fasteners.**

2   Remove the spare tire.

3   Place the shift lever in neutral and make sure that the parking brake is released.

4   Detach the bracket from the front of the rear subframe (see illustration).

12.4 Rear subframe bracket mounting fasteners

12.5 Upper arm link pivot fasteners (A) and balljoint-to-knuckle fasteners (B)

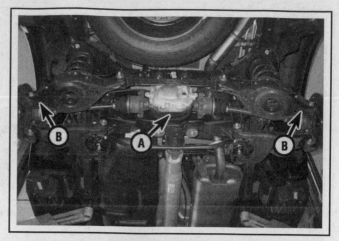

12.10 The locations for the floor jack at the differential (A) and for the jackstands at the lower spring links (B)

12.11 The location of the subframe mounting fasteners (right side shown, left side similar)

5   Remove the upper arm link balljoint-to-knuckle fasteners (see illustration). Pry the ballstud from the knuckle until it is loose. Be careful not to damage the balljoint boot if the arm is to be reused.

6   Remove the upper arm link pivot fasteners with the exception of the front pivot bolt; the front bolt cannot be removed until the subframe is lowered (see illustration 12.5).

7   Remove the brake calipers and secure them to the brake line frame bracket (see Chapter 9).

8   Remove the upper shock absorber mounting fasteners (see Section 8).

9   Disconnect the wheel speed sensor electrical connectors and detach the harnesses from the subframe.

10 Support the rear differential with a floor jack and place jackstands beneath each lower spring link at the outboard ends near the rear knuckles (see illustration). Leave a couple of inches between the jackstands and the links to allow for lowering.

✳✳ WARNING:

Do not raise the vehicle off of the jackstands placed in Step 1 while supporting the rear differential.

11 Remove the subframe mounting bolts from the side of the vehicle

from which the upper arm link is being removed (see illustration). Loosen the subframe bolts on the opposite side approximately one-half inch to allow the subframe to pivot downward.

12 Slowly and carefully lower the floor jack that is supporting the differential approximately two inches, then remove the front pivot bolt.

✳✳ WARNING:

Do not lower the subframe anymore than necessary to remove the upper arm link's front pivot bolt or damage to other components may occur.

13 Installation is the reverse of removal. Tighten the upper arm link pivot fasteners to the torque listed in this Chapter's Specifications. Proceed to Step 31.

➡Note: Raise the lower spring link with a floor jack to simulate normal ride height before tightening the link's mounting fasteners, or tighten them when the wheel is installed and the vehicle is resting on the ground, if possible.

FRONT LOWER LINK

▶ Refer to illustration 12.15

14 Detach the shock absorber from the link (see Section 2).
15 Remove the front lower link balljoint-to-knuckle fasteners (see illustration).
16 Mark the relationship of the link's adjusting cam bolt to the subframe bracket (see illustration 12.24).
17 Remove the link's mounting fasteners then remove the link (see illustration 12.15). Use a soft hammer or equivalent to separate the link from the rear knuckle. Be careful not to damage the balljoint. Use a balljoint separator tool if necessary (see illustration 4.4).
18 Inspect all rubber bushings for wear and damage. If any of the rubber parts are cracked, torn or generally deteriorated, the manufacturer states to replace the link.

➡Note: It may be possible to have the bushing(s) pressed out of the arm by an automotive machine shop or a repair shop that specializes in suspension work. A replacement part may be available as an aftermarket (non-OEM) part, but this could not be confirmed at the time of this manual's writing.

12.15 The front lower link pivot fasteners (A) and the balljoint-to-knuckle fasteners (B)

12.22 Lower spring link and coil spring details:

1   Index marks
2   Link fasteners
3   Floor jack location for lowering link

19 Inspect the balljoint for wear or deterioration (see Section 6).

20 Installation is the reverse of removal. Place the adjusting cam bolt back in the same position to restore the rear alignment to its original setting. Tighten the mounting fasteners to the torque listed in this Chapter's Specifications. Proceed to Step 31.

➡Note: Raise the lower spring link with a floor jack to simulate normal ride height before tightening the link's mounting fasteners, or tighten them when the wheel is installed and the vehicle is resting on the ground, if possible.

REAR LOWER LINK (AND COIL SPRING)

▸ **Refer to illustrations 12.22 and 12.24**

21 Disconnect the electrical connector for the wheel speed sensor and detach the wire harness from the lower spring link.

22 Mark the coil spring and the upper and lower spring seats so that they can all be placed back in their original positions during installation (see illustration).

23 Support the rear lower link and coil spring tension with a floor jack.

24 Mark the relationship of the adjusting cam bolt for the lower link to the subframe bracket on both sides. Hold the cam bolt, then loosen the nut (see illustration).

✳✳ WARNING:

Do not attempt to remove the cam bolt and nut at this time as the link is still under tension from the coil spring.

25 Remove the link mounting fasteners from the rear knuckle (see illustration 12.22).

26 Slowly lower the rear lower link with the floor jack until the spring tension is relieved.

27 Note the position of the coil spring in the lower link as well as the position of the seats (or insulators), then remove all of them.

28 Remove the adjusting cam bolt and nut, then remove the link.

29 Inspect the rubber bushing on the rear knuckle where the link attaches for wear and damage. Refer to Section 14 regarding the bushing in the rear knuckle. Inspect the coil spring seats (insulators) as well.

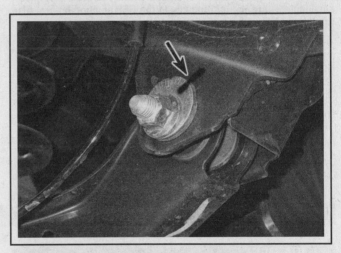

12.24 Index marks on the lower spring link mounting/adjuster bolts (one side shown - mark both sides)

If the seats are cracked, torn or generally deteriorated replace them.

30 Installation is the reverse of removal. Be sure to place the coil spring and seats in the original positions in which they were installed. If new spring seats are used, install them with the arrows (molded in seat) pointing towards the rear knuckle. Place the adjusting cam bolt back in the same position to restore the rear alignment to its original setting. Tighten the mounting fasteners to the torque listed in this Chapter's Specifications. Refer to the torque values listed in the Chapter 9 Specifications for brake related fasteners. Proceed to Step 31.

➡Note: Raise the lower link with a floor jack to simulate normal ride height before tightening the link's mounting fasteners, or tighten them when the wheel is installed and the vehicle is resting on the ground.

ALL LINKS

31 Tighten the wheel lug nuts to the torque listed in the Chapter 1 Specifications.

32 Have the wheel alignment checked and, if necessary, adjusted.

13 Coil spring (rear, Armada models) - removal and installation

※※ WARNING:

Always replace coil springs in pairs - never replace just one of them.

Refer to Section 12 of this Chapter for coil spring removal.

14 Knuckle (rear, Armada models) - removal and installation

※※ WARNING:

The dust created by the brake system is harmful to your health. Never blow it out with compressed air and don't inhale any of it. Do not, under any circumstances, use petroleum-based solvents to clean brake parts. Use brake system cleaner only.

➡Note: On Armada models equipped with a rear auto-leveling suspension, turn the ignition key to the OFF position before raising the vehicle.

1   Loosen the wheel lug nuts, raise the rear of the vehicle and support it securely on jackstands placed under the frame rails. Remove the wheel.

2   Loosen the driveaxle/hub nut (see Chapter 8).

3   Remove the wheel speed sensor, brake disc and the parking brake shoes (see Chapter 9).

4   Remove the parking brake actuator and cable from the knuckle (see Chapter 9).

5   Remove the hub and wheel bearing (see Section 8) and the brake

backing plate.

※※ CAUTION:

Support the driveaxle and do not allow extreme angles on the CV joints or over-extend the inner sliding joint (see Chapter 8).

➡Note: Use a puller or suitable tool if the driveaxle splines are stuck in the wheel hub (see Chapter 8).

6   Remove the rear lower link and coil spring (see Section 12).

7   Detach the front lower link and upper arm link from the rear knuckle (see Section 12), then remove the rear knuckle.

8   Installation is the reverse of removal. Tighten the mounting fasteners to the torque listed in this Chapter's Specifications. Refer to the torque values listed in the Chapter 9 Specifications for brake related fasteners.

➡Note: Raise the rear lower link with a floor jack to simulate normal ride height before tightening the mounting fasteners for the rear suspension components.

15 Steering wheel - removal and installation

※※ WARNING:

The models covered by this manual are equipped with Supplemental Restraint Systems (SRS), more commonly known as airbags. Always disable the airbag system before working in the vicinity of any airbag system components to avoid the possibility of accidental deployment of the airbag(s), which could cause personal injury (see Chapter 12).

REMOVAL

▶ Refer to illustrations 15.3, 15.4a, 15.4b, 15.6 and 15.7

1   The front wheels must be in the straight-ahead position before beginning the procedure, with the key removed.

2   Disconnect the cable from the negative battery terminal (see Chapter 5). Refer to Chapter 12 and disable the airbag system.

3   Remove the small bolt covers from the steering wheel, then remove the airbag module mounting bolts (see illustration).

4   Carefully lift the airbag module, then disconnect the electrical connectors underneath (see illustration).

➡Note: Pull the small locks on the airbag module electrical connectors up to release them (see illustration).

15.3 The airbag module mounting bolts are located on each side of the steering wheel

5   Remove the airbag module from the steering wheel.

※※ WARNING:

Handle the airbag module with care, carry the module with the front cover facing away from your body, and store it in a safe location with the trim side facing up. See the precautions in Chapter 12.

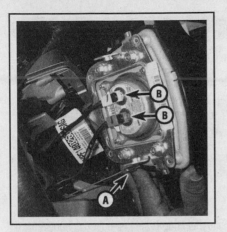

15.4a The horn wire (A) and the two airbag connectors (B)

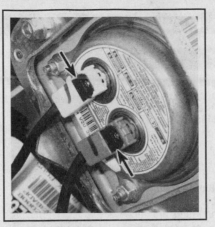

15.4b The airbag connectors are secured by small locks

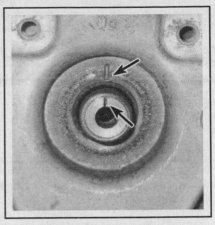

15.6 Index marks on the steering shaft and steering wheel hub (typical shown)

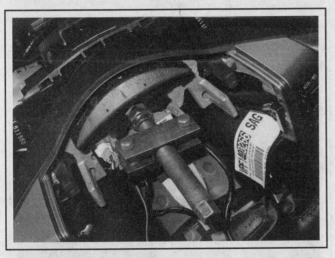

15.7 A puller tool can be used to remove the steering wheel from the steering shaft

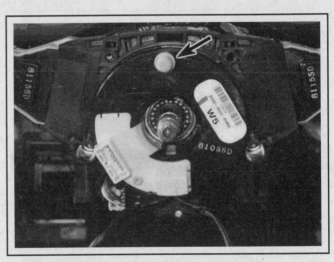

15.9 The clockspring locating pin and position

6   Remove the steering wheel mounting nut, then mark the relationship of the steering wheel hub to the steering shaft if marks don't already exist (see illustration). Make sure all electrical connectors are disconnected; some models may have steering wheel-mounted switches.

7   Wiggle the steering wheel while pulling on it with moderate force to remove it from the steering shaft.

✳✳ CAUTION:

Don't hammer on the shaft or the steering wheel in an attempt to remove the wheel. If it will not come off with moderate effort, use a steering wheel puller to remove it (see illustration).

After the steering wheel has been removed, apply a piece of tape across the airbag clockspring (on the steering column) to keep it centered.

8   If it's necessary to remove the airbag clockspring, remove the steering column covers (see Chapter 11). Disengage the clockspring retaining fingers while detaching it from the steering column, then follow the wiring harnesses and disconnect the electrical connectors.

INSTALLATION

◆ **Refer to illustration 15.9**

9   Installation is the reverse of removal, noting the following points:

a) *Make sure the airbag clockspring is centered with the locating pin at the 12 o'clock position. If necessary, turn the clockspring all the way clockwise until it stops (don't apply too much force), then turn it counterclockwise approximately 2-1/2 turns until the locating pin is at the top (see illustration).*

b) *When installing the steering wheel, align the marks on the shaft and the steering wheel hub.*

c) *Install the steering wheel mounting nut and tighten it to the torque listed in this Chapter's Specifications.*

d) *Connect any electrical connectors to the steering wheel.*

e) *Connect the two airbag connectors and push in their locking tabs, then install the airbag module onto the steering wheel.*

f) *Enable the airbag system (see Chapter 12).*

16 Steering column - removal and installation

➡ Note: On models equipped with Vehicle Dynamic Control, the vehicle will require steering angle sensor calibration after the procedure according to the manufacturer. Special tools are necessary; refer to a dealership service department or a qualified repair location.

REMOVAL

♦ Refer to illustrations 16.6, 16.7, 16.8a and 16.8b

1   Park the vehicle with the wheels pointing straight ahead. Disconnect the cable from the negative battery terminal (see Chapter 5). Disable the airbag system (see Chapter 12).

2   Remove the steering wheel (see Section 15), and the combination switch housing (see Chapter 12). Turn the ignition key to the LOCK position to prevent the steering shaft from turning.

✳✳ **CAUTION:**

If this is not done, the airbag clockspring could be damaged.

3   Remove the knee bolster and the reinforcement behind it (see Chapter 11).

4   Remove the steering column covers (see Chapter 11).

5   Disconnect the shift cable from the column shift lever and the key interlock cable from the steering column, if equipped.

6   Disconnect the electrical connectors for the steering column and detach the harness from the column (see illustration).

7   Mark the relationship of the intermediate shaft coupler to the steering column shaft. Remove the shaft coupler nut and bolt (see illustration). Discard the nut.

8   Remove the steering column mounting fasteners (see illustrations), lower the column and pull it to the rear, making sure nothing is still connected. Separate the intermediate shaft from the steering shaft and remove the column.

INSTALLATION

9   Guide the steering column into position, connect the intermediate shaft coupler, then install the mounting fasteners, but don't tighten them yet.

10 Install the pinch bolt using a new nut and tightening it to the torque listed in this Chapter's Specifications.

11 Tighten the column mounting fasteners to the torque listed in this Chapter's Specifications.

12 The remainder of installation is the reverse of removal.

16.6 The main steering column wiring harness

16.7 Index marks on the intermediate shaft coupler and the steering column shaft (A) and the pinch bolt and nut (B)

16.8a Steering column upper mounting fasteners

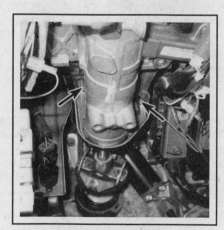

16.8b Steering column lower mounting fastener locations

17 Tie-rod ends - removal and installation

REMOVAL

▸ **Refer to illustrations 17.2, 17.3, and 17.4**

➡ **Note: On Armada models equipped with a rear auto-leveling suspension, turn the ignition key to the OFF position before raising the vehicle.**

1   Loosen the wheel lug nuts, raise the front of the vehicle and support it securely on jackstands. Apply the parking brake and block the rear wheels to keep the vehicle from rolling off the jackstands. Remove the wheel.

2   Loosen the tie-rod end jam nut (see illustration).

3   Mark the relationship of the tie-rod end to the threaded portion of the tie-rod. This will help restore the toe-in setting during reassembly (see illustration).

4   Loosen (but don't remove) the nut on the tie-rod end ballstud and disconnect the tie-rod end from the steering knuckle with a balljoint removal tool or puller (see illustration).

5   Remove the nut and detach the tie-rod end from the steering knuckle. If you're replacing the tie-rod end, unscrew it from the tie-rod, then thread the new one onto the tie-rod to the marked position.

INSTALLATION

6   Connect the tie-rod end to the steering knuckle. Install the nut on the ballstud and tighten it to the torque listed in this Chapter's Specifications. Tighten the jam nut securely. Install the wheel. Lower the vehicle and tighten the lug nuts to the torque listed in the Chapter 1 Specifications.

7   Have the front end alignment checked and, if necessary, adjusted.

17.2 Hold the tie-rod with a wrench while loosening the jam nut

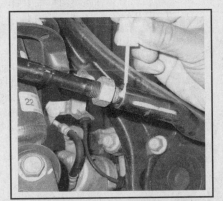

17.3 Mark the position of the tie-rod end in relation to the threads on the inner tie-rod

17.4 Back-off the ballstud nut a few turns, then separate the tie-rod end from the steering knuckle with a balljoint tool or puller (leaving the nut on the ballstud will prevent the tie-rod end from separating violently)

18 Steering gear boots - replacement

▸ **Refer to illustration 18.4**

➡ **Note: On Armada models equipped with a rear auto-leveling suspension, turn the ignition key to the OFF position before raising the vehicle.**

1   Loosen the wheel lug nuts, raise the front of the vehicle and support it securely on jackstands, then remove the wheels. Remove the under-vehicle splash shield.

2   Remove the tie-rod end from the tie-rod (see Section 17).

3   Remove the tie-rod end jam nut.

4   Remove the outer boot clamp with a pair of pliers, then cut off the inner boot (large) clamp and discard it (see illustration).

5   Remove the boot.

6   Place the new clamp on the inner end of the boot.

7   Apply multi-purpose grease to the groove on the tie-rod (where the outer end of the boot is seated).

8   Slide the new boot over the tie-rod and onto the steering gear housing.

9   Make sure the boot isn't twisted, then tighten the inner clamp.

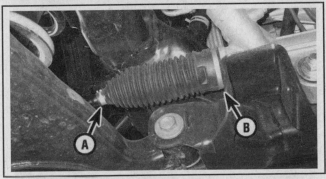

18.4 The outer clamp (A) on the steering gear boot can be squeezed and removed with a pair of pliers; the inner clamp (B) must be cut off

10 Install the outer clamp and tie-rod end jam nut.

11 Install the tie-rod end (see Section 17).

12 Have the front end alignment checked and, if necessary, adjusted.

19 Steering gear - removal and installation

♦ Refer to illustrations 19.5, 19.6 and 19.9

✳✳ WARNING 1:

The models covered by this manual are equipped with Supplemental Restraint Systems (SRS), more commonly known as airbags. Always disable the airbag system before working in the vicinity of any airbag system components to avoid the possibility of accidental deployment of the airbag(s), which could cause personal injury (see Chapter 12).

➡Note: On Armada models equipped with a rear auto-leveling suspension, turn the ignition key to the OFF position before raising the vehicle.

1   With the front wheels pointing straight ahead, loosen the front

19.5 Steering shaft lower pinch bolt (A) and index marks (B)

wheel lug nuts, raise the front of the vehicle and support it securely on jackstands. Apply the parking brake and block the rear wheels. Remove the front wheels.

2   With the ignition key removed, secure the steering wheel in position with the seat belt or a holding tool.

✳✳ CAUTION:

DO NOT allow the steering column shaft to rotate with the steering gear removed or damage to the airbag system could occur.

3   Remove the engine splash shield from under the vehicle.
4   On 4WD models, remove the front axle assembly (see Chapter 8).

➡Note: The driveaxles can remain in place, supported by wire.

5   Mark the relationship of the steering shaft to the steering gear input shaft, then remove the pinch-bolt (see illustration).

➡Note: Do not disturb the small plastic cap on the steering gear input shaft if the steering gear is going to be reinstalled.

6   Place a drain pan under the steering gear. Using a flare-nut wrench, disconnect the pressure and return fluid lines at the steering gear and allow the fluid to drain (see illustration).

7   On 2WD models, remove the front stabilizer bar brackets and lower the bar for clearance (see Section 3).

8   Disconnect the tie-rod ends from the steering knuckles (see Section 17).

9   Remove the steering gear mounting fasteners, then remove the steering gear (see illustration).

10 Installation is the reverse of removal. Be sure to tighten all fasteners to the torque values listed in this Chapter's Specifications. Tighten the wheel lug nuts to the torque listed in Chapter 1.

11 Add power steering fluid to the fluid reservoir, then bleed the air from the system (see Section 21).

12 Have the front end alignment checked and, if necessary, adjusted.

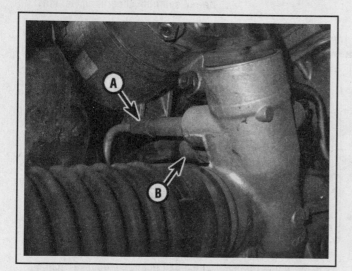

19.6 Power steering gear pressure line (A) and return hose (B)

19.9 Steering gear mounting fasteners

20 Power steering pump - removal and installation

REMOVAL

♦ **Refer to illustrations 20.1, 20.4 and 20.6**

1   Remove the power steering pump reservoir by pulling it up off of its bracket. Pour the fluid out of the reservoir and dispose of it properly, then remove the reservoir bracket (see illustration).

2   Remove the air intake duct (see Chapter 4).

3   Remove the drivebelt (see Chapter 1).

4   Disconnect the pressure sensor electrical connector (see illustration).

5   Detach the pressure line and feed hose from the pump. Discard the sealing washers on both sides of the pressure line fitting. Plug the hoses.

6   Unscrew the mounting fasteners and remove the pump from the vehi-cle, taking care not to spill fluid on the painted surfaces (see illustration).

INSTALLATION

7   Position the pump to the mounting bracket and install the mounting fasteners. Tighten the fasteners to the torque listed in this Chapter's Specifications.

8   Connect the pressure line and feed hose to the pump. Be sure to use new sealing washers on the pressure line fitting and tighten the banjo bolt to the torque listed in this Chapter's Specifications.

9   Install the drivebelt (see Chapter 1).

10   The remainder of installation is the reverse of removal.

11   Fill the power steering reservoir with the recommended fluid (see Chapter 1) and bleed the system following the procedure described in the next Section.

20.1 Remove the power steering reservoir bracket fasteners (one fastener not visible in this photo)

20.4 Power steering pump electrical connector (A), pressure line fitting (B), and feed hose clamp (C)

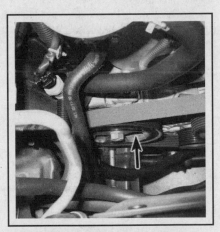

20.6 Access the power steering pump mounting fasteners through the holes in the pulley

21 Power steering system - bleeding

1   Following any operation in which the power steering fluid lines have been disconnected, the power steering system must be bled to remove all air and obtain proper steering performance.

2   With the front wheels in the straight ahead position, check the power steering fluid level and, if low, add fluid until it reaches the Cold mark on the dipstick or reservoir.

3   Start the engine and allow it to run at fast idle. Recheck the fluid level and add more if necessary to reach the Cold mark on the dipstick or reservoir.

4   Bleed the system by turning the wheels from side-to-side, without hitting the stops. This will work the air out of the system. Keep the res-ervoir full of fluid as this is done.

5   When the air is worked out of the system, return the wheels to the straight ahead position and leave the vehicle running for several more minutes before shutting it off. Recheck the fluid level.

6   Road test the vehicle to be sure the steering system is functioning normally and noise free.

7   Recheck the fluid level to be sure it's up to the Hot mark on the dipstick or reservoir while the engine is at normal operating tempera-ture. Add fluid if necessary (see Chapter 1).

22 Wheels and tires - general information

▶ **Refer to illustration 22.1**

Most vehicles covered by this manual are equipped with metric-size fiberglass or steel belted radial tires (see illustration), or inch-pattern light truck tires. Use of other size or type of tires may affect the ride and handling of the vehicle. Don't mix different types of tires, such as radials and bias belted, on the same vehicle as handling may be seriously affected. It's recommended that tires be replaced in pairs on the same axle, but if only one tire is being replaced, be sure it's the same size, structure and tread design as the other.

Because tire pressure has a substantial effect on handling and wear, the pressure on all tires should be checked at least once a month or before any extended trips (see Chapter 1).

Wheels must be replaced if they're bent, dented, leak air, have elongated bolt holes, are heavily rusted, out of vertical symmetry or if the lug nuts won't stay tight. Wheel repairs that use welding or peening are not recommended.

Tire and wheel balance is important to the overall handling, braking and performance of the vehicle. Unbalanced wheels can adversely affect handling and ride characteristics as well as tire life. Whenever a tire is installed on a wheel, the tire and wheel should be balanced by a shop with the proper equipment.

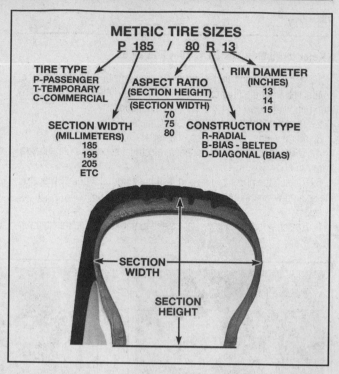

22.1 Metric tire size code

23 Front end alignment - general information

▶ **Refer to illustration 23.1**

A front end alignment (see illustration) refers to the adjustments made to the front wheels so they're in proper angular relationship to the suspension and the ground. Front wheels that are out of proper alignment not only affect steering control, but also increase tire wear.

Getting the proper front wheel alignment is a very exacting process, one in which complicated and expensive machines are necessary to perform the job properly. Because of this, you should have a technician

with the proper equipment to perform these tasks. We will, however, use this space to give you a basic idea of what is involved with front end alignment so you can better understand the process and deal intelligently with the shop that does the work.

Toe-in is the turning in of the front wheels. The purpose of a toe specification is to ensure parallel rolling of the front wheels. In a vehicle with zero toe-in, the distance between the front edges of the wheels will be the same as the distance between the rear edges of the wheels. The actual amount of toe-in is normally only a fraction of an inch. Toe-in is

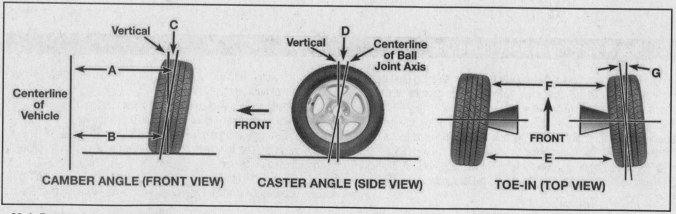

23.1 Front end alignment details:

A minus B = C (degrees camber)
D = degrees camber
E minus F = toe-in (measured in inches)

G = toe-in (expressed in degrees)
A minus B = C (degrees camber)
D = degrees caster

E minus F = toe-in (measured in inches)
G = toe-in (expressed in degrees)

adjusted by turning the tie-rod in the tie-rod end to lengthen or shorten the tie-rod. Incorrect toe-in will cause the tires to wear improperly by making them scrub against the road surface.

Camber is the tilting of the front wheels from vertical when viewed from the front of the vehicle. When the wheels tilt out at the top, the camber is said to be positive (+). When the wheels tilt in at the top the camber is negative (-). The amount of tilt is measured in degrees from the vertical and this measurement is called the camber angle. This angle affects the amount of tire tread which contacts the road and compensates for changes in the suspension geometry when the vehicle is cornering or traveling over an undulating surface. Camber is adjusted by turning the lower control arm pivot bolts, one way or the other, in equal amounts.

Caster is the tilting of the top of the front steering axis from vertical. A tilt toward the rear is positive caster and a tilt toward the front is negative caster. Caster is adjusted by turning the lower control arm pivot bolts, one way or the other, in opposite directions.

When making adjustments to the front end alignment, the caster is set first, then the camber, then the toe-in.

Torque specifications	Ft-lbs (unless otherwise indicated)	Nm

➡ **Note: One foot-pound (ft-lb) of torque is equivalent to 12 inch-pounds (in-lbs) of torque. Torque values below approximately 15 ft-lbs are expressed in inch-pounds, since most foot-pound torque wrenches are not accurate at these smaller values.**

Front suspension

	Ft-lbs	Nm
Hub/bearing assembly-to-steering knuckle bolts	155	210
Lower control arm balljoint pinch bolt	70	95
Lower control arm mounting bolts	98	133
Shock absorber/coil spring assembly lower mounting bolt	99	134
Shock absorber/coil spring assembly upper mounting nuts	22	30
Stabilizer bar link mounting nuts	62	84
Stabilizer bar mounting bracket bolts	94	127
Upper balljoint nut	58	79
Upper control arm mounting bolts/nuts	107	145

Rear suspension

	Ft-lbs	Nm
Hub and bearing assembly-to-rear knuckle bolts (Armada models)	111	150
Front lower link		
Pivot fasteners	101	137
Pinch bolt/nut	70	95
Leaf spring		
Front mounting fasteners	103	140
Rear mounting fasteners	63	86
Shackle-to-spring mounting fasteners	63	86
U-bolt nuts	89	120
Shock absorber mounting fasteners		
Titan	111	150
Armada	129	175
Rear lower link		
Pivot fasteners to subframe	101	137
Pivot fasteners to knuckle	129	175
Stabilizer bar link nuts	65	88
Stabilizer bar mounting bracket bolts	25	34
Upper arm link		
Pivot fasteners	101	137
Pinch bolt/nut	70	95

Torque specifications (continued)	Ft-lbs (unless otherwise indicated)	Nm

Note: One foot-pound (ft-lb) of torque is equivalent to 12 inch-pounds (in-lbs) of torque. Torque values below approximately 15 ft-lbs are expressed in inch-pounds, since most foot-pound torque wrenches are not accurate at these smaller values.

Steering

Airbag module	82 in-lbs	9.3
Power steering pressure line banjo bolt	44	60
Power steering pump mounting bolts	48	65
Power steering pump pulley nut	45	61
Steering column mounting fasteners	12 in-lbs	1.4
Steering column shaft-to-intermediate shaft coupler bolt/nut	20	27
Steering gear mounting fasteners	140	190
Steering shaft-to-steering gear input shaft pinch bolt	20	27
Steering wheel nut	25	34
Tie-rod end ballstud nut	63	85

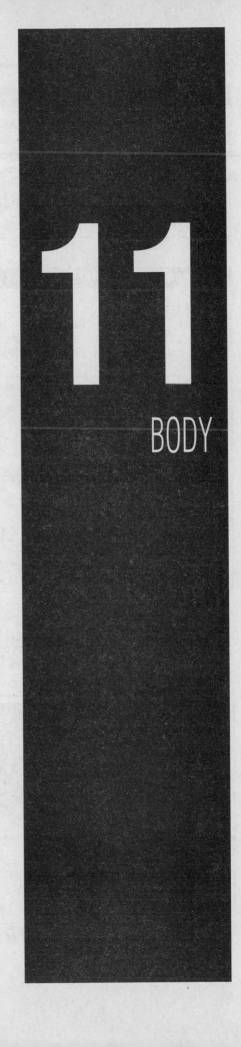

11

BODY

Section

1 General information

❋❋ WARNING:

The models covered by this manual are equipped with Supplemental Restraint Systems (SRS), more commonly known as airbags. Always disable the airbag system before working in the vicinity of any airbag system components to avoid the possibility of accidental deployment of the airbags, which could cause personal injury (see Chapter 12).

Certain body components are particularly vulnerable to accident damage and can be unbolted and repaired or replaced. Among these parts are the hood, doors, tailgate, liftgate, bumpers and front fenders.

Only general body maintenance practices and body panel repair procedures within the scope of the do-it-yourselfer are included in this Chapter.

2 Repair minor paint scratches

No matter how hard you try to keep your vehicle looking like new, it will inevitably be scratched, chipped or dented at some point. If the metal is actually dented, seek the advice of a professional. But you can fix minor scratches and chips yourself. Buy a touch-up paint kit from a dealer service department or an auto parts store. To ensure that you get the right color, you'll need to have the specific make, model and year of your vehicle and, ideally, the paint code, which is located on a special metal plate under the hood or in the door jamb.

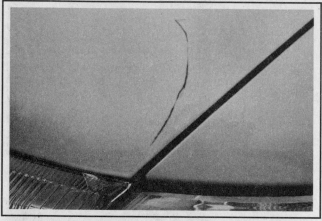

Make sure the damaged area is perfectly clean and rust free. If the touch-up kit has a wire brush, use it to clean the scratch or chip. Or use fine steel wool wrapped around the end of a pencil. Clean the scratched or chipped surface only, not the good paint surrounding it. Rinse the area with water and allow it to dry thoroughly

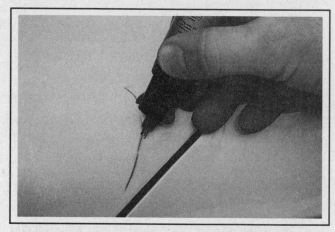

Thoroughly mix the paint, then apply a small amount with the touch-up kit brush or a very fine artist's brush. Brush in one direction as you fill the scratch area. Do not build up the paint higher than the surrounding paint

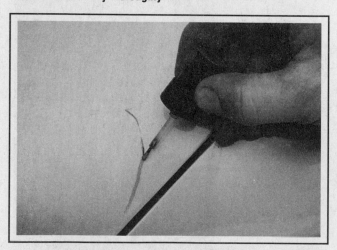

If the vehicle has a two-coat finish, apply the clear coat after the color coat has dried

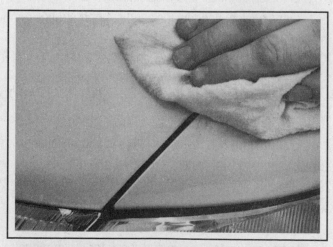

Wait a few days for the paint to dry thoroughly, then rub out the repainted area with a polishing compound to blend the new paint with the surrounding area. When you're happy with your work, wash and polish the area

3   Body repair - minor damage

PLASTIC BODY PANELS

The following repair procedures are for minor scratches and gouges. Repair of more serious damage should be left to a dealer service department or qualified auto body shop. Below is a list of the equipment and materials necessary to perform the following repair procedures on plastic body panels.

Wax, grease and silicone removing solvent
Cloth-backed body tape
Sanding discs
Drill motor with three-inch disc holder
Hand sanding block
Rubber squeegees
Sandpaper
Non-porous mixing palette
Wood paddle or putty knife
Curved-tooth body file
Flexible parts repair material

Flexible panels (bumper trim)

1   Remove the damaged panel, if necessary or desirable. In most cases, repairs can be carried out with the panel installed.

2   Clean the area(s) to be repaired with a wax, grease and silicone removing solvent applied with a water-dampened cloth.

3   If the damage is structural, that is, if it extends through the panel, clean the backside of the panel area to be repaired as well. Wipe dry.

4   Sand the rear surface about 1-1/2 inches beyond the break.

5   Cut two pieces of fiberglass cloth large enough to overlap the break by about 1-1/2 inches. Cut only to the required length.

6   Mix the adhesive from the repair kit according to the instructions included with the kit, and apply a layer of the mixture approximately 1/8-inch thick on the backside of the panel. Overlap the break by at least 1-1/2 inches.

7   Apply one piece of fiberglass cloth to the adhesive and cover the cloth with additional adhesive. Apply a second piece of fiberglass cloth to the adhesive and immediately cover the cloth with additional adhesive in sufficient quantity to fill the weave.

8   Allow the repair to cure for 20 to 30 minutes at 60-degrees to 80-degrees F.

9   If necessary, trim the excess repair material at the edge.

10 Remove all of the paint film over and around the area(s) to be repaired. The repair material should not overlap the painted surface.

11 With a drill motor and a sanding disc (or a rotary file), cut a "V" along the break line approximately 1/2-inch wide. Remove all dust and loose particles from the repair area.

12 Mix and apply the repair material. Apply a light coat first over the damaged area; then continue applying material until it reaches a level slightly higher than the surrounding finish.

13 Cure the mixture for 20 to 30 minutes at 60-degrees to 80-degrees F.

14 Roughly establish the contour of the area being repaired with a body file. If low areas or pits remain, mix and apply additional adhesive.

15 Block sand the damaged area with sandpaper to establish the actual contour of the surrounding surface.

16 If desired, the repaired area can be temporarily protected with several light coats of primer. Because of the special paints and techniques required for flexible body panels, it is recommended that the vehicle be taken to a paint shop for completion of the body repair.

STEEL BODY PANELS

◗ **See photo sequence**

Repair of dents

17 When repairing dents, the first job is to pull the dent out until the affected area is as close as possible to its original shape. There is no point in trying to restore the original shape completely as the metal in the damaged area will have stretched on impact and cannot be restored to its original contours. It is better to bring the level of the dent up to a point that is about 1/8-inch below the level of the surrounding metal. In cases where the dent is very shallow, it is not worth trying to pull it out at all.

18 If the backside of the dent is accessible, it can be hammered out gently from behind using a soft-face hammer. While doing this, hold a block of wood firmly against the opposite side of the metal to absorb the hammer blows and prevent the metal from being stretched.

19 If the dent is in a section of the body which has double layers, or some other factor makes it inaccessible from behind, a different technique is required. Drill several small holes through the metal inside the damaged area, particularly in the deeper sections. Screw long, self-tapping screws into the holes just enough for them to get a good grip in the metal. Now pulling on the protruding heads of the screws with locking pliers can pull out the dent.

20 The next stage of repair is the removal of paint from the damaged area and from an inch or so of the surrounding metal. This is easily done with a wire brush or sanding disk in a drill motor, although it can be done just as effectively by hand with sandpaper. To complete the preparation for filling, score the surface of the bare metal with a screwdriver or the tang of a file or drill small holes in the affected area. This will provide a good grip for the filler material. To complete the repair, see the Section on filling and painting.

Repair of rust holes or gashes

21 Remove all paint from the affected area and from an inch or so of the surrounding metal using a sanding disk or wire brush mounted in a drill motor. If these are not available, a few sheets of sandpaper will do the job just as effectively.

22 With the paint removed, you will be able to determine the severity of the corrosion and decide whether to replace the whole panel, if possible, or repair the affected area. New body panels are not as expensive as most people think and it is often quicker to install a new panel than to repair large areas of rust.

23 Remove all trim pieces from the affected area except those which will act as a guide to the original shape of the damaged body, such as headlight shells, etc. Using metal snips or a hacksaw blade, remove all loose metal and any other metal that is badly affected by rust. Hammer the edges of the hole in to create a slight depression for the filler material.

24 Wire-brush the affected area to remove the powdery rust from the surface of the metal. If the back of the rusted area is accessible, treat it with rust inhibiting paint.

25 Before filling is done, block the hole in some way. This can be done with sheet metal riveted or screwed into place, or by stuffing the hole with wire mesh.

26 Once the hole is blocked off, the affected area can be filled and painted. See the following subsection on filling and painting.

These photos illustrate a method of repairing simple dents. They are intended to supplement *Body repair - minor damage* in this Chapter and should not be used as the sole instructions for body repair on these vehicles.

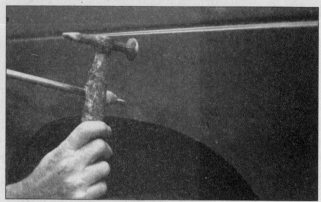

1 If you can't access the backside of the body panel to hammer out the dent, pull it out with a slide-hammer-type dent puller. Tap with a hammer near the edge of the dent to help 'pop' the metal back to its original shape, about 1/8-inch below the surface of the surrounding metal

2 Using coarse-grit sandpaper, remove the paint down to the bare metal. Clean the repair area with wax/silicone remover.

3 Following label instructions, mix up a batch of plastic filler and hardener, then quickly press it into the metal with a plastic applicator. Work the filler until it matches the original contour and is slightly above the surrounding metal

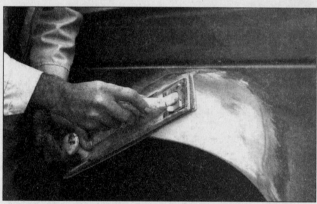

4 Let the filler harden until you can just dent it with your fingernail. File, then sand the filler down until it's smooth and even. Work down to finer grits of sandpaper - always using a board or block - ending up with 360 or 400 grit

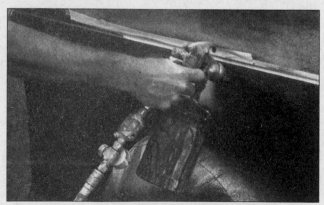

5 When the area is smooth to the touch, clean the area and mask around it. Apply several layers of primer to the area. A professional-type spray gun is being used here, but aerosol spray primer works fine

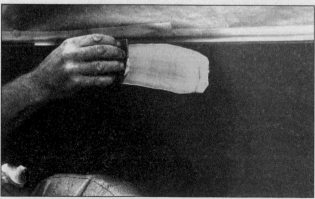

6 Fill imperfections or scratches with glazing compound. Sand with 360 or 400-grit and re-spray. Finish sand the primer with 600 grit, clean thoroughly, then apply the finish coat. Don't attempt to rub out or wax the repair area until the paint has dried completely (at least two weeks)

Filling and painting

27 Many types of body fillers are available, but generally speaking, body repair kits which contain filler paste and a tube of resin hardener are best for this type of repair work. A wide, flexible plastic or nylon applicator will be necessary for imparting a smooth and contoured finish to the surface of the filler material. Mix up a small amount of filler on a clean piece of wood or cardboard (use the hardener sparingly). Follow the manufacturer's instructions on the package, otherwise the filler will set incorrectly.

28 Using the applicator, apply the filler paste to the prepared area. Draw the applicator across the surface of the filler to achieve the desired contour and to level the filler surface. As soon as a contour that approximates the original one is achieved, stop working the paste. If you continue, the paste will begin to stick to the applicator. Continue to add thin layers of paste at 20-minute intervals until the level of the filler is just above the surrounding metal.

29 Once the filler has hardened, the excess can be removed with a body file. From then on, progressively finer grades of sandpaper should be used, starting with a 180-grit paper and finishing with 600-grit wet-or-dry paper. Always wrap the sandpaper around a flat rubber or wooden block, otherwise the surface of the filler will not be completely flat. During the sanding of the filler surface, the wet-or-dry paper should be periodically rinsed in water. This will ensure that a very smooth finish is produced in the final stage.

30 At this point, the repair area should be surrounded by a ring of bare metal, which in turn should be encircled by the finely feathered edge of good paint. Rinse the repair area with clean water until all of the dust produced by the sanding operation is gone.

31 Spray the entire area with a light coat of primer. This will reveal any imperfections in the surface of the filler. Repair the imperfections with fresh filler paste or glaze filler and once more smooth the surface with sandpaper. Repeat this spray-and-repair procedure until you are satisfied that the surface of the filler and the feathered edge of the paint are perfect. Rinse the area with clean water and allow it to dry completely.

32 The repair area is now ready for painting. Spray painting must be carried out in a warm, dry, windless and dust free atmosphere. These conditions can be created if you have access to a large indoor work area, but if you are forced to work in the open, you will have to pick the day very carefully. If you are working indoors, dousing the floor in the work area with water will help settle the dust that would otherwise be in the air. If the repair area is confined to one body panel, mask off the surrounding panels. This will help minimize the effects of a slight mismatch in paint color. Trim pieces such as chrome strips, door handles, etc., will also need to be masked off or removed. Use masking tape and several thickness of newspaper for the masking operations.

33 Before spraying, shake the paint can thoroughly, then spray a test area until the spray painting technique is mastered. Cover the repair area with a thick coat of primer. The thickness should be built up using several thin layers of primer rather than one thick one. Using 600-grit wet-or-dry sandpaper, rub down the surface of the primer until it is very smooth. While doing this, the work area should be thoroughly rinsed with water and the wet-or-dry sandpaper periodically rinsed as well. Allow the primer to dry before spraying additional coats.

34 Spray on the top coat, again building up the thickness by using several thin layers of paint. Begin spraying in the center of the repair area and then, using a circular motion, work out until the whole repair area and about two inches of the surrounding original paint is covered. Remove all masking material 10 to 15 minutes after spraying on the final coat of paint. Allow the new paint at least two weeks to harden, then use a very fine rubbing compound to blend the edges of the new paint into the existing paint. Finally, apply a coat of wax

4 Body repair - major damage

1 Major damage must be repaired by an auto body shop specifically equipped to perform body and frame repairs. These shops have the specialized equipment required to do the job properly.

2 If the damage is extensive, the frame must be checked for proper alignment or the vehicle's handling characteristics may be adversely affected and other components may wear at an accelerated rate.

3 Due to the fact that all of the major body components (hood, fenders, etc.) are separate and replaceable units, any seriously damaged components should be replaced rather than repaired. Sometimes the components can be found in a wrecking yard that specializes in used vehicle components, often at considerable savings over the cost of new parts.

5 Upholstery, carpets and vinyl trim - maintenance

UPHOLSTERY AND CARPETS

1 Every three months remove the floormats and clean the interior of the vehicle (more frequently if necessary). Use a stiff whiskbroom to brush the carpeting and loosen dirt and dust, then vacuum the upholstery and carpets thoroughly, especially along seams and crevices.

2 Dirt and stains can be removed from carpeting with basic household or automotive carpet shampoos available in spray cans. Follow the directions and vacuum again, then use a stiff brush to bring back the "nap" of the carpet.

3   Most interiors have cloth or vinyl upholstery, either of which can be cleaned and maintained with a number of material-specific cleaners or shampoos available in auto supply stores. Follow the directions on the product for usage, and always spot-test any upholstery cleaner on an inconspicuous area (bottom edge of a backseat cushion) to ensure that it doesn't cause a color shift in the material.

4   After cleaning, vinyl upholstery should be treated with a protectant.

➡**Note: Make sure the protectant container indicates the product can be used on seats - some products may make a seat too slippery.**

❋❋ CAUTION:

Do not use protectant on vinyl-covered steering wheels.

5   Leather upholstery requires special care. It should be cleaned regularly with saddlesoap or leather cleaner. Never use alcohol, gaso-line, nail polish remover or thinner to clean leather upholstery.

6   After cleaning, regularly treat leather upholstery with a leather conditioner, rubbed in with a soft cotton cloth. Never use car wax on leather upholstery.

7   In areas where the interior of the vehicle is subject to bright sunlight, cover leather seating areas of the seats with a sheet if the vehicle is to be left out for any length of time.

VINYL TRIM

8   Don't clean vinyl trim with detergents, caustic soap or petroleum-based cleaners. Plain soap and water works just fine, with a soft brush to clean dirt that may be ingrained. Wash the vinyl as frequently as the rest of the vehicle.

9   After cleaning, application of a high-quality rubber and vinyl protectant will help prevent oxidation and cracks. The protectant can also be applied to weather-stripping, vacuum lines and rubber hoses, which often fail as a result of chemical degradation, and to the tires.

6   Fastener and trim removal

▸ **Refer to illustration 6.4**

1   There are a variety of plastic fasteners used to hold trim panels, splash shields and other parts in place in addition to typical screws, nuts and bolts. Once you are familiar with them, they can usually be removed without too much difficulty.

2   The proper tools and approach can prevent added time and expense to a project by minimizing the number of broken fasteners and/or parts.

3   The following illustrations show various types of fasteners that are typically used on most vehicles and how to remove and install them (see illustrations). Replacement fasteners are commonly found at most auto parts stores, if necessary.

4   Trim panels are typically made of plastic and their flexibility can help during removal. The key to their removal is to use a tool to pry the panel near its retainers to release it without damaging surrounding areas or breaking-off any retainers. The retainers will usually snap out of their designated slot or hole after force is applied to them. Stiff plastic tools designed for prying on trim panels are available at most auto parts stores (see illustration). Tools that are tapered and wrapped in protective tape, such as a screwdriver or small pry tool, are also very effective when used with care.

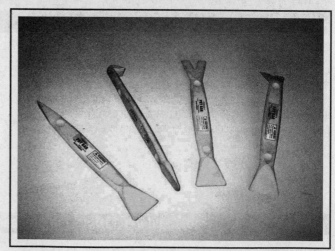

6.4 These small plastic pry tools are ideal for prying off trim panels

Fasteners

This tool is designed to remove special fasteners. A small pry tool used for removing nails will also work well in place of this tool

A Phillips head screwdriver can be used to release the center portion, but light pressure must be used because the plastic is easily damaged. Once the center is up, the fastener can easily be pried from its hole

Here is a view with the center portion fully released. Install the fastener as shown, then press the center in to set it

This fastener is used for exterior panels and shields. The center portion must be pried up to release the fastener. Install the fastener with the center up, then press the center in to set it

This type of fastener is used commonly for interior panels. Use a small blunt tool to press the small pin at the center in to release it . . .

. . . the pin will stay with the fastener in the released position

Reset the fastener for installation by moving the pin out. Install the fastener, then press the pin flush with the fastener to set it

This fastener is used for exterior and interior panels. It has no moving parts. Simply pry the fastener from its hole like the claw of a hammer removes a nail. Without a tool that can get under the top of the fastener, it can be very difficult to remove

7   Hinges and locks - maintenance

Once every 3000 miles, or every three months, the hinges and latch assemblies on the doors, hood and tailgate (or liftgate) should be given a few drops of light oil or lock lubricant. The door latch strikers should also be lubricated with a thin coat of grease to reduce wear and ensure free movement. Lubricate the door and tailgate (or liftgate) locks with spray-on graphite lubricant.

8   Windshield and fixed glass - replacement

Replacement of the windshield and fixed glass requires the use of special fast-setting adhesive/caulk materials and some specialized tools and techniques. These operations should be left to a dealer service department or a shop specializing in glass work.

9 Hood - removal, installation and adjustment

➡Note: The hood is heavy and somewhat awkward to remove and install - at least two people should perform this procedure.

REMOVAL AND INSTALLATION

◆ **Refer to illustration 9.4**

1 Use blankets or pads to cover the cowl area of the body and the fenders. This will protect the body and paint as the hood is lifted off.

2 Scribe alignment marks around the hinge flanges to insure proper alignment during installation (paint or a permanent-type felt-tip marker also will work for this).

3 Disconnect the windshield washer hoses and any electrical connectors from the hood.

4 Have an assistant support one side of the hood. Take turns removing the hinge-to-hood bolts and lift off the hood (see illustration).

5 Installation is the reverse of removal.

ADJUSTMENT

◆ **Refer to illustrations 9.9 and 9.10**

6 Fore-and-aft and side-to-side adjustment of the hood is done by moving the hood in relation to the hinge flanges after loosening the bolts.

7 Scribe or trace a line around the entire hinge plate so you can judge the amount of movement (see illustration 9.4).

8 Loosen the bolts and move the hood into correct alignment. Move it only a little at a time. Tighten the hinge bolts and carefully lower the hood to check the alignment.

9 If necessary after installation, the entire hood latch assembly can be adjusted up-and-down as well as from side-to-side on the radiator support so the hood closes securely and flush with the fenders. To make the adjustment, scribe a line around the hood latch mounting bolts to provide a reference point, then loosen them and reposition the latch assembly, as necessary (see illustration). Following adjustment, retighten the mounting bolts.

10 Finally, adjust the hood bumpers on the hood, so when closed, it is flush with the fenders (see illustration).

11 The hood latch assembly, as well as the hinges, should be periodically lubricated with white, lithium-base grease to prevent binding and wear.

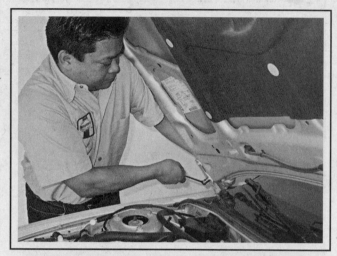

9.4 Support the hood with your shoulder while removing the hood mounting bolts

9.9 Loosen the hood latch bolts, then move the latch as necessary to adjust the hood

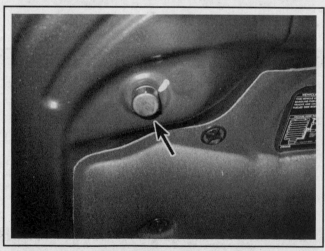

9.10 Twist the hood bumpers in-or-out to make fine adjustments to the hood closed height

10 Radiator grille - removal and installation

▶ **Refer to illustrations 10.1, 10.2 and 10.3**

1   Open the hood and remove the retainers securing the upper part of the radiator grille to the body (see illustration).

2   From under the vehicle, remove the pushpins securing the left and right-hand lower filler panel, then remove the filler panels (see illustration).

3   Pull the radiator grille outward until the clips at each outboard end release from the body (see illustration).

4   Installation is the reverse of removal.

10.1 To remove the retainers mounting the grille to the body, twist them 45-degrees and pull them out

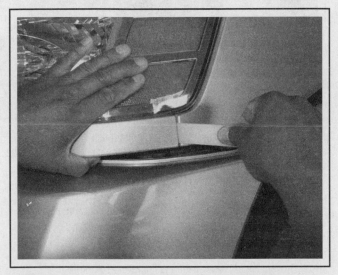

10.2 After removing the fasteners, carefully pry off the filler panels

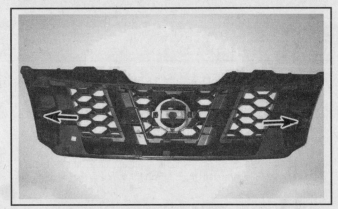

10.3 The two grille mounting clip locations (seen here from the back side)

11 Hood latch and release cable - removal and installation

☀☀ WARNING:

The models covered by this manual are equipped with Supplemental Restraint Systems (SRS), more commonly known as airbags. Always disable the airbag system before working in the vicinity of any airbag system components to avoid the possibility of accidental deployment of the airbags, which could cause personal injury (see Chapter 12).

LATCH

▶ **Refer to illustration 11.1**

1   Remove the bolts and detach the latch assembly (see illustration 9.9). Unhook the spring and pry the cable end from the latch (see illustration).

2   Installation is the reverse of removal. Adjust the latch so the hood engages securely when closed and the hood bumpers are slightly compressed (see Section 9).

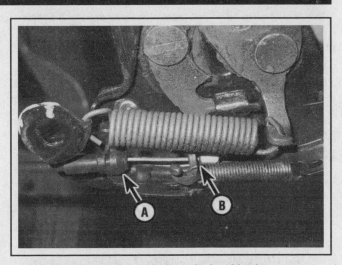

11.1 To disconnect the cable from the hood latch mechanism, disengage the cable housing end (A) from the slot in the latch and twist the cable end (B) out of the latch arm

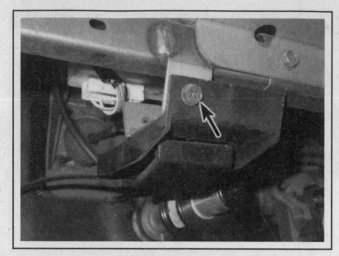

11.5a Hood release handle mounting fastener

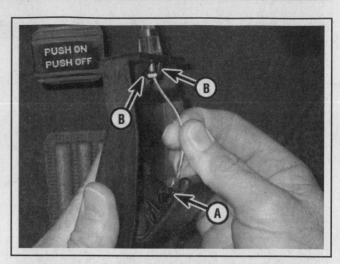

11.5b Pass the cable through the slot in the release handle (A), then squeeze the tangs (B) and detach the cable casing from the handle bracket

RELEASE CABLE

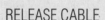

♦ **Refer to illustrations 11.5a and 11.5b**

3 Disconnect the release cable from the hood latch assembly as described in Step 1.

4 Unclip the release cable from the radiator support clips.

5 Remove the driver's side knee bolster (see Section 28). Remove the mounting fastener securing the hood release handle to the underside of the instrument panel, then detach the cable from the handle (see illustrations).

6 Attach a length of wire to the interior end of the cable to assist with the installation of the new cable.

7 Trace the cable forward to the grommet where the cable goes through the firewall and dislodge the grommet (push it through to the engine compartment side). Working in the engine compartment, pull the old cable through the firewall.

8 Disconnect the guide wire from the old cable and fasten it to the new cable.

9 With the new cable attached to the wire, pull the wire back through the firewall until the new cable reaches the release handle. Make sure that the grommet is properly seated on both sides of the hole in the firewall.

10 The remainder of installation is the reverse of removal.

12 Bumper - removal and installation

✳✳ WARNING:

The models covered by this manual are equipped with Supplemental Restraint Systems (SRS), more commonly known as airbags. Always disable the airbag system before working in the vicinity of any airbag system components to avoid the possibility of accidental deployment of the airbags, which could cause personal injury (see Chapter 12).

➡Note: Some trim levels include a chromed steel center section of the front bumper, while on other models this part is plastic. The bumper cover replacement procedure is similar for both types.

FRONT BUMPER

1 Remove the fasteners securing the bottom engine cover or skid plate, then remove it.

2 Remove the fog lamps if equipped (see Chapter 12).

Steel type

3 Remove the radiator grille (see Section 10).

4 Remove the lower front valance fasteners from the bottom of the bumper and remove the valance (if equipped).

5 Remove the lower intake grille fasteners and remove the intake grille from the bumper.

6 Remove the front bumper side bracket fasteners and remove the brackets.

7 Remove the upper and lower bumper mounting fasteners and remove the bumper.

8 Installation is the reverse of removal. Tighten the mounting fasteners securely.

Plastic type

♦ **Refer to illustrations 12.9 and 12.12**

9 Remove the pushpins and mounting screws from under the intake grille area (see illustration). Remove the license plate and bracket.

10 Remove the radiator grille (see Section 10).

11 If equipped, remove the fasteners securing the bumper filler panels, then remove the panels (see illustration 10.2).

12 On each side of the front bumper cover, remove the fasteners securing the cover to the fenderwell liner and lower body (see illustration 13.5). Pull back the front portion of the fenderwell liner to access the screws securing the cover to the body (see illustration).

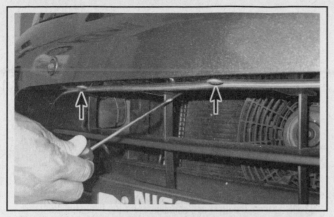

12.9 Use a small screwdriver to release the pushpins under the intake grille, then remove the lower mounting screws

12.12 Remove the fender-to-body bolts

12.17 Remove the trailer hitch mounting bolts and remove the hitch

13 Disconnect any wiring harnesses or any other components that would interfere with removal of the bumper.

14 Remove the remaining bumper cover fasteners at the top and bottom, then with the help of an assistant, carefully detach the bumper cover.

15 Installation is the reverse of removal. Tighten the retaining fasteners securely.

REAR BUMPER

Titan models

▶ **Refer to illustrations 12.17, 12.19a and 12.19b**

16 Disconnect the electrical connectors for the license plate lights and sonar sensors if equipped.

17 Remove the bolts securing the tow hitch (see illustration) to the frame and remove the hitch.

➡ **Note: Disconnect the trailer harness or plug if it is mounted to the hitch.**

18 Pry the step pad up and disconnect the clips from under the bumper and remove the pads.

19 Remove the fasteners securing the bumper to the rear bumper reinforcement (see illustrations) and remove the bumper.

12.19a Remove the fasteners securing the bumper to the bumper reinforcement . . .

12.19b . . . then remove the remaining mounting fasteners (left side shown)

20 Remove the bumper reinforcement fasteners and remove the reinforcement (if necessary).

21 Installation is the reverse of removal. Tighten the retaining bolts or screws securely.

Armada models

2009 and earlier models

22 Remove the bolts securing the tow hitch (if equipped) to the frame and remove the hitch.

➡**Note: Disconnect the trailer harness or plug if it is mounted to the hitch.**

23 Remove the lower bumper fascia reinforcement screws and remove the rear bumper reinforcement.

24 Disconnect the electrical connectors for the license plate lights and sonar sensors (if equipped).

25 Remove the license plate lamps from the retainers and remove the lamps (see Chapter 12).

26 Remove the sonar sensors from the retainers (if equipped) and remove the sensors.

27 Disconnect the step pad clips from under the bumper and remove the pad.

28 Remove the bolts securing the bumper to the rear bumper reinforcement and remove the bumper.

29 Installation is the reverse of removal. Tighten the retaining bolts or screws securely.

2010 models

30 Remove the rear taillight housing (see Chapter 12).

31 Remove the bolts securing the tow hitch (if equipped) to the frame and remove the hitch.

➡**Note: Disconnect the trailer harness or plug if it is mounted to the hitch.**

32 Remove the lower bumper fascia reinforcement screws and remove the rear bumper reinforcement.

33 Disconnect the electrical connectors for the license plate lights and sonar sensors (if equipped).

34 Remove the screws securing the bumper fascia and remove the fascia as an assembly.

➡**Note: When sliding the fascia out it may be necessary to unclip the sonar sensor harness and each sensor from the fascia.**

35 Installation is the reverse of removal. Tighten the retaining bolts or screws securely.

13 Front fender - removal and installation

▶ **Refer to illustration 13.5**

1 Loosen the wheel lug nuts, raise the vehicle, support it securely on jackstands and remove the front wheel.

2 Refer to Chapter 12 and remove the headlight assembly.

3 Remove the mudguard fasteners and mudguard(s) (if equipped).

4 Remove the outer fender protector fasteners and protector (if equipped).

5 Remove the plastic pushpins and fasteners securing the plastic fenderwell to the fender (see illustration). The fenderwell liner does not need to be completely removed from the vehicle, just remove the fasteners at the fender.

6 Remove the fender-to-body bolts in the front of the fenderwell (see illustration 12.12).

7 Open the door and remove the one fender bolt at the top and one at the bottom of the door jamb.

8 At the rocker panel area, remove the two bolts securing the fender.

9 Remove the mounting bolts securing the top of the fender.

10 Detach the fender. It's a good idea to have an assistant support the fender while it's being moved away from the vehicle to prevent damage to the surrounding body panels.

11 Installation is the reverse of the removal procedure. Tighten all nuts, bolts and screws securely.

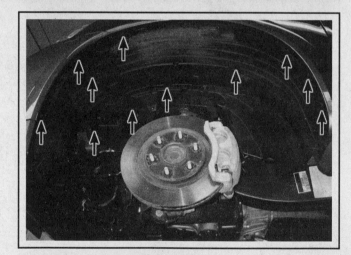

13.5 Fenderwell liner mounting fasteners

14 Cowl cover - removal and installation

▶ **Refer to illustrations 14.2 and 14.3**

1 Pry off the plastic trim cap on the windshield wiper arms, then detach the wiper arm retaining nuts and remove the wiper arms (see Chapter 12).

2 Carefully pry out the clips securing the hood seal to the cowl (see illustration).

3 Pry up the clips securing the ends of the cowl cover (see illustration). Once the cowl cover is raised, disconnect the hose from the windshield washer reservoir attached to the bottom of the cowl cover.

4 Installation is the reverse of removal.

14.2 Pry out the clips and remove the hood seal

14.3 Pry out the pins at each end

15 Door trim panels - removal and installation

FRONT AND REAR DOORS

♦ **Refer to illustrations 15.2, 15.3a, 15.3b, 15.3c, 15.3d and 15.6**

1   Disconnect the cable from the negative terminal of the battery (see Chapter 5).

2   Pry the power switch assembly out of the door panel and disconnect the electrical connectors from the switches (see illustration).

3   Remove all door trim panel retaining screws (see illustrations).

4   Insert a wide putty knife or a special trim panel removal tool between the trim panel and the door to disengage the retaining clips. Work around the outside edge until the panel is free.

➡**Note: Pry at the clip locations only. Prying between the clips will result in distorted or damaged trim panel(s).**

5   Once all of the clips are disengaged, raise the trim panel up and off the door. Disconnect any wiring harness connectors and remove the trim panel from the vehicle.

15.2 Carefully pry up the power window switch assembly from the door

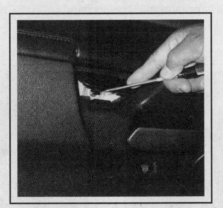

15.3a Pry up this cover. . .

15.3b . . . remove these mounting fasteners . . .

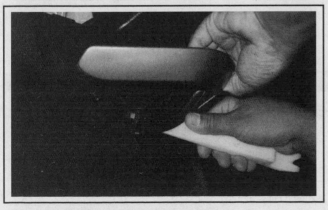

15.3c . . . then carefully pry off the inside door handle escutcheon . . .

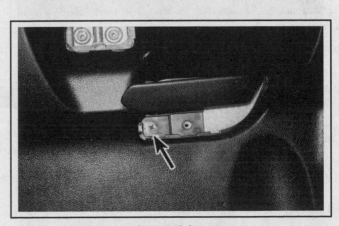

15.3d . . . and remove the remaining screw

6 For access to the inner door, carefully peel back the plastic watershield (see illustration).

7 Prior to installation of the door panel, be sure to reinstall any clips in the panel which may have come out during the removal procedure and remain in the door itself.

8 Connect the wiring harness connectors and place the panel in position on the door. Engage the trim panel with the top of the door first, then push downward on the panel until the clips on the trim panel align with all the holes in the door. Once the clips are aligned with the respective holes, push straight in on the panel until the clips are seated.

9 The remainder of the installation is the reverse of removal

LIFTGATE

▶ **Refer to illustrations 15.10, 15.11, 15.12a and 15.12b**

10 Support the liftgate and detach the liftgate open/close power strut at the liftgate (see illustration).

11 Carefully pry off the upper and side trim panels (see illustration).

12 Remove the liftgate pull handle, then pry out the plastic retaining clips and remove the lower trim panel from the liftgate (see illustrations).

13 Installation is the reverse of the removal procedure.

15.6 Carefully peel back the plastic watershield, it will be necessary to remove the door speaker before the entire watershield can be removed

15.10 Detach the liftgate open/close power strut at the liftgate

15.11 Carefully pry off the upper and side trim panel

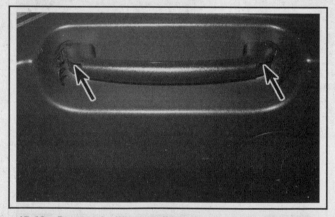

15.12a Remove the liftgate pull handle mounting fasteners. . .

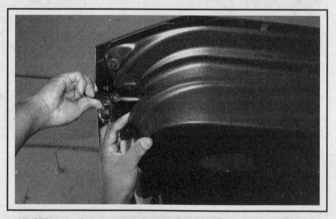

15.12b . . . then pry out the plastic retaining clips and remove the lower trim panel from the liftgate

16 Door - removal, installation and adjustment

➡**Note: The door is heavy and somewhat awkward to remove and install - at least two people should perform this procedure.**

REMOVAL AND INSTALLATION

▶ **Refer to illustrations 16.6 and 16.8**

1 Lower the window completely in the door, then disconnect the cable from the negative terminal of the battery (see Chapter 5).

2 Open the door all the way and support it on jacks or blocks covered with rags to prevent damaging the paint.

3 Remove the door trim panel and watershield as described in Section 15.

4 Disconnect all electrical connections, ground wires and harness retaining clips from the door.

➡**Note: It is a good idea to label all connections to aid the reassembly process.**

16.6 Remove the fastener and detach the door stop strut from the body

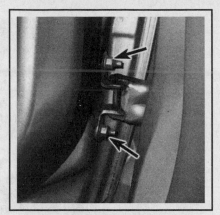

16.8 With the door supported, remove the hinge-to-door nuts (lower hinge shown)

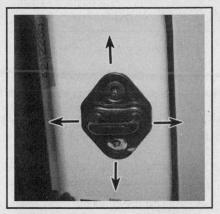

16.12 Adjust the door lock striker by loosening the mounting screws and gently tapping the striker in the desired direction

5   From the door side, detach the rubber conduit between the body and the door. Then pull the wiring harness through the conduit hole and remove the wiring harness from the door.

6   Remove the door stop strut at the body (see illustration).

7   Mark around the door hinges with a pen or a scribe to facilitate realignment during reassembly.

8   With an assistant holding the door, remove the hinge-to-door nuts (see illustration) and lift the door off.

9   Installation is the reverse of removal.

ADJUSTMENT

▶ **Refer to illustration 16.12**

10   Having proper door to body alignment is a critical part of a well functioning door assembly. First check the door hinge pins for excessive play. Fully open the door and lift up and down on the door without lifting the body. If a door has 1/16-inch (1.6 mm) or more excessive play, the hinges should be replaced.

11   Door-to-body adjustments are made by loosening the hinge-to-body bolts or hinge-to-door bolts and moving the door. Proper body alignment is achieved when the top of the doors are parallel with the roof section, the front door is flush with the fender, the rear door is flush with the rear quarter panel and king-cab is flush with the cab and front door and the bottom of the doors are aligned with the lower rocker panel.

12   To adjust the door closed position, scribe a line or mark around the striker plate to provide a reference point, then check that the door latch is contacting the center of the latch striker. If not, adjust the up and down position first (see illustration).

13   Finally, adjust the latch striker sideways position, so that the door panel is flush with either the center pillar, or rear quarter panel or cab, and provides positive engagement with the latch mechanism.

17 Door latch, lock cylinder and handles - removal and installation

※ WARNING:

Wear gloves when working inside the door openings to protect against cuts from sharp metal edges.

1   Remove the door trim panel and peel back the plastic watershield (see Section 15).

DOOR LATCH

▶ **Refer to illustration 17.2**

2   Remove the latch retaining screws from the end of the door, then reach inside the door to release the latch from the control rods (see illustration).

3   On models with power door locks, disconnect the electrical connector.

4   Detach the door latch and (if equipped) the door lock solenoid.

5   Installation is the reverse of removal.

17.2 Remove the latch retaining screws from the end of the door. (A) Is the outside handle lock cylinder retaining bolt

LOCK CYLINDER

6   Detach the electrical connector from the lock cylinder (if equipped).

7   To remove the lock cylinder and/or the outside door handle, remove the access plug at the end of the door, then remove the Torx screw (see illustration 17.2), which will allow the lock cylinder to be angled out of the door while the handle is being pulled. Use a screwdriver to disengage the lock rod and remove the lock cylinder.

OUTSIDE HANDLE

8   With the lock cylinder removed, pull the handle outwards, slide it to the rear and disengage it from the door.

INSIDE HANDLE

▶ **Refer to illustration 17.11**

9   Remove the door trim panel (see Section 15).
10 Release the control rod guide clip.

17.11 Disconnect the control rod from the rear of the inside handle and remove the mounting screws

11 Remove the retaining screws (see illustration), pull the handle free from the door panel and disconnect the control rods from the rear of the inside handle.

12 Installation is the reverse of removal.

18   Door window glass - removal and installation

❊❊ WARNING:

Wear gloves when working inside the door openings to protect against cuts from sharp metal edges.

1   Remove the door trim panel and watershield (see Section 15). Removal and installation of the window glass is essentially the same for front and rear doors (on models so equipped).

2   Lower the glass until the glass track bolts are visible through the holes in the door frame.

3   Place a rag inside the door panel to help prevent scratching the glass during removal.

4   Loosen the two bolts retaining the glass to the window regulator track.

5   Raise the rear of the glass first and lift the glass from the door at an angle.

6   To install, lower the glass into the door, slide it into position and tighten the nuts.

7   The remainder of installation is the reverse of removal.

19   Door window glass regulator - removal and installation

▶ **Refer to illustration 19.4**

❊❊ WARNING:

Wear gloves when working inside the door openings to protect against cuts from sharp metal edges.

➡ **Note: The procedure is the same for both front and rear window regulators.**

1   Remove the door trim panel and the plastic watershield (see Section 15).

2   Remove the window glass assembly (see Section 18).

3   On power operated windows, disconnect the electrical connector from the window regulator motor.

4   Remove the regulator mounting bolts (see illustration).

5   Pull the regulator assembly through the service hole in the door frame to remove it.

6   Installation is the reverse of removal.

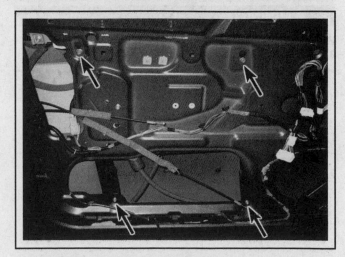

19.4 Regulator mounting bolt locations

20 Mirrors - removal and installation

OUTSIDE MIRRORS

♦ **Refer to illustration 20.2**

1   Pry the cover off, covering the mirror mounting bolts (if equipped).

➡**Note: On some Armada models, the cover is held on with adhesive instead of clips.**

2   Remove the fasteners (see illustration) and detach the mirror from the door.

3   Remove the door trim panel (see Section 15) and unplug the electrical connector.

4   Installation is the reverse of removal.

20.2 Remove the mirror mounting fasteners

INSIDE MIRROR

♦ **Refer to illustration 20.5**

5   Remove the trim cover from the mirror base (see illustration).

6   Loosen the set screw and slide the mirror up and off of the base mount.

7   Disconnect the electrical connector and remove the mirror.

8   Installation is the reverse of removal.

9   If the mounting bracket for the mirror has come off the windshield, it can be reattached with a special mirror adhesive kit available at auto parts stores. Clean the glass and support base thoroughly and follow the directions on the adhesive package, allowing the base to bond overnight before attaching the mirror.

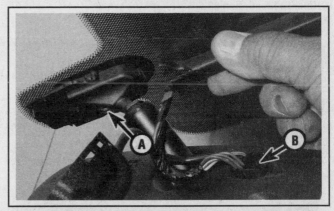

20.5 Remove the upper and lower trim covers, loosen the set screw (A), then slide the mirror off its base and disconnect the electrical connector (B)

21 Liftgate - removal and installation

♦ **Refer to illustrations 21.3 and 21.5**

➡**Note: The liftgate is heavy and somewhat awkward to remove and install - at least two people should perform this procedure.**

1   Open the liftgate and support it fully in this position.

2   Remove the liftgate pull handle, power opener and trim panel from the liftgate (see Section 15).

3   Remove the upper support strut mounting bracket(s) (see illustration).

4   Disconnect the electrical connectors and remove the wiring harness from the liftgate.

5   Remove the liftgate mounting nuts (see illustration). Remove the nuts while at least one assistant, preferably two, helps you hold the liftgate.

6   Installation is the reverse of the removal procedure.

21.3 Remove the upper strut bracket fasteners and bracket

21.5 Remove the liftgate hinge mounting nuts and remove the liftgate - right side shown

22 Liftgate latch, window lock and support struts - removal and installation

1 Remove the liftgate lower trim panel (see Section 15) and watershield.

LATCH

▶ **Refer to illustration 22.3**

2 Disconnect the electrical connections from the latch assembly.
3 Remove the latch mounting fasteners and detach the latch from the liftgate (see illustration).
4 Installation is the reverse of the removal procedure.

WINDOW LOCK

▶ **Refer to illustration 22.6**

5 Detach the electrical connector from the lock.
6 Remove the window lock mounting fasteners and detach the lock from the liftgate (see illustration).

7 Installation is the reverse of the removal procedure.

SUPPORT STRUTS

8 There are two support struts for the liftgate, and two separate struts to support the glass. Open the liftgate or glass and prop it securely in the full open position.
9 Release the small clip at the lower end of the strut, then pull the strut from the mounting ball.
10 Remove the clip securing the upper end of the support strut and detach the strut from the vehicle.
11 Installation is the reverse of the removal procedure.

ADJUSTMENT

12 The closing position of the liftgate can be adjusted by moving the liftgate striker.
13 Loosen the striker mounting bolts, move the striker slightly, retighten the bolts and check the closed position of the liftgate.

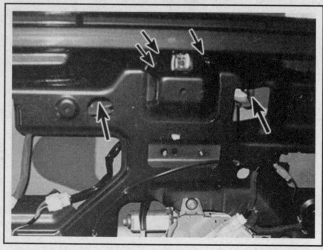

22.3 Liftgate latch mounting fasteners

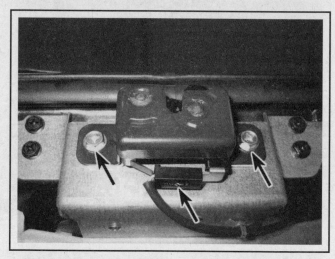

22.6 Disconnect the electrical connector and remove the window lock mounting fasteners

23 Liftgate glass and side window glass - removal and installation

LIFTGATE GLASS

▶ **Refer to illustration 23.1**

1 Open the liftgate glass. Remove the rear spoiler fasteners (see illustration), disconnect the high mount brake light and remove the spoiler.
2 Disconnect the rear window defogger connector.
3 Remove the rear glass support struts.
4 Remove the hinge nuts and remove the glass from the liftgate.
5 To install, slide hinges onto the studs and tighten the nuts securely.
6 The remainder of installation is the reverse of removal.

SIDE WINDOW GLASS

▶ **Refer to illustrations 23.9 and 23.10**

7 Remove the rear interior trim panels (see Section 27).
8 Disconnect the electrical connector at the headliner.
9 Remove the latch bolts on non power side windows (see illustration). On models with power side windows, remove the clip and pull the ballstud out of the side window socket.
10 Remove the front nuts (see illustration) and remove the window.
11 Installation is reverse of removal.

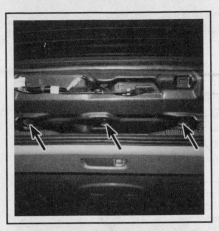

23.1 Remove the rear access plugs and remove the rear spoiler fasteners

23.9 Remove the side window latch bolts - non power window model shown

23.10 Remove the front mounting nuts

---

24 Tailgate and gas stay - removal and installation

GAS STAY

❄ WARNING:

Some models are equipped with a gas stay mounted behind the right taillight housing. It prevents the tailgate from falling open unrestrained when lowering it. If removal is required, it must only be removed when the tailgate is closed.

1 Remove the right taillight housing (see Chapter 12).
2 Close the tailgate. Release the clips at each end of the gas stay, then remove the stay from the mounting ball at each end.
3 Installation is the reverse of removal.

TAILGATE

◆ Refer to illustrations 24.5 and 24.6

4 Remove the gas stay, if so equipped (see Steps 1 and 2).
5 Open the tailgate and detach the retaining cables (see illustration).
6 Lower the tailgate until the flat on the left side hinge pin aligns with the slot in the hinge pocket. Lift the tailgate out of the pocket. With the help of an assistant to support the weight, withdraw the right hinge pin from the body and remove the tailgate from the vehicle (see illustration).
7 Installation is the reverse of removal.

➡Note: Apply some white grease to the mating parts of the tailgate hinge assembly before installation.

24.5 Lift the spring retainer up with a screwdriver and slide the cable end off the bolt

24.6 Align the flat on the right side hinge pin with the slot in the hinge pocket and lift the tailgate off the vehicle

25 Tailgate latch, lock cylinder and handle - removal and installation

▶ **Refer to illustrations 25.1, 25.2, 25.3 and 25.5**

1   Open the tailgate and remove the bed liner panel (see illustration).

2   Remove the tailgate access panel (see illustration).

3   Pop open the plastic retaining clips and detach the rods from the handle (see illustration).

4   Remove the mounting nuts and detach the handle from the tailgate.

5   To remove the lock cylinder, remove the mounting bolt (see illustration) and slide the lock out from the handle assembly.

6   To remove the latch, simply remove the bolts and withdraw the latch from the side of the tailgate with the control rod attached.

➡**Note: If you are removing both latch assemblies, it will be necessary to support the tailgate from below, since the tailgate support cables will be removed at the same time.**

7   Installation is the reverse of removal. Tighten all fasteners securely.

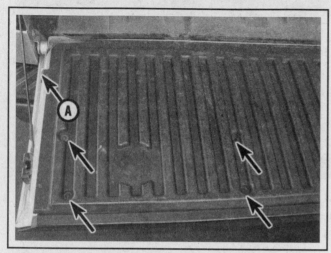

25.1 Remove the tailgate bed liner fasteners and pushpins (A) - left side shown, right side is the same

25.2 Remove the access panel mounting fasteners

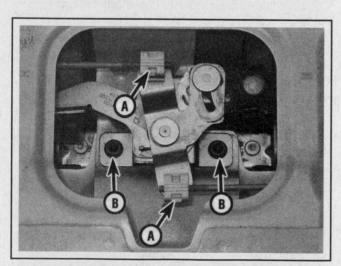

25.3 Tailgate control rods (A) and the handle mounting nuts (B)

25.5 Remove the lock cylinder retaining bolt and remove the lock cylinder

26 Center console - removal and installation

▶ Refer to illustrations 26.2, 26.4, 26.5, 26.6a and 26.6b

1   Disconnect the cable from the negative terminal of the battery

(see Chapter 5) and set the parking brake.

2   Open the center arm rest, remove the upper fastener covers and remove the fasteners (see illustration).

3   Unscrew the knob from the shift lever.

4   Disconnect all electrical connectors connected to the main console box, then remove the box mounting screws (see illustration).

5   Remove the rear cup holder and the lower rear mounting screws (see illustration).

6   Use a trim tool to pry out the rear trim, the two lower screw covers at the rear and the two up front near the base of the instrument panel and remove the screws (see illustrations).

7   Remove the center console from the vehicle.

8   Installation is the reverse of the removal procedure.

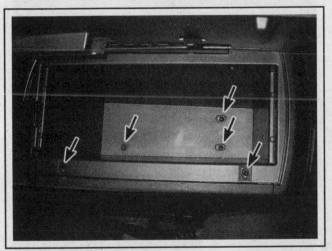

26.2 Remove the console retaining screws inside of the arm rest

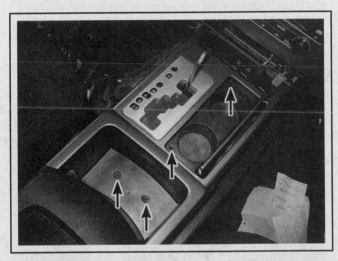

26.4 Remove the center and top console retaining screws

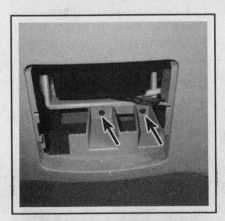

26.5 Remove the cup holder assembly and remove the console retaining screws

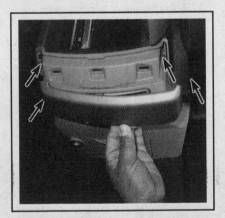

26.6a Remove the upper arm rest rim and lower rear console screws

26.6b Remove the lower front trim cover and remove the console retaining screw - right side shown

27 Rear interior trim panels - removal and installation

▶ **Refer to illustrations 27.2, 27.3, 27.4, 27.6, 27.7 and 27.9**

1   Remove the third row seats (see Section 31).

2   Lift out the rear storage box and pry out the liftgate kick plate (see illustration).

3   Remove the rear luggage lamp fasteners, lower the lamp and disconnect the electrical connector (see illustration).

4   Using a trim tool, carefully pry the upper trim panel down and slide the seat belt from the panel (see illustration).

5   Pry up each rear door kick plate and remove the kick plates.

6   Pry the rear liftgate switch and trim from the upper side panel (see illustration).

7   Remove the cargo net hooks, tie downs, seat belt mounts, power outlet, lower mounting bolts and lower trim panel (see illustration).

8   Start from the rear and carefully pry the rear trim panel out using a trim tool until the entire lower panel can be removed.

9   Remove the upper seat belt mounts and hook (see illustration), then carefully pry the upper trim panel out.

10   Installation is the reverse of the removal procedure.

27.2 Pry up and lift out the liftgate kick plate

27.3 Remove the rear luggage lamp fasteners

27.4 Pry the upper trim panel out using a trim tool

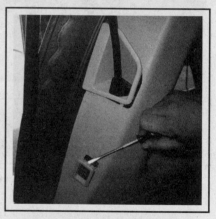

27.6 Carefully pry out the liftgate close switch and power open/close strut trim

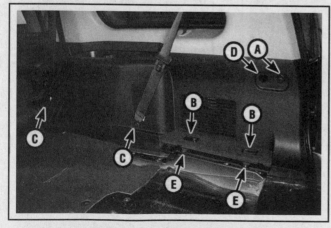

27.7 Rear trim panel details (right side shown, left side similar)

A Cargo net hook	D Power outlet
B Tie downs	E Lower mounting bolts
C Lower seat belt mounts	

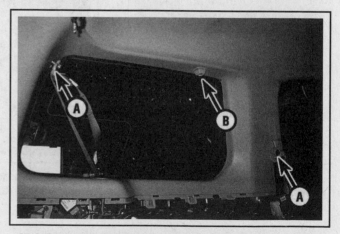

27.9 Rear trim panel details (left side shown, right side similar)

A Upper seat belt mounts	B Upper hook

28 Dashboard trim panels - removal and installation

✳✳ WARNING:

The models covered by this manual are equipped with Supplemental Restraint Systems (SRS), more commonly known as airbags. Always disable the airbag system before working in the vicinity of any airbag system components to avoid the possibility of accidental deployment of the airbags, which could cause personal injury (see Chapter 12).

INSTRUMENT CLUSTER BEZEL

▶ **Refer to illustration 28.6**

1   Disconnect the cable from the negative terminal of the battery (see Chapter 5).
2   On models equipped with tilt steering columns, tilt the steering wheel down as far as possible.
3   Remove the knee bolster (see Step 8).
4   Remove the driver's side vent (illustration 30.10a).
5   Remove the steering column covers (see Section 29).
6   Carefully pry the cluster bezel out from the instrument panel (see illustration).

7   Installation is the reverse of removal.

KNEE BOLSTER

▶ **Refer to illustrations 28.8 and 28.9**

8   Remove the fasteners securing the driver's knee bolster and pull it outward away from the dash (see illustration). Disconnect any electrical connectors at the rear of the knee bolster and detach it from the instrument panel.
9   If the knee bolster reinforcement panel needs to be removed for any reason, remove the retaining bolts (see illustration) and take down the panel.
10 Installation is the reverse of removal.

CENTER TRIM PANEL

▶ **Refer to illustrations 28.12 and 28.13**

11 Disconnect the cable from the negative terminal of the battery (see Chapter 5).
12 Pull out on the lower center panel to release it, then disconnect any electrical connectors behind the panel (see illustration).

28.6 Carefully remove the cluster bezel trim out and away from the instrument cluster

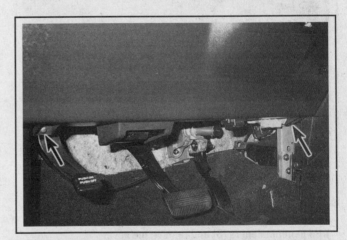

28.8 Remove the knee bolster lower fasteners

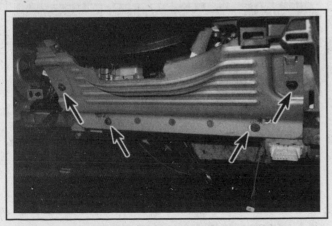

28.9 Reinforcement panel mounting fastener locations

28.12 Carefully pull the lower center trim panel out to disengage the clips

13 Remove the center trim panel mounting screws (see illustration) from the opening.

14 Carefully pull the center trim panel forward, disconnect all the electrical connectors from the back side and remove the panel.

15 Installation is the reverse of removal.

GLOVE BOX

▶ **Refer to illustrations 28.16, 28.17a, 28.17b and 28.17c**

16 Remove the lower cover pushpins, trim mounting screws and remove the cover (see illustration).

17 With the glove box open, remove the fuse panel cover, glove box pins, four screws at the top, striker screws (if equipped), and pull the glove box housing and lower trim panel from the instrument panel (see illustrations).

18 Installation is the reverse of the removal procedure.

KICK PANELS

19 Open the door and pry up the kick plate(s) from the door opening.

20 Remove the kick panel plastic fastener from the upper corner of the panel using a trim tool and remove the kick panel.

21 Installation is the reverse of the removal procedure.

28.13 Remove the center trim panel fasteners, carefully pry around the center trim with a trim tool to disengage the mounting clips and remove the trim panel

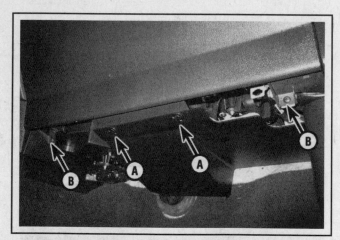

28.16 Remove the lower cover pushpins (A) and the lower trim panel fasteners (B) and remove the cover

28.17a From underneath the glove box, carefully pry the glove box pins back . . .

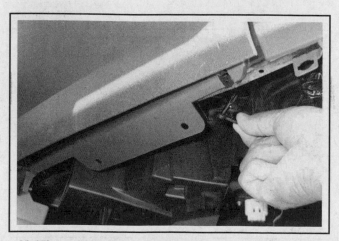

28.17b . . . and out from the glove box

28.17c Remove the lower trim panel retaining screws and pull the glove box and trim panel out

29 Steering column covers - removal and installation

♦ Refer to illustration 29.1

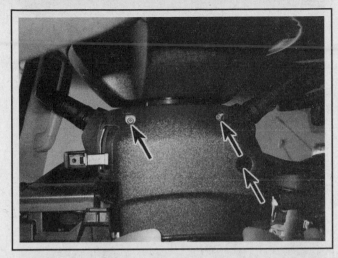

29.1 Remove the screws in the lower column cover, then detach and lift off the upper cover

❊❊ WARNING:

The models covered by this manual are equipped with Supplemental Restraint Systems (SRS), more commonly known as airbags. Always disable the airbag system before working in the vicinity of any airbag system components to avoid the possibility of accidental deployment of the airbags, which could cause personal injury (see Chapter 12).

1   Remove the screws and detach the lower half of the steering column cover (see illustration).
2   Pull the upper column cover straight up and off.
3   Installation is the reverse of removal.

30 Instrument panel - removal and installation

♦ Refer to illustrations 30.9, 30.10a, 30.10b, 30.12, 30.13 and 30.14

❊❊ WARNING:

The models covered by this manual are equipped with Supplemental Restraint Systems (SRS), more commonly known as airbags. Always disable the airbag system before working in the vicinity of any airbag system components to avoid the possibility of accidental deployment of the airbags, which could cause personal injury (see Chapter 12).

➡Note: This is a difficult procedure for the home mechanic, involving tedious disassembly and the disconnection/reconnection of numerous electrical connectors. If you do attempt this procedure, make sure you take good notes and mark all matching connectors (and their mounting points) to aid reassembly.

1   Disconnect the cable from the negative terminal of the battery (see Chapter 5).
2   Remove the center console (see Section 26).
3   Remove the steering column covers (see Section 29) and lower the steering column (see Chapter 10).
4   Remove all the dashboard trim panels and glove box (see Section 28).
5   Remove the instrument cluster (see Chapter 12).
6   Remove the radio unit and heater/air conditioner controls (see Chapter 12 and Chapter 3).

7   Remove the kick panels at each side of the instrument panel. The panels simply pull out after removing the retaining screw at the bottom and the door sill trim.
8   Remove the left and right trim strips along the interior of each windshield post.
9   Pry the defrost grille up using a trim tool and remove the upper mounting fasteners and dash speakers (see illustration). Disconnect and remove the optical sensor (if equipped).

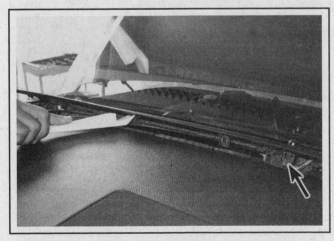

30.9 Carefully pry the defrost vent out and disconnect the optical sensor

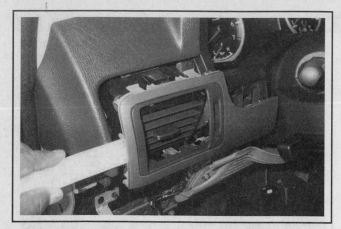

30.10a Pry the driver's side vent out using a trim tool

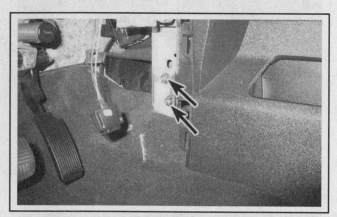

30.12 Remove the lower center fasteners - driver's side shown

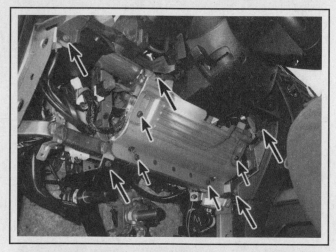

30.14 Remove the lower driver's side instrument panel mounting fasteners

10 On 2007 and earlier models, pry the side vent top covers off and remove the vent mounting fasteners. On all models, pry the side vents (see illustrations) out from the passenger's side center trim panel.

11 Remove the passenger's side airbag (see Chapter 12).

12 Remove the screws from the lower center of the instrument panel (see illustration).

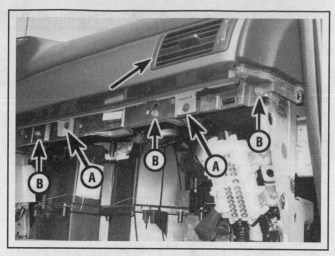

30.10b Pry the passenger's side vent out, then remove the side trim and instrument panel fasteners

A Passenger's side center trim panel fasteners
B Passenger's side instrument panel fasteners

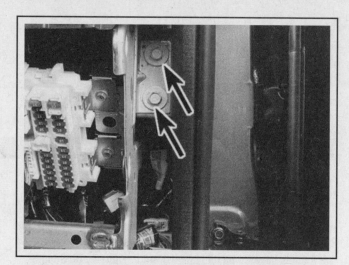

30.13 Remove the instrument panel end fasteners - passenger's side shown

13 Remove the fasteners at each side securing the main instrument panel to the cowl support beam (see illustration).

14 Remove driver's side mounting screws (see illustration).

15 Remove the center mounting screws.

16 Remove the passenger's side mounting screws (see illustration 30.10b).

17 Remove the two floor-to-instrument panel braces.

18 Once you're sure all electrical connectors are tagged and disconnected, start to pull up the main panel. If there is any resistance, check for fasteners you may have overlooked. Don't force removal on any panels.

19 Removal of the cowl support beam is a second difficult procedure. Many electrical connectors remain to disconnect, and most harnesses are clipped or clamped to this beam. Unless you have to access the heating/air conditioning unit, don't remove the beam.

20 Installation is the reverse of the removal procedure. Make sure you have accounted for all fasteners and electrical connectors before installing the trim panels.

31 Seats - removal and installation

FRONT SEATS

▶ Refer to illustrations 31.3a and 31.3b

> ❋❋ **WARNING:**
>
> The models covered by this manual are equipped with Supplemental Restraint Systems (SRS), more commonly known as airbags. Always disable the airbag system before working in the vicinity of any airbag system components to avoid the possibility of accidental deployment of the airbags, which could cause personal injury (see Chapter 12).

1 Position the seat so that all four mounting bolts can be accessed and removed, then disconnect the battery (see Chapter 5) if equipped with side airbags.

> ❋❋ **WARNING:**
>
> The front seats on some models are equipped with side-impact airbags at the upper outside of the seatback. Refer to Chapter 12 to disable the airbag system before working on front seats.

2 If equipped with power seats, disconnect the electrical connectors to the seat.
3 Detach the trim caps or covers and remove the mounting bolts (see illustrations).
4 Remove the front seat(s) from the vehicle.
5 Installation is the reverse of the removal procedure.

SECOND ROW SEATS (ARMADA MODELS)

Outboard seats

▶ Refer to illustration 31.7

6 Lift the handle and tilt the seat forward.
7 Detach the trim cover and remove the fasteners (see illustration).
8 Remove the outboard seat(s) from the vehicle.
9 Installation is the reverse of the removal procedure.

Center seat

▶ Refer to illustration 31.10

10 Tilt the seat forward and remove the fasteners (see illustration).
11 Remove the seat from the vehicle.
12 Installation is the reverse of the removal procedure.

31.3a Remove the retaining fasteners from the front of the seat . . .

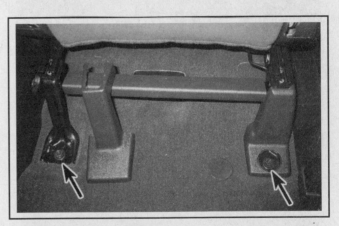

31.3b . . . and from the rear

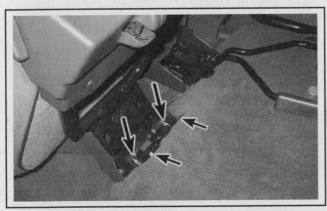

31.7 Remove the outboard seat mounting fasteners and remove the seats

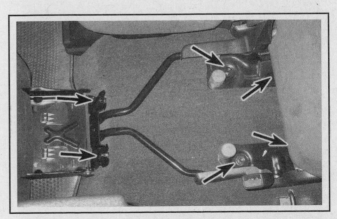

31.10 Remove the center seat mounting fasteners and remove the seats

THIRD ROW SEATS (ARMADA MODELS)

▶ **Refer to illustrations 31.13 and 31.15**

13 Detach the trim covers from the front base anchors and remove the fasteners (see illustration).

14 Remove the pushpin at the end of each seat and release the elastic band from the end of the seats. Remove the seat belt buckle from the cushions.

15 Place the seat(s) into the cargo position and remove the fasteners (see illustration).

16 Remove the front seat(s) from the vehicle.

17 Installation is the reverse of the removal procedure.

REAR SEAT (TITAN MODELS)

▶ **Refer to illustration 31.18**

18 Place the seat into the stowed position and remove the fasteners (see illustration).

19 Position the seat track in the most forward position, then fold the seat back down to access the rear mounting bolts.

20 Pull the seatback release strap to release the seatback and remove the seat.

21 Installation is the reverse of the removal procedure.

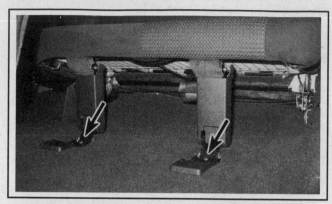

31.13 Remove the seat front mounting fasteners - left side shown, right side similar

31.15 Remove the rear mounting fasteners and remove the seat(s)

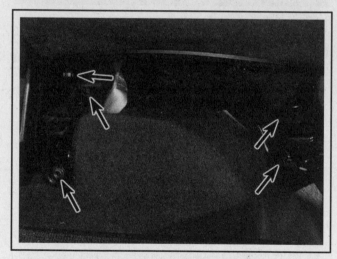

31.18 Remove the rear seat mounting fasteners

32 Rear cab window, glass and regulator (Titan models) - removal and installation

WINDOW GLASS ASSEMBLY

Removal

1 Using a trim tool, carefully pry off the rear window trim.

2 Remove the overhead console (see Chapter 12) and disconnect the electrical connections.

3 Remove the sun visor mounting screws and remove the sun visors.

4 Remove the upper handle fasteners and remove the handles (if equipped).

5 Remove the striker cover, striker fasteners and remove the strikers (if equipped).

6 Remove the rear dome lamp (see Chapter 12) and disconnect the electrical connection.

7 Starting from the rear, carefully pull the rear headliner down, disconnecting the rear clips.

8 Using a trim tool, pry the rear side trim panel out and remove the panels.

9 Remove the rear seat (see Section 31).

10 Remove the rear panel mounting nuts, plastic push pin fasteners and remove the panels.

11 Remove the watershield. Lower the window and remove the window glass to regulator mounting bolts.

12 Raise the window by hand and tape the window into place. Disconnect the rear window defogger connection.

13 Remove the rear window mounting nuts, all the way around the window.

14 Pull the assembly out starting from the top and lift the assembly out at an angle.

Installation

15 Clean the window opening and apply new butyl seal to the window assembly.

16 Lift the window assembly into place, engaging the bottom clips on to the back panel and tighten the mounting nuts securely. After the assembly has been installed, reset the limit switch (see Steps 24 through 29).

17 The remainder of installation is the reverse of removal.

WINDOW REGULATOR

✳✳ WARNING:

Wear gloves when working inside the openings to protect against cuts from sharp metal edges.

Removal

18 Remove the rear window assembly see Steps 1 through 14.

19 Disconnect the power window motor/regulator electrical connections.

20 Remove the window motor/regulator mounting fasteners and remove the regulator and motor assembly.

Installation

21 Install the regulator and motor assembly into the opening and lower the assembly.

22 Connect the electrical connections and install the mounting fasteners. Tighten the fasteners securely. After the assembly been installed, reset the limit switch (see Steps 24 through 29).

23 The remainder of installation is the reverse of removal.

Limit switch resetting

24 Raise the glass to the top of the channel.

25 Find the power window motor reset switch at the base of the window motor and note its position. Press and hold the reset switch while lowering the glass to the bottom.

26 Release the switch when the window is at the bottom.

27 Check the reset switch to make sure it has returned to its original position.

➡**Note: If the switch is not in the correct position, pull the switch out.**

28 Raise the window to the top.

✳✳ CAUTION:

Do not raise the window automatically until after this has been performed.

NOTES

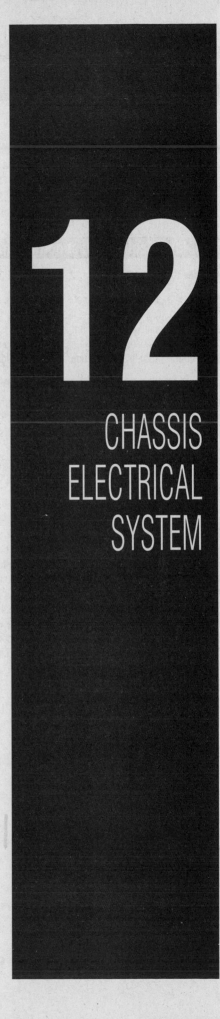

12

CHASSIS
ELECTRICAL
SYSTEM

Section

1 General information

The electrical system is a 12-volt, negative ground type. Power for the lights and all electrical accessories is supplied by a lead/acid-type battery that is charged by the alternator.

This Chapter covers repair and service procedures for the various electrical components not associated with the engine. Information on the battery, alternator, ignition system and starter motor can be found in Chapter 5.

It should be noted that when portions of the electrical system are serviced, the negative cable should be disconnected from the battery to prevent electrical shorts and/or fires.

2 Electrical troubleshooting - general information

▶ **Refer to illustrations 2.5a, 2.5b, 2.6 and 2.9**

A typical electrical circuit consists of an electrical component, any switches, relays, motors, fuses, fusible links or circuit breakers related to that component and the wiring and connectors that link the component to both the battery and the chassis. To help you pinpoint an electrical circuit problem, wiring diagrams are included at the end of this Chapter.

Before tackling any troublesome electrical circuit, first study the appropriate wiring diagrams to get a complete understanding of what makes up that individual circuit. Trouble spots, for instance, can often be narrowed down by noting if other components related to the circuit are operating properly. If several components or circuits fail at one time, chances are the problem is in a fuse or ground connection, because several circuits are often routed through the same fuse and ground connections.

Electrical problems usually stem from simple causes, such as loose or corroded connections, a blown fuse, a melted fusible link or a failed relay. Visually inspect the condition of all fuses, wires and connections in a problem circuit before troubleshooting the circuit.

If test equipment and instruments are going to be utilized, use the diagrams to plan ahead of time where you will make the necessary connections in order to accurately pinpoint the trouble spot.

The basic tools needed for electrical troubleshooting include a circuit tester or voltmeter (a 12-volt bulb with a set of test leads can also be used), a continuity tester, which includes a bulb, battery and set of test leads, and a jumper wire, preferably with a circuit breaker incorporated, which can be used to bypass electrical components (see illustrations). Before attempting to locate a problem with test instruments, use the wiring diagram(s) to decide where to make the connections.

VOLTAGE CHECKS

Voltage checks should be performed if a circuit is not functioning properly. Connect one lead of a circuit tester to either the negative battery terminal or a known good ground. Connect the other lead to a connector in the circuit being tested, preferably nearest to the battery or fuse (see illustration). If the bulb of the tester lights, voltage is present, which means that the part of the circuit between the connector and the battery is problem free. Continue checking the rest of the circuit in the same fashion. When you reach a point at which no voltage is present, the problem lies between that point and the last test point with voltage. Most of the time the problem can be traced to a loose connection.

➡**Note: Keep in mind that some circuits receive voltage only when the ignition key is in the Accessory or Run position.**

FINDING A SHORT

One method of finding shorts in a circuit is to remove the fuse and connect a test light or voltmeter in place of the fuse terminals. There should be no voltage present in the circuit. Move the wiring harness from side-to-side while watching the test light. If the bulb goes on,

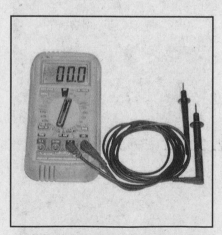

2.5a The most useful tool for electrical troubleshooting is a digital multimeter that can check volts, amps, and test continuity

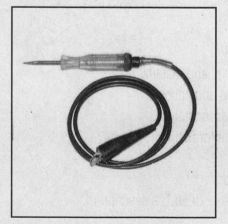

2.5b A test light is a very handy tool for checking voltage

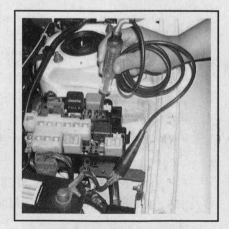

2.6 In use, a basic test light's lead is clipped to a known good ground, then the pointed probe can test connectors, wires or electrical sockets - if the bulb lights, the part being tested has battery voltage

there is a short to ground somewhere in that area, probably where the insulation has rubbed through. The same test can be performed on each component in the circuit, even a switch.

GROUND CHECK

Perform a ground test to check whether a component is properly grounded. Disconnect the battery and connect one lead of a continuity tester or multimeter (set to the ohms scale), to a known good ground. Connect the other lead to the wire or ground connection being tested. If the resistance is low (less than 5 ohms), the ground is good. If the bulb on a self-powered test light does not go on, the ground is not good.

CONTINUITY CHECK

A continuity check is done to determine if there are any breaks in a circuit - if it is passing electricity properly. With the circuit off (no power in the circuit), a self-powered continuity tester or multimeter can be used to check the circuit. Connect the test leads to both ends of the circuit (or to the power end and a good ground), and if the test light comes on the circuit is passing current properly (see illustration). If the resistance is low (less than 5 ohms), there is continuity; if the reading is 10,000 ohms or higher, there is a break somewhere in the circuit. The same procedure can be used to test a switch, by connecting the continuity tester to the switch terminals. With the switch turned On, the test light should come on (or low resistance should be indicated on a meter).

FINDING AN OPEN CIRCUIT

When diagnosing for possible open circuits, it is often difficult to

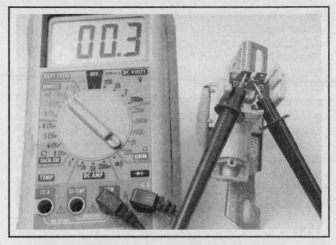

2.9 With a multimeter set to the ohms scale, resistance can be checked across two terminals - when checking for continuity, a low reading indicates continuity, a high reading indicates lack of continuity

locate them by sight because the connectors hide oxidation or terminal misalignment. Merely wiggling a connector on a sensor or in the wiring harness may correct the open circuit condition. Remember this when an open circuit is indicated when troubleshooting a circuit. Intermittent problems may also be caused by oxidized or loose connections.

Electrical troubleshooting is simple if you keep in mind that all electrical circuits are basically electricity running from the battery, through the wires, switches, relays, fuses and fusible links to each electrical component (light bulb, motor, etc.) and to ground, from which it is passed back to the battery. Any electrical problem is an interruption in the flow of electricity to and from the battery.

3 Fuses and fusible links - general information

FUSES

▸ **Refer to illustrations 3.1a, 3.1b and 3.3**

The electrical circuits of the vehicle are protected by a combination of fuses, circuit breakers and fusible links. The main fuse/relay panel is

in the engine compartment (see illustration), while the interior fuse/relay panel is located inside the passenger compartment (see illustration). Each of the fuses is designed to protect a specific circuit, and the various circuits are identified on the fuse panel itself.

Several sizes of fuses are employed in the fuse blocks. There are small, medium and large sizes of the same design, all with the same

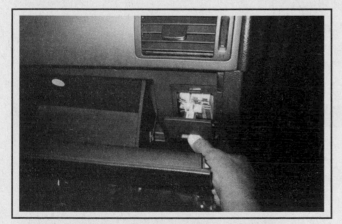

3.1a The interior fuse box is located under the right (passenger's) side of the instrument panel, under a cover

3.1b The engine compartment fuse and fusible link box is located behind the battery

blade terminal design. The medium and large fuses can be removed with your fingers, but the small fuses require the use of pliers or the small plastic fuse-puller tool found in most fuse boxes.

If an electrical component fails, always check the fuse first. The best way to check the fuses is with a test light. Check for power at the exposed terminal tips of each fuse. If power is present at one side of the fuse but not the other, the fuse is blown. A blown fuse can also be identified by visually inspecting it (see illustration).

Be sure to replace blown fuses with the correct type. Fuses (of the same physical size) of different ratings may be physically interchangeable, but only fuses of the proper rating should be used. Replacing a fuse with one of a higher or lower value than specified is not recommended. Each electrical circuit needs a specific amount of protection. The amperage value of each fuse is molded into the top of the fuse body.

If the replacement fuse immediately fails, don't replace it again until the cause of the problem is isolated and corrected. In most cases, this will be a short circuit in the wiring caused by a broken or deteriorated wire.

FUSIBLE LINKS

Some circuits are protected by fusible links. The links are used in circuits which are not ordinarily fused, or which carry high current, such as the circuit between the alternator and the starter motor. Fusible links, which are usually several wire gauges smaller in size than the

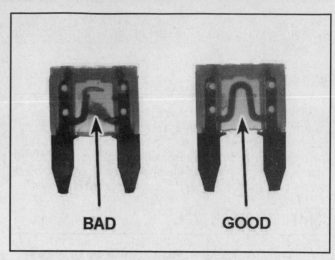

3.3 When a fuse blows, the element between the terminals melts

circuit that they protect, are designed to melt if the circuit is subjected to more current than it was designed to carry. If you have to replace a blown fusible link, make sure that you replace it with one of the same specification. If the replacement fusible link blows in the same circuit, make sure that you troubleshoot the circuit in which the fusible link melted BEFORE installing another fusible link.

Circuit breakers - general information

Circuit breakers protect certain circuits, such as the power windows or heated seats. Depending on the vehicle's accessories, there may be one or two circuit breakers, located in the fuse/relay box in the engine compartment.

Because the circuit breakers reset automatically, an electrical overload in a circuit breaker-protected system will cause the circuit to fail momentarily, then come back on. If the circuit does not come back on, check it immediately.

For a basic check, pull the circuit breaker up out of its socket on the fuse panel, but just far enough to probe with a voltmeter. The breaker should still contact the sockets. With the voltmeter negative lead on a good chassis ground, touch each end prong of the circuit breaker with the positive meter probe. There should be battery voltage at each end. If there is battery voltage only at one end, the circuit breaker must be replaced.

Some circuit breakers must be reset manually.

Relays - general information

Several electrical accessories in the vehicle, such as the fuel injection system, horns, starter, and fog lamps use relays to transmit the electrical signal to the component. Relays use a low-current circuit (the control circuit) to open and close a high-current circuit (the power circuit). If the relay is defective, that component will not operate properly. Most relays are mounted in the engine compartment and interior fuse/relay boxes (see illustrations 3.1a and 3.1h).

6 Electrical connectors - general information

Most electrical connections on these vehicles are made with multiwire plastic connectors. The mating halves of many connectors are secured with locking clips molded into the plastic connector shells. The mating halves of some large connectors, such as some of those under the instrument panel, are held together by a bolt through the center of the connector.

To separate a connector with locking clips, use a small screwdriver to pry the clips apart carefully, then separate the connector halves. Pull only on the shell, never pull on the wiring harness as you may damage the individual wires and terminals inside the connectors. Look at the connector closely before trying to separate the halves. Often the locking clips are engaged in a way that is not immediately clear. Additionally, many connectors have more than one set of clips.

Each pair of connector terminals has a male half and a female half.

When you look at the end view of a connector in a diagram, be sure to understand whether the view shows the harness side or the component side of the connector. Connector halves are mirror images of each other, and a terminal shown on the right side end-view of one half will be on the left side end-view of the other half.

It is often necessary to take circuit voltage measurements with a connector connected. Whenever possible, carefully insert a small straight pin (not your meter probe) into the rear of the connector shell to contact the terminal inside, then clip your meter lead to the pin. This kind of connection is called "backprobing." When inserting a test probe into a terminal, be careful not to distort the terminal opening. Doing so can lead to a poor connection and corrosion at that terminal later. Using the small straight pin instead of a meter probe results in less chance of deforming the terminal connector.

Most electrical connectors have a single release tab that you depress to release the connector

The single release tab might be on the side of the connector instead of on top (or on bottom!)

Some connectors have two release tabs that you must squeeze to release the connector

Some connectors use wire retainers that you squeeze to release the connector

Critical connectors often employ a sliding lock (1) that you must pull out before you can depress the release tab (2)

Here's another sliding-lock style connector, with the lock (1) and the release tab (2) on the side of the connector

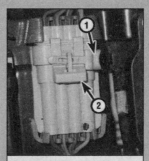

On some connectors the lock (1) must be pulled out to the side and removed before you can depress the release tab (2)

Some critical connectors, like the multi-pin connectors at the Powertrain Control Module employ pivoting locks that must be flipped open

7 Remote keyless entry fob - battery replacement and matching the transmitter to the vehicle

BATTERY REPLACEMENT

▶ **Refer to illustration 7.1**

1 To replace the transmitter battery, carefully pry open the keyless entry fob by inserting a coin into the notch in the body of the transmitter (see illustration) and separate the upper and lower halves of the fob.
2 Carefully pry out the old battery with a small screwdriver.

❊❊ CAUTION:

Do not touch the circuit board or battery terminal connection inside the key fob.

3 Installation is the reverse of removal. Make sure the two halves of the cover snap together tightly.

MATCHING THE TRANSMITTER TO THE VEHICLE

4 Get both transmitters (or more, if you have more; up to five can be programmed). Shut the doors.
5 Place the ignition key into the ignition lock cylinder and pull it back out. Do this at least seven times within a ten second period. The hazard flasher lights should blink twice.
➡**Note: The key must be inserted and removed completely each time. Also, if this is done too fast, it won't work.**

6 Install the key again and turn it to the Accessory position. Push one of the buttons on the remote; the hazard flasher lights will blink twice again. The old code is now erased and the new one programmed in. If

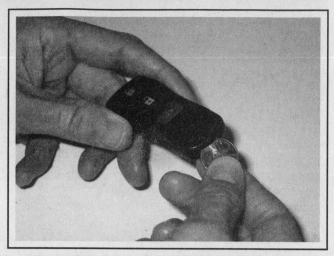

7.1 Using a coin, carefully pry the halves of the transmitter apart

another remote is going to be programmed, proceed to the next Step.
7 Have the next remote transmitter to be programmed ready. Push the driver's door Unlock button, then press the Lock button. Now push any button on the remote; the hazard flasher lights will blink twice. The old code is now erased from this remote, and the new one is programmed in.
8 If another remote is going to be programmed, repeat Step 7. You can match up to five transmitters to the vehicle.
9 To exit the programming mode, open the driver's door.

8 Ignition switch and key lock cylinder - replacement

Because a new ignition key lock cylinder and ignition switch come with new ignition keys, which must be programmed with a factory scan tool, we don't recommend that you attempt to replace the ignition key lock assembly at home.

9 Steering column switches - replacement

▶ **Refer to illustration 9.3**

❊❊ WARNING:

The models covered by this manual are equipped with Supplemental Restraint Systems (SRS), more commonly known as airbags. Always disable the airbag system before working in the vicinity of any airbag system components to avoid the possibility of accidental deployment of the airbags, which could cause personal injury (see Section 27).

1 Disconnect the cable from the negative battery terminal (see Chapter 5). The left multifunction switch on the steering column controls the lighting and turn signals, while the switch on the right of the

column controls the Wipe/Wash functions, including the operation of the rear wiper/washer on Armada models. Each switch can be replaced independently of the other.

2 Remove the steering column covers (see Chapter 11).
3 Press in the two clips and pull out the switch (see illustration).
4 Installation is the reverse of removal.

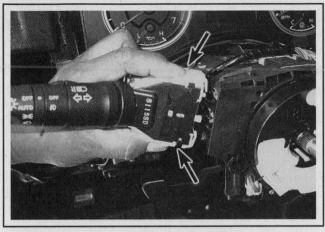

9.3 Squeeze the two clips to release the switch (turn/headlight or wiper/washer switch) from the column

10 Dashboard switches - replacement

▸ **Refer to illustration 10.5**

✳✳ WARNING:

The models covered by this manual are equipped with Supplemental Restraint Systems (SRS), more commonly known as airbags. Always disable the airbag system before working in the vicinity of any airbag system components to avoid the possibility of accidental deployment of the airbags, which could cause personal injury (see Section 27).

1 Disconnect the cable from the negative battery terminal (see Chapter 5).
2 On driver's side switches, remove the driver's knee bolster (see Chapter 11).
3 On center dash switches, remove the center trim panel (see Chapter 11).
4 Disconnect the electrical connector from the switch being replaced.
5 Depending on the switch being replaced, either remove the switch mounting screws and detach the switch from the panel or use a small screwdriver to release the clips and pull out the switch (see illustration).

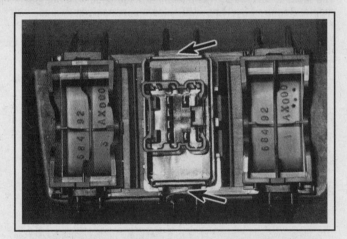

10.5 Release these clips to free the switch from the panel

➥**Note: It may be necessary to remove the knee bolster reinforcement panel (see Chapter 11) to disconnect the switch connector.**

6 Installation is the reverse of removal.

11 Instrument cluster - removal and installation

▸ **Refer to illustration 11.3**

✳✳ WARNING:

The models covered by this manual are equipped with Supplemental Restraint Systems (SRS), more commonly known as airbags. Always disable the airbag system before working in the

vicinity of any airbag system components to avoid the possibility of accidental deployment of the airbags, which could cause personal injury (see Section 27).

1 Disconnect the cable from the negative battery terminal (see Chapter 5).
2 Remove the instrument cluster bezel (see Chapter 11).

3 Remove the retaining screws and pull the cluster forward (see illustration).

4 Unplug the electrical connectors and remove the cluster from the vehicle.

5 Installation is the reverse of the removal procedure.

11.3 Instrument cluster mounting fasteners

12 Radio and speakers - removal and installation

❋❋ WARNING:

The models covered by this manual are equipped with Supplemental Restraint Systems (SRS), more commonly known as airbags. Always disable the airbag system before working in the vicinity of any airbag system components to avoid the possibility of accidental deployment of the airbags, which could cause personal injury (see Section 27).

RADIO

1 Disconnect the cable from the negative battery terminal (see Chapter 5).

All models except 2009 and later Armada

▶ **Refer to illustrations 12.2, 12.3, 12.4 and 12.5**

2 Use a small screwdriver or trim tool to lift up the center bezel (see illustration). The radio controls and A/C heater controls are mounted to the back of the center bezel.

3 Disconnect the electrical connectors (see illustration), remove the center bezel and radio control as an assembly.

4 Remove the radio control mounting fasteners and separate the radio control from the center bezel (see illustration).

5 Remove the radio unit screws and pull the radio unit out of the dash (see illustration).

6 Disconnect the antenna lead and the electrical connectors and remove the radio.

7 Installation is the reverse of removal.

2009 and later Armada models

▶ **Refer to illustrations 12.9 and 12.10**

8 Use a trim tool to pry off the center bezel (see Chapter 11). The radio unit is mounted to the center bezel.

9 Disconnect the electrical connectors (see illustration), remove the radio unit mounting screws and pull the unit out.

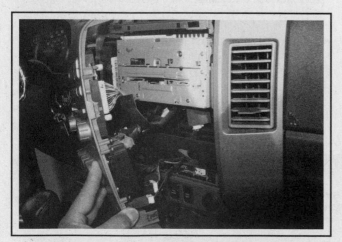

12.2 Use a small screwdriver or trim tool to pry off the center bezel

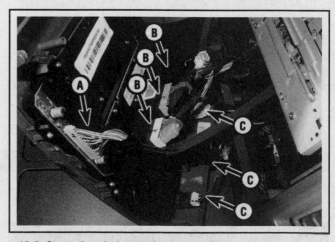

12.3 Center bezel electrical components

A Radio control head electrical connector
B Heating and A/C control head electrical connectors
C Center dash switchesa

12.4 Remove the radio control head fasteners

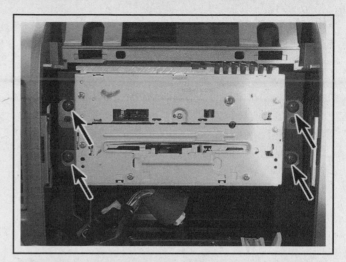

12.5 Radio unit mounting screws - Titan model shown

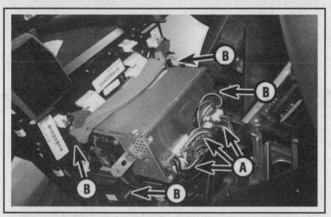

12.9 Disconnect the radio unit wiring (A), remove the mounting fasteners (B), then remove the unit from the center trim panel - Armada model shown

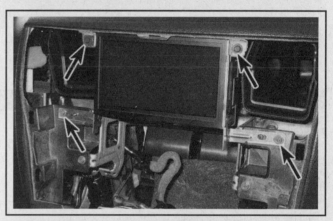

12.10 Radio/navigation display mounting fasteners

10 Remove the radio/navigation display mounting fasteners (see illustration), then remove the display and bracket as an assembly

11 Pull the display forward, disconnect the electrical connectors, remove the display head and separate the head from the mounting bracket.

12 Installation is the reverse of removal.

SPEAKERS

Front tweeter

13 Use a small screwdriver or trim tool to lift up the cover over the tweeter on the instrument panel.

14 Remove the mounting screws and lift out the tweeter. Disconnect the electrical connector.

15 Installation is the reverse of removal.

Center speaker

16 Use a small screwdriver or trim tool to lift up the center speaker cover.

➡Note: The speaker is mounted to the speaker cover.

17 Disconnect the electrical connector. Remove the mounting screws and separate the speaker from the cover.

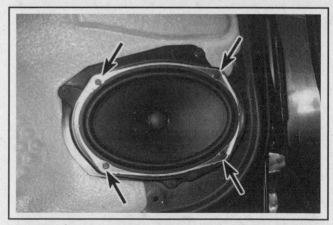

12.20 Speaker mounting fasteners

18 Installation is the reverse of removal.

Door speakers

▶ Refer to illustration 12.20

19 Remove the door trim panel (see Chapter 11).

20 Remove the speaker mounting fasteners (see illustration). Unplug the electrical connector and remove the speaker.

Liftgate speakers

▶ **Refer to illustration 12.22**

21 Remove the liftgate trim panel (see Chapter 11).

22 Remove the speaker mounting fasteners (see illustration). Unplug the electrical connector and remove the speaker.

23 Installation is the reverse of removal.

Sub-woofer speaker

24 On premium-stereo packages in crew-cab models, the vehicle may be equipped with a sub-woofer assembly, mounted under the front driver's seat.

25 Remove the front seat (see Chapter 11).

26 Disconnect the electrical connector, remove the mounting screws and lift out the sub-woofer assembly.

12.22 Liftgate speaker mounting fasteners

13 Antenna - removal and installation

▶ **Refer to illustrations 13.1 and 13.4**

➡**Note: There are two types of antennas used on these models, a grid type and fixed type. The grid type is an integral component of the rear window and side windows. To replace these antennas, the rear window or side window(s) must be replaced.**

1 Remove the antenna mast and bezel (see illustration).

2 Remove the inner fenderwell liner mounting fasteners and pull the rear of the inner fenderwell liner back (see Chapter 11).

3 From inside the vehicle, remove the glove box (see Chapter 11), and disconnect the antenna cable from the connector.

4 Remove the antenna base mounting bolt (see illustration). Pull the base and antenna cable up from the body.

5 Installation is the reverse of the removal. If the cable from the antenna-base connector-to-radio needs to be replaced, remove the audio unit and disconnect the cable from the back of the unit.

6 On models with the satellite radio option, the antenna is mounted on the roof. Because the headliner must be removed for access to the antenna mounting nut, it is recommended that the satellite antenna be serviced at a dealership or other qualified shop.

13.1 Use a small wrench to unscrew the antenna mast

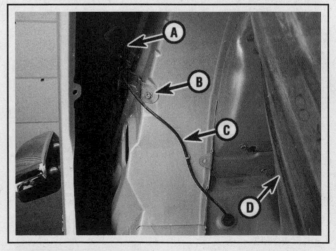

13.4 Fixed antenna details:

A   Antenna mast housing
B   Antenna mast mounting bolt
C   Antenna cable
D   Inner fenderwell liner (pulled back)

14 Rear window defogger - check and repair

1 The rear window defogger consists of a number of horizontal heating elements baked onto the inside surface of the glass. Power is supplied through two fuses and a relay in the IPDM relay box in the engine compartment. A defogger switch on the instrument panel controls the defogger grid.

2 Small breaks in the element can be repaired without removing the rear window.

CHECK

▶ **Refer to illustrations 14.5, 14.6 and 14.8**

3 Turn the ignition and defogger switches to the ON position.

4 Using a voltmeter, place the positive probe against the defogger grid positive side and the negative probe against the ground side. If battery voltage is not indicated, check that the ignition switch is On and that the feed and ground wires are properly connected. Check the two fuses, defogger switch, defogger relay and related wiring. The dealer can scan the body control module if necessary. If voltage is indicated, but all or part of the defogger doesn't heat, proceed with the following tests.

5 When measuring voltage during the next two tests, wrap a piece of aluminum foil around the tip of the voltmeter positive probe and press the foil against the heating element with your finger (see illustration). Place the negative probe on the defogger grid ground terminal.

6 Check the voltage at the center of each heating element (see illustration). If the voltage is 5 to 6 volts, the element is okay (there is no break). If the voltage is 0 volts, the element is broken between the center of the element and the positive end. If the voltage is 10 to 12 volts, the element is broken between the center of the element and the ground side. Check each heating element.

7 If none of the elements are broken, connect the negative probe to a good chassis ground. The voltage reading should stay the same, if it doesn't the ground connection is bad.

8 To find the break, place the voltmeter negative probe against the defogger ground terminal. Place the voltmeter positive probe with the foil strip against the heating element at the positive side and slide it

toward the negative side. The point at which the voltmeter deflects from several volts to zero is the point where the heating element is broken (see illustration).

REPAIR

▶ **Refer to illustration 14.14**

9 Repair the break in the element using a repair kit specifically for this purpose, such as DuPont paste No. 4817 (or equivalent). The kit includes conductive plastic epoxy.

10 Before repairing a break, turn off the system and allow it to cool for a few minutes.

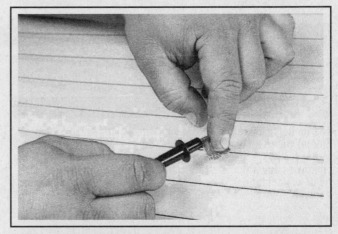

14.5 When measuring the voltage at the rear window defogger grid, wrap a piece of aluminum foil around the negative probe of the voltmeter and press the foil against the wire with your finger

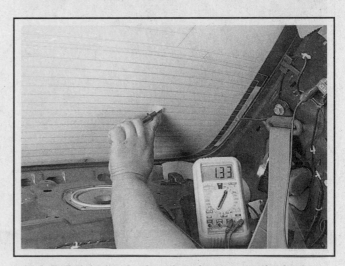

14.8 To find the break, place the voltmeter negative lead against the defogger ground terminal, place the voltmeter positive lead with the foil strip against the heat wire at the positive terminal end and slide it toward the negative terminal end. The point at which the voltmeter deflects from several volts to zero volts is the point at which the wire is broken

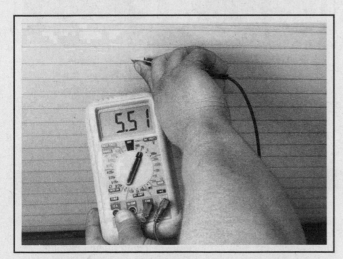

14.6 To determine if a heating element has broken, check the voltage at the center of each element - if the voltage is 6-volts, the element is unbroken

11 Lightly buff the element area with fine steel wool, then clean it thoroughly with rubbing alcohol.

12 Use masking tape to mask off the area being repaired.

13 Thoroughly mix the epoxy, following the kit instructions.

14 Apply the epoxy material to the slit in the masking tape, overlapping the undamaged area about 3/4-inch on either end (see illustration).

15 Allow the repair to cure for 24 hours before removing the tape and using the system.

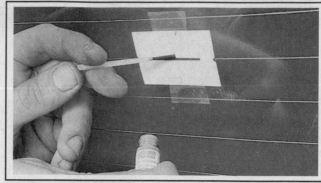

14.14 To use a defogger repair kit, apply masking tape to the inside of the window at the damaged area, then brush on the special conductive coating

15 Headlight housing - removal and installation

▶ Refer to illustrations 15.2 and 15.3

✳✳ WARNING:

The models covered by this manual are equipped with Supplemental Restraint Systems (SRS), more commonly known as airbags. Always disable the airbag system before working in the vicinity of any airbag system components to avoid the possibility of accidental deployment of the airbags, which could cause personal injury (see Section 27).

1 Remove the radiator grille (see Chapter 11).

2 Remove the headlight housing upper mounting fasteners (see illustration).

3 Remove the front corner inner fenderwell liner mounting screws (see Chapter 11, Section 13) and pull the liner back, then remove the housing lower mounting fastener (see illustration).

➡**Note: On 2007 and later models remove the front bumper (see Chapter 11).**

4 Lift the headlight housing up, disconnect the electrical connectors at the back of the headlight housing and remove the headlight housing.

5 Installation is the reverse of the removal procedure.

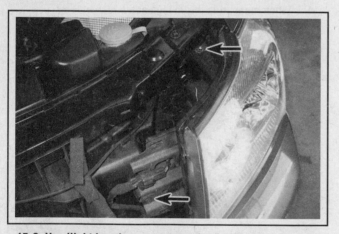

15.2 Headlight housing upper mounting fasteners

15.3 Headlight housing lower mounting fastener

16 Headlight bulb - replacement

▶ Refer to illustration 16.2

✳✳ WARNING:

These models are equipped with halogen gas-filled bulbs, which are under pressure and may shatter if the surface is scratched or the bulb is dropped. Wear eye protection and handle the bulbs

carefully, grasping only the base whenever possible. Do not touch the surface of the bulb with your fingers because the oil from your skin could cause it to overheat and fail prematurely. If you do touch the bulb surface, clean it with rubbing alcohol.**

1 Remove the front corner inner fenderwell mounting screws (see Chapter 11, Section 13) and pull the liner back.

2   Reach up behind the headlight housing and disconnect the electrical connector for the bulb to be replaced (see illustration).

3   Rotate the bulb counterclockwise to remove it from the housing.

4   Without touching the glass with your bare fingers, insert the new bulb assembly into the headlight housing and rotate the bulb clockwise to lock it into the housing.

5   Plug in the electrical connector. Test headlight operation before reinstalling the inner fender liner mounting fasteners.

16.2 Disconnect the electrical connector (A) for the bulb to be replaced, rotate the bulb counterclockwise and remove it from the housing

17 Headlights - adjustment

▶ **Refer to illustrations 17.1 and 17.2**

➡**Note: It is important that the headlights are aimed correctly. If adjusted incorrectly they could blind the driver of an oncoming vehicle and cause a serious accident or seriously reduce your ability to see the road. The headlights should be checked for proper aim every 12 months and any time a new headlight is installed or front end body work is performed. It should be emphasized that the following procedure is only an interim step that will provide temporary adjustment until the headlights can be adjusted by a properly equipped shop.**

1   These models are equipped with only one adjustment screw on the back of the headlight housing (see illustration). This screw adjusts only the vertical aiming of the headlights; horizontal aiming is not adjustable.

2   There are several methods of adjusting the headlights. The simplest method requires an open area with a blank wall and a level floor (see illustration).

3   Position masking tape vertically on the wall in reference to the vehicle centerline and the centerlines of both headlights.

4   Position a horizontal tape line in reference to the centerline of all the headlights.

➡**Note: It may be easier to position the tape on the wall with the vehicle parked only a few inches away.**

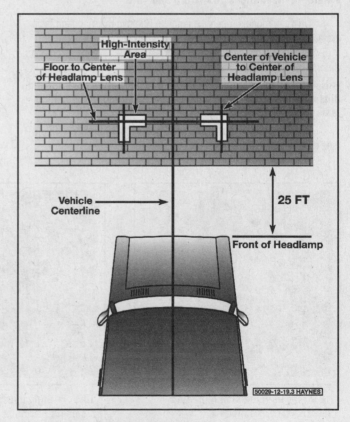

17.1 Headlight housing adjustment screw

17.2 Headlight adjustment details

5 Adjustment should be made with the vehicle parked 25 feet from the wall, sitting level, the gas tank half-full and no unusually heavy load in the vehicle.

6 Starting with the low beam adjustment, position the high intensity zone so it is two inches below the horizontal line. Turn the adjustment screws until the desired level has been achieved.

7 With the high beams on, the high intensity zone should be verti- cally centered with the exact center just below the horizontal line.

➡**Note: It may not be possible to position the headlight aim exactly for both high and low beams. If a compromise must be made, keep in mind that the low beams are the most used and have the greatest effect on driver safety.**

8 Have the headlights adjusted by a dealer service department at the earliest opportunity.

18 Bulb replacement

FRONT SIDE MARKER/TURN SIGNAL/PARK LIGHTS

▶ **Refer to illustration 18.1**

1 The front turn signal and park light and the side marker light are both mounted in the headlight housing. The round bulb is the turn/park bulb and the small bulb is the side marker (see illustration).

2 Remove the front corner inner fenderwell liner mounting fasteners (see Chapter 11, Section 13) and pull the liner back.

3 Reach behind the headlight housing and twist the side marker or turn signal light bulb-holder counterclockwise to remove it. Pull the bulb straight out of the socket. Installation is the reverse of the removal procedure.

TAIL AND BACK-UP LIGHTS

▶ **Refer to illustrations 18.4, 18.5 and 18.6**

4 On Titan models, open the tailgate. Remove the mounting fasten- ers and pull the taillight housing from the bed side (see illustration).

5 On Armada models, open the liftgate and remove the two inboard mounting fasteners and remove the taillight housing (see illustration).

➡**Note: When reinstalling the light housing, align the projecting pins with the holes in the body before installing the mounting fasteners.**

6 Remove the bulb socket from the housing and replace the bulb (see illustration).

LICENSE PLATE LIGHT

▶ **Refer to illustration 18.8**

7 On Titan models, pull the housing from the bumper. Pull the bulb straight out to replace it.

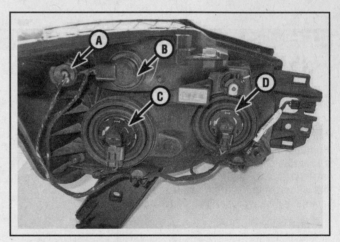

18.1 Headlight housing details

A	Side marker lamp bulb	C	Headlamp low beam
B	Parking/turn signal lamp bulb	D	Headlamp high beam

18.4 Taillight housing mounting fasteners - Titan models

18.5 Taillight housing mounting fasteners - Armada models

18.6 Replace the bulbs in the taillight housing by twisting the bulb holder counterclockwise

8   On Armada models, unsnap the housing from the bumper (see illustration). Remove the bulb holder and replace the bulb.

HIGH-MOUNTED BRAKE LIGHT

▶ **Refer to illustrations 18.9 and 18.10**

9   On Titan models, pry out the two plastic covers (see illustration) at the rear of the interior roof headliner for access to the two mounting nuts. From outside the vehicle, pull the high-mounted brake light assembly out enough to twist out the bulb holders and replace the bulbs. Installation is the reverse of removal.

10   On Armada models, open the tailgate and pry out the plastic covers (see illustration) at the rear of the interior roof for access to the mounting nuts. Pull the high-mounted brake light assembly out enough to twist out the bulb holders and replace the bulbs. Installation is the reverse of removal.

INSTRUMENT CLUSTER ILLUMINATION

11   The instrument cluster lights are part of the circuit board, and not replaceable.

18.8 Unsnap the housing from the bumper

INTERIOR LIGHTS

▶ **Refer to illustrations 18.12a and 18.12b**

12   Remove the lenses for the map lights or dome light by prying the cover off with a small screwdriver (see illustrations). Replace the bulb.

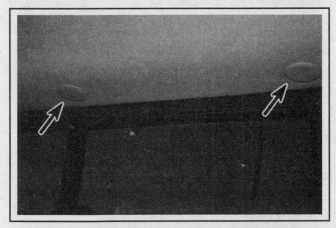

18.9 Pry the plastic covers out from the rear of the headliner for access to the high-mounted brake light screws (Titan models)

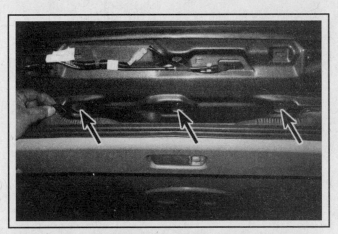

18.10 Open the tailgate and pry out the plastic covers at the rear of the interior roof for access to the mounting nuts

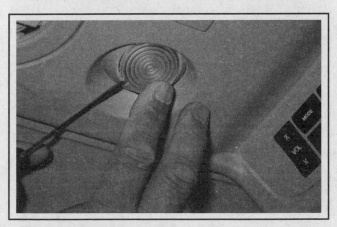

18.12a Use a small screwdriver to pry loose the lens cover from the map light

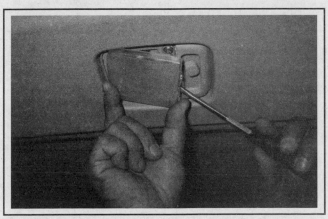

18.12b Carefully pry the lens cover off the dome light using a small-blade screwdriver

FOG LIGHTS

▶ **Refer to illustration 18.13**

13 From below, disconnect the electrical connector on the back of the fog light housing (see illustration), at the rear of the front bumper. Using a clean rag, twist the bulb counterclockwise out of the socket.

14 Installation is the reverse of removal.

✺✺ CAUTION:

Do not touch the surface of the new bulb with your fingers because the oil from your skin could cause it to overheat and fail prematurely. If you do touch the bulb surface, clean it with rubbing alcohol.

18.13 Disconnect the electrical connector for the bulb to be replaced, rotate the bulb counterclockwise and remove it from the housing

19 Horn - replacement

▶ **Refer to illustration 19.2**

1 Remove the grille for access to the horn (see Chapter 11).

2 Disconnect the electrical connector at the horn (see illustration).

3 Remove the mounting fastener securing the horn to the body.

➡ **Note: Some models have two horns on the same bracket.**

4 Installation is the reverse of removal.

19.2 Disconnect the electrical connector and remove the mounting fastener

20 Wiper motors - replacement

WINDSHIELD WIPER MOTOR

▶ **Refer to illustrations 20.2 and 20.5**

1 Disconnect the cable from the negative battery terminal (see Chapter 5).

2 Remove the wiper arm retaining nuts (see illustration).

3 Mark the relationship of the wiper arms to their shafts, then remove the wiper arms.

4 Remove the cowl cover (see Chapter 11).

5 Disconnect the electrical connector from the windshield wiper motor (see illustration), then remove the cowl support bracket.

6 Remove the mounting bolts and remove the wiper drive/motor assembly from the vehicle.

7 Remove the bolts/nuts securing the wiper motor to the drive assembly. Note the position of the motor spacer for reassembly.

8 Installation is the reverse of removal.

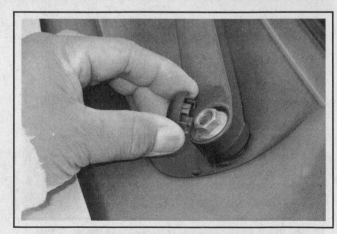

20.2 Pry off the cap, remove the windshield wiper arm nut, then mark the position of the arm to the shaft

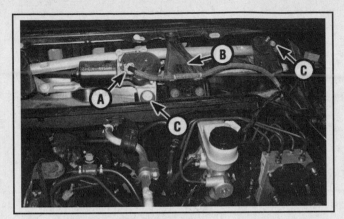

20.5 Wiper motor mounting details

A   Wiper motor electrical connector
B   Cowl support bracket
C   Wiper motor and linkage assembly

REAR WIPER MOTOR

▶ **Refer to illustration 20.11**

9   Disconnect the cable from the negative battery terminal (see Chapter 5).
10 Remove the trim cap from the rear wiper arm.
11 Remove the rear wiper arm retaining nut (see illustration).

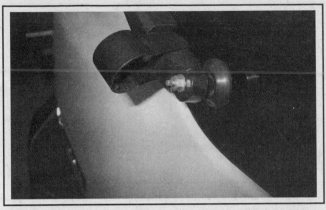

20.11 Pry up the cap, remove the rear wiper arm nut, then mark the position of the arm to the shaft

12 Remove the liftgate trim panel and window lock assembly (see Chapter 11).
13 Disconnect the electrical connector from the rear wiper motor, remove the mounting bolts, then detach the motor from the liftgate.
14 Installation is the reverse of removal. When reattaching the wiper arm/blade assembly, align the arm so that the wiper blade is resting against the stop.

21 Power liftgate motor - replacement

▶ **Refer to illustration 21.4**

1   Open the liftgate and support it fully in this position.
2   With the liftgate supported, detach the liftgate open/close power strut at the liftgate (see illustration 15.10 in Chapter 11).
3   Remove the left rear interior trim panels (see Chapter 11).
4   Disconnect the electrical connector from the liftgate motor, remove the mounting fasteners and detach the motor from the body (see illustration).
5   The liftgate motor must be initialized if the motor has been replaced or the battery has been disconnected.
6   To initialize, close the liftgate. Open the liftgate with the automatic open operation.

➡ **Note: Do not stop the liftgate until the door is fully opened.**

7   Close the liftgate.
8   The remainder of installation is the reverse of removal.

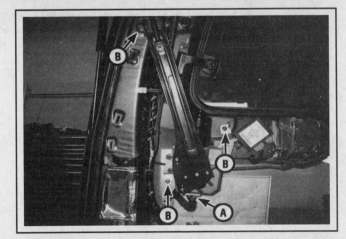

21.4 Disconnect the electrical connector (A) from the liftgate motor and remove the mounting fasteners (B)

22 DVD entertainment system - removal and installation

⁂ **WARNING:**

The models covered by this manual are equipped with Supplemental Restraint Systems (SRS), more commonly known as airbags. Always disable the airbag system before working in the vicinity of any airbag system components to avoid the possibil-

ity of accidental deployment of the airbags, which could cause personal injury (see Section 27).

1   Disconnect the cable from the negative battery terminal (see Chapter 5).

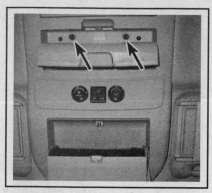

22.5a Remove the overhead console front fasteners . . .

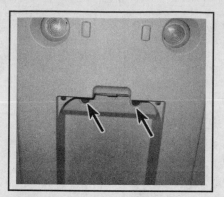

22.5b . . . middle fasteners . . .

22.5c . . . and rear fasteners and lower the unit from the headliner

DVD PLAYER

2   Open the center console arm rest, remove the retaining screws and pull the storage bin out from the center console.

3   Remove the DVD player mounting screws, lift the player up, disconnect the electrical connectors and remove the player from the console.

4   Installation is reverse of removal.

DVD VIDEO MONITOR

▶ **Refer to illustrations 22.5a, 22.5b and 22.5c**

5   Remove the roof console mounting screws (see illustrations) and lower the assembly.

6   Disconnect the monitor electrical connector.

7   Remove the video monitor housing mounting fasteners and separate the monitor housing from the roof console.

8   Remove the video monitor hinge screws and remove the monitor.

9   Installation is the reverse of removal.

23 Cruise control system - description and check

All models have an electronically-controlled throttle body - there is no accelerator cable (or cruise control cable). When you select the speed that you want to maintain, the PCM controls vehicle speed by opening and closing the throttle plate by means of a computer-controlled solenoid (motor) inside the throttle body.

The diagnostic procedures for troubleshooting the cruise control system are beyond the scope of this manual, but if the system can't be set, or the set speed doesn't cancel when the brake pedal is depressed, check the fuses. Start with the fuses in the engine compartment fuse and relay box, then check the fuses in the under-dash fuse and relay box. If the set speed doesn't cancel when the CANCEL button is depressed, check the fuse for that circuit.

Other than checking fuses, the diagnostic procedures for troubleshooting the cruise control system on these models are beyond the scope of this manual. A dealer service department should handle any further testing.

24 Power window system - general information

The power window system operates electric motors, mounted on the doors, which lower and raise the windows. The system consists of the control switches, the motors, regulators, glass mechanisms and associated wiring.

The power windows can be lowered and raised from the master control switch by the driver or by the switch located at the passenger window. Each window has a separate motor that is reversible. The position of the control switch determines the polarity and therefore the direction of operation.

The circuit is protected by fuses and a circuit breaker. Check the fuses in the fuse panel. Each motor is equipped with an internal circuit breaker; this prevents one stuck window from disabling the whole system. Refer to the wiring diagrams at the end of Chapter 12. Problems within this system can only be diagnosed with a factory scan tool. If you have eliminated the obvious causes of a problem, have the vehicle checked at a dealership service department or other properly equipped repair shop.

25 Power door lock system - general information

1   The power door lock system operates the power door motors, which are integral components of the door latch units in each door. The system consists of a fuse (in the engine compartment fuse and relay box), the Body Control Module (BCM), the instrument cluster, the control switches (in each of the front doors), the power door motors and the electrical wiring harnesses connecting all of these components.

2   The lock mechanisms in the door latch units are actuated by a reversible electric motor in each door. When you push the door lock switch to LOCK, the motor operates one way and locks the latch mechanism. When you push the door lock switch the other way, to the UNLOCK position, the motor operates in the other direction, unlocking the latch mechanism. Because the motors and lock mechanisms are an integral part of the door latch units, they cannot be repaired. If a door lock motor or lock mechanism fails, replace the door latch unit (see Chapter 11).

3   Even if you don't manually lock the doors or press the door lock switch to the LOCK position before driving, the instrument cluster automatically locks the doors when the vehicle speed exceeds 15 mph, as long as all the doors are closed and the accelerator pedal is depressed.

➡**Note: You can turn off this feature if you don't want the doors to lock automatically. Refer to your owner's manual.**

4   Some vehicles have an optional Intelligent Key system that allows you to lock and unlock the doors from outside the vehicle. The intelligent key system consists of the transmitter (the electronic push-button "key") and a receiver located on the instrument cluster. The receiver, which operates all the time, is protected by a fuse in the engine compartment fuse and relay box. Vehicles are shipped from the factory with two transmitters but, if you want to purchase extra units, the receiver can actually handle up to five vehicle access codes.

5   Some features of the door lock system on these vehicles rely on resources that they share with other electronic modules through the Programmable Communications Interface (PCI) data bus network. Professional diagnosis of these modules and the PCI data bus network requires the use of a CONSULT-III (proprietary factory) scan tool and factory diagnostic information. At-home repairs are therefore limited to inspecting the wiring for bad connections and for minor faults that can be easily repaired. If you are unable to locate the trouble using the following general steps, consult your dealer service department.

6   Always check the circuit fuses (in the engine compartment fuse and relay box) first. Refer to the wiring diagrams at the end of Chapter 12. Problems within this system can only be diagnosed with a factory scan tool. If you have eliminated the obvious causes of a problem, have the vehicle checked at a dealership service department or other properly equipped repair shop.

➡**Note: It's common for wires to break in the harness between the body and the door because repeatedly opening and closing the door fatigues and eventually breaks the wires.**

26 Sunroof - general information

1   The sunroof is powered by a single motor located in the roof behind the overhead console. The power circuit is protected by a fuse located in the engine compartment power distribution center. When sunlight isn't desired, an interior sliding panel can be closed.

2   The sunroof switch (tilt and slide) sends an operation signal to the sunroof motor CPU encoder when the switches are pressed. Power is supplied to the motor from the Body Control Module (BCM) located under the instrument panel. The front door switch detects the open/close condition and sends an operating signal to the BCM. The sunroof will retain power for 45 seconds after the key has been turned off to operate the system. The retained power can be cancelled by opening the front door, turning the ignition switch to ON again or the 45 seconds has expired.

3   With the ignition On but the engine Off, operate the sunroof control switch through the tilt and slide functions.

4   Listen carefully for the sound of the sunroof motor running in the roof.

5   If the motor can be heard but the sunroof glass doesn't move, there's probably a problem with the drive mechanism.

6   If the sunroof does not operate and no sound comes from the motor, check the fuses (in the interior fuse panel and in the engine compartment power distribution center).

7   If there's voltage at the switch, disconnect it. Check the switch for continuity in all its operating positions. If the switch does not have continuity, replace it. If you have eliminated the obvious causes of a problem, have the vehicle checked at a dealership service department or other properly equipped repair shop.

27 Airbag system - general information

1   These models are equipped with a Supplemental Restraint System (SRS), more commonly known as airbags, designed to protect the driver and the passenger from serious injury in the event of a head-on or side collision. All models have a diagnostic control unit, located on the floor under the center console.

✳✳ WARNING:

If your vehicle is ever involved in a flood, or the interior carpeting is soaked for any reason, disconnect the battery and do not start the vehicle until the airbag system can be checked by your dealer. If the SRS system is subjected to flooding, the airbags could go off upon starting the vehicle, even without an accident taking place.

AIRBAG MODULES

2   The airbag modules consist of a housing incorporating the cushion (airbag) and inflator unit. The inflator assembly is mounted on the back of the housing over a hole through which gas is expelled, inflating the bag almost instantaneously when an electrical signal is sent from the system. The specially wound wire on the driver's side that carries this signal to the module is called a "clockspring." The clockspring is a flat, ribbon-like electrically conductive tape that is wound many times so that it can transmit an electrical signal regardless of steering wheel position. Airbag modules are located in the steering wheel, on the passenger side above the glove box and head-level airbags located along the roof rails (side curtain airbags).

CONTROL UNIT AND SENSORS

▸ **Refer to illustration 27.3a and 27.3b**

3 The diagnosis/sensor unit contains an on-board microprocessor which monitors the operation of the system, and also contains a crash sensor. It checks this system every time the vehicle is started, causing the "AIRBAG" light to go on then off, if the system is operating properly. If there is a fault in the system, the light will go on and stay on and the unit will store fault codes indicating the nature of the fault. If the AIRBAG light goes on and stays on, the vehicle should be taken to your dealer immediately for service. The diagnosis/sensor unit is located under the center console (see illustration). The crash zone sensor is located on the radiator support (see illustration) and the side curtain airbags sensor (satellite crash sensor) is in each door "B" pillar.

OPERATION

4 For the airbag(s) to deploy, the impact sensor(s) must be activated. When this condition occurs, the circuit to the airbag inflator is closed and the airbag inflates.

SELF-DIAGNOSIS SYSTEM

5 A self-diagnosis circuit in the SRS unit displays a light on the instrument panel when the ignition switch is turned to the On position. If the system is operating normally, the light should go out after about five seconds. If the light doesn't come on, or doesn't go out after a short time, or if it comes on while you're driving the vehicle, or if it blinks at any time, there's a malfunction in the SRS system. Have it inspected and repaired as soon as possible. Do not attempt to troubleshoot or service the SRS system yourself. Even a small mistake could cause the SRS

27.3a The airbag system diagnostics/ sensor is located under the floor center console

27.3b The crash zone sensor is located at the front of the vehicle on the radiator support

system to malfunction when you need it.

SERVICING COMPONENTS NEAR THE SRS SYSTEM

6 Nevertheless, there are times when you need to remove the steering wheel, radio or service other components on or near the dashboard. At these times, you'll be working around components and wire harnesses for the SRS system.

✳✳ WARNING:

Do not use electrical test equipment on airbag system wires; it could cause the airbag(s) to deploy. ALWAYS DISABLE THE SRS SYSTEM BEFORE WORKING NEAR THE SRS SYSTEM COMPONENTS OR RELATED WIRING.

DISABLING THE SRS SYSTEM

✳✳ WARNING 1:

Any time you are working in the vicinity of airbag wiring or components, DISABLE THE SRS SYSTEM.

✳✳ WARNING 2:

An auxiliary voltage input device (memory saver) must not be used when working near airbag system components.

7 To disable the airbag system, perform the following steps:
  a) *Turn the steering wheel to the straight-ahead position and turn the ignition switch to the Lock position, then remove the key.*
  b) *Disconnect the battery negative and positive cables, then wait ten minutes before proceeding with any work. Refer to the* **Cautions** *in Chapter 5, Section 1.*
  c) *Before touching any airbag system component, ground yourself to a metal part of the vehicle to discharge any static electricity built up in your body.*

ENABLING THE SYSTEM

8 After you've disabled the airbag and performed the necessary service, reconnect the two-pin airbag connector into the two-pin clockspring connector (driver's side), the SRS main harness (passenger's side) or the side-impact airbag. Reinstall the lid to the underside of the steering wheel or reinstall the glove box/trim panel or upper trim panels.

9 To enable the airbag system, perform the following steps:
  a) *Turn the Ignition switch to the On position.*
  b) *Make sure nobody is inside the vehicle.*
  c) *Connect the battery cable.*
  d) *Turn the ignition to the Off position, then with your body out of the path of the airbag, turn the ignition switch to the On position. Confirm that the airbag warning light is functioning properly.*
  e) *Take the vehicle to a dealer service department or other qualified repair facility and have the airbag system checked and the diagnostic light canceled, if it remains lit.*

REMOVAL AND INSTALLATION

> ### ✳✳ WARNING:
>
> **The bolts used throughout the airbag system to mount the airbag modules, diagnosis sensor unit, crash zone sensor and satellite sensors have a special coating. These bolts are designed to be used once. Replace them with new factory bolts, and never use a substitute fastener.**

Driver's side airbag and clockspring

10 Refer to Chapter 10, Section 14, for removal and installation of the driver's side airbag and clockspring.

> ### ✳✳ WARNING:
>
> **When installing the clockspring, be sure to follow the centering instructions carefully.**

Passenger side airbag

11 Disable the airbag system (see Step 7).

12 Refer to Chapter 11 and remove the passenger-side lower dash panel and the glove box.

13 Remove the two crossmember-to-airbag module mounting nuts, then unlock and disconnect the two-pin connector.

14 Remove the instrument panel assembly from the vehicle (see Chapter 11).

15 Remove the special nuts and remove the unit from the instrument panel.

> ### ✳✳ CAUTION:
>
> **The airbag assembly is heavier than it looks - use both hands when removing it from the instrument panel.**

16 Installation is the reverse of the removal procedure. Tighten the bolts to 93 inch-lbs (10.5 Nm).

Side curtain airbags

17 Disable the airbag system as described earlier in this Section.

18 The side curtain airbags are concealed beneath the door pillar trim pieces. Remove the covers of the door pillars.

19 Disconnect the airbag wiring.

20 The side curtain airbag is a long one piece unit. Remove the screws and detach the airbag from the retaining clips.

> ### ✳✳ WARNING 1:
>
> **Make sure to ground your body using a special wrist strap or a similar device connected to a solid ground on the vehicle's body. Place the airbag module in a safe place with the trim panel side facing up.**

> ### ✳✳ WARNING 2:
>
> **If the side curtain airbag is dropped, it must be replaced.**

21 Installation is the reverse of removal.

Impact seat belt retractors

22 All models are equipped with pyrotechnic (explosive) units in the front seat belt retracting mechanisms for both the lap and shoulder belts. During an impact that would trigger the airbag system, the airbag control unit also triggers the seat belt retractors. When the pyrotechnic charges go off, they accelerate the retractors to instantly take up any slack in the seat belt system to more fully prepare the driver and front seat passenger for impact.

23 The airbag system should be disabled any time work is done to or around the seats.

> ### ✳✳ CAUTION:
>
> **Never strike the pillars or floorpan with a hammer or use an impact-driver tool in these areas unless the system is disabled.**

28 Intelligent Power Distribution Module (IPDM) - description, check and replacement

DESCRIPTION

1 The Intelligent Power Distribution Module (IPDM) is a solid state device that controls various relays and circuits when commands are received from the Powertrain Control Module (PCM) and/or the Body Control Module (BCM). The circuits under its control are:

Headlights
Parking lights
Tail lights/license plate lights
Fog lights
Windshield wipers
Heated mirror relay
Air conditioning compressor clutch
Starter relay
Cooling fan relay
Horn relay
Rear window defogger relay (Armada and Titan King Cab models)

CHECK

2 Although the IPDM is usually very reliable, it must always be factored in to any diagnosis of the circuits under its control. Thorough testing of the unit requires a proprietary Nissan scan tool, but a simple test, called the Auto Active Test, can help you determine the possible source of a problem with some of the circuits under its control. The circuits checked in this test include the:

Windshield wiper circuit
Tail/parking/license plate light circuits
Fog light circuit
Headlight circuit
Air conditioning compressor clutch circuit
Engine cooling fan circuit
Rear window defogger (Armada)

3 Lift the windshield wipers from the windshield and close the right front door. Make sure the ignition switch is in the Off position.

4   To initiate the Auto Active Test, turn the ignition switch to the On position and depress the left front door switch 10 times within 20 seconds, then turn the ignition switch to the Off position.

5   Within 10 seconds, turn the ignition switch back to the On position. The horn should beep once, signifying the start of the test.

6   When the test begins, the following sequence of events should happen (and the sequence of events should repeat three times):

Titan models

The rear window defogger should turn on for 10 seconds (crew cab models only)

The windshield wiper should operate on low speed for 5 seconds, then high speed for 5 seconds

The parking lights/daytime running lights (if equipped)/tail lights/ license plate lights/fog lights should come on for 10 seconds

The headlight low-beams should come on for 20 seconds, then the High-beams should flash on and off 5 times

The air conditioning compressor clutch should engage (click on and off) 5 times

The engine cooling fan should come on for 10 seconds

Armada models

The rear window defogger should turn on for 10 seconds

The windshield wipers should operate on low speed for 5 seconds, then high speed for 5 seconds

The parking lights/tail lights/license plate lights should come on for 10 seconds

The fog lights should come on for 10 seconds

The headlight low-beams should come on for 20 seconds, then the High-beams should flash on and off 5 times

The air conditioning compressor clutch should engage (click on and off) 5 times

The electric engine cooling fan should come on for 10 seconds

DIAGNOSIS

Wipers, parking lights/daytime running lights (if equipped)/ tail lights/license plate lights/fog lights

7   If any of these systems do not operate during the Auto Active Test, the problem could be caused by:

   a) *Wiper motor or the circuit between IPDM and wiper motor faulty*
   b) *Wiper motor ground problem*
   c) *Light bulb or the circuit between IPDM and light faulty*
   d) *Light bulb/housing ground problem*
   e) *Faulty IPDM*

8   If the system in question does operate during the Auto Active Test but doesn't operate under normal conditions, the problem could be a faulty switch, a faulty Body Control Module (BCM), or the circuit between the two.

Air conditioning compressor clutch

9   If the compressor clutch doesn't operate during the Auto Active Test, the problem could be caused by:

   a) *Compressor clutch or the circuit between IPDM and compressor clutch faulty*
   b) *Faulty IPDM*

10 If the compressor clutch does operate during the Auto Active Test but doesn't operate under normal conditions, the problem could be a faulty switch, a faulty Body Control Module (BCM), a faulty PCM,

a fault in the circuit between the PCM and the BCM, or a fault in the circuit between the PCM and the IPDM.

Electric engine cooling fan

11 If the engine cooling fan doesn't operate during the Auto Active Test, the problem could be caused by:

   a) *Cooling fan motor or the circuit between cooling fan motor and IPDM faulty*
   b) *Faulty IPDM*

12 If the engine cooling fan does operate during the Auto Active Test but doesn't operate under normal conditions, the problem could be a faulty PCM, a faulty coolant temperature sensor, the circuit between the coolant temperature sensor and the PCM, or the circuit between the PCM and the IPDM.

Rear window defogger

13 If the rear window defogger doesn't operate during the Auto Active Test, the problem could be caused by:

   a) *Rear window defogger grid or the circuit between the rear window defogger and IPDM faulty*
   b) *Rear window defogger relay faulty*
   c) *Faulty IPDM*

14 If the rear window defogger does operate during the Auto Active Test but doesn't operate under normal conditions, the problem could be a faulty switch, a faulty Body Control Module (BCM), or the circuit between the two.

REPLACEMENT

▶ **Refer to illustration 28.17**

➡**Note: The IPDM is located in the right rear corner of the engine compartment.**

15 Disconnect the cable from the negative terminal of the battery (see Chapter 5).

16 Remove the cover from the IPDM.

17 Push in on the two retainers on the side of the IPDM (see illustration), pull the IPDM up and disconnect the electrical connectors, then remove it from the vehicle.

18 Installation is the reverse of removal.

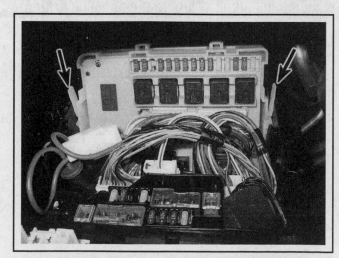

28.17 Squeeze these two retainers to release the IPDM

29 Body Control Module (BCM) - general information

▶ **Refer to illustration 29.2**

The Body Control Module (BCM) receives inputs from various switches and sensors and sends commands, some in the form of multiplex voltage signals, to corresponding components to operate them. Some circuits are controlled by the BCM in conjunction with the IPDM (see Section 28) and/or the Powertrain Control Module (PCM) (see Chapter 6). The circuits under BCM control include the:

Combination switch system
Signal buffer system
Power consumption control system
Auto light system
Turn signal and hazard warning light system
Headlight system
Fog light system
Daytime running lights system
Interior illumination system
Interior illumination battery saver system
Step light system
Windshield wiper/washer system
Rear window wiper/washer system
Warning chime system
Power door lock system
Power window system
Nissan anti-theft system (NATS)
Vehicle security system
Rear window defogger system
Remote keyless entry system
Intelligent Key system
Retained accessory power (RAP) system
Tire pressure monitoring system

The BCM is located under the driver's side of the instrument panel (see illustration). Removal and installation of the BCM is not covered in this manual because special equipment is required to diagnose it and the systems it controls. Additionally, if the BCM requires replacement, it must be programmed with the same special equipment before it will work. So, diagnosis and replacement of the BCM must be performed at a dealer service department or other qualified repair shop equipped with the necessary tool.

29.2 The Body Control Module is located under the driver's side of the instrument panel, to the right of the steering column

30 Wiring diagrams - general information

Since it isn't possible to include all wiring diagrams for every year and model covered by this manual, the following diagrams are those that are typical and most commonly needed.

Prior to troubleshooting any circuits, check the fuses and circuit breakers (if equipped) to make sure they are in good condition. Make sure the battery is properly charged and has clean, tight cable connections (see Chapter 1).

When checking the wiring system, make sure that all electrical connectors are clean, with no broken or loose pins. When unplugging an electrical connector, do not pull on the wires, only on the connector housings themselves.

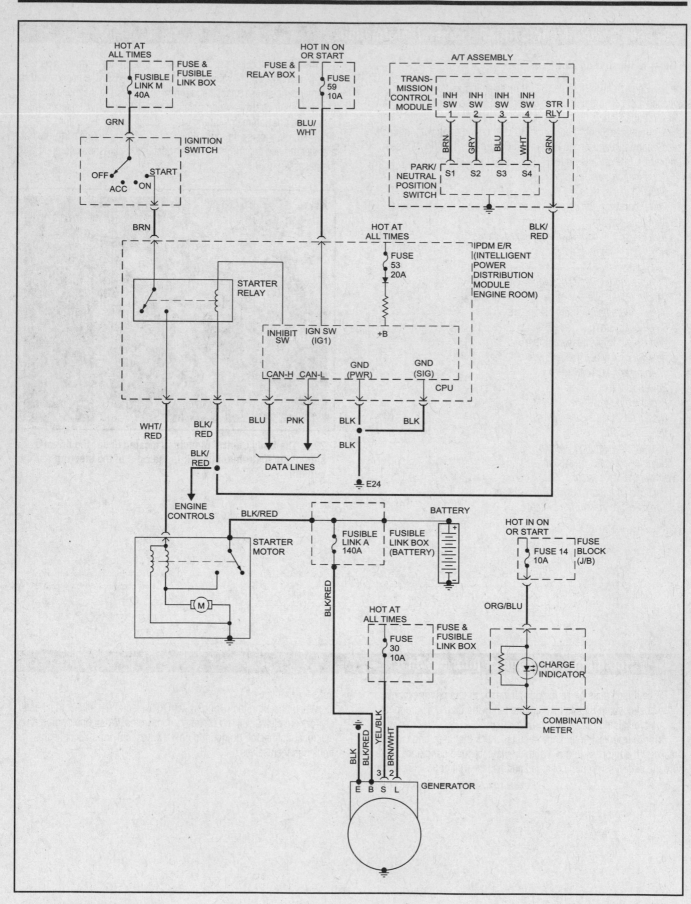

Starting and charging systems

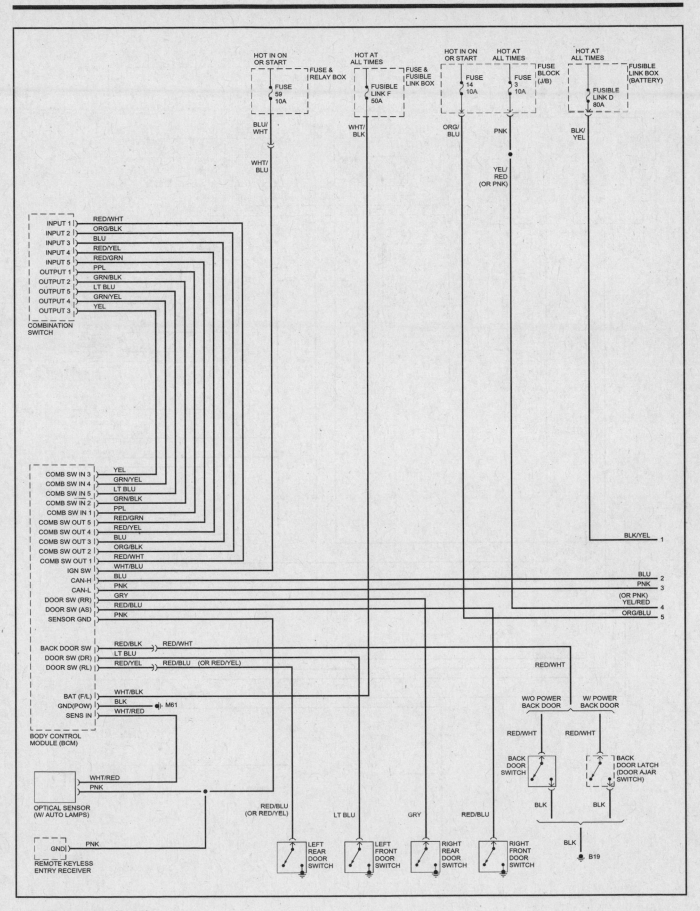

Headlight system (1 of 2)

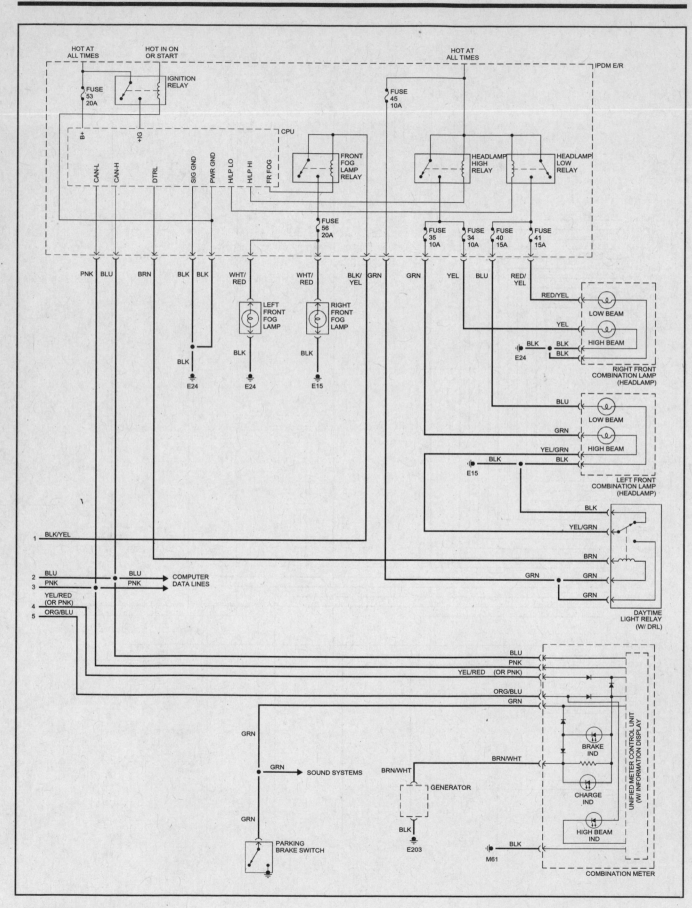

Headlight system (2 of 2)

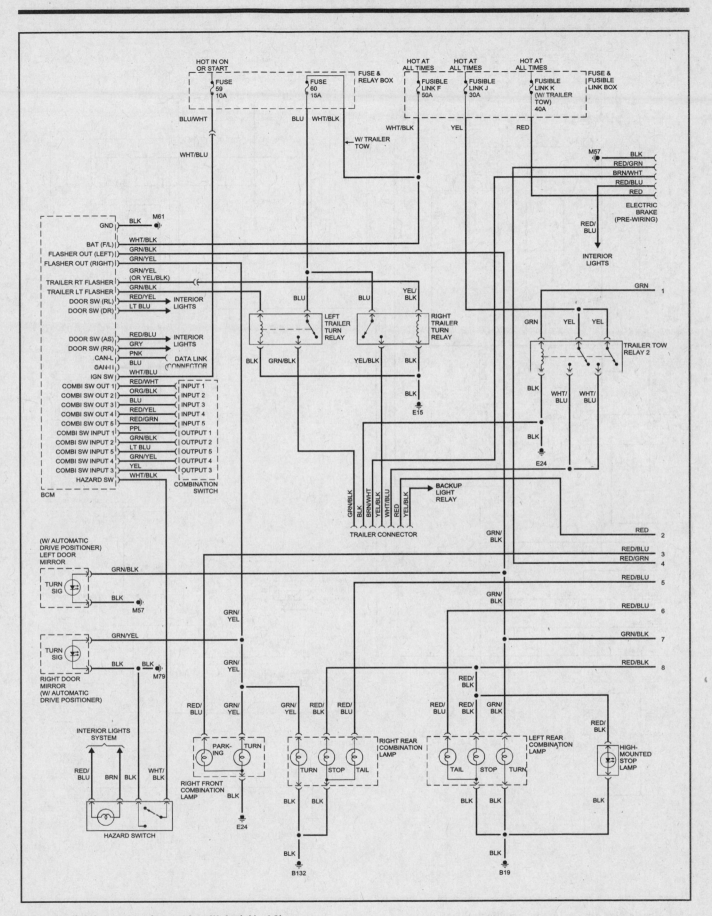

Exterior lighting system (except headlights) (1 of 2)

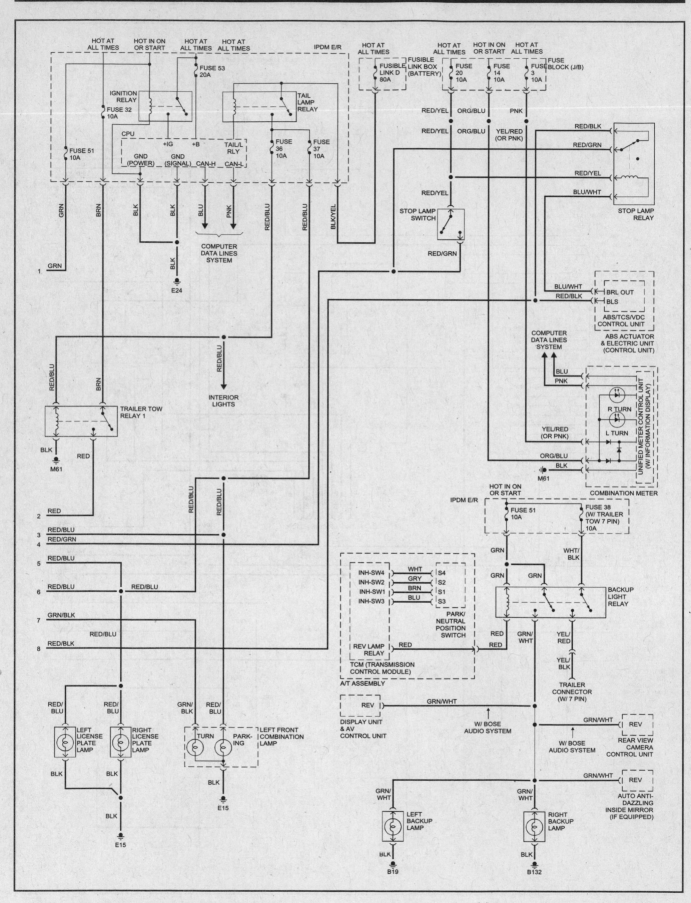

Exterior lighting system (except headlights) (2 of 2)

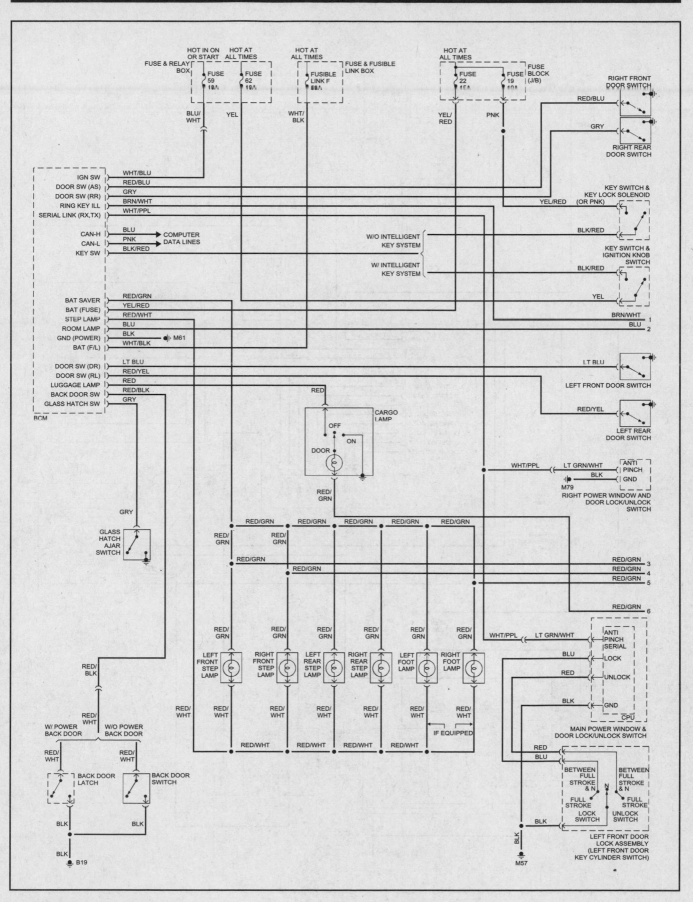

Interior lighting system (1 of 3)

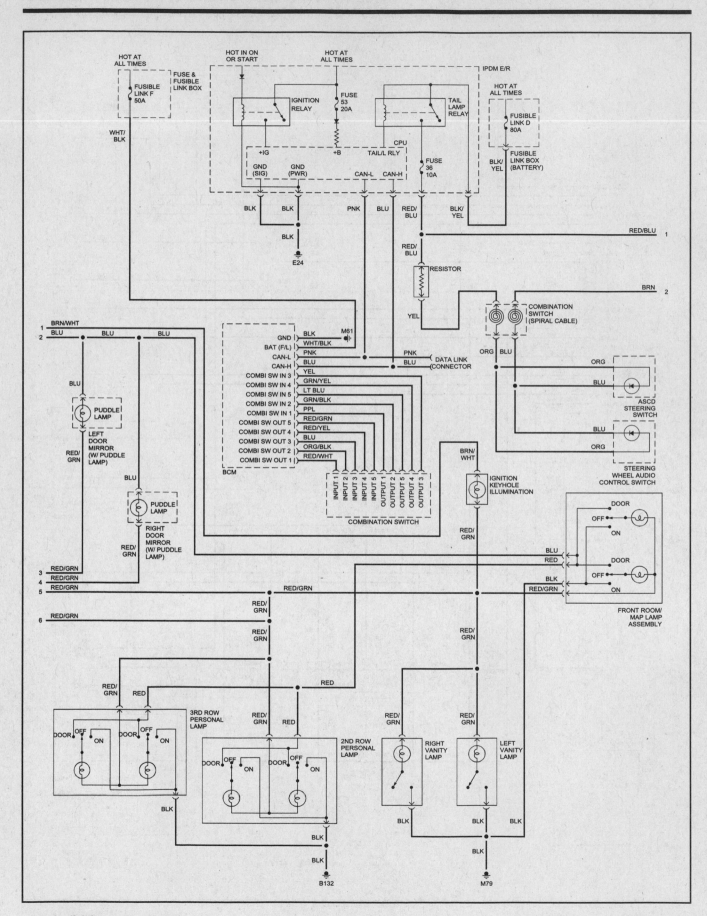

Interior lighting system (2 of 3)

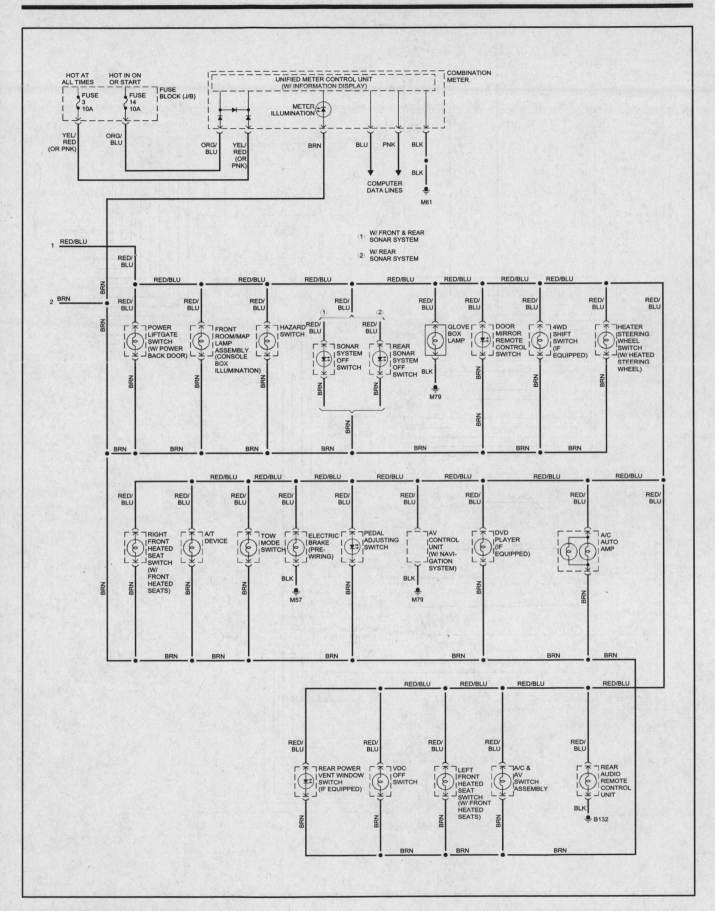

Interior lighting system (3 of 3)

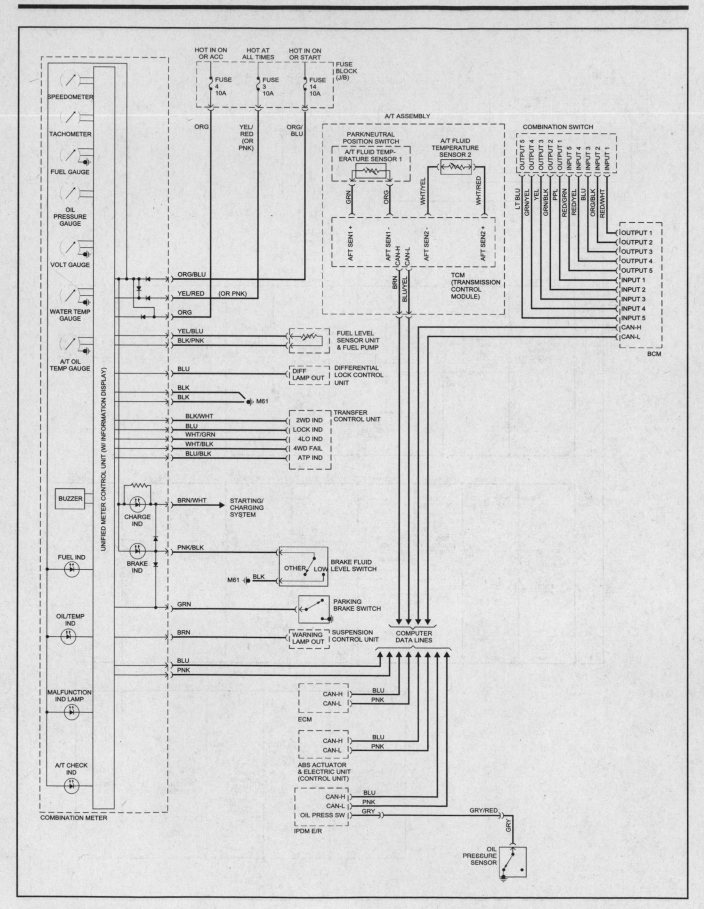

Warning lights and gauges

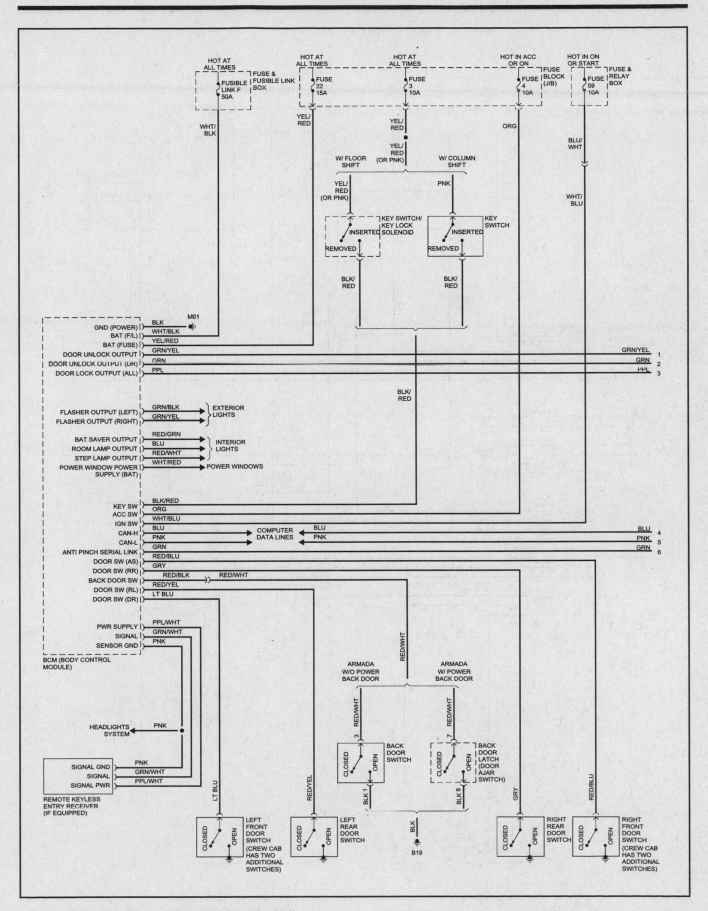

Power door locks system - without Intelligent Key Unit

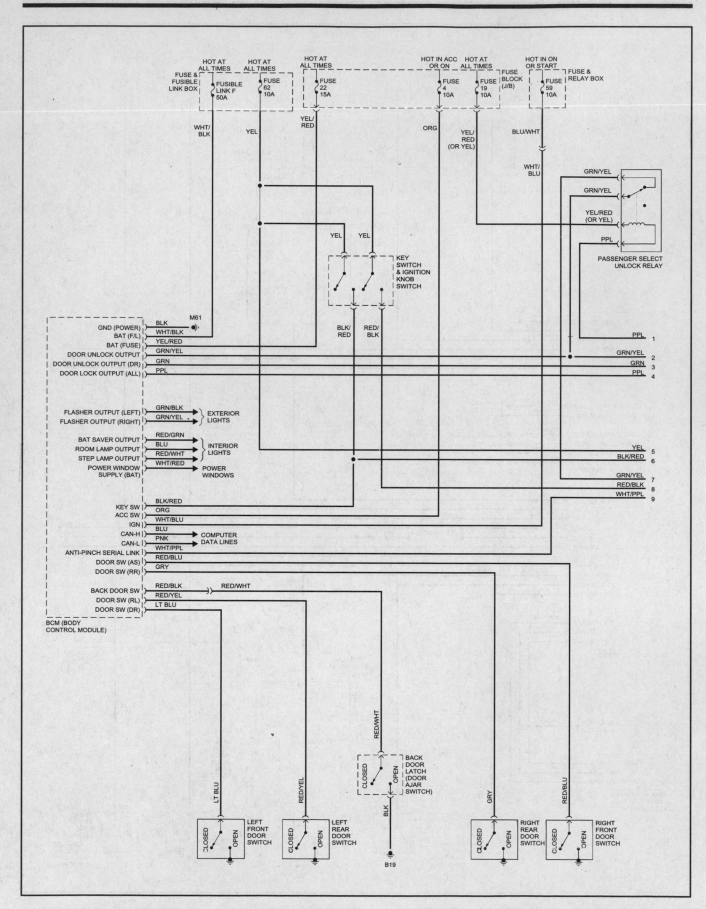

Power door locks system - Armada, with Intelligent Key Unit (1 of 3)

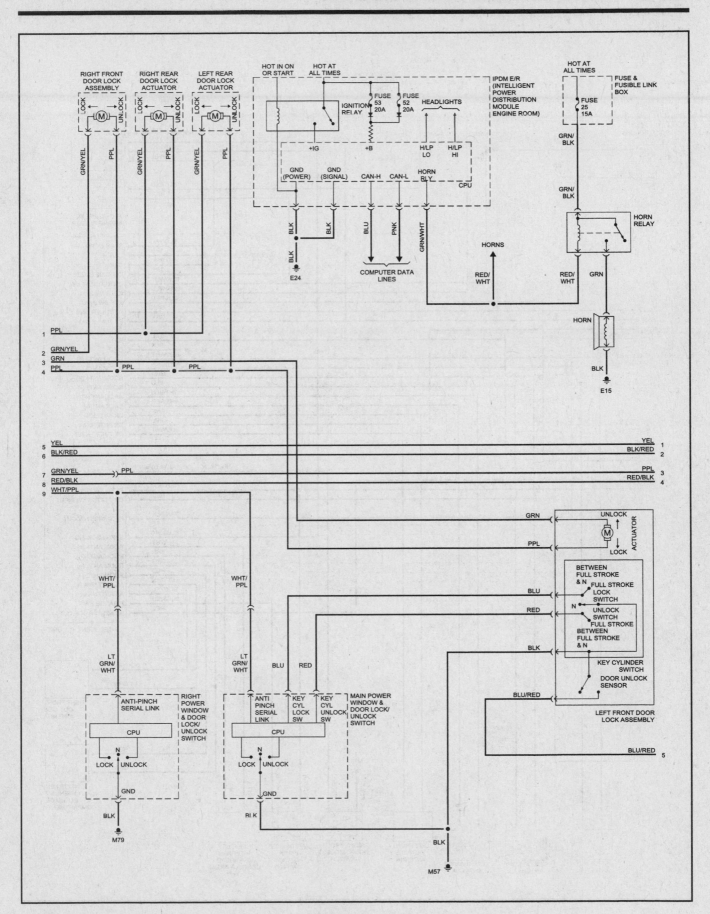

Power door locks system - Armada, with Intelligent Key Unit (2 of 3)

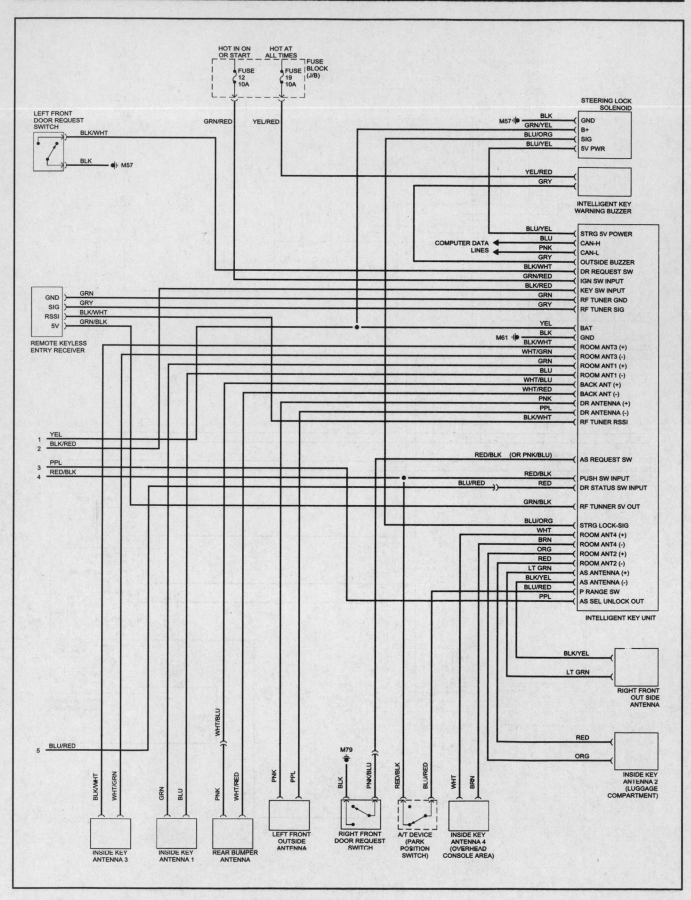

Power door locks system - Armada, with Intelligent Key Unit (3 of 3)

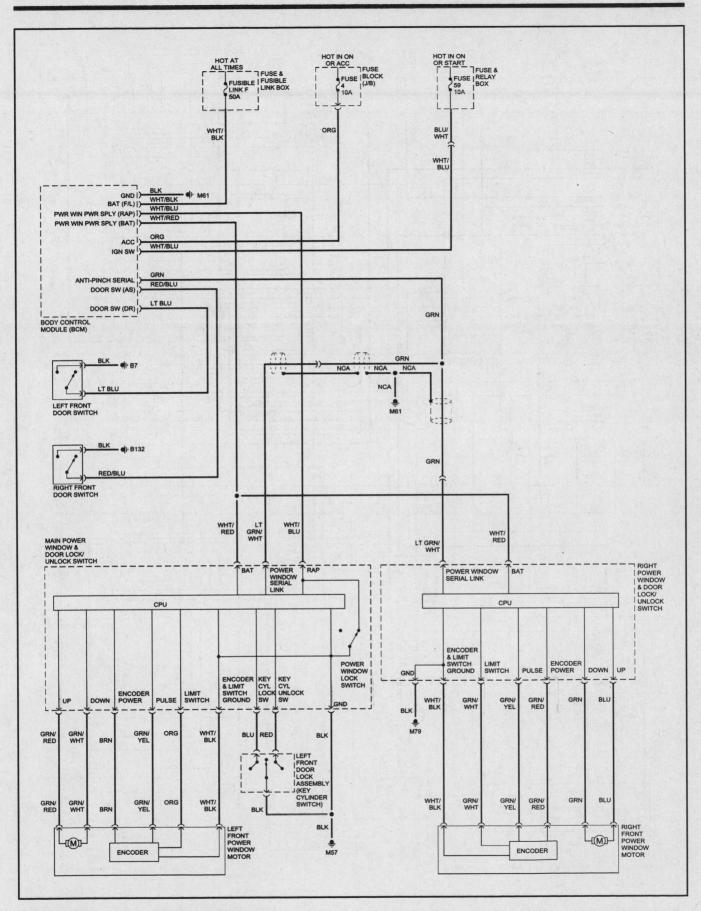

Power windows system - Titan King Cab models

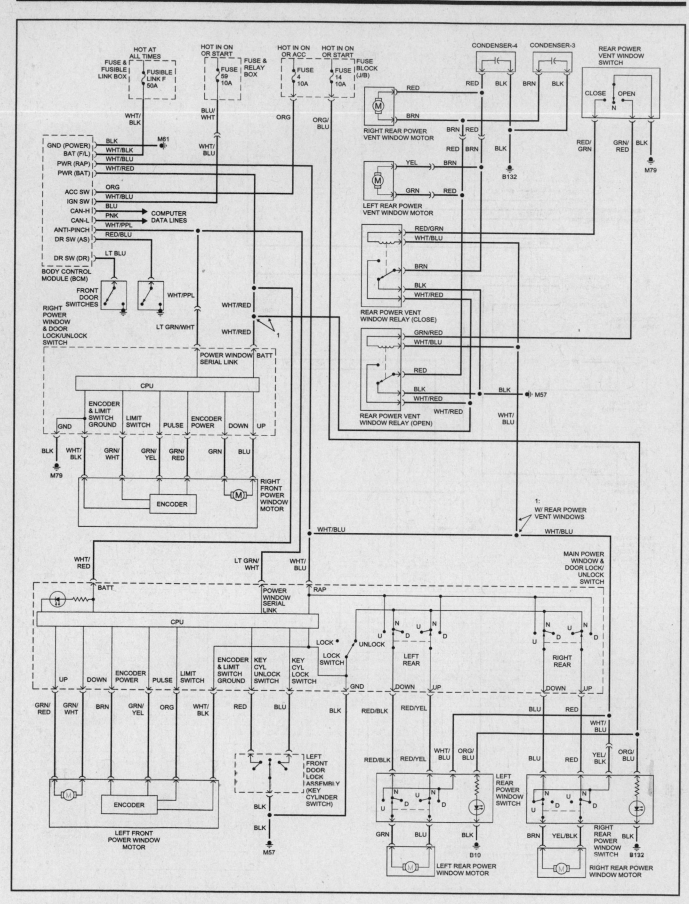

Power windows system - Titan Crew Cab/Armada models

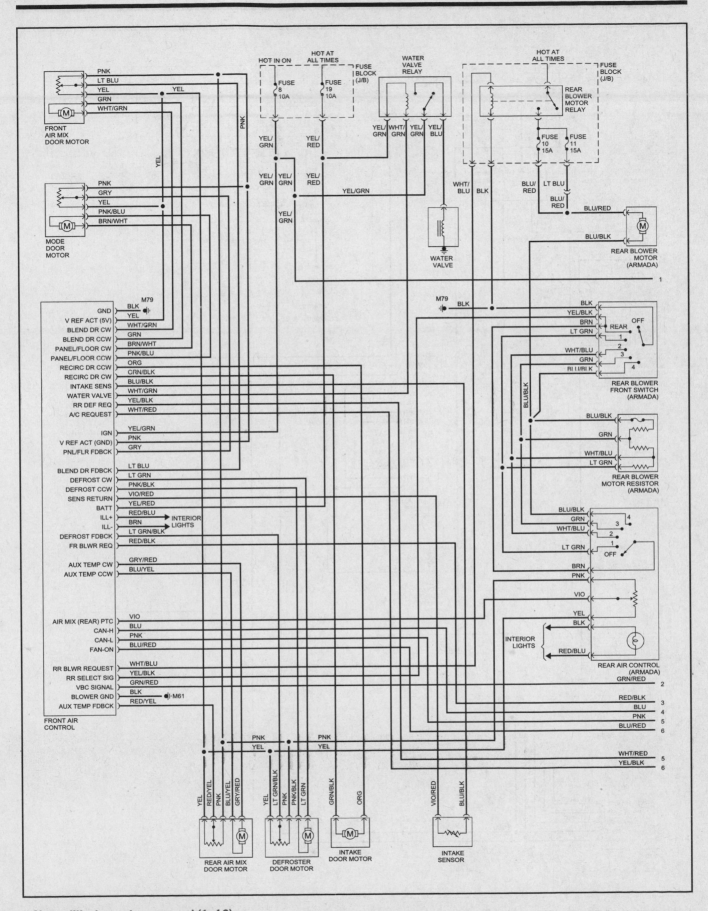

Air conditioning system - manual (1 of 2)

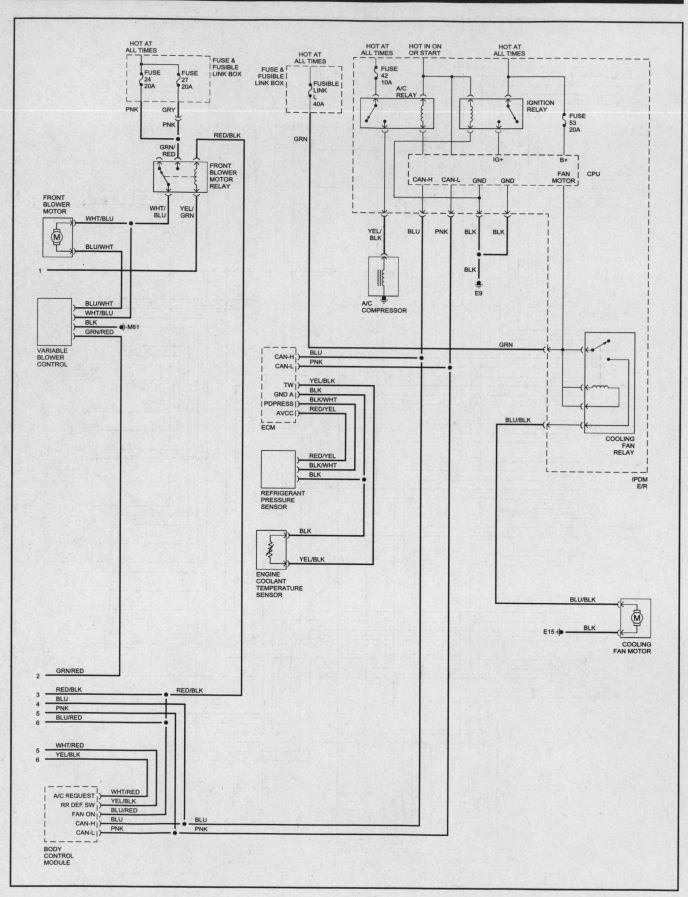

Air conditioning system - manual (2 of 2)

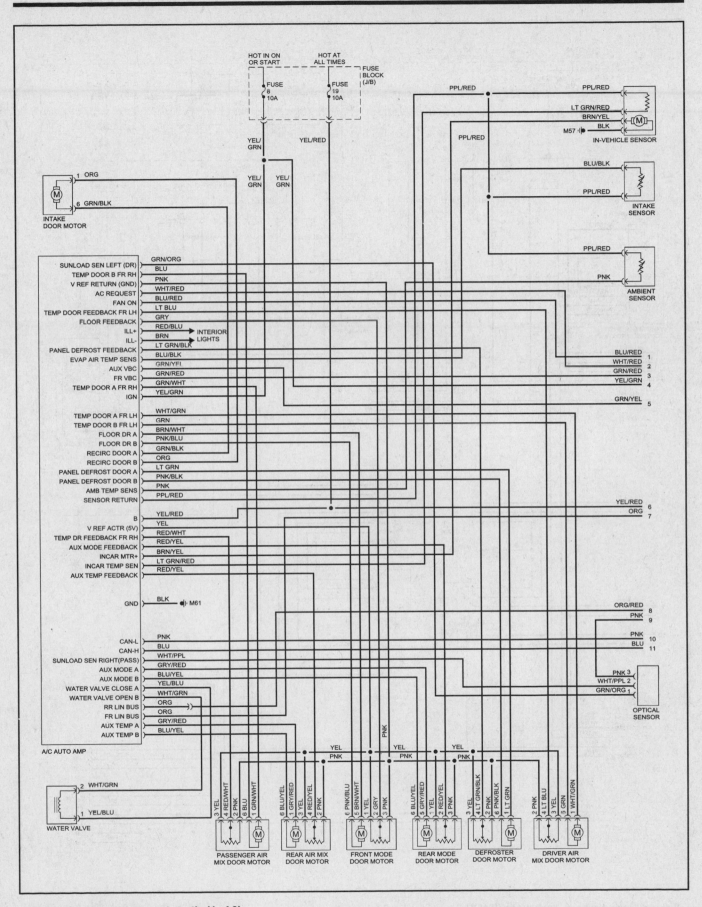

Air conditioning system - automatic (1 of 2)

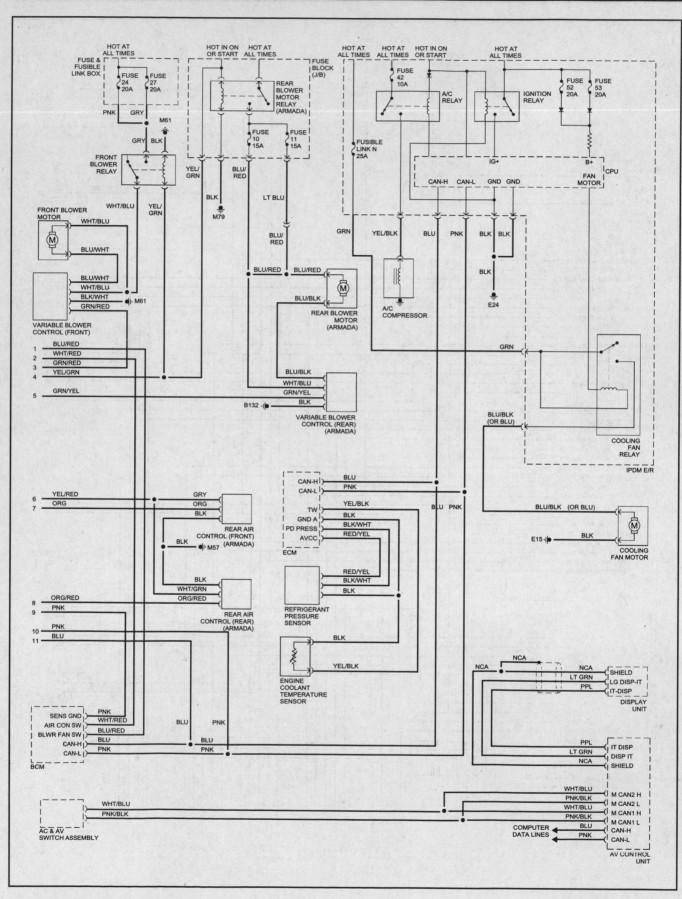

Air conditioning system - automatic (2 of 2)

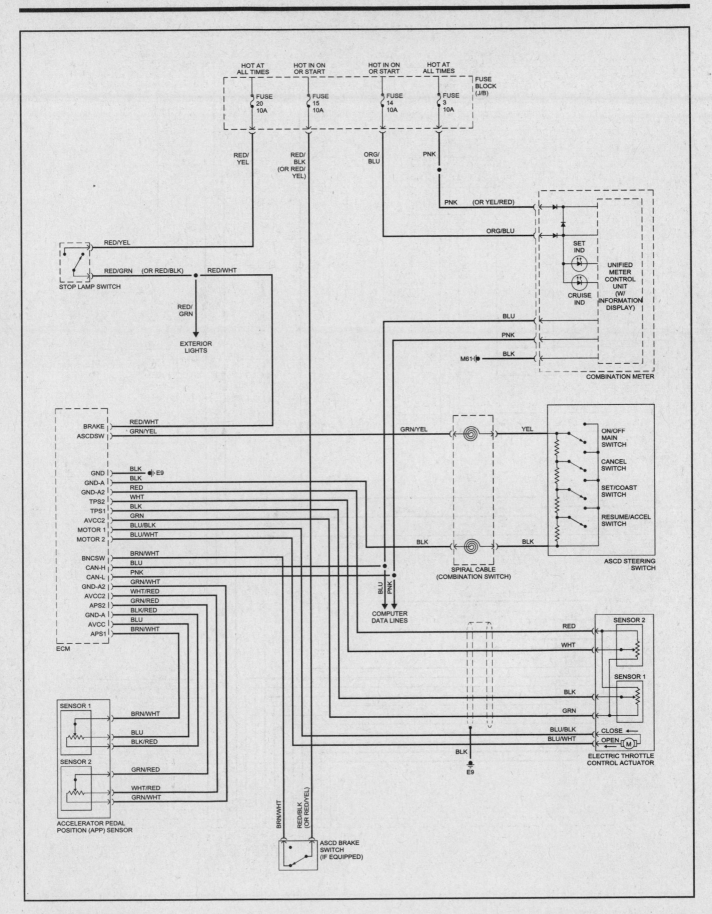

Cruise control system

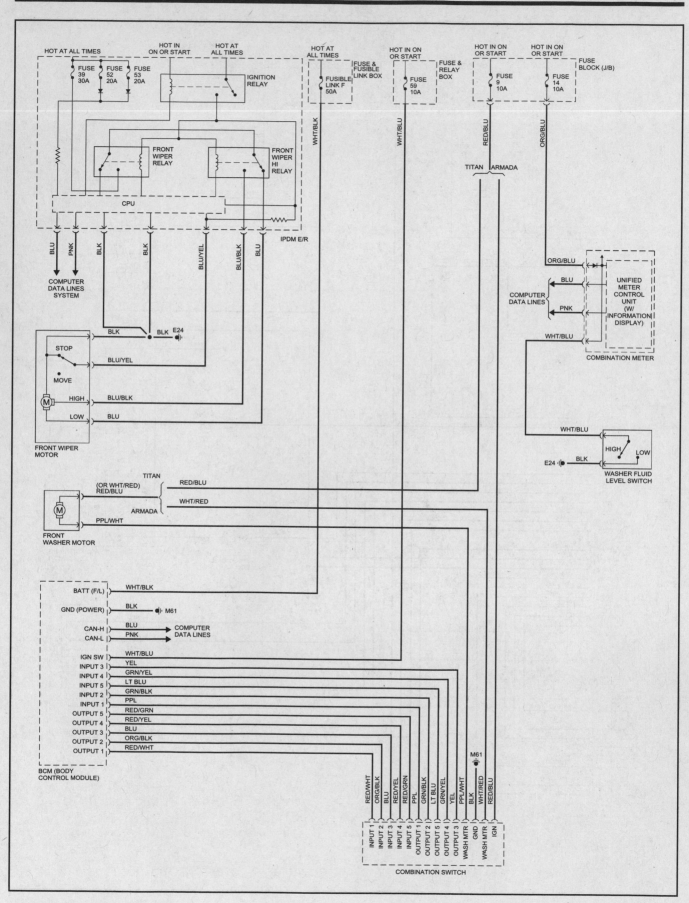

Windshield wiper/washer system

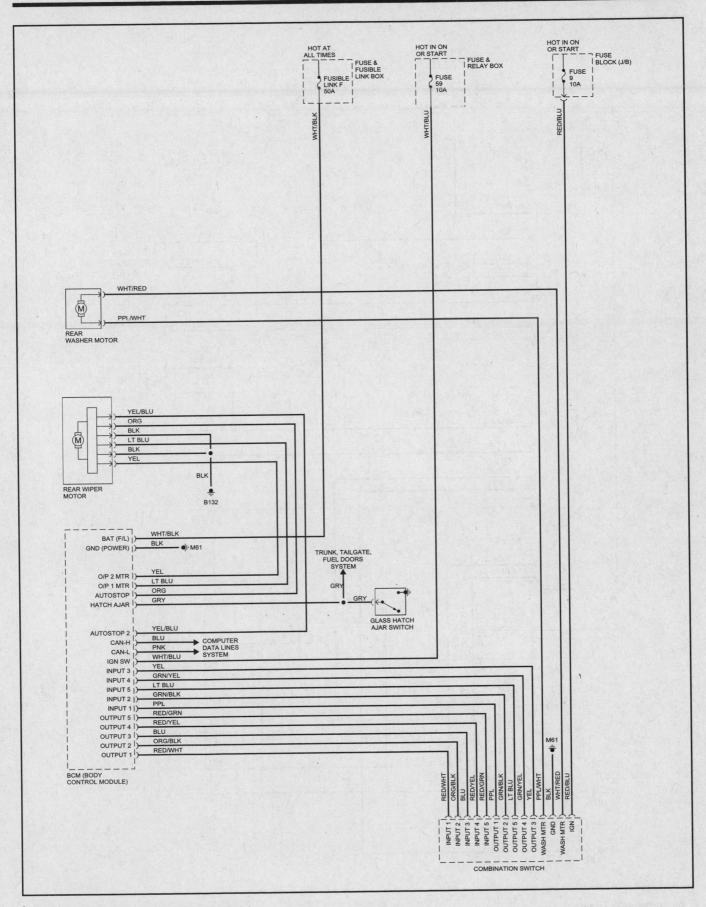

Rear window wiper/washer system (Armada)

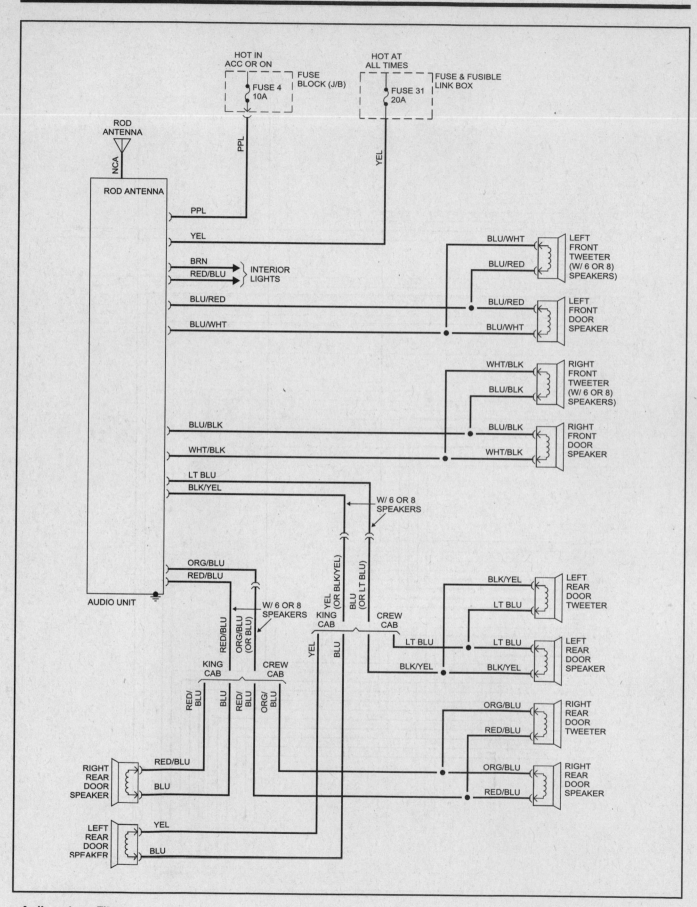

Audio system - Titan

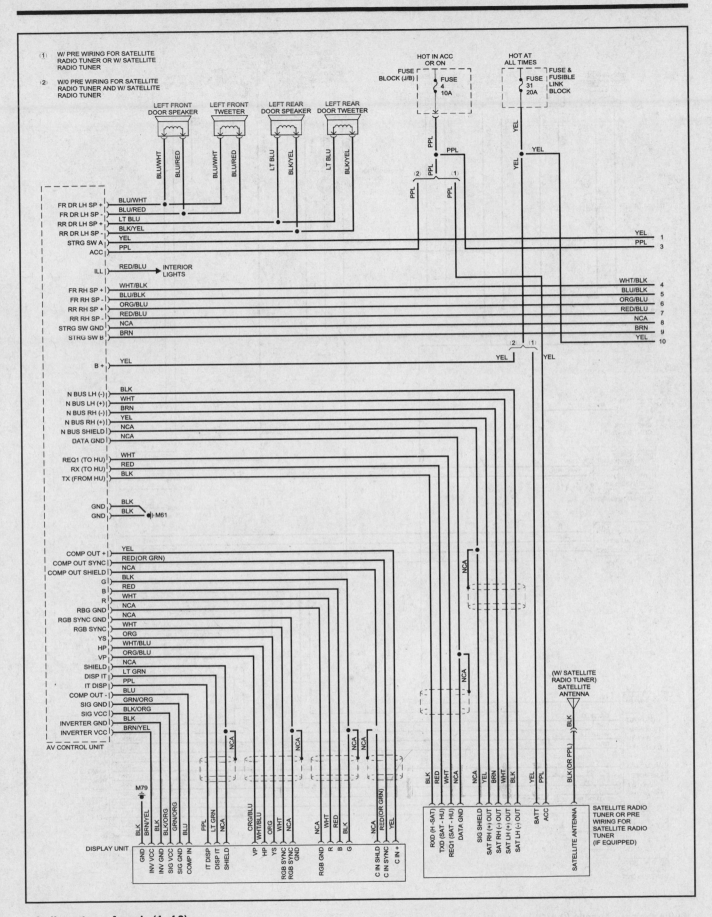

Audio system - Armada (1 of 2)

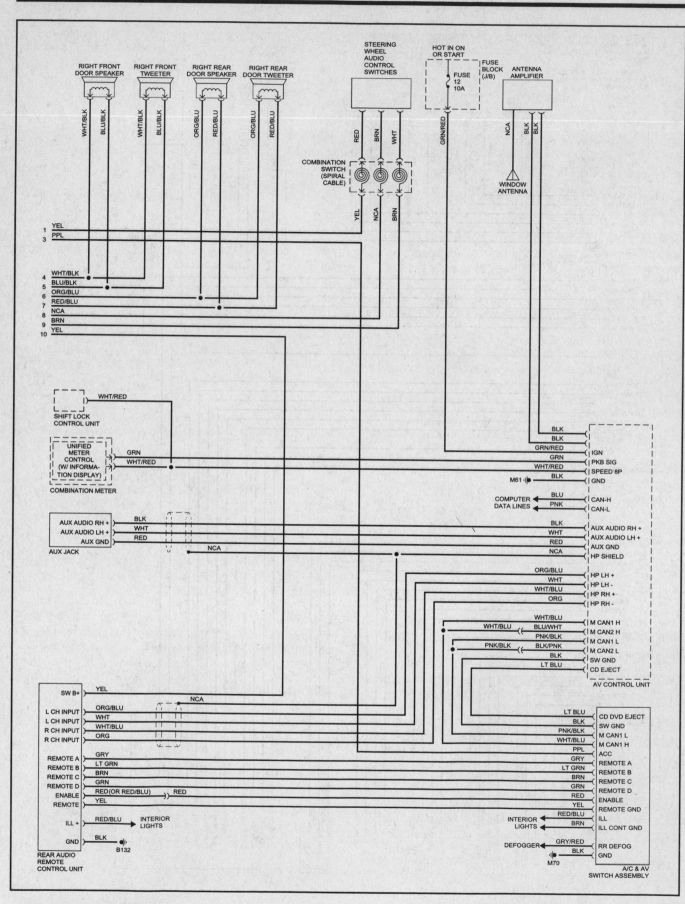

Audio system - Armada (2 of 2)

GLOSSARY

AIR/FUEL RATIO: The ratio of air-to-gasoline by weight in the fuel mixture drawn into the engine.

AIR INJECTION: One method of reducing harmful exhaust emissions by injecting air into each of the exhaust ports of an engine. The fresh air entering the hot exhaust manifold causes any remaining fuel to be burned before it can exit the tailpipe.

ALTERNATOR: A device used for converting mechanical energy into electrical energy.

AMMETER: An instrument, calibrated in amperes, used to measure the flow of an electrical current in a circuit. Ammeters are always connected in series with the circuit being tested.

AMPERE: The rate of flow of electrical current present when one volt of electrical pressure is applied against one ohm of electrical resistance.

ANALOG COMPUTER: Any microprocessor that uses similar (analogous) electrical signals to make its calculations.

ARMATURE: A laminated, soft iron core wrapped by a wire that converts electrical energy to mechanical energy as in a motor or relay. When rotated in a magnetic field, it changes mechanical energy into electrical energy as in a generator.

ATMOSPHERIC PRESSURE: The pressure on the Earth's surface caused by the weight of the air in the atmosphere. At sea level, this pressure is 14.7 psi at 32°F (101 kPa at 0°C).

ATOMIZATION: The breaking down of a liquid into a fine mist that can be suspended in air.

AXIAL PLAY: Movement parallel to a shaft or bearing bore.

BACKFIRE: The sudden combustion of gases in the intake or exhaust system that results in a loud explosion.

BACKLASH: The clearance or play between two parts, such as meshed gears.

BACKPRESSURE: Restrictions in the exhaust system that slow the exit of exhaust gases from the combustion chamber.

BAKELITE: A heat resistant, plastic insulator material commonly used in printed circuit boards and transistorized components.

BALL BEARING: A bearing made up of hardened inner and outer races between which hardened steel balls roll.

BALLAST RESISTOR: A resistor in the primary ignition circuit that lowers voltage after the engine is started to reduce wear on ignition components.

BEARING: A friction reducing, supportive device usually located between a stationary part and a moving part.

BIMETAL TEMPERATURE SENSOR: Any sensor or switch made of two dissimilar types of metal that bend when heated or cooled due to the different expansion rates of the alloys. These types of sensors usually function as an on/off switch.

BLOWBY: Combustion gases, composed of water vapor and unburned fuel, that leak past the piston rings into the crankcase during normal engine operation. These gases are removed by the PCV system to prevent the buildup of harmful acids in the crankcase.

BRAKE PAD: A brake shoe and lining assembly used with disc brakes.

BRAKE SHOE: The backing for the brake lining. The term is, however, usually applied to the assembly of the brake backing and lining.

BUSHING: A liner, usually removable, for a bearing; an anti-friction liner used in place of a bearing.

CALIPER: A hydraulically activated device in a disc brake system, which is mounted straddling the brake rotor (disc). The caliper contains at least one piston and two brake pads. Hydraulic pressure on the piston(s) forces the pads against the rotor.

CAMSHAFT: A shaft in the engine on which are the lobes (cams) which operate the valves. The camshaft is driven by the crankshaft, via a belt, chain or gears, at one half the crankshaft speed.

CAPACITOR: A device which stores an electrical charge.

CARBON MONOXIDE (CO): A colorless, odorless gas given off as a normal byproduct of combustion. It is poisonous and extremely dangerous in confined areas, building up slowly to toxic levels without warning if adequate ventilation is not available.

CARBURETOR: A device, usually mounted on the intake manifold of an engine, which mixes the air and fuel in the proper proportion to allow even combustion.

CATALYTIC CONVERTER: A device installed in the exhaust system, like a muffler, that converts harmful byproducts of combustion into carbon dioxide and water vapor by means of a heat-producing chemical reaction.

CENTRIFUGAL ADVANCE: A mechanical method of advancing the spark timing by using flyweights in the distributor that react to centrifugal force generated by the distributor shaft rotation.

CHECK VALVE: Any one-way valve installed to permit the flow of air, fuel or vacuum in one direction only.

CHOKE: A device, usually a moveable valve, placed in the intake path of a carburetor to restrict the flow of air.

CIRCUIT: Any unbroken path through which an electrical current can flow. Also used to describe fuel flow in some instances.

CIRCUIT BREAKER: A switch which protects an electrical circuit from overload by opening the circuit when the current flow exceeds a predetermined level. Some circuit breakers must be reset manually, while most reset automatically.

COIL (IGNITION): A transformer in the ignition circuit which steps up the voltage provided to the spark plugs.

COMBINATION MANIFOLD: An assembly which includes both the intake and exhaust manifolds in one casting.

COMBINATION VALVE: A device used in some fuel systems that routes fuel vapors to a charcoal storage canister instead of venting them into the atmosphere. The valve relieves fuel tank pressure and allows fresh air into the tank as the fuel level drops to prevent a vapor lock situation.

COMPRESSION RATIO: The comparison of the total volume of the cylinder and combustion chamber with the piston at BDC and the piston at TDC.

CONDENSER: 1. An electrical device which acts to store an electrical charge, preventing voltage surges. 2. A radiator-like device in the air conditioning system in which refrigerant gas condenses into a liquid, giving off heat.

CONDUCTOR: Any material through which an electrical current can be transmitted easily.

CONTINUITY: Continuous or complete circuit. Can be checked with an ohmmeter.

COUNTERSHAFT: An intermediate shaft which is rotated by a mainshaft and transmits, in turn, that rotation to a working part.

CRANKCASE: The lower part of an engine in which the crankshaft and related parts operate.

CRANKSHAFT: The main driving shaft of an engine which receives reciprocating motion from the pistons and converts it to rotary motion.

CYLINDER: In an engine, the round hole in the engine block in which the piston(s) ride.

CYLINDER BLOCK: The main structural member of an engine in which is found the cylinders, crankshaft and other principal parts.

CYLINDER HEAD: The detachable portion of the engine, usually fastened to the top of the cylinder block and containing all or most of the combustion chambers. On overhead valve engines, it contains the valves and their operating parts. On overhead cam engines, it contains the camshaft as well.

DEAD CENTER: The extreme top or bottom of the piston stroke.

DETONATION: An unwanted explosion of the air/fuel mixture in the combustion chamber caused by excess heat and compression, advanced timing, or an overly lean mixture. Also referred to as "ping".

DIAPHRAGM: A thin, flexible wall separating two cavities, such as in a vacuum advance unit.

DIESELING: A condition in which hot spots in the combustion chamber cause the engine to run on after the key is turned off.

DIFFERENTIAL: A geared assembly which allows the transmission of motion between drive axles, giving one axle the ability to turn faster than the other.

DIODE: An electrical device that will allow current to flow in one direction only.

DISC BRAKE: A hydraulic braking assembly consisting of a brake disc, or rotor, mounted on an axle, and a caliper assembly containing, usually two brake pads which are activated by hydraulic pressure. The pads are forced against the sides of the disc, creating friction which slows the vehicle.

DISTRIBUTOR: A mechanically driven device on an engine which is responsible for electrically firing the spark plug at a predetermined point of the piston stroke.

DOWEL PIN: A pin, inserted in mating holes in two different parts allowing those parts to maintain a fixed relationship.

DRUM BRAKE: A braking system which consists of two brake shoes and one or two wheel cylinders, mounted on a fixed backing plate, and a brake drum, mounted on an axle, which revolves around the assembly.

DWELL: The rate, measured in degrees of shaft rotation, at which an electrical circuit cycles on and off.

ELECTRONIC CONTROL UNIT (ECU): Ignition module, module, amplifier or igniter. See Module for definition.

ELECTRONIC IGNITION: A system in which the timing and firing of the spark plugs is controlled by an electronic control unit, usually called a module. These systems have no points or condenser.

END-PLAY: The measured amount of axial movement in a shaft.

ENGINE: A device that converts heat into mechanical energy.

EXHAUST MANIFOLD: A set of cast passages or pipes which conduct exhaust gases from the engine.

FEELER GAUGE: A blade, usually metal, or precisely predetermined thickness, used to measure the clearance between two parts.

FIRING ORDER: The order in which combustion occurs in the cylinders of an engine. Also the order in which spark is distributed to the plugs by the distributor.

FLOODING: The presence of too much fuel in the intake manifold and combustion chamber which prevents the air/fuel mixture from firing, thereby causing a no-start situation.

FLYWHEEL: A disc shaped part bolted to the rear end of the crankshaft. Around the outer perimeter is affixed the ring gear. The starter drive engages the ring gear, turning the flywheel, which rotates the crankshaft, imparting the initial starting motion to the engine.

FOOT POUND (ft. lbs. or sometimes, ft.lb.): The amount of energy or work needed to raise an item weighing one pound, a distance of one foot.

FUSE: A protective device in a circuit which prevents circuit overload by breaking the circuit when a specific amperage is present. The device is constructed around a strip or wire of a lower amperage rating than the circuit it is designed to protect. When an amperage higher than that stamped on the fuse is present in the circuit, the strip or wire melts, opening the circuit.

GEAR RATIO: The ratio between the number of teeth on meshing gears.

GENERATOR: A device which converts mechanical energy into electrical energy.

HEAT RANGE: The measure of a spark plug's ability to dissipate heat from its firing end. The higher the heat range, the hotter the plug fires.

HUB: The center part of a wheel or gear.

HYDROCARBON (HC): Any chemical compound made up of hydrogen and carbon. A major pollutant formed by the engine as a byproduct of combustion.

HYDROMETER: An instrument used to measure the specific gravity of a solution.

INCH POUND (inch lbs.; sometimes in.lb. or in. lbs.): One twelfth of a foot pound.

INDUCTION: A means of transferring electrical energy in the form of a magnetic field. Principle used in the ignition coil to increase voltage.

INJECTOR: A device which receives metered fuel under relatively low pressure and is activated to inject the fuel into the engine under relatively high pressure at a predetermined time.

INPUT SHAFT: The shaft to which torque is applied, usually carrying the driving gear or gears.

INTAKE MANIFOLD: A casting of passages or pipes used to conduct air or a fuel/air mixture to the cylinders.

JOURNAL: The bearing surface within which a shaft operates.

KEY: A small block usually fitted in a notch between a shaft and a hub to prevent slippage of the two parts.

MANIFOLD: A casting of passages or set of pipes which connect the cylinders to an inlet or outlet source.

MANIFOLD VACUUM: Low pressure in an engine intake manifold formed just below the throttle plates. Manifold vacuum is highest at idle and drops under acceleration.

MASTER CYLINDER: The primary fluid pressurizing device in a hydraulic system. In automotive use, it is found in brake and hydraulic clutch systems and is pedal activated, either directly or, in a power brake system, through the power booster.

MODULE: Electronic control unit, amplifier or igniter of solid state or integrated design which controls the current flow in the ignition primary circuit based on input from the pick-up coil. When the module opens the primary circuit, high secondary voltage is induced in the coil.

NEEDLE BEARING: A bearing which consists of a number (usually a large number) of long, thin rollers.

OHM: (Ω) The unit used to measure the resistance of conductor-to-electrical flow. One ohm is the amount of resistance that limits current flow to one ampere in a circuit with one volt of pressure.

OHMMETER: An instrument used for measuring the resistance, in ohms, in an electrical circuit.

OUTPUT SHAFT: The shaft which transmits torque from a device, such as a transmission.

OVERDRIVE: A gear assembly which produces more shaft revolutions than that transmitted to it.

OVERHEAD CAMSHAFT (OHC): An engine configuration in which the camshaft is mounted on top of the cylinder head and operates the valve either directly or by means of rocker arms.

OVERHEAD VALVE (OHV): An engine configuration in which all of the valves are located in the cylinder head and the camshaft is located in the cylinder block. The camshaft operates the valves via lifters and pushrods.

OXIDES OF NITROGEN (NOx): Chemical compounds of nitrogen produced as a byproduct of combustion. They combine with hydrocarbons to produce smog.

OXYGEN SENSOR: Use with the feedback system to sense the presence of oxygen in the exhaust gas and signal the computer which can reference the voltage signal to an air/fuel ratio.

PINION: The smaller of two meshing gears.

PISTON RING: An open-ended ring with fits into a groove on the outer diameter of the piston. Its chief function is to form a seal between the piston and cylinder wall. Most automotive pistons have three rings: two for compression sealing; one for oil sealing.

PRELOAD: A predetermined load placed on a bearing during assembly or by adjustment.

PRIMARY CIRCUIT: the low voltage side of the ignition system which consists of the ignition switch, ballast resistor or resistance wire, bypass, coil, electronic control unit and pick-up coil as well as the connecting wires and harnesses.

PRESS FIT: The mating of two parts under pressure, due to the inner diameter of one being smaller than the outer diameter of the other, or vice versa; an interference fit.

RACE: The surface on the inner or outer ring of a bearing on which the balls, needles or rollers move.

REGULATOR: A device which maintains the amperage and/or voltage levels of a circuit at predetermined values.

RELAY: A switch which automatically opens and/or closes a circuit.

RESISTANCE: The opposition to the flow of current through a circuit or electrical device, and is measured in ohms. Resistance is equal to the voltage divided by the amperage.

RESISTOR: A device, usually made of wire, which offers a preset amount of resistance in an electrical circuit.

RING GEAR: The name given to a ring-shaped gear attached to a differential case, or affixed to a flywheel or as part of a planetary gear set.

ROLLER BEARING: A bearing made up of hardened inner and outer races between which hardened steel rollers move.

ROTOR: 1. The disc-shaped part of a disc brake assembly, upon which the brake pads bear; also called, brake disc. 2. The device mounted atop the distributor shaft, which passes current to the distributor cap tower contacts.

SECONDARY CIRCUIT: The high voltage side of the ignition system, usually above 20,000 volts. The secondary includes the ignition coil, coil wire, distributor cap and rotor, spark plug wires and spark plugs.

SENDING UNIT: A mechanical, electrical, hydraulic or electro-magnetic device which transmits information to a gauge.

SENSOR: Any device designed to measure engine operating conditions or ambient pressures and temperatures. Usually electronic in nature and designed to send a voltage signal to an on-board computer, some sensors may operate as a simple on/off switch or they may provide a variable voltage signal (like a potentiometer) as conditions or measured parameters change.

SHIM: Spacers of precise, predetermined thickness used between parts to establish a proper working relationship.

SLAVE CYLINDER: In automotive use, a device in the hydraulic clutch system which is activated by hydraulic force, disengaging the clutch.

SOLENOID: A coil used to produce a magnetic field, the effect of which is to produce work.

SPARK PLUG: A device screwed into the combustion chamber of a spark ignition engine. The basic construction is a conductive core inside of a ceramic insulator, mounted in an outer conductive base. An electrical charge from the spark plug wire travels along the conductive core and jumps a preset air gap to a grounding point or points at the end of the conductive base. The resultant spark ignites the fuel/air mixture in the combustion chamber.

SPLINES: Ridges machined or cast onto the outer diameter of a shaft or inner diameter of a bore to enable parts to mate without rotation.

TACHOMETER: A device used to measure the rotary speed of an engine, shaft, gear, etc., usually in rotations per minute.

THERMOSTAT: A valve, located in the cooling system of an engine, which is closed when cold and opens gradually in response to engine heating, controlling the temperature of the coolant and rate of coolant flow.

TOP DEAD CENTER (TDC): The point at which the piston reaches the top of its travel on the compression stroke.

TORQUE: The twisting force applied to an object.

TORQUE CONVERTER: A turbine used to transmit power from a driving member to a driven member via hydraulic action, providing changes in drive ratio and torque. In automotive use, it links the driveplate at the rear of the engine to the automatic transmission.

TRANSDUCER: A device used to change a force into an electrical signal.

TRANSISTOR: A semi-conductor component which can be actuated by a small voltage to perform an electrical switching function.

TUNE-UP: A regular maintenance function, usually associated with the replacement and adjustment of parts and components in the electrical and fuel systems of a vehicle for the purpose of attaining optimum performance.

TURBOCHARGER: An exhaust driven pump which compresses intake air and forces it into the combustion chambers at higher than atmospheric pressures. The increased air pressure allows more fuel to be burned and results in increased horsepower being produced.

VACUUM ADVANCE: A device which advances the ignition timing in response to increased engine vacuum.

VACUUM GAUGE: An instrument used to measure the presence of vacuum in a chamber.

VALVE: A device which control the pressure, direction of flow or rate of flow of a liquid or gas.

VALVE CLEARANCE: The measured gap between the end of the valve stem and the rocker arm, cam lobe or follower that activates the valve.

VISCOSITY: The rating of a liquid's internal resistance to flow.

VOLTMETER: An instrument used for measuring electrical force in units called volts. Voltmeters are always connected parallel with the circuit being tested.

WHEEL CYLINDER: Found in the automotive drum brake assembly, it is a device, actuated by hydraulic pressure, which, through internal pistons, pushes the brake shoes outward against the drums.

A

MASTER INDEX

NOTES

WITHDRAWN